STUDIES IN
LATE ANTIQUITY AND EARLY ISLAM

23

THE "CONSTITUTION OF MEDINA"

STUDIES IN
LATE ANTIQUITY AND EARLY ISLAM

23

THE "CONSTITUTION OF MEDINA"

MUḤAMMAD'S FIRST LEGAL DOCUMENT

MICHAEL LECKER

THE DARWIN PRESS, INC.
PRINCETON, NEW JERSEY
2004

Library of Congress Control Number: 2004112422

ISBN 0-87850-148-7

The paper in this book is acid-free neutral pH stock and meets the guidelines for permanence and durability of the Committee on Production Guidelines for Book Longevity of the Council on Library Resources.

Printed in the United States of America

CONTENTS

Preface

The monograph presented here to students of Arabic and Islam is dedicated to the most significant document that has survived from the time of the Prophet Muḥammad, namely the so-called "Constitution of Medina". Although the original document was not preserved and is only known from literary sources, it is widely acknowledged as authentic and as dating back to the time of the Prophet.[1] Given its importance and wide acceptance it is surprising that so little scholarly effort has so far gone into the interpretation of the document, which is replete with difficult words and expressions. It was felt that any progress achieved in the study of this document would enrich the resources available for the study of early Islam.

Like a first love, one always returns to one's doctoral thesis. Most of the research behind this study was carried out some two decades ago when I was writing my Ph.D. thesis at the Hebrew University of Jerusalem under the close supervision of M.J. Kister.[2] At that time the evidence supporting the emendation *umma/amana* (§28) did not seem to be convincing, which is probably the reason why my findings have taken so long to appear. Meanwhile new evidence has emerged that in my opinion supports this emendation.

Fortunately for me, research on my Ph.D. thesis coincided with the convening of an international workshop in Jerusalem, followed by the first in a series of colloquia entitled "From Jāhiliyya to Islam". As early as in October 1979 the interpretation of the said *umma/amana* clause was the topic of my very first scholarly lecture. I recall G.H.A. Juynboll's warm welcome of my argument (as well as his discreet correction of a glaring error in Arabic). At

[1] See, for example, Humphreys, *Islamic History: A Framework for Inquiry*, 92, who quotes in detail Wellhausen's arguments in favour of its authenticity. This is followed (92–98) by a useful critical summary of certain aspects covered in research until 1974.

[2] M. Lecker, *On the Prophet Muḥammad's Activity in Medina*, Jerusalem: The Hebrew University, 1982. (In Hebrew.)

a colloquium on *ḥadīth* convened in Cambridge in 1985 by the late Martin Hinds and Patricia Crone I presented a paper entitled "On the Participation of the Main Jewish Clans in the Document Known as 'The Constitution of Medina'". An extended version of its first part is now published.[3] An early draft of the paper was read in 1980 by Michael Zwettler, who was among the workshop participants; I am indebted to him for his valuable comments. Excursus C ("The Recensions of the Kitāb") was presented in 1988 at the *ḥadīth* colloquium convened in Oxford by the late Martin Hinds, Patricia Crone and G.H.A. Juynboll. It is my pleasant duty to thank the organizers and participants for their helpful comments. Simon Hopkins and Uri Rubin read the Arabic text and its translation and kindly shared their insights with me. I am grateful to Lawrence I. Conrad for many acute remarks and comments.

[3]Lecker, "Wāqidī's Account on the Status of the Jews of Medina".

Introduction

The present monograph offers an edited version and interpretation of the earliest and most important document from the time of Muḥammad. The document is often referred to as the "Constitution of Medina". Although this is a misnomer, it appears at the title of this monograph because it is widespread. The document is referred to throughout this study by the neutral Arabic term "Kitāb".

Detailed attention has been dedicated to the Kitāb by Muḥammad Ḥamīdullāh, who often employed political science terminology. In an article published in 1969[4] he described the Kitāb as "the earliest written constitution, promulgated by a sovereign for his own statal conduct, both in internal and foreign affairs". It preceded the Magna Carta by several centuries; its second clause, according to Ḥamīdullāh, is "the declaration of independence, be that against the pagan Mecca, Byzantine empire, Iran or any other state in the world". Ten clauses were "devoted to social insurance" (i.e. the ransoming of captives and the payment of blood-money), and it was "the first step to abolish nationalities based on the accidents of birth, such as the identity of birth-place, language, race, colour of skin etc."[5] I find

[4] "The Earliest Written Constitution of a State in the World". His book *The First Written Constitution in the World* is not available to me.

[5] The same views can be found in an article that appeared more than three decades earlier: see Ḥamīdullāh, "Aqdam dustūr". The author gave (99) due credit to the Christian Orientalists who studied the document: *wa-qad ḥasaba lahā l-naṣārā l-ūrubbiyyūna mina l-ḥisāb akthar mimmā ḥasaba l-mu'arrikhūna l-muslimūna wa-ʿallaqū ʿalayhā ahammiyya kabīra.* See also *idem*, *Le Prophète de l'Islam*, I, 124: "Si c'est la constitution du premier Etat musulman, c'est également la première constitution écrite d'un Etat dans le monde entier". Zein al-Abdin, "The Political Significance of the Constitution of Medina", 152, says: "The set of rules stated in the Agreement were [*sic*] the natural beginning for the centralised administration which emerged in Arabia. That is why it may not be a wild exaggeration to call it 'The First Written Constitution in the World'".

this terminology, above all the term "constitution", rather disorienting. The document is sometimes referred to more appropriately as *ʿahd al-umma*.

In 1889 J. Wellhausen published a short study of the Kitāb entitled *Muhammads Gemeindeordnung von Medina*, which was included in his monograph about Medina on the eve of Islam.[6] I. Goldziher, with reference to the preservation of written documents in the context of fabricated *ḥadīth*, was very sceptical regarding the possibility that such documents were at all authentic and assumed that written documents were produced to support certain legal practices. In his own words:

> In order to fix certain legal norms, recourse was had not only to the fabrication of oral traditions but also to the production of written documents which were to be taken as the expression of the wishes of the Prophet.[7]

Goldziher himself acknowledged that had Wellhausen's monograph on Medina reached him before the second volume of *Muslim Studies* went to press, "the results of that work would have been used for the first chapters of the study of *ḥadīth*".[8] Indeed, Goldziher's conclusions are too sweeping. The Kitāb, which goes back to the early days of Islam, was preserved more or less in its original form.

In 1974 M. Gil published a study of certain aspects of the Kitāb, in particular Muḥammad's presumed plot against the Jews.[9] In two studies published in 1964 and 1978, respectively, R.B. Serjeant unconvincingly argued for the division of the Kitāb into separate documents. In his interpretation he employed ethnological data relating to contemporary Yemen, in addition to comparative evidence from the primary sources.[10] In 1982

[6]Wellhausen, *Skizzen*, IV, 65–83. An English version of this short study appeared as an excursus in Wensinck, 128–38.

[7]*Muslim Studies*, II, 57. Concerning the authenticity of the Prophet's letters and treaties, Serjeant ("Early Arabic Prose", 131) is of the opinion that their majority is "to be considered authentic notwithstanding inconsistencies in the reportage of some and the possibility of occasional tampering or 'improvement'".

[8]*Muslim Studies*, II, 13. He did however manage to include passing references to Wellhausen's work (*ibid.*, 57 n. 1, 328 n. 6). That Goldziher's work would have been affected by Wellhausen's study is evident from the former's discussion of *man aḥdatha fīhā ḥadathan* which he renders "he who introduces new things into this town"; *ibid.*, II, 26–27. Cf. below, §25.

[9]Gil, "The Constitution of Medina".

[10]Serjeant, "The 'Constitution of Medina'"; *idem*, "The *sunnah jāmiʿah*". For a succinct presentation of his views see his "Early Arabic Prose", 134–39, where he refers to

the English version of A. Goto's study on the Kitāb appeared.[11] In 1985 U. Rubin wrote a short study on the Kitāb, possibly in the wake of my Ph.D. thesis (Jerusalem 1982).[12] In 1988 J.B. Simonsen included a chapter on the Kitāb in his monograph on Islamic taxation.[13] Several other scholars have commented on certain aspects of the Kitāb, and their views will be discussed or referred to in this monograph.

The Kitāb defines the relationship between the members of three groups: the Muhājirūn or the Qurashīs who came to Medina in the first wave of emigration; the Anṣār or the former idol worshippers of Medina who converted to Islam; and some of the Jews of Medina. It includes the legal framework prepared by Muḥammad for his activity shortly after the *hijra*. At that time the main Jewish clans were still the dominant political and military power in Medina. The rapid growth of Muḥammad's community and the progress of the cause of Islam soon rendered much of this legal framework irrelevant. Yet the document was preserved, along with many letters of Muḥammad, by those who realized that they were precious remnants from the time of the Arabian Prophet.

This monograph aims at forming a new basis for the study of the Kitāb, while adding yet another item to the growing inventory of studies about the life of Muḥammad. Future research will involve the utilization of more sources and the preparation of a good map of early Islamic Medina. The study of Islamic history should not be carried out in a void, and it is hoped that geographical and archaeological evidence will contribute to a better understanding of this crucial period in the history of the world.

The Kitāb is a unified document rather than a series of documents. It is made of two clearly defined parts, one including the treaty of the Mu'minūn, or the Muhājirūn and the Anṣār, and another including a non-belligerency treaty with the Jews. The Arabs of Medina who were still idol worshippers were not part of it, and the same is true of the majority of the Jews of Medina, including the main Jewish tribes Naḍīr, Qurayẓa and Qaynuqā'. Only

---

the Kitāb as the "Eight Documents". Serjeant also wrote "Unity of the Ummah and the Sunnah Jāmi'ah in the First Century of Islam", in *Journal for Islamic Studies/Tydskrif vir Islamkunde* 9 (1989), 23–47; the study is not available to me. There is frequent reference to the Kitāb in Serjeant's "Sunnah, Qur'ān, 'Urf".

[11] The Japanese original was published in 1977; Goto, "The Constitution of Medina".

[12] Rubin, "The 'Constitution of Medina'".

[13] Simonsen, *Studies in the Genesis and Early Development of the Caliphal Taxation System*, 39–46.

one Jewish tribe of some weight, the Thaʿlaba b. al-Fiṭyawn, participated in the Kitāb.

The legal formulae used in the Kitāb presumably reflect the customary law and legal practices of Yathrib on the eve of Islam regarding blood vengeance. These formulae do not appear to have survived in the sources — indeed a whole corpus of legal documents in Arabic was probably lost[14] — although many legal practices survived the transition from Jāhiliyya to Islam. The tribal system remained in place; as long as there were tribes there were also agreements, formal and informal, guaranteeing common responsibility and cooperation between their members. The tribes handled matters of blood vengeance among themselves with little intervention from the central or provincial government. If the evidence on such matters in the literary sources is poor, it only means that compilers and historians had other priorities.

[14] Cf. Lecker, "A Pre-Islamic Endowment Deed in Arabic Regarding al-Waḥīda in the Ḥijāz".

Chapter 1

Text and Translation

The following abbreviations were used in the edition of the text:[1]

AU — Abū ʿUbayd, *Amwāl*, 260–64 no. 518.
AU, fragment — Abū ʿUbayd, *Amwāl*, 166 nos. 328–29.
AU1 — Abū ʿUbayd, *Amwāl*, ed. Muḥammad Ḥāmid al-Fiqī, Cairo AH 1353, 202–205 (noted only in the case of differences with AU).
AU/DK1 — Abū ʿUbayd, *Amwāl*, MS Dār al-Kutub, Ḥadīth 2282 (copied in Damascus, AH 1346), 216–21; the fragment, 132.
AU/DK2 — Abū ʿUbayd, *Amwāl*, MS Dār al-Kutub, Ḥadīth 2534, 85a–87a.
AU/DK3 — Abū ʿUbayd, *Amwāl*, MS Dār al-Kutub, Ḥadīth 2558 (*riwāyat ʿAlī b. ʿAbd al-ʿAzīz al-Baghawī ʿanhu*).
AU/Zah. — Abū ʿUbayd, *Amwāl*, MS Ẓāhiriyya, Ḥadīth 310; photocopy in the Staatsbibliothek Berlin (MSS simulata orient. 32), I, 85b–87a.
Fa. — Zamakhsharī, *Fāʾiq*, II, 25–26.
Fa. (India) — Zamakhsharī, *Fāʾiq*, Hyderabad 1324/1906, I, 221–22.
Fa. (India MS) — Zamakhsharī, *Fāʾiq*, MS Osmania University 1614 (copied in AH 1134), 85b.
IH — Ibn Hishām, *Sīra*, II, 147–50.

[1]The selection of manuscripts is unsystematical and is probably unrepresentative. Several sources that have a complete or nearly complete recension of the Kitāb guide us to its general form. Yet it was found that the consultation of sources that only include a partial version of the Kitāb was beneficial. However, the mention of each omission in the partial versions would have cluttered the apparatus unnecessarily. Some differences were considered insignificant and were left out.

IH/DK — Ibn Hishām, *Sīra*, MS Dār al-Kutub, H 7083 (copied in AH 862), 100b–101b.
IH/Berl. — Ibn Hishām, *Sīra*, MS Staatsbibliothek Berlin (Sprenger 93), 334–37.[2]
IJ — a fragment quoted from Ibn Jurayj in Abū ʿUbayd, *Amwāl*, 166–67 no. 330.
IK — Ibn Kathīr, *Bidāya*, III, 224–26.
IQ — Ibn Qayyim, *Aḥkām*, II, 835–37.
ISN — Ibn Sayyid al-Nās, *ʿUyūn al-athar*, I, 197–98.
ISN2 — Ibn Sayyid al-Nās[2], *ʿUyūn al-athar*, I, 318–20.
ISN/Berl. — Ibn Sayyid al-Nās, *ʿUyūn al-athar*, MS Staatsbibliothek Berlin (Sprenger 122), 60a–61a.
IT — Ibn Taymiyya, *al-Ṣārim al-maslūl*, 62–64.
Maq. — al-Maqrīzī, *Imtāʿ al-asmāʿ*, MS Dār al-Kutub 886, V, 1035–36.
Maw. — al-Mawṣilī, *Wasīla*, IV,ii 105–10.
Mis. — Ibn Ḥudayda, *Miṣbāḥ muḍīʾ*, II, 5–10.
Mis.1 — Ibn Ḥudayda, *Miṣbāḥ muḍīʾ*, MS Hakim Muzahir (India), 75a–76b (only partially compared).
Mis.2 — Ibn Ḥudayda, *Miṣbāḥ muḍīʾ*, MS Mumtāz al-ʿulamāʾ, Muḥammad Taqī, 130 Ḥadīth, 117b–119a.
MT — a fragment in *Manāl al-ṭālib*, 227.
ND — a fragment in *Nathr al-durr*, I, 222–23.
Nuw. — Nuwayrī, *Nihāyat al-arab*, XVI, 348–51.
Qast. — a fragment in Qasṭallānī, *Mawāhib laduniyya*, II, 270.
Qast.1 — Qasṭallānī, *Mawāhib laduniyya*, MS Br. Lib. Or. 5477, 142b.
Wüst. — Ibn Hishām, *Sīra*, ed. F. Wüstenfeld, Göttingen 1858, I.i, 341–44.
Zan. — Ibn Zanjawayh, *Amwāl*, II, 466–70 no. 750.
Zan.1 — Ibn Zanjawayh, *Amwāl*, MS Burdur 183, 70b–71b.
Zurq. — al-Zurqānī, *Sharḥ ʿalā l-mawāhib al-laduniyya*, IV, 168–69.

[2]Sprenger remarked about these volumes of Ibn Hishām's *Sīra* (nos. 93 and 94): "This is the most carefully written Arabic Ms. I have ever seen".

Ibn Isḥāq's Version

كتاب رسول الله صلعم الذي كتبه بين المهاجرين والأنصار وموادعة يهود
قال ابن إسحاق: وكتب رسول الله صلى الله عليه وسلم كتابا بين المهاجرين والأنصار وادع فيه يهود وعاهدهم وأقرهم على دينهم وأموالهم وشرط لهم واشترط عليهم
قال ابن إسحاق: حدثني عثمان بن محمد بن الأخنس بن شريق قال: أخذت من آل عمر بن الخطاب هذا الكتاب، كان مقرونا بكتاب الصدقة الذي كتب عمر للعمال، كتب:
بسم الله الرحمن الرحيم

١. هذا كتاب من محمد النبي بين المؤمنين والمسلمين من قريش ويثرب ومن تبعهم فلحق بهم وجاهد معهم
٢. إنهم أمة واحدة من دون الناس
٣. المهاجرون من قريش على ربعتهم، يتعاقلون بينهم، وهم يفدون عانيهم بالمعروف واالقسط بين المؤمنين
٤. وبنو عوف على ربعتهم، يتعاقلون معاقلهم الأولى، وكل طائفة منهم تفدي عانيها بالمعروف والقسط بين المؤمنين
٥. وبنو الحارث على ربعتهم، يتعاقلون معاقلهم الأولى، وكل طائفة منهم تفدي عانيها بالمعروف والقسط بين المؤمنين
٦. وبنو ساعدة على ربعتهم، يتعاقلون معاقلهم الأولى، وكل طائفة منهم تفدي عانيها بالمعروف والقسط بين المؤمنين
٧. وبنو جشم على ربعتهم، يتعاقلون معاقلهم الأولى، وكل طائفة منهم تفدي عانيها بالمعروف والقسط بين المؤمنين
٨. وبنو النجار على ربعتهم، يتعاقلون معاقلهم الأولى، وكل طائفة منهم تفدي عانيها بالمعروف والقسط بين المؤمنين
٩. وبنو عمرو بن عوف على ربعتهم، يتعاقلون معاقلهم الأولى، وكل طائفة منهم تفدي عانيها بالمعروف والقسط بين المؤمنين
١٠. وبنو النبيت على ربعتهم، يتعاقلون معاقلهم الأولى، وكل طائفة منهم تفدي عانيها بالمعروف والقسط بين المؤمنين
١١. وبنو الأوس على ربعتهم، يتعاقلون معاقلهم الأولى، وكل طائفة منهم تفدي عانيها بالمعروف والقسط بين المؤمنين
١٢. وإن المؤمنين لا يتركون مفرحا بينهم أن يعطوه بالمعروف في فداء أو عقل
١٣. ولا يحالف مؤمن مولى مؤمن دونه
١٤. وإن المؤمنين المتقين على من بغى منهم أو ابتغى دسيعة ظلم أو إثم أو عدوان أو فساد بين المؤمنين، وإن أيديهم عليه جميعاً ولو كان ولد أحدهم
١٥. ولا يقتل مؤمن مؤمنا في كافر ولا ينصر كافرا على مؤمن

١٦ . وإن ذمة الله واحدة ، يجير عليهم أدناهم
١٧ . وإن المؤمنين بعضهم موالي بعض دون الناس
١٨ . وإنه من تبعنا من يهود فإن له النصر والأسوة ، غير مظلومين ولا متناصر عليهم
١٩ . وإن سلم المؤمنين واحدة ، لا يسالم مؤمن دون مؤمن في قتال في سبيل الله إلا على سواء وعدل بينهم
٢٠ . وإن كل غازية غزت معنا يعقب بعضها بعضا
٢١ . وإن المؤمنين يبيء بعضهم عن بعض بما نال دماءهم في سبيل الله
٢٢ . وإن المؤمنين المتقين على أحسن هذا واقومه
٢٣ . وإنه لا يجير مشرك مالا لقريش ولا نفسا ولا يحول دونه على مؤمن
٢٤ . وإنه من اعتبط مؤمنا قتلا عن بينة فإنه قود يد ، إلا أن يرضى ولي المقتول ، وإن المؤمنين عليه كافة ولا يحل لهم إلا قيام عليه
٢٥ . وإنه لا يحل لمؤمن أقر بما في هذه الصحيفة وآمن بالله واليوم الآخر أن ينصر محدثا ولا يؤويه ، وإنه من نصره أو آواه فإن عليه لعنة الله وغضبه يوم القيامة ، ولا يؤخذ منه صرف ولا عدل
٢٦ . وإنكم مهما اختلفتم فيه من شيء فإن مرده إلى الله وإلى محمد
٢٧ . وإن اليهود ينفقون مع المؤمنين ما داموا محاربين
٢٨ . وإن يهود بني عوف أمة مع [أمنة من] المؤمنين ، لليهود دينهم وللمسلمين دينهم ، مواليهم وأنفسهم ، إلا من ظلم وأثم ، فإنه لا يوتغ إلا نفسه وأهل بيته
٢٩ . وإن ليهود بني النجار مثل ما ليهود بني عوف
٣٠ . وإن ليهود بني الحارث مثل ما ليهود بني عوف
٣١ . وإن ليهود بني ساعدة مثل ما ليهود بني عوف
٣٢ . وإن ليهود بني جشم مثل ما ليهود بني عوف
٣٣ . وإن ليهود بني الأوس مثل ما ليهود بني عوف
٣٤ . وإن ليهود بني ثعلبة مثل ما ليهود بني عوف ، إلا من ظلم وأثم ، فإنه لا يوتغ إلا نفسه وأهل بيته
٣٥ . وإن جفنة بطن من ثعلبة كأنفسهم
٣٦ . وإن لبني الشطيبة مثل ما ليهود بني عوف
٣٧ . وإن البر دون الاثم
٣٨ . وإن موالي ثعلبة كأنفسهم
٣٩ . وإن بطانة يهود كأنفسهم
٤٠ . وإنه لا يخرج منهم أحد إلا باذن محمد
٤١ . وإنه لا ينحجز على ثأر جرح
٤٢ . وإنه من فتك فبنفسه وأهل بيته ، إلا من ظلم
٤٣ . وإن الله على أبر هذا
٤٤ . وإن على اليهود نفقتهم وعلى المسلمين نفقتهم
٤٥ . وإن بينهم النصر على من حارب أهل هذه الصحيفة
٤٦ . وإن بينهم النصح والنصيحة
٤٧ . والبر دون الاثم

٤٨ . وإنه لن يأثم امرؤ بحليفه وإن النصر للمظلوم
٤٩ . وإن يثرب حرام جوفها لأهل هذه الصحيفة
٥٠ . وإن الجار كالنفس، غير مضار ولا آثم
٥١ . وإنه لا تجار حرمة إلا بإذن أهلها
٥٢ . وإنه ما كان بين أهل هذه الصحيفة من حدث أو اشتجار يخاف فساده، فإن مرده إلى الله وإلى محمد
٥٣ . وإن الله على أتقى ما في هذه الصحيفة وأبره
٥٤ . وإنه لا تجار قريش ولا من نصرها
٥٥ . وإن بينهم النصر على من دهم يثرب
٥٦ . وإذا دعوا إلى صلح يصالحونه ويلبسونه، فإنهم يصالحونه ويلبسونه، وإنهم إذا دعوا إلى مثل ذلك، فإنه لهم على المؤمنين، إلا من حارب في الدين، على كل أناس حصتهم من جانبهم الذي قبلهم
٥٧ . وإن يهود الأوس مواليهم وأنفسهم على مثل ما لأهل هذه الصحيفة، مع البر المحسن من أهل هذه الصحيفة
٥٨ . وإن البر دون الاثم
٥٩ . لا يكسب كاسب إلا على نفسه
٦٠ . وإن الله على أصدق ما في هذه الصحيفة وأبره
٦١ . وإنه لا يحول هذا الكتاب دون ظالم وآثم
٦٢ . وإنه من خرج آمن ومن قعد آمن [بالمدينة]، إلا من ظلم وأثم
٦٣ . وإن الله جار لمن بر واتقى ومحمد رسول الله
٦٤ . وإن أولاهم بهذه الصحيفة البر المحسن

Ibn Isḥāq's Version with Variants

كتاب رسول الله صلعم الذي كتبه بين المهاجرين والأنصار وموادعة يهود[1]

1) كتاب . . . , Wüst. IH/DK IH IT Mis.1 om.; IK فصل في عقده عليه السلام الألفة بين المهاجرين والأنصار بالكتاب الذي أمر به فكتب بينهم والمؤاخاة التي أمرهم بها وقررهم عليها وموادعته اليهود الذين كانوا بالمدينة; ISN ذكر الموادعة بين المسلمين واليهود ; Maw. كتابه بين المهاجرين والأنصار ; Mis.1 om.

قال[1] ابن إسحاق : [2] وكتب[3] رسول الله صلى الله عليه وسلم[4] كتابا[5] بين المهاجرين والأنصار وادع[6] فيه يهود[7] وعاهدهم وأقرهم على دينهم وأموالهم[8] وشرط لهم واشترط عليهم[9]

1) IK وقال ; IK IT ad. محمد 2) IT ad. يعني في أول ما قدم النبي صلى الله عليه وسلم المدينة 3) IK لما هاجر النبي صلى الله عليه وسلم إلى المدينة واستقر بها 4) Wüst. صلعم ; IQ ad. يعني في أول ما قدم المدينة 5) وكتب . . . , Maw. كتب 6) Wüst. IH IK IT; Maw. ISN ووادع 7) IK Mis.2 اليهود 8) دينهم . . . , Maq. أموالهم ودينهم 9) وشرط لهم . . . , Wüst. IK Mis. Mis.1 Mis.2 Maq. IH/DK Maw. IT IQ واشترط عليهم وشرط لهم; IH/Berl. واشترط عليهم واشترط لهم ; Maw. ad. وهذه نسخته

قال ابن إسحاق : حدثني عثمان بن محمد[1] بن الأخنس بن شريق قال : أخذت من آل عمر بن الخطاب هذا الكتاب ، كان مقرونا[2] بكتاب الصدقة الذي كتب عمر للعمال ، كتب : [3]

1) IT ad. بن عثمان 2) IQ معرونا 3) قال ابن إسحاق . . . , IT IQ only

بسم الله الرحمن الرحيم

١ . هذا كتاب[1] من محمد النبي[2] بين[3] المؤمنين والمسلمين[4] من قريش ويثرب ومن تبعهم[5] فلحق[6] بهم وجاهد معهم

1) Maw. الكتاب ; IQ om. 2) IK ad. الأمي; IH IH/Berl. ISN IQ Mis. Mis.1 Mis.2 IH/DK Maw. ad. صلى الله عليه وسلم 3) IQ نبي 4) المؤمنين والمسلمين , IT المسلمين والمؤمنين 5) Maw. معهم 6) Maw. Nuw. ولحق

٢ . إنهم[1] أمة واحدة من دون[2] الناس

1) Maq. إنه (2 من دون , IT IQ دون

٣ . المهاجرون من قريش على ربعتهم[1] يتعاقلون بينهم[2] وهم[3] يفدون عانيهم بالمعروف واالقسط بين[4] المؤمنين[5]

1) IH IT voc. رِبْعَتهم ; Wüst. رَبَعَتهم (2 IT Maw. only. IT ad. معاقلهم الأولى ; IQ ad. بعاقلتهم
الأولى (3 IT IQ om. 4) IQ والعسَطنَينَ (5 بين المؤمنين , IK om.; Mis.2 بين المهاجرين المؤمنين

٤ . وبنو عوف على ربعتهم يتعاقلون معاقلهم[1] الأولى وكل[2] طائفة منهم تفدي[3] عانيها بالمعروف والقسط بين المؤمنين

1) IQ معاقلتهم (2 IH كل (3 Maw. يفدى

٥ . وبنو الحارث[1] على ربعتهم يتعاقلون معاقلهم الأولى وكل طائفة منهم تفدي عانيها بالمعروف والقسط بين المؤمنين[2]

1) IH/DK om. this clause. IH places this clause after the next one. 2) وبنو الحارث..., Maw. Mis. om.

٦ . وبنو ساعدة على ربعتهم يتعاقلون معاقلهم الأولى وكل طائفة منهم تفدي عانيها بالمعروف والقسط بين المؤمنين[1]

1) IH/Berl. repeats here the clause of Banū l-Ḥārith.

٧ . وبنو جشم على ربعتهم يتعاقلون معاقلهم الأولى وكل طائفة منهم تفدي عانيها بالمعروف والقسط بين المؤمنين

٨ . وبنو النجار على ربعتهم يتعاقلون معاقلهم الأولى وكل طائفة منهم تفدي عانيها بالمعروف والقسط بين المؤمنين

٩ . وبنو عمرو بن عوف على ربعتهم يتعاقلون معاقلهم الأولى وكل طائفة منهم تفدي عانيها بالمعروف والقسط بين المؤمنين

١٠ . وبنو النبيت على ربعتهم يتعاقلون معاقلهم الأولى وكل طائفة منهم تفدي عانيها بالمعروف والقسط بين المؤمنين[1]

1) وبنو النبيت . . . , Nuw. om.

١١ . وبنو الأوس على ربعتهم يتعاقلون معاقلهم الأولى وكل طائفة منهم تفدي عانيها بالمعروف والقسط بين المؤمنين[1]

1) وبنو الحارث . . . , IK ثم ذكر كل بطن من بطون الأنصار وأهل كل دار : بني ساعدة وبني جشم وبني النجار وبني عمرو بن عوف وبني النبيت إلى أن قال; ISN وذكر كذلك في بني ساعدة وبني جشم وبني النجار وبني عمرو بن عوف وبني النبيت وبني الأوس; IT IQ ثم ذكر لبطون الأنصار بني الحارث وبني ساعدة وبني جشم وبني النجار وبني عمرو بن عوف وبني الأوس وبني النبيت مثل هذا الشرط ثم قال; Maq. only has بنو عوف بنو النجار بنو الأوس.

١٢ . وإن[1] المؤمنين لا يتركون مفرحا[2] بينهم[3] أن يعطوه بالمعروف في فداء أو عقل[4]

1) IH/Berl. here and systematically in what follows وأنَ 2) ISN/Berl. voc. مَفْرَحًا ; Maw. مفدحا 3) IT IQ منهم 4) أو عقل, IK وعقل; Wüst. IH Maw. ad. قال ابن هشام المفرح المثقل بالدين والعيال قال الشاعر إذا أنت لم تبرح تؤدي أمانةً وتحمل أخرى أفرحتك الودائع; IH has instead of والعيال : والكثير العيال; IH/Berl. has on the margin a variant reading from one Ibn al-Ward: أفدحتك; Maw. ad. قال ابن هشام المفدح هو المثقل بالدين والعيال ; the editor amended المفرج into المفدح

١٣ . ولا[1] يحالف[2] مؤمن مولى مؤمن دونه

1) Wüst. IH وأن لا; Nuw. وإنه لا 2) Wüst. يخالف

١٤ . وإن المؤمنين المتقين على من بغى منهم[1] أو ابتغى دسيعة[2] ظلم أو إثم أو عدوان أو فساد[3] بين المؤمنين، وإن أيديهم عليه[4] جميعا[5] ولو كان ولد أحدهم

1) Maq. عليهم منهم; IH/Berl. adds a variant above منهم : عليهم 2) IK دسيسة 3) Cf. the Persian trans. of Ibn Isḥāq (Ḥamīd., *Mamjūʿa* p. 359), Ḥamīd., no. 1, p. 3: أو إثما أو فسادا 4) IH/DK عليهم 5) IH IH/Berl. ISN Maw. Mis.; IH/DK جميعه; IK جميعهم

١٥ . ولا يقتل مؤمن مؤمنا في كافر ولا ينصر كافرا[1] على مؤمن[2]

1) Wüst. IH; Maq. IH/DK Mis. Mis.2 IK ISN Maw. كافر; ISN/Berl. voc. يُنْصَرُ كافِرٌ 2) IT IQ وإن المؤمنين المتقين . . . , إلى أن قال

١٦ . وإن ذمة الله واحدة، يجير عليهم أدناهم
١٧ . وإن[1] المؤمنين بعضهم موالي[2] بعض دون الناس

1) IT IQ فإن 2) IT IQ مولى

١٨ . وإنه[1] من تبعنا من يهود[2] فإن له النصر والأسوة،[3] غير مظلومين ولا متناصر[4] عليهم

1) ISN وإن ; ISN2 وإنه 2) Nuw. وانه من تهود . . . ,وإنه 3) Maw. الأخوة; Wüst. voc. والإسوَة; Maq. والأسرة 4) IH Nuw. متناصرين

١٩ . وإن سلم المؤمنين واحدة، لا يسالم مؤمن دون[1] مؤمن في قتال في سبيل الله إلا على[2] سواء وعدل[3] بينهم

1) ISN Mis. من دون; ISN/Berl. من was written and then struck out 2) Mis. Mis.2 عن
3) ISN Mis.2 أو عدل

٢٠ . وإن كل غازية غزت معنا يعقب[1] بعضها بعضا

1) Wüst. IH/Berl. IH ISN/Berl. يُعْقب

٢١ . وإن المؤمنين يبيء[1] بعضهم عن بعض[2] بما نال[3] دماءهم[4] في سبيل الله

1) Maw. بنيء 2) بعضهم عن بعض, Maq. Wüst Mis. ISN; IH/DK IH Maw. Mis.2 بعضهم على بعض; IH/Berl. بعضهم على بعض and above على a variant reading was added: عن; IK بعضهم بعضا 3) Maq. لما, and on the margin: يبيء يمنع ويكف من البواء أي المساواة 4) Maq. Mis.2 دماؤهم

٢٢ . وإن المؤمنين[1] المتقين[2] على أحسن هذا[3] واقومه

1) ISN om. but ISN2 has it 2) المؤمنين المتقين, Maq. المتقين المؤمنين 3) IH/DK ISN/Berl.; Maq. voc. هَذَا; IH IK ISN Nuw. Maw. Mis. هدى; Wüst. هُدًى ; Mis.2 voc. هُدْيٍ

٢٣ . وإنه لا يجير[1] مشرك مالا لقريش ولا نفسا ولا يحول دونه على مؤمن

1) Maw. بحير

٢٤ . وإنه من اعتبط[1] مؤمنا قتلا عن بينة[2] فإنه قود يد،[3] إلا[4] أن يرضى ولي المقتول، وإن المؤمنين عليه كافة ولا يحل لهم إلا قيام عليه

1) IK اغتبط 2) Maw. بنبه 3) Maq. ISN Maw.; IH/DK voc. يَدَ; IH Wüst. ISN2 IK Nuw. به; Mis. Mis.2 يديه 4) IK إلى

٢٥ . وإنه لا يحل لمؤمن[1] أقر بما في هذه الصحيفة وآمن بالله[2] واليوم الآخر أن ينصر محدثا ولا يؤويه ، وإنه[3] من نصره أو آواه فإن عليه لعنة الله[4] وغضبه يوم[5] القيامة ، ولا يؤخذ منه صرف ولا عدل

1) Maq. لمؤمن من 2) IH/Berl. بها 3) ISN وإن 4) Mis.2 ad. والملائكة 5) Mis.2 إلى يوم

٢٦ . وإنكم مهما اختلفتم فيه من شيء فإن مرده[1] إلى الله[2] وإلى محمد[3]

1) فإن مرده , IH/DK فأمره 2) IH IK ad. عز وجل 3) Mis.2 رسوله ; Wüst. ad. عليه السلام; IH/Berl. عليه السلام added above the line; IH Mis. ad. صلى الله عليه وسلم ; IK(ص) لا يسالم; IT IQ إلى أن قال , . . . مؤمن

٢٧ . وإن اليهود ينفقون[1] مع المؤمنين ما داموا محاربين[2]

1) Maw. يقفون; ISN IK Maq. يتفقون; ISN2 يثفقون; IQ متفقون 2) Maw. مجاورين; IH/Berl. voc. مُحارَبين; IH/DK محاربون

٢٨ . وإن يهود بني عوف أمة مع المؤمنين ،[1] لليهود دينهم وللمسلمين دينهم ،[2] مواليهم وأنفسهم ، إلا من ظلم وأثم ،[3] فإنه لا يوتغ[4] إلا نفسه وأهل بيته

1) Maw. ad. وإن; وإن . . . . , IT IQ وإن ليهود بني عوف ذمة من المؤمنين 2) ISN ad. بني النجار مثل (!) 3) Wüst. IH/DK ISN أو أثم; IH/Berl. أو أثم is added as a variant on the margin 4) IT IQ IH/DK يوقع

٢٩ . وإن ليهود بني النجار مثل ما ليهود بني عوف
٣٠ . وإن ليهود بني الحارث مثل ما ليهود بني عوف
٣١ . وإن ليهود بني ساعدة مثل ما ليهود بني عوف
٣٢ . وإن ليهود بني جشم مثل ما ليهود بني عوف[1]

1) IH/DK om. this clause

٣٣ . وإن ليهود بني[1] الأوس مثل ما ليهود بني عوف

1) IQ (but not IT) om.

٣٤ . وإن ليهود بني[1] ثعلبة مثل ما ليهود بني عوف، إلا من ظلم وأثم،[2] فإنه لا يوتغ[3] إلا نفسه وأهل بيته

1) IT (but not IQ) om. 2) IH/DK أو أثم (3 IT IQ IH/DK يوقع

٣٥ . وإن جفنة[1] بطن من ثعلبة كأنفسهم[2]

1) IT لحقه; IQ الحـمـه (without diacritical points) 2) IT IQ مثله; IH/Berl. Maw. IH/DK Maq. Nuw. om.

٣٦ . وإن لبني الشطيبة[1] مثل ما ليهود بني عوف

1) Maq. السبطية; IH/Berl. الشَطْبَة and the variant الشُطَيْبَة is added on the margin; IH/DK السطبة; IT Maw. Mis. الشطبة; Mis.1 voc. الشَطْبَة; Mis.2 الشظَبَة; Nuw. الشُّطُنَّة

٣٧ . وإن البر دون الاثم[1]

1) وإن البر . . . , Mis.1. voc. وإن البِـرَ دون الإثْم

٣٨ . وإن موالي[1] ثعلبة كأنفسهم[2]

1) Mis.2 لموالي (2 وإن ليهود بني النجار . . . , IK وإن ليهود بني النجار وبني الحارث وبني ساعدة وبني جشم وبني الأوس وبني ثعلبة وجفنة وبني الشطنة مثل ما ليهود بني عوف; ISN وذكر مثل ذلك ليهود بني النجار وبني الحارث وبني ساعدة وبني جشم وبني الأوس وبني ثعلبة وبني الشطبة وإن جفنة بطن من ثعلبة

٣٩ . وإن بطانة يهود كأنفسهم

٤٠ . وإنه لا يخرج منهم أحد إلا باذن محمد[1]

1) Wüst. ad. عليه السلام; IH IH/Berl. Maw. IH/DK ad. صلى الله عليه وسلم

٤١ . وإنه لا[1] ينحجز[2] على[3] ثأر جرح

1) وإنه لا . . . , IK Maw. IH/DK ولا ; IH/Berl. ولا and a variant reading is added above it: وإنه (2 IK ينحجر ; Maw. يتحجر ; ISN ينجحر but ISN2 has ينحجز; Wüst. IH/Berl. voc. يَنْحَجز ;

Mis.1 voc. يَنْحَجِز . 3) ISNعن

٤٢ . وإنه من فتك[1] فبنفسه[2] وأهل بيته،[3] إلا من ظلم[4]

1) Maw. فتل 2) IH ad. فتك 3) وأهل بيته . . . , IK ISN Maw. Maq. Mis. Mis.1 Mis.2 IH/DK Nuw. om. 4) Mis.1 voc. ظُلِمَ

٤٣ . وإن الله على أبر[1] هذا

1) IK Maw. اثر

٤٤ . وإن على اليهود[1] نفقتهم وعلى المسلمين نفقتهم

1) IH/DK يهود; IH/Berl. يهود, and the variant اليهود is added on the margin

٤٥ . وإن بينهم النصر على من حارب أهل هذه الصحيفة
٤٦ . وإن بينهم النصح والنصيحة
٤٧ . والبر دون الآثم[1]

1) Mis.1 voc. والبِرُ دون الإِثْم

٤٨ . وإنه لن[1] يأثم امرؤ بحليفه[2] وإن النصر للمظلوم[3]

1) Wüst. ISN Mis.2; IH IH/Berl. IK Maw. IH/DK Mis.2 لم 2) IH/Berl. بحليفة 3) Wüst. IH IH/DK Mis. Mis.2 Maw. Maq. ad. وإن اليّهود ينفقون مع المؤمنين ما داموا محاربين; IH/Berl. voc. محارَبين ... ; Maw. مجاورين ...

٤٩ . وإن يثرب حرام جوفها[1] لأهل هذه الصحيفة[2]

1) IK حرفها, var. خوفها; in a footnote this comment was added: وفي النهاية الجرف موضع قريب من المدينة ولعله الأصح 2) وإن بينهم . . . ، وإنه لا يخرج . . . , Nuw. om. IT IQ ثم يقول فيها

٥٠ . وإن الجار كالنفس، غير مضار ولا آثم
٥١ . وإنه لا تجار[1] حرمة إلا بإذن أهلها[2]

1) Maw. تجاز (2 وإنه لا تجار . . . , IT IQ om.

٥٢ . وإنه ما كان بين أهل هذه الصحيفة من حدث أو اشتجار[1] يخاف[2] فساده، فإن مرده إلى الله[3] وإلى محمد[4]

1) IH/DK ISN استجار; حدث . . . , IT حرث أو اشجار; IQ حدث واسحار (2 IT IQ يخشى; Maw. نحاف (3 IH Mis. ad. عز وجل (4 Wüst. ad. رسول الله صلعم; Mis. Mis.1 Mis.2 IH/DK IH Maw. ad. رسول الله صلى الله عليه وسلم; ISN IT IQ ad. صلى الله عليه وسلم ; IK Maq. ad. رسول الله

٥٣ . وإن الله على[1] أتقى[2] ما في هذه الصحيفة وأبره

1) IK ad. من (2 Maq. ابقى; IH/DK اتقا

٥٤ . وإنه لا تجار قريش ولا من نصرها
٥٥ . وإن بينهم النصر على من دهم يثرب
٥٦ . وإذا دعوا إلى صلح يصالحونه ويلبسونه، فإنهم يصالحونه ويلبسونه،[1] وإنهم إذا دعوا[2] إلى مثل ذلك، فإنه[3] لهم على المؤمنين، إلا من حارب في الدين، على كل أناس[4] حصتهم من جانبهم الذي قبلهم[5]

1) IK om.; IH/Berl. ISN/Berl. voc. in both cases ويُلبسونه (2 Maq. voc. twice دُعُوا; Mis.1 voc. دَعَوا . . . دُعُوا (3 ISN فإنهم but ISN2 has فإنه (4 Wüst. ISN ISN/Berl. Maq. Mis.1 Mis.2 Nuw. إنسان but ISN2 has أناس ; IH/DK first أناس was written, then it was written إنسان (5 وإن الله على أتقى . . . , IT IQ om.

٥٧ . وإن يهود الأوس مواليهم[1] وأنفسهم على مثل[2] ما لأهل[3] هذه[4] الصحيفة، مع[5] البر[6] المحسن[7] من أهل هذه[8] الصحيفة[9]

1) IT IQ وموالیهم (2 IH/DK Maw. ad. ذلك (3 IT في (4 ISN om. but ISN2 has it 5) Mis. من (6 IT البار; ISN البراء but ISN2 has البر (7 IT; Wüst. IH Maw. ISN Mis. Maq. المحض ; IH/DK المحصن (8 IH/DK Maw. om. 9) Wüst. ad. قال ابن هشام ويقال مع البر المحسن من أهل هذه الصحيفة، قال ابن اسحاق; ما لأهل . . . , ما في هذه الصحيفة

٥٨ . وإن البر دون الاثم[1]

1) وإن البر . . . , Maw. om.; Mis.1 voc. وإن البَرَ دُون الأَثِم . ; Mis.2 voc. وإن البِرَ دون الأثم

٥٩. لا يكسب[1] كاسب إلا على[2] نفسه

1) لا يكسب . . . , ISN ولا يكتسب 2) Maw. om.

٦٠. وإن الله على أصدق ما في هذه الصحيفة وأبره[1]

1) وإن يهود الأوس . . . , IK om.

٦١. وإنه لا يحول هذا الكتاب دون ظالم وآثم[1]

1) Wüst. Maw. IK IH/DK Maq. أو آثم; ISN Nuw. ولا آثم; ISN/Berl. أو اثم; IH/Berl. ولا اثم and a variant is added between the lines أو; Mis. أو آثم; Mis.1 voc. أو أَثِم; Mis.2 voc. أو آثِمٍ

٦٢. وإنه[1] من خرج[2] آمن ومن قعد آمن[3] [بالمدينة]، إلا من ظلم وأثم[4]

1) Wüst. ISN وإن; IH/Berl. وإنــه and between the lines a variant is added وإن 2) Maq. جرج 3) Maq. om.; آمن . . . آمن, IH/Berl. Mis.1 voc. أَمِنَ . . . أَمِنَ 4) Maq. Wüst. Maw.; IH IK ISN Mis. Mis.1 Mis.2 أو أثم

٦٣. وإن الله جار لمن[1] بر واتقى ومحمد رسول الله[2]

1) Maw. من 2) Wüst. ad. صلعم; IH ISN Maw. Mis.1 Mis.2 IH/DK Maq. ad. صلى الله عليه وسلم; ومحمد . . . , IK om.; وإن المؤمنين عليه . . . , Qast. only ومن ظلم وأثم فإنه لا يوتغ إلا نفسه .

٦٤. وإن أولاهم بهذه الصحيفة البر المحسن[1]

1) وإن . . . , Wüst. Nuw. om.; وإن البر . . . , IT وفيها أشياء أخر

Abū ʿUbayd's Version

وهذا كتاب رسول الله صلى الله عليه وسلم بين المؤمنين وأهل يثرب وموادعته يهودها مقدمه المدينة .
حدثني يحيى بن عبدالله بن بكير وعبدالله بن صالح قالا : حدثنا الليث بن سعد قال : حدثنا عقيل بن خالد عن ابن شهاب أنه قال : بلغني أن رسول الله صلى الله عليه وسلم كتب بهذا الكتاب :

هذا كتاب من محمد النبي رسول الله بين المؤمنين والمسلمين من قريش وأهل يثرب ومن تبعهم فلحق بهم فحل معهم وجاهد معهم

إنهم أمة واحدة دون الناس

المهاجرون من قريش على رباعتهم يتعاقلون بينهم معاقلهم الأولى وهم يفكون عانيهم بالمعروف والقسط بين المؤمنين

وبنو عوف على رباعتهم يتعاقلون معاقلهم الأولى وكل طائفة منهم تفدي عانيها بالمعروف والقسط بين المؤمنين

وبنو الحارث بن الخزرج على رباعتهم يتعاقلون معاقلهم الأولى وكل طائفة منهم تفدي عانيها بالمعروف والقسط بين المؤمنين

وبنو ساعدة على رباعتهم يتعاقلون معاقلهم الأولى وكل طائفة منهم تفدي عانيها بالمعروف والقسط بين المؤمنين

وبنو جشم على رباعتهم يتعاقلون معاقلهم الأولى وكل طائفة منهم تفدي عانيها بالمعروف والقسط بين المؤمنين

وبنو النجار على رباعتهم يتعاقلون معاقلهم الأولى وكل طائفة منهم تفدي عانيها بالمعروف والقسط بين المؤمنين

وبنو عمرو بن عوف على رباعتهم يتعاقلون معاقلهم الأولى وكل طائفة منهم تفدي عانيها بالمعروف والقسط بين المؤمنين

وبنو النبيت على رباعتهم يتعاقلون معاقلهم الأولى وكل طائفة منهم تفدي عانيها بالمعروف والقسط بين المؤمنين

وبنو الأوس على رباعتهم يتعاقلون معاقلهم الأولى وكل طائفة منهم تفدي عانيها بالمعروف والقسط بين المؤمنين

وإن المؤمنين لا يتركون مفرحا منهم أن يعينوه بالمعروف في فداء أو عقل

وإن المؤمنين المتقين أيديهم على كل من بغى عليهم وابتغى منهم دسيعة ظلم أو إثم أو عدوان أو فساد بين المؤمنين وإن أيديهم عليه جميعة ولو كان ولد أحدهم

لا يقتل مؤمن مؤمنا في كافر ولا ينصر كافرا على مؤمن

والمؤمنون بعضهم موالي بعض دون الناس

وإنه من تبعنا من اليهود فإن له المعروف والأسوة ، غير مظلومين ولا متناصر عليهم

وإن سلم المؤمنين واحد، ولا يسالم مؤمن دون مؤمن في قتال في سبيل الله إلا على سواء وعدل بينهم
وإن كل غازية غزت يعقب بعضهم بعضا
وإن المؤمنين المتقين على أحسن هذا وأقومه
وإنه لا يجير مشرك مالا لقريش ولا يعينها على مؤمن
وإنه من اعتبط مؤمنا قتلا فإنه قود، إلا أن يرضى ولي المقتول بالعقل، وإن المؤمنين عليه كافة
وإنه لا يحل لمؤمن أقر بما في هذه الصحيفة أو آمن بالله واليوم الآخر أن ينصر محدثا ولا يؤويه، فمن نصره أو آواه فإن عليه لعنة الله وغضبه إلى يوم القيامة، لا يقبل منه صرف ولا عدل
وإنكم ما اختلفتم فيه من شيء فإن حكمه إلى الله وإلى الرسول
وإن اليهود ينفقون مع المؤمنين ما داموا محاربين
وإن يهود بني عوف ومواليهم وأنفسهم أمة من المؤمنين، لليهود دينهم وللمؤمنين دينهم، إلا من ظلم وأثم، فإنه لا يوتغ إلا نفسه وأهل بيته
وإن ليهود بني النجار مثل ما ليهود بني عوف
وإن ليهود بني الحارث مثل ما ليهود بني عوف
وإن ليهود بني جشم مثل ما ليهود بني عوف
وإن ليهود بني ساعدة مثل ما ليهود بني عوف
وإن ليهود الأوس مثل ما ليهود بني عوف، إلا من ظلم، فإنه لا يوتغ إلا نفسه وأهل بيته
وإنه لا يخرج أحد منهم إلا باذن محمد
على اليهود نفقتهم وعلى المسلمين نفقتهم
وإن بينهم النصر على من حارب أهل هذه الصحيفة
وإن بينهم النصيحة والنصر للمظلوم
وإن المدينة جوفها حرم لأهل هذه الصحيفة
وإنه ما كان بين أهل هذه الصحيفة من حدث يخاف فساده، فإن أمره إلى الله وإلى محمد النبي
وإن بينهم النصر على من دهم يثرب
وإنهم إذا دعوا اليهود إلى صلح حليف لهم، فإنهم يصالحونه، وإن دعونا إلى مثل ذلك، فإنه لهم على المؤمنين، إلا من حارب الدين، وعلى كل أناس حصتهم من النفقة
وإن يهود الأوس ومواليهم وأنفسهم مع البر المحسن من أهل هذه الصحيفة
وإن بني الشطبة بطن من جفنة
وإن البر دون الاثم فلا يكسب كاسب إلا على نفسه
وأن الله على أصدق ما في هذه الصحيفة وأبره
ولا يحول الكتاب دون ظالم ولا آثم
وإنه من خرج آمن ومن قعد آمن، إلا من ظلم وأثم
وإن أولاهم بهذه الصحيفة البر المحسن

Abū ʿUbayd's Version with Variants

وهذا كتاب رسول الله صلى الله عليه وسلم بين المؤمين وأهل يثرب وموادعته يهودها مقدمه المدينة .
حدثني يحيى بن عبدالله بن بُكير وعبدالله بن صالح قالا : حدثنا الليث[1] بن سعد قال : حدثنا عُقَيل بن خالد عن ابن شهاب أنه قال : بلغني أن رسول الله صلى الله عليه وسلم كتب بهذا الكتاب :
هذا كتاب[2] من محمد النبي رسول الله [3]بين المؤمنين والمسلمين[4] من[5] قريش وأهل يثرب[6] ومن تبعهم[7] فلحق بهم فحل معهم [8]وجاهد معهم[9]

1) Zan.1 حدثنا حميد حدثني عبدالله بن صالح حدثني الليث 2) AU الكتاب 3) AU/DK1 (fragment) Zan.1 AU, fragment ad. صلى الله عليه وسلم 4) المؤمنين والمسلمين, IJ المسلمين والمؤمنين 5) AU om. but AU, fragment has it 6) وأهل يثرب, also IJ. Qast. starts here: وأين ذلك من كتابه . . . هذا, IJ عن ابن جريج قال في كتاب النبي صلى الله عليه وسلم بين المسلمين والمؤمنين من قريش وأهل يثرب ومن اتبعهم 7) كتب بين قريش والأنصار كتابا وفي الكتاب: Fa. starts here: بين قريش والأنصار; 8) فحل معهم, IJ om. 9) ومن تبعهم . . . , Qast. Fa. om.

إنهم[1] أمة واحدة دون[2] الناس[3]

1) Zurq. ad. أي الأنصار 2) AU AU/DK1 AU/DK2 Qast. Fa. IJ MT; Zan.1 من دون 3) AU/DK1 om., but AU/DK1 (fragment): الناس

المهاجرون[1] من قريش، على رباعتهم[2] يتعاقلون بينهم[3] معاقلهم الأولى وهم يفكون[4] عانيهم[5] بالمعروف والقسط بين المؤمنين[6]

1) AU والمهاجرون; Qast. Qast.1 Zurq. om. 2) Qast. Fa. MT; AU (after من قريش) قال ابن بكير : على رباعتهم ... AU1 ; ربعاتهم، قال أبو عبيد : والمحفوظ عندنا : رباعتهم AU, fragment ربعاتهم . . . حدثنا عبدالله بن صالح عن الليث ; cf. AU, interpretations, 264: بنو فلان على رباعتهم; AU/DK1 voc. ربَعَاتهم . . . على ربَاعتهم ; AU/DK1 (fragment) ربعاتهم 3) Qast.1 عنهم 4) AU, fragment; AU Zan.1 IJ (?) AU/DK1 AU/DK2 AU/Zah. يـفـدون; AU/DK1 (fragment) يكفون; وهم يفكون , Fa. Qast. MT ND Zurq. ويفكون 5) Zurq. عافيهم 6) AU, AU/DK2 ad. والمسلمين; AU, fragment ends here with the words: ثم ذكر حديثا طويلا في المعاقل

وبنو عوف على رباعتهم يتعاقلون معاقلهم الأولى وكل طائفة منهم[1] تفدي عانيها بالمعروف والقسط بين المؤمنين

1) Zan.1 om.

وبنو الحارث بن الخزرج على رباعتهم يتعاقلون معاقلهم الأولى وكل طائفة منهم تفدي عانيها بالمعروف والقسط بين المؤمنين
وبنو ساعدة على رباعتهم يتعاقلون معاقلهم الأولى وكل طائفة منهم تفدي عانيها بالمعروف والقسط بين المؤمنين
وبنو جشم على رباعتهم يتعاقلون معاقلهم الأولى وكل طائفة منهم تفدي عانيها بالمعروف والقسط بين المؤمنين
وبنو النجار على رباعتهم يتعاقلون معاقلهم الأولى وكل طائفة منهم تفدي عانيها بالمعروف والقسط[1] بين المؤمنين

1) AU AU/DK1 AU/DK 2) بالقسط والمعروف

وبنو عمرو بن عوف على رباعتهم يتعاقلون معاقلهم الأولى وكل طائفة منهم تفدي عانيها بالمعروف والقسط بين المؤمنين
وبنو النبيت على رباعتهم يتعاقلون معاقلهم الأولى وكل طائفة منهم تفدي عانيها بالمعروف والقسط بين المؤمنين
وبنو الأوس[1] على رباعتهم يتعاقلون معاقلهم الأولى وكل طائفة منهم تفدي عانيها بالمعروف والقسط بين المؤمنين [2]

1) Zan.1 وبني أوس 2) وبنو عوف . . . , Fa. Qast. om.

وإن[1] المؤمنين لا يتركون مفرحا[2] منهم أن يعينوه[3] بالمعروف في[4] فداء أو عقل

1) IJ إن 2) IJ مفدوحا; AU notes: وهو واحد والمعنى مفرحا جريج ابن حديث غير وفي : عبيد أبو قال
المثقل بالدين قال أبو عبيد : فالعاني والمفدوح قد تشترك فيه المرأة والرجل وقد يدخل الصغير في معنى العاني;
cf. ISN, interpretations, 199: والمفرح رواه ابن جريج مفرجا . قال أبو عبيد : ومعناهما واحد . وقال
Suhaylī II 252: وذكر أبو عبيد رواية; أبو عبيد : سمعت محمد بن الحسن يقول : هذا يروى بالحاء وبالجيم
من .Fa (4 يعطوه IJ (3 وقال في الكتاب : وألا يترك مفرح :ibid., 251; أخرى مفرج بالجيم

ولا يحالف مؤمن مولى مؤمن دونه[1]

1) دونه ... , AU/Zah. Zan.1 only

وإن المؤمنين المتقين[1] أيديهم[2] على كل[3] من بغى عليهم[4] وابتغى منهم[5] دسيعة ظلم أو إثم أو عدوان[6] أو فساد

بين المؤمنين وإن أيديهم عليه[7] جميعة[8] ولو كان ولد أحدهم[9]

1) Zan.1 والمتقين; Qast.1 om. 2) Zan.1 يد; Zan. om. 3) AU/Zah. Qast. Qast.1 MT ND om. 4) Qast. Qast.1 Fa. (but AU om.); AU/Zah. AU/DK1 Zan.1 وابتغى منهم(5 منهم , Zan.1 أو يبتغا ; Qast. Qast.1 Fa. MT Zan. Zurq. منهم;أو ابتغى, AU/Zah. AU/DK1 ND om.; على . . . , AU/DK2 على من بغا وابتغا (6 أو عدوان, AU/DK1 AU/DK2 only 7) Zan.1 عليهم (8 AU جمعيه; AU/Zah. AU/DK1 Zan.1 جميعه ; AU/DK2 جميعة (9 أو إثم . . . , Fa. Qast. Qast.1 om.

لا يقتل مؤمن مؤمنا في كافر ولا ينصر كافرا[1] على مؤمن[2]

1) AU/DK1 Zan.1 كافر; AU/DK2 first كافر was written then it was struck out and كافرا was written 2) على مؤمن, AU/DK1 AU/DK2

والمؤمنون بعضهم موالي بعض دون الناس
وإنه من تبعنا من اليهود فإن له المعروف والأسوة، غير مظلومين ولا متناصر عليهم

وإن سلم المؤمنين واحد،[1] ولا[2] يسالم مؤمن دون مؤمن في قتال في سبيل الله إلا على سواء وعدل بينهم[3]

1) Cf. Zurq. يذكر ويؤنث (2 Fa. MT لا (3 وأن سلم . . . , Qast. Qast.1 ولإن سلم المؤمنين واحد على سواء وعدل بينهم

وإن كل غازية غزت يعقب[1] بعضهم بعضا

1) AU/DK1 AU/DK2 voc. يُعقِب

وإن المؤمنين المتقين على أحسن هذا[1] وأقومه[2]

1) Zan.1 هُدًا; Zan. هُدى (2 وإن المؤمنين يبيء . . . , Fa. om.

وإنه لا يجير مشرك[1] مالا لقريش ولا يعينها على مؤمن[2]

1) Zan.1 مسرك (2 AU, interpretations, 264: فليس من موادعتهم أن يجيروا أموال أعدائه ولا يعينوهم عليه

وإنه من[1] اعتبط مؤمنا قتلا [2] فإنه[3] قود، إلا أن يرضى ولي[4] المقتول[5] بالعقل، [6] وإن[7] المؤمنين عليه[8] كافة [9]

1) وإنه من, AU/DK1 AU/DK2; Qast. Qast.1 Zurq. ومن 2) Zan.1 ad. عن نبيه; Zan. عن بينة 3) Zurq. Qast. Qast.1 فهو 4) Cf. AU, interpretations, 264: أولياء 5) AU/DK1 AU/DK2 Zan.1 Fa. 6) Zurq. Qast. Qast.1 om . 7) بالعقل . . . , Qast. ومن ظلم وأثم فإنه لا يوتغ إلا نفسه وأولاهم بهذه الصحيفة البر المحسن; Qast. ends here 8) AU عليها 9) وإن المؤمنين . . . , Fa. om .

وإنه لا يحل لمؤمن أقر بما في هذه الصحيفة أو آمن بالله واليوم الآخر أن ينصر محدثا أو[1] يؤويه، فمن نصره أو آواه[2] فإن عليه لعنة الله وغضبه إلى[3] يوم القيامة، لا يقبل منه صرف ولا عدل

1) Zan. AU/DK1 ولا; in AU/DK2 أو was first written and then it was corrected on the margin 2) فمن . . . , AU/DK1 فمن آواه; AU/Zah. (؟) فمن داواه; AU/DK2 فمن نصره او اواه 3) Zan.1 om.

وإنكم ما اختلفتم فيه من شيء فإن حكمه[1] إلى الله[2] وإلى الرسول[3]

1) فإن حكمه, AU/Zah. AU/DK1 فحكمه; AU/DK2 فان حكمه 2) AU AU/DK2 ad. تبارك وتعالى, but Zan.1 om. 3) AU AU/Zah. AU/DK1 AU/DK2 ad . صلى الله عليه وسلم, but Zan.1 has only الرسول; وإن المؤمنين عليه . . . , Fa. om .

وإن اليهود ينفقون[1] مع المؤمنين ما داموا محاربين

1) Fa. MT ND يتفقون; Zan.1 يفقون (the second character without diacritical points); AU/DK1 يممون (only the first character has diacritical points); AU/DK2 نفقون

وإن يهود بني عوف ومواليهم وأنفسهم أمة[1] من المؤمنين، لليهود دينهم وللمؤمنين دينهم، [2] إلا من ظلم وأثم، [3] فإنه لا يوتغ[4] إلا نفسه وأهل بيته

1) وإن . . . , Fa . وإن يهود بني عوف أنفسهم وأموالهم أمنة; MT ND وإن يهود بني عوف أنفسهم ومواليهم وإن يهود بني عوف أمة من المؤمنين لليهود دينهم وللمؤمنين دينهم, Zan . 1 . . . . وإن يهود بني عوف 2) امة 3) Fa . أو أثم 4) Zan . 1 يوقع; ND يوبغ ومواليهم وأنفسهم

وإن ليهود بني النجار مثل ما ليهود بني عوف
وإن ليهود بني الحارث مثل ما ليهود بني عوف

وإن ليهود بني جشم مثل ما ليهود بني عوف
وإن ليهود بني ساعدة مثل ما ليهود بني عوف
وإن ليهود الأوس مثل ما ليهود بني عوف، [1] إلا من ظلم، فإنه لا يوتغ إلا نفسه وأهل بيته

1) ما ليهود بني عوف, Zan. ذلك

وإنه لا يخرج أحد منهم إلا باذن محمد[1]

1) AU AU/Zah. AU/DK1 AU/DK2 Zan.1 ad. صلى الله عليه وسلم

على اليهود نفقتهم وعلى المسلمين نفقتهم[1]

1) على . . . , Zan.1 only

وإن بينهم النصر على من حارب أهل هذه الصحيفة
وإن بينهم[1] النصيحة والنصر للمظلوم

1) Zan.1 ad. النصح

وإن المدينة جوفها حرم لأهل هذه الصحيفة
وإنه ما كان بين أهل هذه الصحيفة من حدث[1] يخاف فساده، فإن أمره إلى الله وإلى محمد النبي

1) Zan.1 ad. أو اشتجار

وإن بينهم النصر على من دهم يثرب
وإنهم إذا دعوا اليهود إلى صلح حليف لهم، [1] فإنهم يصالحونه، وإن دعونا إلى مثل ذلك، فإنه لهم على المؤمنين، إلا من حارب الدين، وعلى كل أناس حصتهم من النفقة[2]

1) Zan.1 ad. بالأسوة 2) وإن ليهود بني النجار . . . , Fa. om.

وإن يهود الأوس ومواليهم وأنفسهم مع البر المحسن[1] من أهل هذه الصحيفة
1) ND المحبين

وإن بني الشطبة بطن من جفنة

وإن البر دون الاثم فلا يكسب كاسب إلا على نفسه
وأن الله على أصدق ما في هذه الصحيفة وأبره
ولا [1] يحول الكتاب دون ظالم[2] ولا آثم[3]

1) AU/DK1; AU Fa. MT ND AU/DK2 لا 2) Fa. MT ND ظلم ظالم 3) Fa. MT ND اثم آثم

وإنه من خرج آمن ومن قعد[1] آمن، إلا من ظلم وأثم[2]

1) Zan.1 ad. بالمدينة 2) Zan.1 إلا من امن إلا ظلم واثم (!); AU/Zah. AU/DK1 om. وأثم but AU/DK2 has it

وإن[1] أولاهم[2] بهذه الصحيفة البر المحسن

1) AU وإلى; AU1 وإن 2) وإن أولاهم , Zurq. Qast. واولاهم

The Versions of Ibn Isḥāq and Abū ᶜUbayd (in Bold Script)

كتاب رسول الله صلعم الذي كتبه بين المهاجرين والأنصار وموادعة يهود

وهذا كتاب رسول الله صلى الله عليه وسلم بين المؤمنين وأهل يثرب وموادعته يهودها مقدمه المدينة

قال ابن إسحاق: وكتب رسول الله صلى الله عليه وسلم كتابا بين المهاجرين والأنصار وادع فيه يهود وعاهدهم وأقرهم على دينهم وأموالهم وشرط لهم واشترط عليهم.

قال ابن إسحاق: حدثني عثمان بن محمد بن الأخنس بن شريق قال: أخذت من آل عمر بن الخطاب هذا الكتاب، كان مقرونا بكتاب الصدقة الذي كتب عمر للعمال، كتب:

حدثني يحيى بن عبدالله بن بكير وعبدالله بن صالح قالا: حدثنا الليث بن سعد قال: حدثنا عقيل بن خالد عن ابن شهاب أنه قال: بلغني أن رسول الله صلى الله عليه وسلم كتب بهذا الكتاب:

بسم الله الرحمن الرحيم

١. هذا كتاب من محمد النبي بين المؤمنين والمسلمين من قريش ويثرب ومن تبعهم فلحق بهم وجاهد معهم

هذا كتاب من محمد النبي رسول الله بين المؤمنين والمسلمين من قريش وأهل يثرب ومن تبعهم فلحق بهم فحل معهم وجاهد معهم

٢. إنهم أمة واحدة من دون الناس

إنهم أمة واحدة دون الناس

٣. المهاجرون من قريش على ربعتهم، يتعاقلون بينهم معاقلهم الأولى، وهم يفدون عانيهم بالمعروف واالقسط بين المؤمنين

المهاجرون من قريش على رباعتهم، يتعاقلون بينهم معاقلهم الأولى، وهم يفكون عانيهم بالمعروف والقسط بين المؤمنين

٤. وبنو عوف على ربعتهم يتعاقلون معاقلهم الأولى، وكل طائفة منهم تفدي عانيها بالمعروف والقسط بين المؤمنين

وبنو عوف على رباعتهم، يتعاقلون معاقلهم الأولى، وكل طائفة منهم تفدي عانيها بالمعروف والقسط بين المؤمنين

٥. وبنو الحارث على ربعتهم، يتعاقلون معاقلهم الأولى، وكل طائفة منهم تفدي عانيها بالمعروف والقسط بين المؤمنين

وبنو الحارث بن الخزرج على رباعتهم، يتعاقلون معاقلهم الأولى، وكل طائفة منهم تفدي عانيها بالمعروف والقسط بين المؤمنين

٦. وبنو ساعدة على ربعتهم، يتعاقلون معاقلهم الأولى، وكل طائفة منهم تفدي عانيها بالمعروف والقسط بين المؤمنين

وبنو ساعدة على رباعتهم، يتعاقلون معاقلهم الأولى، وكل طائفة منهم تفدي عانيها بالمعروف والقسط بين المؤمنين

٧ . وبنو جشم على ربعتهم، يتعاقلون معاقلهم الأولى، وكل طائفة منهم تفدي عانيها بالمعروف والقسط بين المؤمنين

وبنو جشم على رباعتهم، يتعاقلون معاقلهم الأولى، وكل طائفة منهم تفدي عانيها بالمعروف والقسط بين المؤمنين

٨ . وبنو النجار على ربعتهم، يتعاقلون معاقلهم الأولى، وكل طائفة منهم تفدي عانيها بالمعروف والقسط بين المؤمنين

وبنو النجار على رباعتهم، يتعاقلون معاقلهم الأولى، وكل طائفة منهم تفدي عانيها بالمعروف والقسط بين المؤمنين

٩ . وبنو عمرو بن عوف على ربعتهم، يتعاقلون معاقلهم الأولى، وكل طائفة منهم تفدي عانيها بالمعروف والقسط بين المؤمنين

وبنو عمرو بن عوف على رباعتهم، يتعاقلون معاقلهم الأولى، وكل طائفة منهم تفدي عانيها بالمعروف والقسط بين المؤمنين

١٠ . وبنو النبيت على ربعتهم، يتعاقلون معاقلهم الأولى، وكل طائفة منهم تفدي عانيها بالمعروف والقسط بين المؤمنين

وبنو النبيت على رباعتهم، يتعاقلون معاقلهم الأولى، وكل طائفة منهم تفدي عانيها بالمعروف والقسط بين المؤمنين

١١ . وبنو الأوس على ربعتهم، يتعاقلون معاقلهم الأولى، وكل طائفة منهم تفدي عانيها بالمعروف والقسط بين المؤمنين

وبنو الأوس على رباعتهم، يتعاقلون معاقلهم الأولى، وكل طائفة منهم تفدي عانيها بالمعروف والقسط بين المؤمنين

١٢ . وإن المؤمنين لا يتركون مفرحا بينهم أن يعطوه بالمعروف في فداء أو عقل

وإن المؤمنين لا يتركون مفرحا منهم أن يعينوه بالمعروف في فداء أو عقل

١٣ . ولا يحالف مؤمن مولى مؤمن دونه

١٤ . وإن المؤمنين المتقين على من بغى منهم أو ابتغى دسيعة ظلم أو إثم أو عدوان أو فساد بين المؤمنين، وإن أيديهم عليه جميعة ولو كان ولد أحدهم

وإن المؤمنين المتقين أيديهم على كل من بغى عليهم وابتغى منهم دسيعة ظلم أو إثم أو عدوان أو فساد بين المؤمنين، وإن أيديهم عليه جميعة ولو كان ولد أحدهم

١٥ . ولا يقتل مؤمن مؤمنا في كافر ولا ينصر كافرا على مؤمن

لا يقتل مؤمن مؤمنا في كافر ولا ينصر كافرا على مؤمن

١٦ . وإن ذمة الله واحدة، يجير عليهم أدناهم

١٧ . وإن المؤمنين بعضهم موالي بعض دون الناس

والمؤمنون بعضهم موالي بعض دون الناس

١٨ . وإنه من تبعنا من يهود فإن له النصر والأسوة، غير مظلومين ولا متناصر عليهم

وإنه من تبعنا من اليهود فإن له المعروف والأسوة، غير مظلومين ولا متناصر عليهم

١٩ . وإن سلم المؤمنين واحدة، لا يسالم مؤمن دون مؤمن في قتال في سبيل الله إلا على سواء وعدل بينهم

وإن سلم المؤمنين واحد، ولا يسالم مؤمن دون مؤمن في قتال في سبيل الله إلا على سواء وعدل بينهم

٢٠ . وإن كل غازية غزت معنا يعقب بعضها بعضا

وإن كل غازية غزت يعقب بعضهم بعضا

٢١ . وإن المؤمنين يبيء بعضهم عن بعض بما نال دماءهم في سبيل الله

٢٢ . وإن المؤمنين المتقين على أحسن هذا واقومه

وإن المؤمنين المتقين على أحسن هذا وأقومه

٢٣ . وإنه لا يجير مشرك مالا لقريش ولا نفسا ولا يحول دونه على مؤمن

وإنه لا يجير مشرك مالا لقريش ولا يعينها على مؤمن

٢٤ . وإنه من اعتبط مؤمنا قتلا عن بينة فإنه قود يد، إلا أن يرضى ولي المقتول، وإن المؤمنين عليه كافة ولا يحل لهم إلا قيام عليه

وإنه من اعتبط مؤمنا قتلا فإنه قود، إلا أن يرضى ولي المقتول بالعقل، وإن المؤمنين عليه كافة

٢٥ . وإنه لا يحل لمؤمن أقر بما في هذه الصحيفة وآمن بالله واليوم الآخر أن ينصر محدثا ولا يؤويه، وإنه من نصره أو آواه فإن عليه لعنة الله وغضبه يوم القيامة، ولا يؤخذ منه صرف ولا عدل

وإنه لا يحل لمؤمن أقر بما في هذه الصحيفة أو آمن بالله واليوم الآخر أن ينصر محدثا ولا يؤويه، فمن نصره أو آواه فإن عليه لعنة الله وغضبه إلى يوم القيامة، لا يقبل منه صرف ولا عدل

٢٦ . وإنكم مهما اختلفتم فيه من شيء فإن مرده إلى الله وإلى محمد

وإنكم ما اختلفتم فيه من شيء فإن حكمه إلى الله وإلى الرسول

٢٧ . وإن اليهود ينفقون مع المؤمنين ما داموا محاربين

وإن اليهود ينفقون مع المؤمنين ما داموا محاربين

٢٨ . وإن يهود بني عوف أمة مع المؤمنين، لليهود دينهم وللمسلمين دينهم، مواليهم وأنفسهم، إلا من ظلم وأثم، فإنه لا يوتغ إلا نفسه وأهل بيته

وإن يهود بني عوف ومواليهم وأنفسهم أمة من المؤمنين، لليهود دينهم وللمؤمنين دينهم، إلا من ظلم وأثم، فإنه لا يوتغ إلا نفسه وأهل بيته

٢٩ . وإن ليهود بني النجار مثل ما ليهود بني عوف

٣٠ . وإن ليهود بني الحارث مثل ما ليهود بني عوف

٣١ . وإن ليهود بني ساعدة مثل ما ليهود بني عوف

وإن ليهود بني ساعدة مثل ما ليهود بني عوف

٣٢ . وإن ليهود بني جشم مثل ما ليهود بني عوف

وإن ليهود بني جشم مثل ما ليهود بني عوف In AU the Sāʿida appear after the Jusham

٣٣ . وإن ليهود بني الأوس مثل ما ليهود بني عوف
وإن ليهود الأوس مثل ما ليهود بني عوف
٣٤ . وإن ليهود بني ثعلبة مثل ما ليهود بني عوف ، إلا من ظلم وأثم ، فإنه لا يوتغ إلا نفسه وأهل بيته
إلا من ظلم، فإنه لا يوتغ إلا نفسه وأهل بيته
٣٥ . وإن جفنة بطن من ثعلبة كأنفسهم
٣٦ . وإن لبني الشطيبة مثل ما ليهود بني عوف See below after §59
٣٧ . وإن البر دون الاثم
٣٨ . وإن موالي ثعلبة كأنفسهم
٣٩ . وإن بطانة يهود كأنفسهم
٤٠ . وإنه لا يخرج منهم أحد إلا باذن محمد
وإنه لا يخرج أحد منهم إلا باذن محمد
٤١ . وإنه لا ينحجز على ثأر جرح
٤٢ . وإنه من فتك فبنفسه وأهل بيته ، إلا من ظلم
٤٣ . وإن الله على أبر هذا
٤٤ . وإن على اليهود نفقتهم وعلى المسلمين نفقتهم
على اليهود نفقتهم وعلى المسلمين نفقتهم
٤٥ . وإن بينهم النصر على من حارب أهل هذه الصحيفة
٤٦ . وإن بينهم النصح والنصيحة
وإن بينهم النصيحة والنصر للمظلوم
٤٧ . والبر دون الاثم
٤٨ . وإنه لن يأثم امرؤ بحليفه وإن النصر للمظلوم
٤٩ . وإن يثرب حرام جوفها لأهل هذه الصحيفة
وإن المدينة جوفها حرم لأهل هذه الصحيفة
٥٠ . وإن الجار كالنفس ، غير مضار ولا آثم
٥١ . وإنه لا تجار حرمة إلا بإذن أهلها
٥٢ . وإنه ما كان بين أهل هذه الصحيفة من حدث أو اشتجار يخاف فساده ، فإن مرده إلى الله وإلى محمد
وإنه ما كان بين أهل هذه الصحيفة من حدث يخاف فساده، فإن أمره إلى الله وإلى محمد النبي
٥٣ . وإن الله على أتقى ما في هذه الصحيفة وأبره
٥٤ . وإنه لا تجار قريش ولا من نصرها
٥٥ . وإن بينهم النصر على من دهم يثرب
وإن بينهم النصر على من دهم يثرب
٥٦ . وإذا دعوا إلى صلح يصالحونه ويلبسونه ، فإنهم يصالحونه ويلبسونه ، وإنهم إذا دعوا إلى مثل ذلك ، فإنه لهم على المؤمنين ، إلا من حارب في الدين ، على كل أناس حصتهم من جانبهم الذي قبلهم

وإنهم إذا دعوا اليهود إلى صلح حليف لهم، فإنهم يصالحونه، وإن دعونا إلى مثل ذلك، فإنه لهم على المؤمنين، إلا من حارب الدين، وعلى كل أناس حصتهم من النفقة

٥٧ . وإن يهود الأوس مواليهم وأنفسهم على مثل ما لأهل هذه الصحيفة، مع البر المحسن من أهل هذه الصحيفة

وإن يهود الأوس ومواليهم وأنفسهم مع البر المحسن من أهل هذه الصحيفة

٥٨ . وإن البر دون الاثم

٥٩ . لا يكسب كاسب إلا على نفسه

وإن بني الشطبة بطن من جفنة

وإن البر دون الاثم فلا يكسب كاسب إلا على نفسه

٦٠ . وإن الله على أصدق ما في هذه الصحيفة وأبره

وأن الله على أصدق ما في هذه الصحيفة وأبره

٦١ . وإنه لا يحول هذا الكتاب دون ظالم وآثم

ولا يحول الكتاب دون ظالم ولا آثم

٦٢ . وإنه من خرج آمن ومن قعد آمن [بالمدينة]، إلا من ظلم وأثم

وإنه من خرج آمن ومن قعد آمن، إلا من ظلم وأثم

٦٣ . وإن الله جار لمن بر واتقى ومحمد رسول الله

٦٤ . وإن أولاهم بهذه الصحيفة البر المحسن

وإن أولاهم بهذه الصحيفة البر المحسن

Text and Translation of Ibn Isḥāq's Version

§1. *hādhā kitāb min muḥammad al-nabī bayna l-muʾminīna wa-l-muslimīna min quraysh wa-yathrib wa-man tabiʿahum fa-laḥiqa bihim wa-jāhada maʿahum*

THIS IS A COMPACT FROM MUḤAMMAD THE PROPHET BETWEEN THE MUʾMINŪN AND MUSLIMŪN OF QURAYSH AND YATHRIB AND THOSE WHO JOIN THEM AS CLIENTS, ATTACH THEMSELVES TO THEM AND FIGHT THE HOLY WAR WITH THEM.

§2. *innahum umma wāḥida min dūni l-nās*

THEY FORM ONE PEOPLE TO THE EXCLUSION OF OTHERS.

§3. *al-muhājirūn min quraysh ʿalā ribāʿatihim, yataʿāqalūna baynahum wa-hum yafdūna ʿāniyahum bi-l-maʿrūf wa-l-qisṭ bayna l-muʾminīna*

THE MUHĀJIRŪN FROM QURAYSH KEEP TO THEIR TRIBAL ORGANIZATION AND LEADERSHIP, CO-OPERATING WITH EACH OTHER REGARDING BLOOD MONEY [and related matters] AND RANSOMING THEIR CAPTIVES ACCORDING TO WHAT IS CUSTOMARY AND EQUITABLE AMONG THE MUʾMINŪN.

§4. *wa-banū ʿawf ʿalā ribāʿatihim, yataʿāqalūna maʿāqilahumu l-ʾūlā, wa-kull ṭāʾifa minhum tafdī ʿāniyahā bi-l-maʿrūf wa-l-qisṭ bayna l-muʾminīna*

§5–§11. *wa-banū l-ḥārith ʿalā ribāʿatihim, yataʿāqalūna maʿāqilahumu l-ʾūlā, wa-kull ṭāʾifa minhum tafdī ʿāniyahā bi-l-maʿrūf wa-l-qisṭ bayna l-muʾminīna, wa-banū sāʿida... wa-banū jusham... wa-banu l-najjār... wa-banū ʿamr ibn ʿawf... wa-banū l-nabīt... wa-banū l-aws...*

THE BANŪ ʿAWF KEEP TO THEIR TRIBAL ORGANIZATION AND LEADERSHIP, CONTINUING TO CO-OPERATE WITH EACH OTHER IN ACCORDANCE WITH THEIR FORMER MUTUAL AID AGREEMENTS REGARDING BLOOD MONEY [and related matters], AND EVERY SUB-GROUP RANSOMS ITS CAPTIVES ACCORDING TO WHAT IS CUSTOMARY AND EQUITABLE AMONG THE MUʾMINŪN.

THE BANŪ L-ḤĀRITH KEEP TO THEIR TRIBAL ORGANIZATION AND LEADERSHIP. . . .

THE BANŪ SĀʿIDA KEEP TO THEIR TRIBAL ORGANIZATION AND LEADERSHIP. . . .

THE BANŪ JUSHAM KEEP TO THEIR TRIBAL ORGANIZATION AND LEADERSHIP. . . .

THE BANŪ L-NAJJĀR KEEP TO THEIR TRIBAL ORGANIZATION AND LEADERSHIP. . .

THE BANŪ ʿAMR IBN ʿAWF KEEP TO THEIR TRIBAL ORGANIZATION AND LEADERSHIP. . . .

THE BANŪ L-NABĪT KEEP TO THEIR TRIBAL ORGANIZATION AND LEADERSHIP. . . .

THE BANŪ L-AWS KEEP TO THEIR TRIBAL ORGANIZATION AND LEADERSHIP. . . .

§12. *wa-inna l-muʾminīna lā yatrukūna mufraḥan baynahum an yuʿṭūhu bi-l-maʿrūf fī fidāʾ aw ʿaql*

THE MUʾMINŪN SHALL NOT NEGLECT TO GIVE [aid] TO A DEBTOR AMONGST THEM [who is not entitled to support according to tribal law, but will aid him] ACCORDING TO WHAT IS CUSTOMARY IN MATTERS OF RANSOM OR BLOOD MONEY.

§13. *wa-lā yuḥālifu muʾmin mawlā muʾmin dūnahu*

NO MUʾMIN SHALL MAKE AN ALLIANCE WITH AN ALLY OF ANOTHER MUʾMIN TO THE EXCLUSION OF THE LATTER.

§14. *wa-inna l-muʾminīna l-muttaqīna ʿalā man baghā minhum awi btaghā dasīʿat ẓulm aw ithm aw ʿudwān aw fasād bayna l-muʾminīna wa-inna aydiyahum ʿalayhi jamīʿan wa-law kāna walad aḥadihim*

THE GOD-FEARING MUʾMINŪN ARE AGAINST WHOSOEVER OF THEM DEMANDS AN EXCESSIVE SUM OF BLOOD MONEY OR DESIRES A GIFT OF INJUSTICE, SIN, TRANSGRESSION, OR EVIL AMONG THE MUʾMINŪN. THEY SHALL ALL UNITE AGAINST HIM EVEN IF HE IS THE SON OF ONE OF THEM.

§15. *wa-lā yaqtulu muʾmin muʾminan fī kāfir wa-lā yanṣuru kāfiran ʿalā muʾmin*

A MUʾMIN WILL NOT KILL A MUʾMIN IN RETALIATION FOR A NON-BELIEVER AND WILL NOT AID A NON-BELIEVER AGAINST A MUʾMIN.

§16. *wa-inna dhimmata llāh wāḥida yujīru ʿalayhim adnāhum*

THE PROTECTION OF ALLĀH [as extended by the Muʾminūn] IS UNVARYING, [and hence] THE LEAST OF THEM IS ENTITLED TO GRANT PROTECTION THAT IS BINDING FOR ALL OF THEM.

§17. *wa-inna l-muʾminīna baʿḍuhum mawālī baʿḍ dūna l-nās*

THE MUʾMINŪN ARE EACH OTHER'S ALLIES TO THE EXCLUSION OF OTHER PEOPLE.

§18. *wa-innahu man tabiʿanā min yahūd fa-inna lahu l-naṣr wa-l-uswa, ghayr maẓlūmīna wa-lā mutanāṣar ʿalayhim*

THE JEWS WHO JOIN US AS CLIENTS WILL RECEIVE AID AND EQUAL RIGHTS; THEY WILL NOT BE WRONGED, NOR WILL THEIR ENEMIES BE AIDED AGAINST THEM.

§19. *wa-inna silma l-muʾminīna wāḥida lā yusālimu muʾmin dūna muʾmin fī qitāl fī sabīli llāh illā ʿalā sawāʾ wa-ʿadl baynahum*

THE PEACE OF THE MUʾMINŪN IS UNVARYING, [and hence] A MUʾMIN WILL NOT MAKE PEACE TO THE EXCLUSION OF ANOTHER MUʾMIN IN FIGHTING IN THE CAUSE OF ALLĀH, EXCEPT ON THE BASIS OF EQUALITY AND EQUITY BETWEEN THEM.

§20. *wa-inna kull ghāziya ghazat maʿanā yaʿqubu baʿḍuhā baʿḍan*

EACH RAIDING PARTY THAT RAIDS WITH US WILL TAKE TURNS WITH EACH OTHER.

§21. *wa-inna l-muʾminīna yubīʾu baʿḍuhum ʿan baʿḍ bi-mā nāla dimāʾahum fī sabīli llāh*

THE MUʾMINŪN WILL FULLY RETALIATE ON EACH OTHER'S BEHALF IN THE CASE OF DEATH OR INJURY INCURRED WHILE FIGHTING IN THE CAUSE OF ALLĀH.

§22. *wa-inna l-muʾminīna l-muttaqīna ʿalā aḥsan hādhā wa-aqwamihi*

THE GOD-FEARING MUʾMINŪN GUARANTEE THE BEST AND MOST UPRIGHT FULFILMENT OF THIS [treaty].

§23. *wa-innahu lā yujīru mushrik mālan li-quraysh wa-lā nafsan wa-lā yaḥūlu dūnahu ʿalā muʾmin*

A POLYTHEIST WILL NOT GRANT PROTECTION TO ANY PROPERTY OR TO ANY PERSON OF QURAYSH, NOR WILL HE INTERVENE BETWEEN THEM [viz. the property or person] AND A MUʾMIN.

§24. *wa-innahu mani ʿtabaṭa muʾminan qatlan ʿan bayyina fa-innahu qawad yad illā an yarḍā waliyyu l-maqtūl wa-inna l-muʾminīna ʿalayhi kāffa wa-lā yaḥillu lahum illā qiyām ʿalayhi*

SHOULD ANYONE MURDER A MUʾMIN ARBITRARILY, AND SHOULD UNDISPUTED EVIDENCE OF THIS MURDER EXIST, HE WILL BE SLAIN IN RETALIATION, UNLESS THE AGNATIC KIN OF THE DECEASED IS APPEASED [with blood money]. ALL THE MUʾMINŪN ARE [united] AGAINST HIM AND IT IS NOT PERMISSIBLE TO THEM NOT TO ACT AGAINST HIM.

§25. *wa-innahu lā yaḥillu li-muʾmin aqarra bi-mā fī hādhihi l-ṣaḥīfa wa-āmana bi-llāh wa-l-yawmi l-ākhir an yanṣura muḥdithan wa-lā yuʾwiyahu wa-innahu man naṣarahu aw āwāhu fa-inna ʿalayhi laʿnata llāhi wa-ghaḍabahu yawma l-qiyāma wa-lā yuʾkhadhu minhu ṣarf wa-lā ʿadl*

IT IS NOT PERMISSIBLE TO A MUʾMIN WHO ACKNOWLEDGES WHAT IS IN THIS TREATY AND BELIEVES IN ALLĀH AND THE LAST DAY TO SUPPORT A MURDERER OR GIVE HIM SHELTER. UPON WHOEVER SUPPORTS HIM OR GIVES HIM SHELTER IS THE CURSE OF ALLĀH AND HIS WRATH ON THE DAY OF RESURRECTION, AND NEITHER REPENTANCE NOR RANSOM WILL BE ACCEPTED FROM HIM.

§26. *wa-innakum mahmā khtalaftum fīhi min shayʾ fa-inna maraddahu ilā llāh wa-ilā muḥammad*

WHATEVER YOU DIFFER ABOUT SHOULD BE BROUGHT BEFORE ALLĀH AND MUḤAMMAD.

§27. *wa-inna l-yahūd yunfiqūna maʿa l-muʾminīna mā dāmū muḥāribīna*

THE JEWS SHARE EXPENDITURE WITH THE MUʾMINŪN AS LONG AS THEY ARE AT WAR.

§28. *wa-inna yahūd banī ʿawf umma maʿa [amana mina] l-muʾminīna, li-l-yahūd dīnuhum wa-li-l-muslimīna dīnuhum, mawālīhim wa-anfusihim, illā man ẓalama wa-athima fa-innahu lā yūtighu illā nafsahu wa-ahl baytihi*

THE JEWS OF BANŪ ʿAWF ARE SECURE FROM THE MUʾMINŪN. THE JEWS HAVE THEIR RELIGION AND THE MUSLIMŪN HAVE THEIRS. [This applies to] THEIR ALLIES AND THEIR PERSONS. BUT WHOEVER ACTS UNJUSTLY AND SINS WILL ONLY DESTROY HIMSELF AND HIS AGNATES.

§29–§33. *wa-inna li-yahūd banī l-najjār mithl mā li-yahūd banī ʿawf... wa-inna li-yahūd banī l-ḥārith... wa-inna li-yahūd banī sāʿida... wa-inna li-yahūd banī jusham... wa-inna li-yahūd banī l-aws...*

THE JEWS OF THE BANŪ L-NAJJĀR HAVE THE SAME [rights] AS THE JEWS OF BANŪ ʿAWF.

THE JEWS OF BANŪ L-ḤĀRITH HAVE THE SAME [rights] AS THE JEWS OF BANŪ ʿAWF.

THE JEWS OF BANŪ SĀʿIDA HAVE THE SAME [rights] AS THE JEWS OF BANŪ ʿAWF.

THE JEWS OF BANŪ JUSHAM HAVE THE SAME [rights] AS THE JEWS OF BANŪ ʿAWF.

THE JEWS OF BANŪ L-AWS HAVE THE SAME [rights] AS THE JEWS OF BANŪ ʿAWF.

§34. *wa-inna li-yahūd banī thaʿlaba mithl mā li-yahūd banī ʿawf, illā man ẓalama wa-athima fa-innahu lā yūtighu illā nafsahu wa-ahl baytihi*

THE JEWS OF BANŪ THAʿLABA HAVE THE SAME [rights] AS THE JEWS OF BANŪ ʿAWF. BUT WHOEVER ACTS UNJUSTLY AND SINS WILL ONLY DESTROY HIMSELF AND HIS AGNATES.

§35. *wa-inna jafna baṭn min thaʿlaba ka-anfusihim*

THE JAFNA ARE A TRIBAL GROUP OF THE THAʿLABA AND ARE ON A PAR WITH THEM.

§36. *wa-inna li-banī l-shuṭayba mithl mā li-yahūd banī ʿawf.*

THE BANŪ L-SHUṬAYBA HAVE THE SAME [rights] AS THE JEWS OF BANŪ ʿAWF.

§37. *wa-inna l-barr dūna l-āthim*

THE RIGHTEOUS MAN WILL RESTRAIN THE SINNER.

§38. *wa-inna mawāliya thaʿlaba ka-anfusihim*

THE ALLIES OF THE THAʿLABA ARE ON A PAR WITH THEM.

§39. *wa-inna biṭānat yahūd ka-anfusihim*

THE NOMADIC ALLIES OF THE JEWS ARE ON A PAR WITH THEM.

§40. *wa-innahu lā yakhruju minhum aḥad illā bi-idhn muḥammad*

NO-ONE OF THEM [viz. of the Jews' nomadic allies] MAY GO OUT [of Medina] WITHOUT MUḤAMMAD'S PERMISSION.

§41. *wa-innahu lā yunḥajazu ʿalā thaʾr jurḥ*

THERE IS NO REFRAINING FROM RETALIATION FOR A WOUND.

§42. *wa-innahu man fataka fa-bi-nafsihi wa-ahl baytihi, illā man ẓalama*

HE WHO KILLS [someone entitled to security] KILLS HIMSELF AND HIS AGNATES, UNLESS HE [viz. his victim] ACTED UNJUSTLY.

§43. *wa-inna llāh ʿalā abarr hādhā*

ALLĀH GUARANTEES THE MOST RIGHTEOUS FULFILMENT OF THIS [treaty].

§44. *wa-inna ʿalā l-yahūd nafaqatahum wa-ʿalā l-muslimīna nafaqatahum*

INCUMBENT UPON THE JEWS IS THEIR EXPENDITURE AND UPON THE MUSLIMŪN THEIRS.

§45. *wa-inna baynahumu l-naṣr ʿalā man ḥāraba ahl hādhihi l-ṣaḥīfa*

THEY WILL AID EACH OTHER AGAINST WHOSOEVER IS AT WAR WITH THE PEOPLE OF THIS TREATY.

§46. *wa-inna baynahumu l-nuṣḥ wa-l-naṣīḥa*

THERE IS AMONG THEM SINCERE ADVICE AND COUNSEL.

§47. *wa-l-barr dūna l-āthim*

THE RIGHTEOUS MAN WILL RESTRAIN THE SINNER.

§48. *wa-innahu lan yaʾthama mruʾ bi-ḥalīfihi wa-inna l-naṣr li-l-maẓlūm*

A MAN WILL NOT BETRAY HIS CLIENT; AID WILL BE PROVIDED TO HIM WHO HAS BEEN WRONGED.

§49. *wa-inna yathrib ḥarām jawfuhā li-ahl hādhihi l-ṣaḥīfa*

THE JAWF OF YATHRIB IS A ḤARAM FOR THE PEOPLE OF THIS TREATY.

§50. *wa-inna l-jār ka-l-nafs ghayr muḍārr wa-lā āthim*

THE PROTECTED NEIGHBOUR IS LIKE ONE'S SELF, AS LONG AS HE DOES NOT CAUSE DAMAGE OR ACT SINFULLY.

§51. *wa-innahu lā tujāru ḥurma illā bi-idhn ahlihā*

NO PROTECTION WILL BE GRANTED WITHOUT THE PERMISSION OF THE PARTIES TO THIS TREATY.

§52. *wa-innahu mā kāna bayna ahl hādhihi l-ṣaḥīfa min ḥadath awi shtijār yukhāfu fasāduhu, fa-inna maraddahu ilā llāh wa-ilā muḥammad*

EVERY MURDER [or another major crime] OR DISPUTE BETWEEN THE PEOPLE OF THIS TREATY FROM WHICH EVIL IS TO BE FEARED SHOULD BE BROUGHT BEFORE ALLĀH AND MUḤAMMAD.

§53. *wa-inna llāh ʿalā atqā mā fī hādhihi l-ṣaḥīfa wa-abarrihi*

ALLĀH GUARANTEES THE TRUEST AND MOST RIGHTEOUS FULFILMENT OF THE CLAUSES OF THIS TREATY.

§54. *wa-innahu lā tujāru quraysh wa-lā man naṣarahā*

NO PROTECTION WILL BE GRANTED TO QURAYSH NOR TO WHOEVER SUPPORTS THEM.

§55. *wa-inna baynahumu l-naṣr ʿalā man dah(a/i)ma yathrib*

THEY [viz. the participating parties] UNDERTAKE TO AID EACH OTHER AGAINST WHOSOEVER ATTACKS YATHRIB.

§56. *wa-idhā duʿū ilā ṣulḥ yuṣāliḥūnahu wa-yalbasūnahu, fa-innahum yuṣāliḥūnahu wa-yalbasūnahu; wa-innahum idhā daʿaw ilā mithl dhālika fa-innahu lahum ʿalā l-muʾminīna, illā man ḥāraba fī l-dīn; ʿalā kull unās ḥiṣṣatuhum min jānibihimu lladhī qibalahum*

IF THEY [the Jews] ARE CALLED [by the other parties to the treaty] TO CONCLUDE AND ACCEPT (?) AN AGREEMENT, THEY WILL CONCLUDE AND ACCEPT (?) IT; AND IF THEY [the Jews] CALL FOR THE SAME, IT IS INCUMBENT UPON THE MUʾMINŪN TO GIVE IT THEM, WITH THE EXCEPTION OF THOSE FIGHTING FOR RELIGION. EVERYBODY SHOULD PAY THEIR SHARE AT THEIR OWN EXPENSE (?).

§57. *wa-inna yahūda l-aws mawāliyahum wa-anfusahum ʿalā mithl mā li-ahl hādhihi l-ṣaḥīfa maʿa al-barr al-muḥsin min ahl hādhihi l-ṣaḥīfa*

THE JEWS OF AWS, THEIR ALLIES AND THEIR PERSONS, HAVE THE SAME STANDING AS THE PEOPLE OF THIS TREATY, TOGETHER WITH THE RIGHTEOUS AND SINCERE OF THE PEOPLE OF THIS TREATY.

§58. *al-barr dūna l-āthim*

THE RIGHTEOUS MAN WILL RESTRAIN THE SINNER.

§59. *lā yaksibu kāsib illā ʿalā nafsihi*

HE WHO OFFENDS, OFFENDS ONLY AGAINST HIMSELF.

§60. *wa-inna llāh ʿalā aṣdaq mā fī hādhihi l-ṣaḥīfa wa-abarrihi*

ALLĀH GUARANTEES THE MOST LOYAL AND MOST RIGHTEOUS FULFILMENT OF THIS TREATY.

§61. *wa-innahu lā yaḥūlu hādhā l-kitāb dūna ẓālim wa-āthim*

THIS COMPACT DOES NOT INTERVENE TO PROTECT AN UNJUST MAN AND A SINNER.

§62. *wa-innahu man kharaja āmin wa-man qaʿada āmin, illā man ẓalama wa-athima*

HE [of the Jews] WHO GOES OUT [opting not to participate in the compact] IS SAFE AND HE WHO STAYS IS SAFE, EXCEPT HE WHO ACTS UNJUSTLY AND SINS.

§63. *wa-inna llāh jār li-man barra wa-ttaqā wa-muḥammad rasūlu llāh*

ALLĀH IS THE PROTECTOR OF HIM WHO IS RIGHTEOUS AND GOD-FEARING AND SO IS MUḤAMMAD, THE MESSENGER OF GOD.

§64. *wa-inna awlāhum bi-hādhihi l-ṣaḥīfa l-barru l-muḥsin*

THE MOST WORTHY OF THEM [the Jews] TO PARTICIPATE IN THIS TREATY ARE THE RIGHTEOUS AND SINCERE.

Chapter 2

Muʾminūn, Yahūd, Muhājirūn and Muslimūn

According to Ibn Isḥāq's introduction to the Kitāb, it was concluded between the Muhājirūn and the Anṣār and included a non-belligerency treaty with the Jews.[1] But when we turn to the Kitāb itself we only find the Muhājirūn from Quraysh, who are mentioned once, in §3, while the Anṣār as such are not mentioned at all. It appears that the listing of Anṣārī groups in §§4–11 made the specific mention of the Anṣār superfluous.

To judge from the number of times they are mentioned, the Mu'min/Mu'minūn and the Yahūd receive most attention, although according to Ibn Isḥāq's introduction the main contracting parties were the Mu'minūn and the Muslimūn,[2] not the Mu'minūn and the Yahūd. Mu'min/Mu'minūn are mentioned in the Kitāb 28 times in the treaty of the Mu'minūn and three times in the treaty of the Jews, and hence should be considered the most important party. The Yahūd are mentioned twenty times. Muslimūn are mentioned in §1 (and referred to in §2). They are also mentioned in §§28 and 44 (and are presumably referred to in §§45 and 46). Quraysh appear four times — twice, in §§1 and 3, with reference to the tribe in general and twice, in §§23 and 54, with reference to the Quraysh of Mecca. *Ahl hādhihi l-ṣaḥīfa*, or "the people of this treaty", appear four

[1] See also *Manāl al-ṭālib*, 227: *kataba rasūlu llāh ṣ bayna quraysh wa-l-anṣār kitāban, wa-fī l-kitāb (i/a)nnahum umma wāḥida dūna l-nās*. Ibn Sayyid al-Nās, however, presents the Kitāb as a *muwādaʿa* or truce between the Muslimūn and the Yahūd; cf. Gil, 59.

[2] Theoretically, it could be argued that the Kitāb was concluded between the Mu'minūn and Muslimūn on the one hand and *man tabiʿahum…* on the other; but those referred to by *man tabiʿahum…* were a secondary element and not a main contracting party.

times, in §§45, 49, 52 and 57, and include all the groups participating in the Kitāb. *Mushrik* is mentioned once, in §23. Finally, *kāfir* is mentioned in §15 twice.

As to the use of pronouns, the third-person plural is common. The first-person plural appears twice, in §§18 and 20, and points to the main contracting parties, namely the Mu'minūn and Muslimūn, with reference to their dealings with foreign elements. The second-person plural appears in §26 twice. Again, the main contracting parties are addressed, but this time with reference to their internal affairs.

Muhājirūn

An unusual version of §3 is found in the partial text of the Kitāb found in Qasṭallānī's *al-Mawāhib al-laduniyya*.[3] In this version the word al-Muhājirūn is missing. Indeed, the version belongs to Qasṭallānī's text and is not a scribal error. This is shown by the fact that the word is also missing in Qasṭallānī's version as quoted by his commentator, Zurqānī. Moreover, Zurqānī's commentary clearly relates to this unusual version: he says that *innahum* (*umma wāḥida*) refers to the Anṣār, as does the following phrase, *min Quraysh*, that declares the Anṣār a group of Quraysh as if they were of Qurashī descent.[4] But Qasṭallānī's claim that the Anṣār (and not the participants of the Kitāb) formed *umma wāḥida* is unconvincing; in addition, the omission of Muhājirūn is not supported by any other source.

[3]The partial text belongs to Abū 'Ubayd's recension; see below, 191.

[4]The words of Qasṭallānī are given, as they appear in Zurqānī, between brackets: [*wa-ayna dhālika min kitābihi bayna quraysh wa-l-anṣār innahum*] *bi-kasri l-hamza, ayi l-anṣār* [*umma wāḥida dūna l-nās*] *ḥāl mini sm inna* [*min quraysh*] *ṣifa li-umma baʿda ṣifa, ay juz' minhum ka-abnā'ihim wa-ikhwānihim, ʿalā naḥw anta minnī bi-manzilat hārūn min mūsā, yaʿnī anna l-anṣār dūna ghayrihim mina l-nās ṭā'ifa min quraysh, fa-huwa mubālagha fī ttiḥādihim maʿahum ḥattā ka-annahum min naslihim*...; Qasṭallānī, II, 270; Zurqānī, IV, 168:16. Also the subsequent interpretation of the expression *ʿalā ribāʿatihim* makes it clear that according to Qasṭallānī and his commentator Zurqānī, the Muhājirūn do not belong in this clause: [*ʿalā ribāʿatihim*] *bi-kasri l-rā' ay ʿalā stiqāmatihim, yurīdu annahum ʿalā amrihimi lladhī kānū ʿalayhi, wa-ribāʿatu l-rajul sha'nuhu wa-ḥāluhu llatī huwa rābiʿ ʿalayhā ay thābit muqīm, qālahu fī l-nihāya, wa-huwa khabar thānin li-inna, yaʿnī anna l-anṣār maʿa quraysh bāqūna ʿalā ḥālihimi llatī kānū ʿalayhā mina li-ttiḥād wa-l-mawadda.* Admittedly, the words *min Quraysh* appear in §1, and a dittography in §3 cannot be ruled out.

The difference between §3 and §§4–11 is clear: the Muhājirūn had no *ṭawā'if* or sub-groups and functioned as a unified solidarity group, while each of the Anṣārī clans listed in §§4–11 was divided into *ṭawā'if*.[5]

Almost a century after the conclusion of the Kitāb the Quraysh still formed a separate solidarity group within Medinan society. ʿUmar b. ʿAbd al-ʿAzīz, when he officiated as the governor of Medina, arranged the *maʿqula* or mutual blood money obligations of Quraysh; the tribe covered injuries in excess of one third of the blood money due in the case of death. Compensation that amounted to less than one third was to be paid by the offender himself.[6] ʿUmar b. ʿAbd al-ʿAzīz functioned in this case as their chief or regulator.[7]

Another difference between §3 and §§4–11 is that the words *maʿāqilahumu l-'ūlā* only appear in §§4–11. Unlike the Anṣār, the Muhājirūn, a newly formed group, did not have former *maʿāqil*.[8]

The Muhājirūn belong in the Kitāb. This conclusion has obvious implications for the identification of the Mu'minūn and Muslimūn.

[5]Below, 103. Wellhausen remarked (68): "Bei den Emigranten findet sich dieser Unterschied nicht; sie bildeten damals nur erst ein kleines Häuflein, welches nicht noch Unterabteilungen zuliess".

[6]Cf. Ibn Ḥazm, *Muḥallā*, XI, 52: *wa-qad kāna ʿumar b. ʿabd al-ʿazīz allafa maʿqulat quraysh idh kāna amīran ʿalā l-madīna ʿalā annahum yaʿqilūna thultha l-diya fa-mā fawqahā wa-anna mā dūna dhālika yakūnu ʿalā l-jāriḥ fī mālihi.* The *maʿāqil* were the strongest legal bond between an individual and his tribe, and hence can stand for tribal affiliation. A satirical verse of Musāfiʿ b. ʿAbd Manāf al-Jumaḥī addresses Ḥazn b. Abī Wahb al-Makhzūmī, whose family did not belong to Quraysh, with regard to the *maʿāqil*; it was neither in the branches of Quraysh nor in the main body: *fa-lastum fī l-maʿāqili min qurayshin wa-lā fī l-farʿi minhā wa-l-ṣamīmi*; allegedly, Ḥazn's mother, who was also the mother of his brother Hubayra (Jaʿda b. Hubayra's father), was a whore; Ibn al-Kalbī, *Mathālib*, MS Dār al-Kutub (the passage is found in the section on *dhawāt al-rāyāt*, or the prostitutes of pre-Islamic Mecca).

[7]The verb *allafa* suggests a formal agreement among the Qurashī factions, perhaps in the form of a written document. See also *ibid.*, 53: *inna rasūla llāh ṣ allafa bayna l-nās fī maʿāqilihim....*

[8]Below, 92. One assumes that the *maʿāqil* were the first matter agreed upon at the ʿAqaba meeting even before the first Muhājir set foot in Medina. See on this point the penetrating observation of Simonsen, *Studies in the Genesis and Early Development of the Caliphal Taxation System*, 41: "The Constitution of Medina must have been agreed upon in its entirety as only such a coherent and embracing agreement would enable Muhammad and his followers to be absorbed into Medinan society as a unified group".

Muʾminūn and Muslimūn

The Kitāb was concluded between the Mu'minūn and the Muslimūn from Quraysh and Yathrib (Ibn Isḥāq), or between the Mu'minūn and Muslimūn from Quraysh and *ahl yathrib* (Abū ʿUbayd).[9] Together with lesser participants the Mu'minūn and Muslimūn were declared *umma wāḥida*. Some of the participants were associated with a tribe, namely Quraysh, while others were associated with a place, namely Yathrib. There are three possibilities. Either the Muslimūn are from Quraysh, while the Mu'minūn are from Yathrib, or the other way round; or the Muslimūn and Mu'minūn are associated with both Quraysh and Yathrib; or one group is associated with both Quraysh and Yathrib, while the other is only associated with one of them. I shall argue that the last mentioned possibility is the correct one, more precisely that the Mu'minūn were from Quraysh and Yathrib, while the Muslimūn were from Yathrib.

The first-mentioned possibility assumes the existence of a parallelism. Elsewhere in the Kitāb we find an ABBA parallelism: §18 prescribes: *wa-innahu man tabiʿanā min yahūd, fa-inna lahu l-naṣr wa-l-uswa, ghayr maẓlūmīna wa-lā mutanāṣar ʿalayhim.* The root *n-ṣ-r* appears twice, and hence the parallelism is ABBA: *naṣr* = *wa-lā mutanāṣar ʿalayhim*; *uswa* = *ghayr maẓlūmīna.* According to this parallelism, the Mu'minūn are from Yathrib, while the Muslimūn are from Quraysh.[10] But this possibility must be rejected because the Muhājirūn who were "from Quraysh" were among the Mu'minūn: §3 that deals with the Muhājirūn ends with the words *bayna l-muʾminīn.* Should we then opt for a ABAB parallelism, in which case the Mu'minūn are from Quraysh, while the Muslimūn are from Yathrib? This is impossible because §§4–11 that list the Anṣārī clans end with the words *bayna l-muʾminīn.* In other words, both the Anṣār and the Muhājirūn were Mu'minūn.

[9]Cf. *EI*², s.v. *sīra* (W. Raven), 662a: the Kitāb was an agreement between Muḥammad and "the believers and Muslims of Ḳuraysh and Yat̲h̲rib". Hoyland, "Sebeos, the Jews and the Rise of Islam", 95, renders: "This is a writing of Muḥammad... between the believers, (namely) the Muslims of Quraysh and Yathrib and those who follow them...". For the terms Muslim and Mu'min cf. Denny, "Some Religio-Communal Terms and Concepts in the Qur'ān", 36–42.

[10]See a similar ABBA parallelism in the Prophet's treaty with the people of Ayla that prescribes a guarantee of security: *li-yuḥanna b. ruʾba wa-ahl ayla, sufunihim wa-sayyāratihim, fī l-barr wa-l-baḥr*; *Wath.*, 117–18 no. 31; Zurqānī, III, 359:-8. Zurqānī explains (359:-4): *yaʿnī anna l-amān ʿāmm lahum fī jamīʿi l-amākini llatī yakūnūna bihā.*

The Kitāb itself defines Mu'min as the opposite of *kāfir* in §15. The first part of the Kitāb includes the treaty of the Mu'minūn who are the most important party in the Kitāb. The Mu'minūn were *min Quraysh wa-Yathrib*.

However, this was not the case with the Muslimūn. Their status as a main contracting party and their inclusion in the *umma* give them special weight. The Yahūd were neither a main contracting party nor part of the *umma*,[11] although they are mentioned no less than twenty times. The Muslimūn are hardly mentioned at all. Beyond §1 and §2 (where they are referred to) the Muslimūn also appear in §§28 and 44 (and are presumably referred to in §§45 and 46). §§28 and 44, which belong to the treaty of the Jews, prescribe that in the two key areas of *dīn* (§28) and *nafaqa* (§44) the Muslimūn and Yahūd are set apart from each other, which suggests that they are otherwise associated with each other. §28 deals with the Yahūd Banī ʿAwf, probably the most important Jewish group in the Kitāb. The appearance of the Muslimūn in the same clause (*li-l-yahūd dīnuhum wa-li-l-muslimīna dīnuhum*) creates the impression that they were a sub-group of the Yahūd Banī ʿAwf. Given the status of the Muslimūn in the Kitāb one expects Muslimūn to be found among other Jewish groups as well. This is corroborated by §44, where the Muslimūn are not associated with any specific Jewish group.

The Muslimūn and the Yahūd were separated by *dīn* and *nafaqa*. The former may point to the difference or main difference between them: unlike the Yahūd, the Muslimūn were in some way closer to Muḥammad and his cause. Perhaps they were prepared to recognize Muḥammad as the Messenger of Allāh — at least to the Arabs, if not to the whole of mankind. If this analysis, based on the text of the Kitāb itself, is correct, it follows that the Muslimūn were from Yathrib, not from Quraysh and Yathrib.

Perhaps relevant for us here is the use of *muslim* in the sense of "one who makes peace": this was the nickname of Asad b. ʿAbd al-ʿUzzā, who would make peace among quarrelling Qurashīs (*kāna lā yatafāsadu fī quraysh thnāni illā aṣlaḥa baynanhumā*). After him his son and grandson played the same role and were also referred to as *muslim*. Muʿāwiya addressed one of their descendants as *ibn muslim b. muslim*.[12] In the Prophet's letter to the people of Maqnā the Mu'minūn and Muslimūn are called upon to treat

[11] Cf. below, §§28–34.

[12] The man came to the caliph's court in connection with the death of his brother and the caliph was presumably soothing his presumed or real anger; Zubayr b. Bakkār, *Jamharat nasab Quraysh*, 470, 512–13. See also *Khizāna*, III, where the verb *nuslim(u)* is interpreted as *nūqiʿu l-silm bayna l-qawm wa-l-ṣulḥ*.

them kindly.[13] The treaty between Ḥabīb b. Maslama and the people of Ṭiflīs prescribes that if a Muʾmin is unable to proceed in his journey in their land, they should bring him to the nearest party of Muʾminūn and Muslimūn.[14] This evidence may be helpful, but the testimony of the Kitāb regarding the Muslimūn is more important.

Unspecified Participants

Other participants who became part of the *umma* were *man tabiʿahum fa-laḥiqa bihim fa-jāhada maʿahum.* The verb *tabiʿa* reappears in §18: *wa-innahu man tabiʿanā min yahūd* etc. Rather than "to follow", in the present context *tabiʿa* means "to become a client" (of a person or a tribal group). Only one category of people is addressed here, namely clients and prospective clients; *laḥiqa* and *jāhada* refer to the same group.[15] The identity of these clients or of many of them is pointed out by the reappearance of *tabiʿa* in §18: *wa-innahu man tabiʿanā min yahūd....*

According to Ibn ʿAbbās, in the Jāhiliyya a man would attach himself (*yalḥaqu*) to another and become the latter's *tābiʿ* or client. When the master died, his inheritance went to his relatives, while the *tābiʿ* or client received nothing.[16] Another Qurʾān exegete says that the client (referred to by the verb *tabiʿa*) undertook to bequeath to his master a share identical to that of each of his children.[17] The reports on the agreements concluded between masters and clients before Islam vary and probably reflect different circumstances. One assumes that the larger the master's share in the client's inheritance, the more comprehensive his commitment to pay blood money for him.

[13]Ibn Saʿd, I, 276–77: *ammā baʿdu fa-ilā l-muʾminīna wa-l-muslimīna, man aṭlaʿa ahl maqnā bi-khayr fa-huwa khayr lahu, wa-man aṭlaʿahum bi-sharr fa-huwa sharr lahu.* A letter from the caliph ʿAbd al-Malik is addressed *ilā man bi-l-ʿirāq mina l-muʾminīna wa-l-muslimīna*; ʿAskarī, *Awāʾil*, II, 73.

[14]*Wa-in quṭiʿa bi-aḥad mina l-muʾminīna ʿindakum fa-ʿalaykum adāʾuhu ilā adnā fiʾa mina l-muʾminīna wa-l-muslimīna.*

[15]In Abū ʿUbayd's version, *wa-jāhada maʿahum* is preceded by: *fa-ḥalla maʿahum.*

[16]Ṭabarī, *Tafsīr*, V, 34:25, interpretation of Qurʾān 4,33, *wa-lladhīna ʿaqadat aymānukum.* The right to inherit is closely linked to matters of blood money.

[17]Ṭabarī, *Tafsīr*, V, 34:23 (al-Ḍaḥḥāk): *kāna l-rajul yatbaʿu l-rajul fa-yuʿāqiduhu: in muttu fa-laka mithl mā yarithu baʿḍu wuldī; wa-hādhā mansūkh.* Yet another says that the master received one sixth of the client's inheritance; Bayḍāwī, I, 90:6: *mawālī l-muwālāt, kāna l-ḥalīf yūrathu l-suds min māl ḥalīfihi.*

The plural form *taba'* is synonymous with *mawālin* in the sense of "clients". They were considered people of impure lineage, and hence of inferior social status. Both terms are antonymous with *ṣamīm*, "one having pure lineage".[18] The people of pure lineage differ from the *taba'* in that they are capable of defending themselves without relying on others. *Tābi'* is also synonymous with *ḥalīf* in the sense of client, as opposed to *ṣamīm* and *mujīr*.[19]

Laḥiqa appears to be a near synonym of *tabi'a*, in which case it does not add a new category of participants to the Kitāb.[20] Alternatively it could mean "to join", "to be attached to". *Laḥiqa* in the Prophet's treaty with 'Amr b. Ma'bad al-Juhanī indicates that whoever joins the main contracting party receives the same right (i.e. a guarantee of security) as the main party.[21] In the context of war, *laḥiqa* seems to indicate the joining of relatively weak tribal units to stronger ones.[22]

---

[18] *Naqā'iḍ*, I, 323: *yā ḍabba ghayrukumu l-ṣamīmu wa-antumu taba'un idhā 'udda l-ṣamīmu mawālī.*

[19] Ibn Kathīr, *Bidāya*, III, 137 (← the *Maghāzī* of al-Umawī): when the Prophet returned from Ṭā'if, al-Akhnas b. Sharīq told him: ... *inna ḥalīf quraysh lā yujīru 'alā ṣamīmihā*; see below, 116. In the same context Abū Sufyān is supposed to have asked al-Muṭ'im b. 'Adī: ... *a-mujīr aw tābi'*, or "are you a man granting security or a client?"

[20] Cf. the report just quoted: "... a man would attach himself (*yalḥaqu*) to another and become his client (*tābi'*)...".

[21] Ibn Sa'd, I, 271–72: ... *fa-innahu āmin bi-amāni llāhi wa-amān muḥammad... wa-man laḥiqa bihim fa-inna lahu mithl mā lahum.* Cf. *laja'a* in the treaty of Hilāl al-Aslamī; below, 144.

[22] *'Iqd*, V, 216:11: ... *wa-da'at [taghlib] l-namir b. qāsiṭ fa-nḍammat ilā banī kulayb wa-ṣārū yadan ma'ahum 'alā bakr, wa-laḥiqat bihim ghufayla.* On the Ghufayla or the 'Āmir b. Qāsiṭ see Ibn Ḥazm, *Ansāb*, 300. Also *'Iqd*, V, 248:2: *taḥālafat asad wa-ṭay' wa-ghaṭafān, wa-laḥiqat bihim ḍabba wa-'adī....* In the context of the Ḥudaybiyya expedition *laḥiqa* refers to the bedouins who joined Muḥammad: *wa-kharaja rasūlu llāh ṣ bi-man ma'ahu mina l-muhājirīna wa-l-anṣār wa-man laḥiqa bihi mina l-'arab*; Ibn Hishām, III, 322.

Chapter 3

The Jewish Participants

The Jews are mentioned for the first time in §18, *wa-innahu man tabiʿanā min yahūd*.... But this clause does not mark the beginning of their treaty, since it is a single clause concerning Jews amidst clauses dealing with Muʾminūn. Besides, it concerns prospective members rather than actual ones.

The Jews reappear in §27, *wa-inna l-yahūd yunfiqūna*...that opens the second part of the Kitāb or the treaty of the Jews.[1] With regard to the division of the Kitāb one should follow the references to Muʾminūn and Yahūd: as long as the Muʾminūn are the subject, we are still in the treaty of the Muʾminūn; when the Yahūd become the subject (with the exception of §18), we are in the treaty of the Jews in the latter part of the Kitāb. In this part the Muʾminūn are mentioned three times (§§27, 28 and 56), invariably in clauses the subject of which is Yahūd that define the rights and duties of the Jews in relation to the Muʾminūn.[2] It is noteworthy that the first part of the Kitāb has both Muʾmin and Muʾminūn (with the exception of §24, the singular Muʾmin appears only in negative sentences), whereas the second part only has the plural Yahūd but not the singular Yahūdī (although in some clauses the subject is in the singular).

[1]Perhaps §27 is misplaced (cf. below, 184), in which case §28 becomes the first clause in the treaty of the Jews.

[2]It is therefore hard to accept Hoyland's assumption that "the term 'believer' is used throughout..., seemingly referring to all parties; Muslim... and Jew... are only used when a distinction needs to be made. One should perhaps, then, regard the term as including the Jews among, rather than distinguishing them from, all other monotheists, 'believers' being the general appellation and Muslim and Jew specific cases thereof"; Hoyland, "Sebeos, the Jews and the Rise of Islam", 95.

The division of the Kitāb into two parts is also reflected in the two lists of participants found in it, listing the Mu'minūn and Yahūd groups, respectively. As one can expect in one and the same document, there is a great deal of correspondence between the lists, for example the Banū ʿAwf in the former list (§4) correspond to the Yahūd Banī ʿAwf in the latter (§28). The existence of a separate part dealing with the Jews is also reflected in Ibn Isḥāq's introduction to the Kitāb.[3] As has already been mentioned, the *ahl hādhihi l-ṣaḥīfa* who appear in the second part of the Kitāb are all those who took part in it.

The identity of the Jewish participants is much disputed. I argue that the majority of the Jews of Medina, including the main Jewish tribes Naḍīr, Qurayẓa and Qaynuqāʿ who are not mentioned in the Kitāb, were not party to it. This does not mean that the main Jewish tribes had no agreements whatsoever with Muḥammad; on the contrary, after the *hijra* the Naḍīr, Qurayẓa and Qaynuqāʿ concluded separate treaties with him. But these were basic non-belligerency treaties mainly including security arrangements, unlike the far-reaching commitments undertaken by the Jews who did participate in the Kitāb.[4] The rather limited Jewish participation in the Kitāb means that it is far less significant with regard to the Prophet's relationship with the Jews of Medina than has previously been thought.

[3]The existence of two distinct parts was noticed by Khadduri, *War and Peace in the Law of Islam*, 206: "The first part of the treaty deals with the relations of the Madīna tribes; the latter with the alliance with the Jews". Ḥamīdullāh considered the treaty of the Jews a separate treaty perhaps concluded after the battle of Badr; see his "The Earliest Written Constitution", 13; *idem*, *Le Prophète de l'Islam*, I, 124–25. Ḥamīdullāh published this theory as early as 1937; see "Aqdam dustūr", 105–106 (where the latter part of the Kitāb is called *dustūr al-yahūd*). Ḥamīdullāh refers to the fact that the *Lisān al-ʿarab*, s.v. *r-b-ʿ*, uses two different expressions with reference to the Kitāb: it says once *wa-fī kitābihi li-l-muhājirīna wa-l-anṣār* (VIII, 107b), and then *fī kitāb rasūli llāhi ṣ li-yahūd* (VIII, 108a). But the differences probably go back to the sources quoted in the *Lisān*. Moreover, the quotation that follows the mention of *kitāb rasūli llāhi ṣ li-yahūd* includes a variant reading of a word found in the first part of the Kitāb, i.e. the treaty of the Mu'minūn, and not in the treaty of the Jews: *ʿalā ribʿatihim* [*sic*]. Ḥamīdullāh also says that Abū Dāwūd reports in his *Sunan* that this document (*ṣaḥīfa*), i.e. the one which according to Ḥamīdullāh was the separate treaty of the Jews, was concluded after Badr. But there is no evidence that the *ṣaḥīfa* mentioned by Abū Dāwūd is identical with the Kitāb; see his *Sunan*, II, 138 (*bāb kayfa kāna ikhrāju l-yahūd mina l-madīna*).

[4]See Lecker, "Did Muḥammad Conclude Treaties with the Jewish Tribes", 34.

The First Six Groups

The Kitāb includes two lists of participants. In what follows the groups are juxtaposed in order to demonstrate the extent of agreement between the lists:

Banū ʿAwf	Yahūd Banī ʿAwf
Banū l-Ḥārith	Yahūd Banī l-Ḥārith
Banū Sāʿida	Yahūd Banī Sāʿida
Banū Jusham	Yahūd Banī Jusham
Banū l-Najjār	Yahūd Banī l-Najjār
Banū ʿAmr b. ʿAwf	——
Banū l-Nabīt	——
Banū l-Aws	Yahūd Banī l-Aws
——	Yahūd Banī Thaʿlaba
——	Jafna
——	Banū l-Shuṭayba

Although the three main Jewish tribes are not mentioned, the prevailing theory ever since Wellhausen wrote his short study on the Kitāb has been that the document included all the inhabitants of Medina.[5] Medieval Muslim

[5]Wellhausen (74) said: "Medina wird... als eine einheitliche Umma verfasst... Gleichwol gehören nicht bloss die Gläubigen dazu, sondern auch alle die ihnen folgen und sich ihnen anschliessen und mit ihnen kämpfen ... d.h. alle Bewohner von Medina". Wellhausen, *The Arab Kingdom*, 11–12, says that "it is not only the Faithful who belong to the Umma, but also all who ally themselves with them and fight along with them, i.e. all the inhabitants of Medina.... There are still heathens among the Ansâr, and they are not excluded, but expressly included. The Jews are also included, though they have not so close a connection with the Umma as the Muhâjira and the Ansâr, and have not exactly the same rights and obligations". Wellhausen was followed by Buhl, *Leben*, 210–11. See also *EI*^{2}, s.v. Muḥammad (F. Buhl—A.T. Welch): "Muḥammad's task was to form a united community out of these heterogeneous elements" [i.e. the Muhājirūn, the Anṣār and the Jews, including the three main Jewish tribes]; Paret, "Ummah", says: "After he had finally broken off relations with the pagan Meccans and migrated with his followers to Madīna, he created a new community there. He went beyond the circle of Muslims proper and included those citizens of Madīna who had not yet heeded his religious appeal in one political combination. 'The constitution of the community of Madīna', in which this unification is laid down in writing, expressly states that the citizens of the town, including the Jews, now form an umma.... The predominantly political character of this new umma was however only a makeshift. As soon as Muḥammad felt himself firmly established and had successfully attacked the pagan Meccans, he was able to exclude from his politico-religious community the Madīnese (especially the Jews) who had not yet adopted his religion".

writers were of the same opinion concerning the participation of the three main Jewish tribes in the Kitāb.[6]

Wellhausen (75) explained away the lack of mention of the main Jewish tribes, at the same time proposing an interpretation of the crucial phrase "Yahūd Banī so-and-so". He argued that the Jews of Medina, together with the remnants of the older Arab population attached to them (i.e. the Arabs, mainly of the Balī tribe, who had been there before the settlement of the Aws and Khazraj), were included in the *umma* as clients (*Beisassen*) of the Anṣār among whom they lived. In other words, according to Wellhausen, by the time the Kitāb was concluded the Jews had lost their independence and had become clients of Anṣārī clans; the phrase "Yahūd Banī so-and-so" reflects the fact that the "Banū so-and-so" were the masters of the Jewish clans attached to them in client status. Wellhausen rejected Sprenger's view that the Jews of the Kitāb were converts to Judaism from among the Aws and Khazraj, since he suspected that there were not many such converts; the Kitāb dealt with Jewish clans, not with individuals, Wellhausen argued.[7] As for the Jewish members of the Aws and Khazraj, he argued that they were included in the Kitāb together with their clans. Wellhausen did express some doubts regarding the participation of the Naḍīr and Qurayẓa: they were independent and only loosely connected to the Aws. Yet he argued that these two tribes should be identified with Yahūd Banī l-Aws and Yahūd Banī Thaʿlaba, respectively.[8]

Almost every student of early Islamic history has accepted Wellhausen's assumption regarding the purport of the phrase "Yahūd Banī so-and-so". Gil (63), for example, said: "The Jews belong to the *ummah*, since they

---

[6] *Sīra ḥalabiyya*, II, 90:7, interprets "Yahūd" in Ibn Isḥāq's introduction to the Kitāb as a reference to the Qaynuqāʿ, Qurayẓa and Naḍīr; Abū ʿUbayd, *Amwāl*, 266 no. 519; *Mawrid al-ẓamʾān*, 150b: *thumma inna rasūla llāh ṣ kataba kitāban bayna l-muhājirīna wa-l-anṣār wādaʿa fīhi* [so far the introduction to the Kitāb, but in what follows the word *yahūd* is replaced by:] *banī qaynuqāʿ wa-banī qurayẓa wa-banī l-naḍīr, ay ṣālaḥahum ʿalā an lā yuḥāribahum wa-lā yuʾdhiyahum wa-an lā yuʿīnū ʿalayhi aḥadan wa-annahu in dahamahu bihā ʿaduww naṣarūhu* [and at this point we return to the introduction of the Kitāb:] *wa-ʿāhadahum wa-aqarrahum ʿalā dīnihim.* Ibn Taymiyya, *Ṣārim*, 64, identifies the Qaynuqāʿ with the Yahūd Banī ʿAwf of the Kitāb.

[7] "Indessen haben unsere Juden... viel zu viel Autonomie und Konsistenz; es ist überhaupt nur von Judenschaften, nicht von einzelnen Juden die Rede".

[8] Wellhausen identified the Banū l-Aws with the Aws Allāh and the Banū Thaʿlaba with the Thaʿlaba b. ʿAmr b. ʿAwf (a subdivision of the ʿAmr b. ʿAwf). His identification was based on geographical data: he claimed that the Naḍīr and Qurayẓa lived between the Aws Allāh and the Thaʿlaba b. ʿAmr b. ʿAwf. I shall argue that while his former identification is correct, the Thaʿlaba of the Kitāb are the Thaʿlaba b. al-Fiṭyawn.

are clients of Muslim clans. The Jews of Banū ʿAwf are *ummatun maʿa ʾl-muʾminīna*, and so are the others, as belonging to their respective Muslim patrons". Yet while accepting Wellhausen's interpretation of the phrase and his overall concept regarding Medinan society, some scholars had other ideas concerning the identification of the main Jewish tribes on the list of Jewish participants. Wensinck (56 n. 3) argued that the Qaynuqāʿ comprised four of the Yahūd Banī so-and-so groups (al-Najjār, al-Ḥārith, Sāʿida and Jusham), while Hirschberg argued that all five Yahūd Banī so-and-so groups that belonged to the Khazraj — that is, these four in addition to the Yahūd Banī ʿAwf — correspond to the Qaynuqāʿ.[9] However, deviating from Wellhausen's view, Hirschberg (139) argued that the Naḍīr and Qurayẓa, unlike the Qaynuqāʿ, were not clients of the Arabs, and hence were not party to the Kitāb. In his opinion the Jewish groups in the Kitāb were remnants of the Jewish population in northern Medina that had been driven out by clans of the Aws; these remnants lived among the Aws as clients.

Adopting Wellhausen's interpretation of the phrase Yahūd Banī so-and-so, Watt (194) wrote:

> By about the time of the *hijra* all the lesser Jewish clans or groups in as-Samhūdī's list had lost their identity, or at least had ceased to be of political importance. They are not mentioned in the primary sources for the career of Muḥammad. When the Constitution of Medina deals with them they are simply "the Jews of an-Najjār", "the Jews of al-Ḥārith" and so on.

Rubin stated (7):

> The fact that these groups do not have any definite tribal affinity of their own seems to indicate that for some reason they lost their separate tribal organization, and unlike the greater Jewish tribes they became closely associated with various Arab tribes among whom they dwelt. At least some of these nameless mixed groups seem to be identical with the Jews of the "Constitution" where they are called "the Jews of such-and-such an Arab tribe".

Gil (61) wrote:

> Very important is the point noticed by Wellhausen (68), that the document makes no mention at all of the Khazraj... though

[9] Hirschberg, 140, 300 n. 10.

> it does mention five clans known definitely as belonging to the Khazraj. This may be the case in regard to the main Jewish tribes.

In other words, according to Gil, they were part of the Kitāb. Watt (227) was also of the opinion that the main Jewish tribes participated in the Kitāb. Referring to the fact that they were not mentioned in it he concluded:

> If this is so, the document in its present form might belong to the period after the elimination of Qurayẓah.[10]

Watt's assumption should be rejected on the basis of the Kitāb's unity.[11]

Goto (13) did not think that the Naḍīr, Qurayẓa and Qaynuqā' were referred to as Yahūd Banī so-and-so: "The view is hardly acceptable", he said, because of the appearance of "the name of a fourth tribe, which had to be much smaller than the three", namely the Banū Tha'laba. Rubin (10) argued correctly that the main Jewish tribes are not in the Kitāb, although Muḥammad "did wish to establish close relations with these tribes as well".

Elsewhere I have argued that on the eve of the *hijra* the Naḍīr and Qurayẓa were not clients of the Aws and Khazraj.[12] It follows that they could not have been included in the Kitāb as Yahūd Banī so-and-so, assuming that the phrase indicates client status. The same is true of the Qaynuqā'.[13]

Wellhausen stressed[14] that, contrary to Sprenger's view, the Jewish groups in the Kitāb were not converts to Judaism — such converts remained members of their Arab clans — but proper Jewish clans.[15] Rubin (6,9)

---

[10] Rubin, 7 n. 8, found Watt's explanation concerning the absence of the main Jewish tribes from the Kitāb unlikely. Goitein, *Studies in Islamic History and Institutions*, 128 n. 2, rejected Watt's assumption that the Kitāb "was promulgated after year 5 of the *hijra*".

[11] See Appendix B.

[12] Lecker, "Wāqidī's Account on the Status of the Jews of Medina".

[13] Below, 57.

[14] Above, 50.

[15] See Sprenger, *Leben*, III, 23 n. 2: "Es ist hier nicht die Rede von geborenen Juden, sondern von Arabern der genannten Stämme, welche in mosaischen Glauben erzogen worden sind". He refers here to *Nūr al-nibrās*, I, 650. The text in this source is as follows: *qawluhu wa-inna yahūd banī 'awf, wa-ka-dhālika yahūd banī l-najjār wa-banī l-ḥārith wa-banī sā'ida wa-banī jusham wa-banī l-aws wa-banī tha'laba, wa-ka-dhālika ghayr dhālika min qabā'ili l-anṣār: i'lam anna l-yahūd banū isrā'īl, wa-jumlat man kāna minhum bi-l-madīna wa-khaybar innamā hum banū qurayẓa wa-l-naḍīr wa-banū qaynuqā', ghayr anna fī l-aws wa-l-khazraj man qad tahawwada, wa-kāna min nisā'ihim man tandhuru idhā waladat in 'āsha waladuhā an tuhawwidahu li-anna l-yahūd kānū ahl 'ilm wa-kitāb, wa-*

agreed with Wellhausen that the Yahūd Banī so-and-so were genuine Jewish groups:

> It is inconceivable that the indigenous Jews who formed nearly half the population of Medina[16] should be totally excluded from a document designed to make Medina an indivisible unity.

He concluded:

> ...The phrase "*Yahūd Banī...*" refers to nameless Jewish groups, who, unlike the great Jewish tribes, did not have a territory of their own, nor a distinct tribal affinity. They had *ḥilf* relations with various Arab tribes in whose territory they dwelt and by whose names they used to be called.

Regarding the identity of the Yahūd groups Rubin referred to a passage in Samhūdī on *jummāʿ*, or groups from various tribes,[17] that inhabited different villages (or perhaps towns) in the Medina area. However, the first five groups on the list of Jewish participants match the five branches of the Khazraj and it is doubtful that each Khazraj branch had a *jummāʿ* of its own.

The nine Jewish groups of the Kitāb should be divided into two sub-groups: six groups that have counterparts (albeit in a different order) on the list found at the beginning of the Kitāb and three groups lacking such counterparts. There was of course a close link between the components of the six pairs, e.g. Banū ʿAwf and Yahūd Banī ʿAwf.

There are several alternatives for interpreting the phrase "Yahūd Banī so-and-so":

1. The proselytes alternative rejected by Wellhausen: the Yahūd Banī so-and-so were the Jewish members of the Banū so-and-so; in other words, they were those among the Arab clans who converted to Judaism or were descendants of such converts.

---

fī hāʾulāʾi l-abnāʾi lladhīna tahawwadū nazalat ʿlā ikrāha fī l-dīnʾ, ḥīna arāda ābāʾuhum ikrāhahum ʿalā l-islām fī aḥadi l-aqwāl, qālahu l-suhaylī. In Sprenger's wake, Krehl, *Leben*, 145, rendered the relevant clauses of the Kitāb thus: "Die Juden von dem Stamme ʿAuf..., Die Juden, welche zu dem Stamme al-Nadshshâr gehören...".

[16] There are no reliable statistics. See the same estimate in Wensinck, 4; but cf. *ibid.*, 28.

[17] On the term see Lecker, "Muḥammad at Medina", 43.

2. The client clan alternative adopted by Wellhausen: the Yahūd Banī so-and-so were members of Jewish clans the name of which was unspecified in keeping with Arab custom regarding clients.

3. The individual client alternative: they were Jewish individuals living among the Anṣār as clients.

4. Any combination of the above alternatives.

The Yahūd Banī Thaʿlaba are our starting point since they are the only Yahūd Banī so-and-so group that does not have an Arab counterpart. Consequently they should be identified with the Jewish tribe of Thaʿlaba (b. al-Fiṭyawn).[18] In this case Yahūd Banī Thaʿlaba were simply "the Jewish Banū Thaʿlaba", not "the Jews who were the clients of the Arab Banū Thaʿlaba". Similarly, *yahūd banī qurayẓa wa-l-naḍīr*[19] were simply the Jewish Qurayẓa and Naḍīr, and *naṣārā banī taghlib*[20] were the Christian Banū Taghlib.[21]

However, since the Thaʿlaba are an exception on the list of Jewish groups, we should not adopt this interpretation with regard to the other Yahūd Banī so-and-so groups, since this would assume the existence of many Jewish proselytes among the Arabs of Medina. Such an assumption is contradicted by the evidence on the rampant idol worship in Medina on the eve of Islam that indicates that the majority of the Aws and Khazraj were idol worshippers.[22] The interpretations of Qur'ān 2,144, where Muḥammad is instructed to turn in prayer to Mecca (*qad narā taqalluba wajhika fī l-samā'i...*), have it that when the Prophet arrived at Medina, the majority of its inhabitants was Jewish. God instructed him to turn to Jerusalem, and consequently the Jews rejoiced.[23] But even if these interpretations are historical, they do

[18]Below, 75f.

[19]Suyūṭī, *Durr*, I, 88:3.

[20]ʿAbd al-Razzāq, VI, 72.

[21]This interpretation was adopted by Sharon, *Revolt: The Social and Military Aspects*, 164 n. 53, 166. Note the peculiar expression *yahūd al-anṣār*, i.e. the Jewish Anṣār or the Anṣār who were Jewish; Lecker, "A Note on Early Marriage Links", 24n, 26; *idem*, *Muslims, Jews and Pagans*, 52. For a man of the Yahūd Banī ʿAmr b. ʿAwf who was either of the ʿAmr b. ʿAwf or their client see *ibid.*

[22]Lecker, "Idol Worship in Pre-Islamic Medina (Yathrib)"; *idem*, "Was Arabian Idol Worship Declining on the Eve of Islam?". Cf. Watt, "Economic and Social Aspects of the Origin of Islam", 95–96, 100, who speaks of "vague monotheism" in pre-Islamic Medina.

[23]See e.g. Ṭabarī, *Tafsīr*, II, 13:-7. Wensinck (28) qualifies this statement by remarking: "Tradition tends to depict the Jews as being powerful to demonstrate that the cause of Allah overcomes all opposition".

not prove that there were many proselytes among the Aws and Khazraj. Evidence of such proselytes is scarce, even with regard to the Jews' close friends, the Aws Allāh.[24] Some of the evidence on this sensitive matter may have been suppressed; but even if more former Jews were to be found among the Aws and Khazraj, their number is unlikely to have been large.[25]

Having said that, it must be observed that according to passages found in Ibn Isḥāq, Suhaylī and Burhān al-Dīn al-Ḥalabī, the phrase Yahūd Banī so-and-so refers to converts to Judaism; but these passages have a limited evidential power with regard to the identity of most of the Jewish groups in the Kitāb.

Ibn Isḥāq's list of the Jewish adversaries of the Prophet includes people from the Jewish clans Naḍīr, Qurayẓa, Qaynuqāʿ and Thaʿlaba b. al-Fiṭyawn, in addition to several Yahūd Banī so-and-so groups, among them the Yahūd Banī l-Najjār who appear in the Kitāb:

> The names of the Jewish adversaries: About that time the Jewish rabbis showed hostility to the apostle in envy, hatred and malice, because God had chosen His apostle from among the Arabs. They were joined by men from the al-Aws and al-Khazraj who had obstinately clung to their heathen religion.[26] They were hypocrites, clinging to the polytheism of their fathers denying the resurrection; yet when Islam appeared and their people flocked to it they were compelled to pretend to accept it to save their lives. But in secret they were hypocrites whose inclination was towards the Jews because they considered the apostle a liar and strove against Islam.... These are the names of those Jews: from the Banū al-Naḍīr.... From Banū Thaʿlaba b. al-Fiṭyawn.... From Banū Qaynuqāʿ.... From Banū Qurayẓa.... From Yahūd Banī Zurayq.... From Yahūd Banī Ḥāritha.... From Yahūd Banī ʿAmr b. ʿAwf.... From Yahūd Banī l-Najjār....[27]

[24]Lecker, *Muslims, Jews and Pagans*, 41–45.

[25]On children from the Aws and Khazraj raised by the Jews see Lecker, "ʿAmr b. Ḥazm al-Anṣārī and Qurʾān 2,256". See also the next page.

[26]*Sic.* In the context of a passage entitled *al-aʿdāʾ min yahūd* we must assume that *shirk* here refers to Judaism.

[27]Guillaume, *The life of Muhammad*, 239–40 (who systematically omitted the word Yahūd from his translation of the passage); Ibn Hishām, II, 160–63: ... *wa-nḍāfa ilayhim rijāl mina l-aws wa-l-khazraj mimman kāna ʿasā ʿalā jāhiliyyatihi fa-kānū ahl nifāq ʿalā dīn ābāʾihim mina l-shirk wa-l-takdhīb bi-l-baʿth, illā anna l-islām qaharahum bi-ẓuhūrihi wa-jtimāʿ qawmihim ʿalayhi. Fa-ẓaharū bi-l-islām wa-ttakhadhūhu junna mina l-qatl wa-*

The passage clearly points to people from the Aws and Khazraj (*wa-nḍāfa ilayhim rijāl mina l-Aws wa-l-Khazraj*) who were Jewish. This refers to those listed after the members of the major Jewish tribes, i.e. from Yahūd Banī Zurayq onwards. The Zurayq and Najjār belong to the Khazraj, the Ḥāritha and ʿAmr b. ʿAwf belong to the Aws.

Suhaylī's commentary on the above passage from Ibn Isḥāq shows that for him too the Yahūd groups consisted of converts to Judaism:

> And the phrases: and from Yahūd Banī Zurayq, and from Yahūd Banī Ḥāritha, and he mentioned clans of the Anṣār: indeed, the Jews are the Banū Isrāʾīl [the Children of Israel], and all of those of them who were in Medina and Khaybar were the Qurayẓa, Naḍīr and Qaynuqāʿ. But among the Aws and Khazraj there were people who converted to Judaism. Some of their women would vow when they gave birth to a child, that if he survived, they would make him a Jew because they considered the Jews people of knowledge and owners of a sacred book. The following Qurʾān verse was revealed with regard to these children: "There is no compulsion in religion" (Qurʾān 2,256). Their parents wanted, according to one account, to force them to embrace Islam.[28]

Suhaylī must have had in mind a limited phenomenon among the Aws and Khazraj, or the literature concerning Qurʾān 2,256 was all he had to go by. In any case, in his view Ibn Isḥāq speaks of people from the Aws and Khazraj.

The following passage from Burhān al-Dīn al-Ḥalabī's commentary on the *sīra* by Ibn Sayyid al-Nās (entitled *Nūr al-nibrās*)[29] relates to the Kitāb

---

nāfaqū fī l-sirr. Wa-kāna hawāhum maʿa yahūd li-takdhībihimi l-nabī ṣ wa-juḥūdihimi l-islām... minhum....

[28]Suhaylī, II, 289: *...wa-qawluhu: wa-min yahūd banī zurayq wa-min yahūd banī ḥāritha, wa-dhakara qabāʾil mina l-anṣār; wa-innamā l-yahūd banū isrāʾīl, wa-jumlat man kāna minhum bi-l-madīna wa-khaybar innamā hum banū qurayẓa wa-banū l-naḍīr wa-banū qaynuqāʿ; ghayra anna fī l-aws wa-l-khazraj man qad tahawwada, wa-kāna min nisāʾihim man tandhuru idhā waladat in ʿāsha waladuhā an tuhawwidahu, li-anna l-yahūd ʿindahum ahl ʿilm wa-kitāb; wa-fī hāʾulāʾi l-abnāʾi lladhīna tahawwadū nazalat 'lā ikrāha fī l-dīn', arāda ābāʾuhum ikrāhahum ʿalā l-islām fī aḥadi l-aqwāl....* Suhaylī is quoted in Gil, "The Origin of the Jews of Yathrib", 210. Gil also quotes al-Yaʿqūbī with regard to Jewish converts among the Aws and Khazraj; Lecker, "Judaism Among Kinda and the *Ridda* of Kinda", 635.

[29]MS Kılıç Ali, no. 768, 349b. See *GAL*, II, 67, 71; *GAL S*, II, 77. This source was employed by Sprenger; see above, 52n.

itself and not to the list of Muḥammad's Jewish adversaries. It reveals a close affinity to the passage quoted above from the much earlier work of Suhaylī, which reduces its importance. In any case, having enumerated some of the Yahūd Banī so-and-so groups, al-Ḥalabī stated that they were people from the Aws and Khazraj:

> And the words: Yahūd Banī ʿAwf, Yahūd Banī l-Najjār, al-Ḥārith, Sāʿida, Jusham, al-Aswad [!], Thaʿlaba and others (*wa-ka-dhālika ghayr dhālika*) from the clans (*qabāʾil*) of the Anṣār: You should know that the Jews are the Banū Isrāʾīl, and all of them who were in Medina and Khaybar were their nobles (*aʿyānuhum*), the Qurayẓa, Naḍīr and Qaynuqāʿ. But among the Aws and Khazraj there were people who converted to Judaism (*man qad tahawwada*)....

These passages notwithstanding, the number of Jewish converts among the Aws and Khazraj was too small to substantiate the Jewish converts alternative on its own. Still, some of the Yahūd Banī so-and-do may have been converts from the Aws and Khazraj, although most of them were not.

Yahūd Banī ʿAwf, Qaynuqāʿ and Ghuṣayna

The Yahūd Banī ʿAwf were probably the most important Yahūd group that had an Arab counterpart: they figure at the beginning of the list of the Yahūd groups, and as we shall see the rights granted to them were the model followed with regard to the other Yahūd groups. Among the Jewish clans living in Medina before the settlement of the Aws and Khazraj we find the Banū ʿAwf,[30] but they could not have been identical with the Yahūd Banī ʿAwf since the latter had a counterpart on the list of Arab participants.

If we were to identify the Yahūd Banī ʿAwf with a specific Jewish tribe, assuming that due to its client status the Jewish tribe was called after its masters rather than by its proper name, the Qaynuqāʿ would be the natural candidates because they were closely associated with the Banū ʿAwf of the Khazraj. Ibn Taymiyya stated that the Qaynuqāʿ were the clients (*ḥulafāʾ*) of the Banū ʿAwf and consequently identified them with the Yahūd Banī ʿAwf of the Kitāb. Ibn Taymiyya and others were drawing the logical conclusion from the reports on the siege and expulsion of the Qaynuqāʿ.[31]

[30] *Aghānī*, XIX, 95:11; *Aghānī* (Dār al-Kutub), XXII, 109.

[31] Ibn Taymiyya, *Ṣārim*, 64: *wa-kāna banū qaynuqāʿ, wa-humu l-mujāwirūna bi-l-madīna wa-hum raḥṭ ʿabdillāh b. salām, ḥulafāʾ banī ʿawf b. al-khazraj... l-raḥṭi lladhīna budiʾa bihim fī hādhihi l-ṣaḥīfa*. See also below, 146n.

But this identification is wrong, since the Qaynuqāʿ were strong militarily and were not clients but allies of the ʿAwf; had they been part of the Kitāb, they would have appeared in it with their proper name. The Qaynuqāʿ are often referred to in the sources by their name and there is no evidence that they were ever called "the Jews (i.e. the Jewish clients) of the Banū ʿAwf". When ʿAbdallāh b. Ubayy demanded that the Prophet spare the Qaynuqāʿ and let them go into exile, he called them his *mawālī* (glossed as *ḥulafāʾ*) and told Muḥammad of their military exploits: 400 men without coats of mail and 300 wearing such coats defended him "from the whole world".[32] *Mawālin* and *ḥulafāʾ* can be either "allies" or "clients", but in this case the former rendering should be adopted.

The two leaders of the ʿAwf, ʿAbdallāh b. Ubayy and ʿUbāda b. al-Ṣāmit of the Ḥublā and the Qawāqil(a), respectively, adopted different attitudes towards the Qaynuqāʿ. The former clung to his alliance with them, whereas the latter abandoned it. Ibn Ubayy's dependence on his Jewish allies is emphasized in this context: while ʿUbāda renounced his many Jewish allies (he said to the Prophet: *inna lī mawāliya min yahūd kathīr ʿadaduhum*), Ibn Ubayy declared that he feared the vicissitudes of fortune (*innī rajul akhāfu l-dawāʾir*),[33] i.e. he feared that the Jews might eventually gain the upper hand, and hence refused to renounce his allies. The historian puts in the Prophet's mouth the following ironical response: "Abū l-Ḥubāb [Ibn Ubayy is addressed by his *kunya*, as a token of respect], the alliance with the Jews about which you were so stingy with regard to ʿUbāda b. al-Ṣāmit is given to you alone".[34] Significantly, the Qaynuqāʿ who lived in their own territory owned fortresses.[35]

To conclude, the Qaynuqāʿ were not identical with the Yahūd Banī ʿAwf. It follows that like the Naḍīr and Qurayẓa, they were not part of the Kitāb.

---

[32]See e.g. Ṭabarī, II, 480:14 [I, 1361]: ... *yā muḥammad, aḥsin fī mawāliyya — wa-kānū ḥulafāʾa l-khazraj... arbaʿumiʾat ḥāsir wa-thalāthumiʾat dāriʿ qad manaʿūnī mina l-aswad wa-l-aḥmar...*; cf. *The History of al-Ṭabarī*, VII, trans. Watt and McDonald, 86: "Muhammad, treat my *mawālī* well.... 400 men without armour and 300 hundred with coats of mail, who defended me from the Arab and the non-arab alike, and you would mow them down in a single morning? By God, I do not feel safe and am afraid of what the future may have in store".

[33]Cf. Qurʾān 5,52: ... *yaqūlūna: nakhshā an tuṣībanā dāʾiratun.*

[34]*Mā bakhulta bihi min wilāyat yahūd ʿalā ʿubāda b. al-ṣāmit fa-huwa ilayka dūnahu*; Ṭabarī, *Tafsīr*, VI, 177–78, interpretation of Qurʾān 5,51. ʿUbāda is wrongly said here to have been of the Banū l-Ḥārith b. al-Khazraj.

[35]See Lecker, "Muḥammad at Medina", 38–39.

This probably leaves us with the Balī as the only possible identification of the Yahūd Banī ʿAwf or most of them; this must have been the case with regard to the other Yahūd Banī so-and-so groups that have counterparts in the list of Arab groups.

The Balī who were scattered in the Sāfila or Lower Medina and the ʿĀliya or Upper Medina are particularly suitable candidates for us here since they were clients and most of them were Jewish. Judaism was widespread among the Balawīs in Qubāʾ in the ʿĀliya where they were the clients of the dominant clan that lived there, the ʿAmr b. ʿAwf (Aws).[36] Admittedly, the ʿAmr b. ʿAwf listed among the Arab groups have no counterpart on the list of Jewish groups, but the evidence on the Balawīs in Qubāʾ is valuable nonetheless. Among these Balawīs were the Ḥishna, who had been forced to convert to Judaism before being admitted into the castle of Taymāʾ.[37] Still in the ʿĀliya we find among the Aws Allāh a Judaised Balawī clan called Murīd (or Murayd).[38] Also the Zayd Allāt (see below) were presumably of the Balī. They were among the Jewish clans of Medina, and since they were clients of the ʿAwf b. al-Khazraj they provide an example of Jewish clients outside Qubāʾ who were attached to a branch of the Khazraj.

That not all of the Balawīs in Medina were Jewish is shown by the example of Kaʿb b. ʿUjra al-Balawī, who owned an idol.[39] Kaʿb belonged to a branch of the Balī called Suwād b. Murayy b. Irāsha,[40] but he is said to have adopted the pedigree (*intasaba... fī*) of the ʿAmr b. ʿAwf.[41] The custodians of the idol al-Saʿīda, located on Mt. Uḥud, were the Banū l-ʿAjlān[42] who are identical with the Balawī ʿAjlān.[43]

As a rule the Balī clans were clients of either the Aws or Khazraj. They had been clients of the Jewish tribes, but by the Islamic era became clients of the more recent Arab settlers. According to Ibn ʿAbd al-Barr, the clans of

[36]Lecker, *Muslims, Jews and Pagans*, 135: "Many, if not all of the Balawīs, converted to Judaism at some stage". The words "if not all" are superfluous. See also Wellhausen, 12–13, summing up the lists of the Jewish tribes and of the Arab tribes associated with them: "Man sieht, die Grenze schwankt. Manche arabische Geschlechter, die bei den Juden wohnten, wurden mehr oder weniger judaisirt, manche jüdische Geschlechter waren arabischen Ursprungs". The Zayd Allāt (below, 63–66) with their pagan name belong to the latter category.

[37]Lecker, *Muslims, Jews and Pagans*, 66–67.

[38]*Ibid.*, 45–46.

[39]Lecker, "Idol Worship in Pre-Islamic Medina (Yathrib)", 340–41.

[40]Dāraquṭnī, *al-Muʾtalif wa-l-mukhtalif*, III, 1234–35; Caskel, I, 329.

[41]Dāraquṭnī, *al-Muʾtalif wa-l-mukhtalif*, III, 1235.

[42]Ibn Ḥabīb, *Muḥabbar*, 316–17.

[43]See Caskel, II, 144, s.v. al-ʿAǧlān b. Ḥāriṯa, and below.

the Balī living in Medina included the ʿAjlān, the Unayf and the Ghuṣayna, all of whom were clients (*ḥulafāʾ*) of the Anṣār. He then quotes al-Zubayr b. Bakkār's statement that they were the clients of the ʿAmr b. ʿAwf of the Aws and were "whole tribes from the Balī among the Anṣār" (*wa-hiya qabāʾil bi-asrihā min balī fī l-anṣār*). Ibn ʿAbd al-Barr's mention of two Balawī individuals is followed by his comment that their *ʿashāʾir* were not clients,[44] i.e. the other members of their original tribes who lived outside Medina were free-born. Now while the ʿAjlān and the Unayf were indeed clients of the ʿAmr b. ʿAwf,[45] the Ghuṣayna were clients of the ʿAwf b. al-Khazraj.

The best-known Balawī client of the ʿAwf was Ghuṣayna's al-Mujadhdhar b. Dhiyād al-Balawī; more precisely, he was a *ḥalīf* or client of the Sālim/Qawāqil(a) subdivision of the ʿAwf.[46] Typically, the sources record his link with the ʿAwf in more than one way; not every medieval author was knowledgeable enough or interested in the minute details of Anṣārī genealogy. One source says that al-Mujadhdhar was a client of the Anṣār, more precisely of the Sālim b. ʿAwf;[47] another says in more general terms that he was a client of the ʿAwf b. al-Khazraj.[48] Elsewhere it is said that

---

[44]Ibn ʿAbd al-Barr, *Inbāh*, 122. He was probably reflecting sensitivities of Andalusians originating from these *ʿashāʾir*.

[45]On these two clans, and on the above-mentioned Ḥishna, see Lecker, *Muslims, Jews and Pagans*, 62–71, 135–44.

[46]In Gil, "The Medinan Opposition to the Prophet", 79, read al-Mujadhdhar instead of Mujdhir. Al-Mujadhdhar's biography provides a curious link between pre-Islamic and early Islamic Medina. Al-Ḥārith b. Suwayd b. al-Ṣāmit from the Ḥabīb, a subdivision of the ʿAmr b. ʿAwf, killed al-Mujadhdhar in the battle of Uḥud and fled to Mecca. Ibn Hishām explains that al-Mujadhdhar had killed al-Ḥārith's father, Suwayd b. al-Ṣāmit, in one of the battles between the Aws and Khazraj; Ibn Hishām, II, 167; Wāqidī, I, 303–305 (in the context of the Muslims killed at Uḥud). Muḥammad's uncompromising order that al-Ḥārith be executed in retaliation for the killing demonstrated that for him the aristocratic murderer and his victim, a former client, were on the same level. This impression is corroborated by the remote family link between al-Ḥārith and Muḥammad: the former's grandmother Laylā was the sister of Salmā who gave birth to Muḥammad's grandfather, ʿAbd al-Muṭṭalib. It is of course no accident that the executioner, ʿUwaym b. Sāʿida, was himself a Balawī; Lecker, *Muslims, Jews and Pagans*, 63–67.

[47]Ibn Hishām, II, 282.

[48]Ibn Ḥabīb, *Mughtālīna*, 150. Ibn al-Kalbī, *Nasab Maʿadd*, II, 709, has two contradictory statements regarding the Ghuṣayna. First he says wrongly that they were clients of the ʿAmr b. ʿAwf *b. Mālik b. al-Aws*; then he says correctly that they were the clients of the ʿAwf b. al-Khazraj. The words "b. Mālik b. al-Aws" should probably be attributed to a scribal error since elsewhere we find, in a quotation from Ibn al-Kalbī's *Jamhara* regarding the Ghuṣayna: *ḥilfuhum fī banī ʿAmr b. ʿAwf* (without *b. Mālik b. al-Aws*); see

al-Mujadhdhar was the client of the Qawāqil,[49] which is probably another way of saying that he was the client of the Sālim.

Let us take a close look at Samhūdī's chapter on the tribal territories of the Anṣār, most of which he quoted from Ibn Zabāla's lost book on the history of Medina. Sālim and Ghanm, sons of ʿAwf b. ʿAmr b. ʿAwf b. al-Khazraj, lived in the court called Dār Banī Sālim. There were three fortresses in this court: al-Muzdalif, which belonged to (or "was [re]built by") the Companion ʿItbān b. Mālik and had belonged before him to Mālik b. al-ʿAjlān al-Sālimī (the brother of ʿItbān's grandfather); al-Shammākh (the owners of which are unspecified), which was outside the houses of the Sālim to the south (*kāna khārijan ʿan buyūt banī sālim min jihati l-qibla*); and finally "the fortress of the Qawāqil" (*uṭum al-qawāqil*) on the edge of the houses of the Sālim opposite al-ʿAṣaba; it belonged to the Sālim b. ʿAwf.[50]

The Sālim had a clear advantage over their brothers, the Ghanm. The court carried their name and they owned at least two of its fortresses if not all three. In the confusion surrounding the definition of the tribal nickname al-Qawāqil, the statement that *uṭum al-qawāqil* belonged to the Sālim b. ʿAwf sticks out as solid evidence: the dominant element in the court, the Sālim, were probably the original Qawāqil.

The advent of Islam changed the balance of power in the court. The dominant line was no longer that of the descendants of the pre-Islamic hero Mālik b. al-ʿAjlān, now represented by his brother's grandson, ʿItbān b. Mālik, but that of ʿUbāda b. al-Ṣāmit, who rose to prominence after the *hijra*. According to his pedigree, ʿUbāda was of the Ghanm.[51] However, his mother was a great-granddaughter of Mālik b. al-ʿAjlān from the Sālim.[52] It

---

Tawḍīḥ al-mushtabih, VI, 428–29. Ibn Mākūlā, I, 185, similarly quoting Ibn al-Kalbī, says about the Ghuṣayna: *wa-ḥilfuhum fī banī ʿAwf b. al-Khazraj.*

[49]Ibn Qudāma, *Istibṣār*, 327.

[50]Samhūdī, I, 199; Lecker, *Muslims, Jews and Pagans*, 126 n. 178. *Maghānim*, 352, s.v. al-Qawāqil and 381, s.v. al-Muzdalif, says about these two fortresses that they were built by Sālim and Ghanm, sons of ʿAwf. The former belonged to the Sālim and the latter to Mālik b. al-ʿAjlān. Mālik belonged to the Sālim and it is not clear why the Ghanm should be mentioned as the builders. Samhūdī (III, 819–21, 877–78) reports that the ruins of al-Muzdalif, the fortress of ʿItbān b. Mālik, are north of the larger mosque of the Sālim that was also known (probably not simultaneously) as Masjid al-Jumuʿa or "the Friday mosque", Masjid ʿĀtika and Masjid al-Wādī. Their smaller mosque, the one consecrated by the Prophet, was at the foot (*aṣl*) of al-Muzdalif. Cf. Lecker, *Muslims, Jews and Pagans*, 95–96.

[51]ʿUbāda b. al-Ṣāmit b. Qays b. Aṣram b. Fihr b. Thaʿlaba b. Ghanm b. ʿAwf b. ʿAmr b. ʿAwf b. al-Khazraj. This is the pedigree given in Ibn Saʿd, III, 546, 621.

[52]*Ibid.*, III, 546.

appears that ʿUbāda's descendants attempted to present him as a member of the Qawāqil. For example, in one pedigree of ʿUbāda[53] the name "Sālim" was added between Ghanm and ʿAwf (making ʿUbāda one of the Sālim);[54] or the Qawāqil are said to include both the Ghanm and the Sālim sons of ʿAwf b. ʿAmr b. ʿAwf b. al-Khazraj.[55]

We now return to al-Mujadhdhar's clan, Ghuṣayna. Ghuṣayna was their "mother", while "their father" or eponym was al-Mujadhdhar's great-great-grandfather, ʿAmr b. ʿAmmāra[56] whose pedigree goes back to Farrān (or Farān) b. Balī.[57] Hence it could be said of al-Mujadhdhar and a fellow Ghuṣaynī of his that they were from the Banū Farrān.[58] Perhaps the Ghuṣayna were linked to the descendants of Farrān known as *al-quyūn*, or "the blacksmiths", who were among the inhabitants of Maʿdin Banī Sulaym in Najd.[59]

The Ghuṣayna included some early supporters of Muḥammad, and hence could have been on Muḥammad's side shortly after the *hijra* when the Kitāb was concluded: al-Mujadhdhar and three other members of the Ghuṣayna

[53] Which is different from the one quoted earlier in other details as well.

[54] Ibn ʿAsākir, XXVI, 175.

[55] Ibn Saʿd, III, 546. An even more unusual claim can be found in the entry of another member of the Ghanm, al-Nuʿmān b. Mālik: his grandfather is said to have been the Qawqal after whom the Ghanm and the Sālim were called Qawāqil(a); Ibn Saʿd, III, 548.

[56] For the vocalization of this name see *Tawḍīḥ al-mushtabih*, I, 345; Ibn Mākūlā, I, 184–85. Bakrī, I, 28, says that they were the descendants of Suwād b. Murayy b. Irāsha; cf. Caskel, I, 329.

[57] Ibn Hishām, II, 352. The insertion of "Ghuṣayna" in al-Mujadhdhar's paternal pedigree between Mālik and ʿAmr is erroneous; cf. *Iṣāba*, V, 770–71 no. 7732; Ibn Saʿd, III, 552.

[58] Ibn Qudāma, *Istibṣār*, 202.

[59] Bakrī, III, 1013, s.v. Fārān: *maʿdin ḥadīd bi-manāzil banī sulaym.* Bakrī's geographical dictionary provides some information about them; Lecker, *Banū sulaym*, 198–201; Bakrī, I, 28: *wa-aqāma bi-maʿdin sulaym farrān b. balī fī ṭāʾifa min balī, wa-hum banū l-akhtham... b. sulaym, wa-humu lladhīna yuqālu lahumu l-quyūn, wa-yazʿumūna anna aṣlahum min balī, maʿa unās wajadūhum hunāka mina l-ʿāriba l-ʾūlā, min banī fārān b. ʿamr b. ʿimlīq.* More specifically, the *quyūn* in question were the ʿUjayba b. ʿĀmir b. ʿAbīla b. Qismīl b. Fārān b. Balī; Caskel, I, 329 (who has ʿAjība, Qasmīl). ʿUjayba's descendants were the blacksmiths who were among (*fī*) the Sulaym; they are called Banū Jusham (read: al-Akhtham); Ibn al-Kalbī, *Nasab Maʿadd*, II, 705–706. *Muqtaḍab*, 341, has here: Jushaym; Abū ʿUbayd, *Nasab*, 371, has: Khuthaym (which could be a variant of al-Akhtham). Regarding *al-quyūn* from the Sulaym see also *Takmilat al-ikmāl*, IV, 177 (*... mina l-quyūn min banī jusham b. ʿawf b. ʿuṣayya*). *Qayn* usually means a blacksmith but could also mean a goldsmith; Ibn al-Athīr, *Nihāya*, IV, 135, s.v.: *wa-huwa l-ḥaddād wa-l-ṣāʾigh.* One wonders whether the Ghuṣayna were connected to the Qaynuqāʿ who were allied with the ʿAwf b. al-Khazraj.

fought at Badr.[60] Moreover, one of them, Yazīd b. Thaʿlaba, participated in the last ʿAqaba meeting prior to the *hijra*.[61]

There were close links between the Ghuṣayna and the ʿAwf. The Ghuṣayna lived near the ʿAwf, more precisely near the Sālim: the statement that the Sālim (and their brothers, the Ghanm) lived in the court called Dār Banī Sālim is followed by a reference to the mosque of the Ghuṣayna: it is reported that the Ghuṣayna, a clan (*ḥayy*) of the Balī whose members were the clients of the Sālim, settled near the mosque of the Ghuṣayna.[62]

There were marriage links between the Ghuṣayna and the ʿAwf, more precisely the Ghanm. Khawla bint al-Ṣāmit of the Ghanm (ʿUbāda b. al-Ṣāmit's sister) was married to the above-mentioned Yazīd b. Thaʿlaba of the Ghuṣayna;[63] al-Mujadhdhar's sister was married to a member of the Ghanm.[64]

In sum, the Ghuṣayna who were the clients of the Banū ʿAwf and were presumably Jewish, on a par with most of the Balawīs that lived in Medina before the settlement of the Aws and Khazraj, may well have been among the Yahūd Banī ʿAwf.

ʿAbdallāh b. Salām and the Zayd Allāt

The famous Jewish convert ʿAbdallāh b. Salām could have been one of the Yahūd Banī ʿAwf. ʿAbdallāh probably embraced Islam together with several relatives of his who appear in the sources. There are conflicting claims concerning his conversion. According to his descendants, it took place in Minā before the *hijra*.[65] Ibn Isḥāq quotes the story of his conversion from a member of ʿAbdallāh's family (*baʿḍ ahlihi*),[66] i.e. a descendant of his who

---

[60]Wāqidī, I, 167–68.

[61]Ibn Hishām, II, 108.

[62]Samhūdī, I, 199–200. An abridged version of this report is found in *Khulāṣat al-wafā*, 172. Cf. Lecker, *Muslims, Jews and Pagans*, 126 n. 178. The mosque of the Ghuṣayna was reportedly among the mosques in which the Prophet prayed; *Manāsik*, 399 (the data in the accompanying note are inaccurate). In Ibn Shabba, *Taʾrīkh al-madīna*, I, 64, 65, read instead of ʿUḍayya: Ghuṣayna. Also Ibn Shabba, *Taʾrīkh al-madīna*^{2}, I, 46, 47, has ʿUḍayya. Ghuṣayna's proximity to the Sālim is confirmed by the details of the above-mentioned murder of Suwayd b. al-Ṣāmit; Wāqidī, I, 303: their court faced that of the Sālim from the east (*wijāh banī sālim ilā maṭlaʿi l-shams*).

[63]Ibn Saʿd, VIII, 377.

[64]*Ibid.*, III, 548. Although the Ghuṣayna were themselves clients, they had at least one client of their own; *Iṣāba*, IV, 427.

[65]Suyūṭī, *Khaṣāʾiṣ*, I, 358–59; *Majmaʿ al-zawāʾid*, IX, 326. The report goes back to Muḥammad b. Ḥamza b. Yūsuf b. ʿAbdallāh b. Salām ← his father.

[66]Ibn Hishām, II, 163.

was Ibn Isḥāq's contemporary. The story is less favourable to ʿAbdallāh since it dates his conversion to the Prophet's first days in Medina. The two stories have in common the circumstances in which ʿAbdallāh heard of the Prophet's arrival: in both he heard the news when he was at the top of a palm tree; in the former he threw himself down, while in the latter he only said *allāhu akbar*. The witness to this was his mother or his paternal aunt, Khālida bint al-Ḥārith, respectively. The witness' reaction was the same: a remark that had Moses appeared, ʿAbdallāh would not have received him with more enthusiasm.

ʿAbdallāh's children, whose involvement in transmitting the story is not concealed, attempted to secure for their famous father the best possible place in the Islamic past by claiming an early conversion. Their interests coincided with those of Islamic scholarship at large, since ʿAbdallāh was a significant witness to Muhḥammad's truthfulness. But it is doubtful that we should accept the family's testimony, especially since it clashes with another claim that is even less favourable to ʿAbdallāh:[67] his conversion took place in AH 8, or alternatively two years before the Prophet's death.[68] Beside the obvious tendency to prefer a non-family claim, support for the later date can be found in Ibn Isḥāq's list of the Prophet's Jewish adversaries, where ʿAbdallāh concludes the list of adversaries from the Qaynuqāʿ. The details attached to his name in the report on his later conversion exclude the possibility that another ʿAbdallāh b. Salām is meant here.[69] It appears that after the *hijra* ʿAbdallāh was involved in actions against the Prophet. At any rate, this refutes the family's claims that he converted before the *hijra* or shortly thereafter. Obviously, Ibn Isḥāq did not bother to synchronize the reports he quoted from his informants, which is often advantageous for research.

It was the Prophet himself who reportedly accepted ʿAbdallāh's conversion, replacing his former name with an Islamic one.[70] This probably accounts for the fact that, together with his sons Yūsuf and Muḥammad,

---

[67]ʿAbdallāh was involved in politics at the time of the Rāshidūn. For example, before the arrival of the Egyptian rebels, ʿAbdallāh used to demand the Qurashī leaders not to kill ʿUthmān; he also warned ʿAlī against going to Iraq; Ibn ʿAsākir, XXXIX, 351. But his political role does not seem to have affected the claims regarding his conversion.

[68]*Iṣāba*, IV, 118 no. 4728.

[69]Ibn Hishām, II, 161–62. ʿAbdallāh is not found in the much shorter parallel list in Balādhurī, *Ansāb*, I, 285.

[70]Ibn Hishām, II, 163–64.

ʿAbdallāh is listed among the *mawālī* of the Banū Hāshim.[71] Whatever link was established between the Prophet and ʿAbdallāh upon the latter's conversion, he was and remained a client of the ʿAwf or of a specific clan among the ʿAwf: reportedly he was one of the clients (*ḥulafāʾ*) of the ʿAwf b. al-Khazraj,[72] or (more precisely) of the Qawāqil.[73]

Clientage bonds remained in force for generations. Two pertinent examples, both relating to the descendants of former Jews, can be adduced. ʿAbdallāh b. Salām's great-grandson, Muḥammad b. Ḥamza b. Yūsuf b. ʿAbdallāh b. Salām (above, 63n), was still the client of the Anṣār (*ḥalīf al-anṣār*).[74] Abū l-Ḥārith Ṣāliḥ b. Ḥassān al-Naḍīrī (or al-Naḍarī), a transmitter of *ḥadīth* who flourished in the first half of the second century AH, was a client of the Aws (*min ḥulafāʾi l-aws*).[75] Since by Ṣāliḥ's time the Naḍīr tribe had ceased to exist, *ḥulafāʾ* in this context are clients, not allies. Incidentally, this would be a fine example of an Arabian clientage *par excellence* that probably began at the time of Muḥammad and continued into the second Islamic century. The clientage may have been established when the Naḍīr went into exile; Ṣāliḥ's father or grandfather must have been among the few who stayed behind.

In the list of the Prophet's Jewish adversaries and elsewhere ʿAbdallāh b. Salām is considered one of the Qaynuqāʿ. This, however, creates a contradiction: if indeed they were militarily strong and were the allies of the ʿAwf rather than their clients, how could ʿAbdallāh have been the client of the ʿAwf? One could argue that he and his family were an exception, but there is evidence that ʿAbdallāh was not a member of the Qaynuqāʿ.

In the section of his book dealing with the pre-Islamic history of Medina Samhūdī includes a list of the Jewish tribes that remained in Medina when the Aws and Khazraj settled there. Among them were the Banū Zayd Allāt, about whom Samhūdī's source, Ibn Zabāla, remarks that they were the clan of ʿAbdallāh b. Salām and that their territory was close to that of the Ghuṣayna (*raht ʿabdillāh b. salām, kānū qarīban min banī ghuṣayna*). This is immediately followed by the mention of the Qaynuqāʿ, who lived elsewhere.

---

[71] Khalīfa, *Ṭabaqāt*, 8. The list is followed by another including the *ḥulafāʾ* of the Banū Hāshim.

[72] *Fatḥ al-bārī*, VII, 197:3.

[73] *Iṣāba*, IV, 118: *ḥalīf al-qawāqil mina l-khazraj al-isrāʾīlī thumma l-anṣārī*. Regarding his son, Muḥammad, it is reported less specifically that he was a client of the Khazraj (*al-khazrajī al-anṣārī, ḥalīf lahum*); *Istīʿāb*, III, 1374.

[74] *Tahdhīb al-kamāl*, XXV, 96–97 no. 5166.

[75] Ibn Saʿd, *Qism mutammim*, 450 (printed: al-Naḍrī); Samʿānī, V, 503–504, s.v. al-Naḍīrī; *Tahdh.*, IV, 385.

Aware of the problematic nature of Ibn Zabāla's account, Samhūdī hastens to add that according to Bukhārī's *Ṣaḥīḥ* and contrary to what Ibn Zabāla said, the Qaynuqāʿ were ʿAbdallāh's *rahṭ* (i.e. family or tribe).[76]

Again, the less favourable version is to be preferred. The Zayd Allāt and the Qaynuqāʿ were two distinct tribes living in different places; ʿAbdallāh belonged to the former, who were the neighbours of the Ghuṣayna.[77]

A clue regarding the identification of the Zayd Allāt can perhaps be derived from the pedigree of their neighbours, the Ghuṣayna, who were of the Farrān. Ghuṣayna's eponym, ʿAmr b. ʿAmmāra, was a descendant of Taym b. Irāsha b. ʿĀmir b. ʿAbīla b. Qismīl b. Farrān b. Balī.[78] Also the Unayf, one of the Balawī clans living in Qubāʾ, were the descendants of Taym b. Irāsha.[79] Along the same genealogical line we find a brother of Irāsha called Zayd[80] or Zaydallāh[81] or Zayd Allāt.[82] The appearance of the name in a genealogical line of Balī known to have been represented in Medina suggests a possible identification of the Zayd Allāt.

In sum, the Zayd Allāt to whom ʿAbdallāh b. Salām belonged were probably a clan of the Balī that converted to Judaism several generations before Islam. ʿAbdallāh b. Salām, who was still a Jew at that time, and the Zayd Allāt may well have been among the Yahūd Banī ʿAwf.

Labīd b. al-Aʿṣam and Yahūd Banī Zurayq

Labīd b. al-Aʿṣam, who reportedly bewitched the Prophet, is on the list of the Prophet's Jewish adversaries, where he figures as a member of Yahūd Banī Zurayq.[83] Labīd is of interest for us here because the Zurayq are part of the Jusham, one of the Khazraj subdivisions that participated in the Kitāb.

[76] Samhūdī, I, 164. An abridged version of Ibn Zabāla's statement (without the reference to Zayd Allāt's location) is found in Ibn Rusta, 62:7. The Zayd Allāt may be identical with the Banū Zayd listed among the *qabāʾil banī isrāʾīl* that were in Medina when the Aws and Khazraj settled there; *Aghānī*, XIX, 95:10; *Aghānī* (Dār al-Kutub), XXII, 109.

[77] Like every other tribe, Jewish or otherwise, the Qaynuqāʿ were made of subdivisions; for a sub-group of the Qaynuqāʿ see Lecker, "Ḥudhayfa b. al-Yamān", 160–61. One could argue that the Zayd Allāt were a subdivision of the Qaynuqāʿ; in this case they must have been relatively recent converts to Judaism since their name still included that of a deity.

[78] Dāraquṭnī, *al-Muʾtalif wa-l-mukhtalif*, I, 286, s.v. Bathīra; Caskel, I, 329.

[79] Ibn al-Kalbī, *Nasab Maʿadd*, II, 706–708; Caskel, I, 329.

[80] Caskel, I, 329.

[81] Yāqūt, V, 37a, s.v. Maʾrib.

[82] Bakrī, I, 27, 30.

[83] Rubin, 8 = Ibn Hishām, II, 162. Also Lecker, "The Bewitching of the Prophet Muḥammad"; Cook, "The Prophet Muḥammad, Labīd Al-Yahūdī and the Commentaries to *Sūra* 113".

Rubin (8) argued that Labīd belonged to a Jewish group having *ḥilf* relations with the Zurayq and living among them. This argument supports Rubin's view regarding the identity of the Yahūd Banī so-and-so in general.[84] But do we really have a group here? It is true that the Yahūd Banī Zurayq reportedly bewitched (plural) Muḥammad,[85] but the plural form probably relates to Labīd and his family. One account has it that the tool of witchcraft was actually prepared by Labīd's sisters,[86] while in another the witches are identified as Labīd's daughters.[87] The latter claim is doubtful, since Labīd was still a young lad (see below).

There is no unanimity regarding Labīd's status. A late compiler struggles with the conflicting claims that he was from the Yahūd Banī Zurayq or, alternatively, a man of the Zurayq who was a *ḥalīf* (client) of the Jews and a *munāfiq* or hypocrite. His harmonizing solution is that those who called him a Jew pointed to his substance, while those who called him a *munāfiq* pointed to his appearance.[88] Elsewhere Labīd is said to have been a client of (*wa-kāna ḥalīfan fī*) the Zurayq,[89] in other words, a non-Zuraqī. Finally, an account that does not specify the bewitcher's name calls him a man of the Anṣār.[90] Three cousins from the Zurayq (Qays b. Miḥṣan, al-Ḥārith b. Qays and Jubayr b. Iyās) are also mentioned in different versions of this report.[91] The location of Bīr Dharwān that was linked to the bewitching in the territory of the Zurayq and the tribal affiliation of the three Zuraqīs leave no room for doubt that the affair was connected to the Banū Zurayq.[92]

Curiously, Labīd is listed among the prominent Jews (*ʿuẓamāʾ yahūd*) of the Qurayẓa.[93] One could argue that Labīd was one of the Quraẓīs who were spared because they had not yet reached the age of puberty, and then he became a client of the Zurayq. But at least two people on the same list were

---

[84] Above, 52f.

[85] Rubin, 8 = ʿAbd al-Razzāq, XI, 14.

[86] Ibn Saʿd, II, 197.

[87] Qurṭubī, *Tafsīr*, XX, 259.

[88] *Sīra shāmiyya*, III, 600. There may not be a difficulty here: one is sometimes referred to as al-Yahūdī even after one's conversion to Islam.

[89] Ibn Saʿd, II, 197.

[90] *Ibid.*, II, 199.

[91] *Ibid.*, II, 197–98; III, 591–92.

[92] On the settlement of the Banū Zurayq in Dharwān see Samhūdī, I, 206:9. One source (quoted in *Sīra shāmiyya*, III, 598:1; Suyūṭī, *Durr*, VI, 418:3) calls the well Biʾr Maymūn. Unfortunately, the owner of the well is only referred to as *Abū Fulān* ("father of so-and-so"); ʿAbd al-Razzāq, XI, 14. His real name was concealed so as to protect the family's prestige.

[93] Balādhurī, *Ansāb*, I, 285.

actually of the Qaynuqāʿ,[94] and it appears that one cannot consider Labīd a Quraẓī on the basis of this testimony. A *ḥadīth* of ʿĀʾisha has it that Labīd was a Jewish slave of the Prophet (*ghulām yahūdī yakhdumuhu*).[95] Now before the females and young children of the Qurayẓa were sold into slavery, the Prophet took his own share, the fifth part. Some he manumitted, some he handed out as gifts and some he gave to whomever he pleased (as slaves).[96] Muḥammad may well have kept some of the young slaves to himself, but Labīd was not one of them. The survivors from the Qurayẓa are known as such; had Labīd been one of them, we would have heard about it.

Neither was he of the Zurayq themselves. The *nisba* al-Saḥūlī attached to his name probably indicates that he was originally a Yemenite of the Ḥimyar. In other words, he was a foreigner associated with the Zurayq as a client.[97] One assumes that he was not a client of the Zurayq as a whole but of a specific person among them.

In sum, the case of Labīd shows that among the Yahūd Banī so-and-so one can expect to find not only converts from among the Aws and Khazraj and Jewish Balawī groups in client status, but also individual Jews (or small Jewish families) living as clients amidst the Anṣārī groups.

Yahūd Banī Ḥāritha

The Yahūd Banī Ḥāritha, although they are not listed in the Kitāb, included a variety of groups and individuals, and hence contribute to a better understanding of the phrase Yahūd Banī so-and-so.

The Ḥāritha were a subdivision of the Nabīt (Aws) alongside the ʿAbd al-Ashhal, Ẓafar and several lesser groups. The Ḥāritha adopted independent policies among the Nabīt. At some point the ʿAbd al-Ashhal together with the nomadic Sulaym besieged the Ḥāritha, but through the intercession of other subdivisions of the Aws, namely the ʿAmr b. ʿAwf and the Khaṭma, the besieged Ḥāritha were allowed to go into exile and lived in the

[94] Below, 72f.

[95] Rubin, 8 ("servant") = Suyūṭī, *Durr*, VI, 417:27. The same words (*anna ghulāman yahūdiyyan kāna yakhdumu l-nabī*) are used with regard to another Jewish slave who was probably a young boy: he fell ill, the Prophet visited him, called on him to become a Muslim and the boy's father ordered him to obey; *Iṣāba*, IV, 379 no. 5254, s.v. ʿAbd al-Qaddūs al-Isrāʾīlī.

[96] *Fa-akhadha khumusan fa-kāna yuʿtiqu minhu wa-yahabu minhu wa-yukhdimu minhu man arāda*; Wāqidī, II, 523:15.

[97] Lecker, "The Bewitching of the Prophet Muḥammad", 567–68.

Jewish settlement of Khaybar.[98] This indicates a particularly close relationship between the Ḥāritha and the Jews, which is in fact true of the Nabīt as a whole. When the Ḥāritha returned from Khaybar a year later, they settled in the Yathrib village or town northwest of Medina (that gave its name to the whole vicinity). The village was inhabited by Jews described as *jummāʿ*,[99] who "excelled the rest of the Jews in nobility, wealth and power".[100] The exile in Khaybar that was caused by internal strife within the Nabīt is not identical with another exile to Khaybar, in this case of the Nabīt, that took place some time before the battle of Buʿāth. Under military pressure from the Khazraj the Aws tried to make an alliance with Quraysh against the Khazraj. When this attempt failed, the Nabīt went to Khaybar and remained there for a year. Samhūdī argues that Nabīt's stay in Khaybar is in fact identical to that of the Ḥāritha, since the latter were part of the former; but actually we have here two events with different backgrounds.[101] The Ḥāritha were not among the Nabīt clans that set out to Mecca in an attempt to make an alliance with Quraysh,[102] and in the battle of Buʿāth they followed an independent policy. Before fighting broke out, they informed the Khazraj that they did not wish to fight against them and sent them twelve hostages.[103]

According to Muḥayyiṣa b. Masʿūd (the murderer of Ibn Sunayna, see below), quoted with a family *isnād* through his son and grandson, at times of famine the people of Medina (or, more specifically, his family or clan) would go to Khaybar, and sometimes to Fadak and Taymāʾ.[104] Muḥayyiṣa, his elder brother Ḥuwayyiṣa and their cousin ʿAbdallāh b. Sahl belonged to a subdivision of the Ḥāritha called Majdaʿa b. Ḥāritha.[105] It is no accident that the Prophet sent another member of the Majdaʿa, Abū Ḥathma, to Khaybar as an evaluator of its produce of dates for the purpose of taxation

---

[98]Samhūdī, I, 192.

[99]Above, 53.

[100]Lecker, "Muḥammad at Medina", 41–42, 56. In an earlier round of the internal strife within the Nabīt, the Ḥāritha managed to expel their brothers ʿAbd al-Ashhal, who went to the land of the Sulaym; Samhūdī, I, 191–92; Lecker, *Banū sulaym*, 104.

[101]Samhūdī, I, 216. That a period of one year appears in both stories could result from contamination. Alternatively, it may have been the standard period of exile in pre-Islamic Medina.

[102]Ibn Ḥabīb, *Munammaq*, 269.

[103]*Aghānī*, XV, 163:-5; *Aghānī* (Dār al-Kutub), XVII, 123–24.

[104]Wāqidī, II, 713. This is reported by way of introduction to the story on the murder of ʿAbdallāh b. Sahl.

[105]Ibn Qudāma, *Istibṣār*, 241–46 (the famous Muḥammad b. Maslama belonged to the same subdivision). See also Ibn Ḥazm, *Ansāb*, 341–42.

(*khāriṣ*).[106] Beside being skillful in calculations the tax collector must have been intimately acquainted with Khaybar and its people.

Ibn Sunayna was one of the Yahūd Banī Ḥāritha. This information is found in a story of the "old times — new times" type that is not uncommon in Islamic literature. Stories of this type not only record past events, but also allow the descendants of their protagonists to present their ancestors in the best possible light as acting for the sake of Islam against their own interests. The need to correct images was most strongly felt in the case of those who had had close relations with the Jews.

Ibn Sunayna, a merchant and a *ḥalīf* or client of Ḥuwayyiṣa b. Masʿūd, embraced Islam, and hence the epithet al-Yahūdī in his case means "the former Jew". He was murdered by Muḥayyiṣa.[107] Ibn Sunayna was a non-Ḥārithī client of Ḥuwayyiṣa; his only protector was his master, the murderer's brother. Obviously, Muḥayyiṣa did not fear retaliation since the duty to avenge Ibn Sunayna's blood was his and his brother's. Ḥuwayyiṣa was shocked: according to Arabian values, murdering one's client — or indeed, harming someone entitled to one's protection — was degrading, and in this case it was also economically imprudent.

The affair of Ibn Sunayna is comparable to that of Udhayna, a Jewish merchant from Najrān who was under the protection (*jiwār*) of ʿAbd al-Muṭṭalib. When he was killed, his protector exacted his blood money and handed it over to Udhayna's cousin.[108]

---

[106] Ibn Qudāma, *Istibṣār*, 246–47.

[107] Wāqidī, I, 190:3, 191–92; Ṭabarī, II, 491 [I, 1372–73] (*rajul min tujjār yahūd kāna yulābisuhum wa-yubāyiʿuhum*); Ibn Hishām, III, 62 (variants: Subayna/Shubayna). Elsewhere Ibn Sunayna is said less accurately to have been of the Banū Ḥāritha; Balādhurī, *Ansāb*, I, 285:-2 (he is called here: Abū Sunayna). Gil, "The Origin of the Jews of Yathrib", 211, says: "There is special mention of Jews among the Banū Ḥāritha, which designation apparently applied to the Banū Qayla, i.e. both Aws and Khazraj" (Abū ʿAwāna, *Musnad*, IV, 163: *... wa-ajlā rasūlu llāh ṣ yahūda l-madīna kullahum min banī qaynuqāʿ wa-hum qawm ʿabdillāh b. salām raḍiya llāh ʿanhu wa-yahūd banī ḥāritha wa-kull yahūdī kāna bi-l-madīna*). But Ibn Sunayna's Ḥāritha were no doubt the Ḥāritha of the Nabīt, not the Banū Qayla.

[108] Lecker, "A Note on Early Marriage Links", 37. Also comparable are the affairs of a Jew from Taymāʾ and another from Wādī l-Qurā. Both of them were wine merchants who traded in northern Arabia under the protection (*jiwār*) of two nomadic tribes. When the Jewish *jār* of one tribe was murdered by the other tribe, retaliation took the form of murdering the Jewish *jār* of the aggressors; *Aghānī*, XII, 124; *Aghānī* (Dār al-Kutub), XIV, 2–4.

Kināna b. Ṣūriyā was also of the Yahūd Banī Ḥāritha; he appears as such on Ibn Hishām's list of the Prophet's Jewish adversaries, while elsewhere he figures as one of the doctors (*aḥbār*) of the Qaynuqāʿ who embraced Islam outwardly (*nifāqan*).[109] It seems that we have here one and the same person having two tribal affiliations, perhaps due to a shift in his pedigree sometime after the *hijra*.

Since his father's name Ṣūriyā(ʾ) is a typical Jewish name, one assumes that he was not an Arab of the Ḥāritha but rather their non-Ḥārithī Jewish client. In this case his status was identical to that of Ibn Sunayna.

Yahūd Banī Ḥāritha and Banū Murāna

At an unspecified time the Prophet expelled from Medina the Yahūd Banī Ḥāritha and all the other Jews.[110] The fact that the Yahūd Banī Ḥāritha are specifically mentioned with regard to the expulsion indicates that they were the most significant group among those expelled.[111]

The Yahūd Banī Ḥāritha owned land, which contradicts the claim that the Yahūd Banī so-and-so groups did not have a territory of their own. ʿUmar's estate Thamgh, which he declared a *ṣadaqa* or charitable endowment,[112] was reportedly obtained from the Yahūd Banī Ḥāritha.[113] In the context of the dispute over the first charitable endowment in Islam it is reported on the authority of Muḥammad b. Kaʿb al-Quraẓī that the Prophet declared as charitable endowments the estates bequeathed to him by the Jew Mukhayrīq 22 months after the *hijra*, while ʿUmar declared

[109]Ibn Hishām, II, 175, 162. In Balādhurī, *Ansāb*, I, 285:7, Kināna b. Ṣūb.rā (var. Ṣūriyā) is listed among the Qaynuqāʿ leaders. Kināna b. Ṣuwayrāʾ of the Naḍīr, mentioned favourably in Wāqidī, I, 365, 371, is another person, although the name Ṣuwayrāʾ appears to be a corruption of Ṣūriyā(ʾ); see Ṭabarī, II, 552:13 [I, 1450].

[110]Lecker, "Muḥammad at Medina", 56, 58.

[111]For mention of Yahūd Banī Ḥāritha alongside the main Jewish tribes see Ibn Junghul, I, 255a, with regard to AH 2: *wa-fīhā khadaʿa l-mushrikūna min ahli l-madīna wa-l-yahūdi lladhīna bihā min banī qaynuqāʿ wa-bani l-naḍīr wa-bani qurayẓa wa-yahūd banī ḥāritha wa-ṣānaʿū l-muslimīna wa-aẓhara ṭāʾigh kathīra* [read: *wa-aẓharat ṭawāʾif kathīra*] *mina l-yahūd wa-l-muskhrikīna l-islām wa-hum munāfiqūn fī l-bāṭin.*

[112]Sometimes it is confused with ʿUmar's land in Khaybar; cf. Dāraquṭnī, *Sunan*, IV, 186 (*Kitāb al-aḥbās*; ...*ʿan ʿumar annahu aṣāba arḍan bi-khaybar yuqālu lahā thamgh...*). See also below, 82.

[113]Lecker, "Muḥammad at Medina", 56; Samhūdī, IV, 1165, s.v. Thamgh: ... *aṣāba arḍan min yahūd banī ḥāritha yuqālu lahā thamgh.* See also Aḥmad², VIII, 224–25 no. 6078. Bakrī, I, 346, s.v. Thamgh, locates it opposite (*tilqāʾ*) Medina and reports that ʿUmar declared it a charitable endowment when, following an excursion there, he missed a prayer. *Lisān al-ʿarab*, VIII, 423b, locates it in Medina.

Thamgh a charitable endowment upon his return from the expedition of Khaybar in AH 7.[114] In other words, according to Ibn Kaʿb al-Quraẓī the credit belongs to Muḥammad. If this is historical,[115] it could serve as a *terminus ante quem* for the expulsion of the Yahūd Banī Ḥāritha who were the former owners of Thamgh. But their expulsion could even have taken place several years earlier.[116] The circumstances of this takeover of land are obscure, and ʿUmar may have become the owner of Thamgh in a different manner.[117] In any case, the Yahūd Banī Ḥāritha owned land.

Another Jewish group living near or inside the territory of the Ḥāritha, namely the Murāna, owned a fortress that was located in Thamgh.[118] Since the place-name Thamgh is associated with both the Yahūd Banī Ḥāritha and the Murāna, the two groups could have been one and the same. However, the Murāna could also have been part of the Yahūd Banī Ḥāritha.

Yahūd Banī l-Najjār and Silsila b. Barhām

Unlike the Yahūd Banī Ḥāritha, the Yahūd Banī l-Najjār appear in the Kitāb. In Ibn Hishām's list of Muḥammad's Jewish adversaries we find one of them, Silsila b. Barhām.[119] Silsila b. Abrāhām ("and some say: Bahrām, but the former is more accurate") in Balādhurī's list of Jewish leaders (*ʿuẓamāʾ yahūd*) is probably the same person, although Balādhurī lists him as a Quraẓī. It is reported that Silsila embraced Islam outwardly (literally: "he had recourse to the Islamic faith").[120] Silsila b. Barhām, Rāfiʿ

[114] Samhūdī, IV, 1166. Samhūdī, who quotes this report from Ibn Shabba, does not specify the latter's *isnād*. *Fatḥ al-bārī*, V, 299:18, says that Ibn Shabba's *isnād* is weak; but this verdict belongs to the sphere of *jarḥ wa-taʿdīl* and has no bearing on the usefulness of this report for modern research. On the dispute see also Lecker, "Muḥammad at Medina", 29–30; below, 81f.

[115] Cf. Ibn Shabba, *Taʾrīkh al-madīna*, I, 175 (← Wāqidī): the Prophet declared al-Aʿwāf (and six other estates) charitable endowments (*waqafa*) in AH 7.

[116] Cf. the expulsion of the Thaʿlaba in AH 3; below, 77.

[117] Cf. Lecker, "Muḥammad at Medina", 29; Samhūdī, IV, 1166: Thamgh was given to ʿUmar by Muḥammad and the former bought land adjacent to it from some Jews.

[118] Lecker, "Muḥammad at Medina", 58; Samhūdī, IV, 1165, s.v. Thamgh; 1241, s.v. al-Shabʿān; I, 165:6 (printed: Murāba); *Maghānim*, 199, s.v. al-Shabʿān; Yāqūt, III, 322a, s.v. al-Shabʿān (the two last mentioned sources quote Naṣr); Naṣr, *Amkina*, 79a: *uṭum li-l-yahūd bi-l-madīna fī diyār usayd b. muʿāwiya*. The wording suggests that the Usayd b. Muʿāwiya are a tribal group, but they could not be identified.

[119] Ibn Hishām, II, 162.

[120] *Wa-kāna silsila mutaʿawwidhan*; Balādhurī, *Ansāb*, I, 285:17. It will be recalled that Labīd b. al-Aʿṣam is also listed by Balādhurī as a Quraẓī; Balādhurī's text seems to be garbled.

b. Ḥuraymila and Rifāʿa b. Zayd b. al-Tābūt, listed by Balādhurī as Quraẓīs, appear elsewhere among the doctors (*aḥbār*) of the Qaynuqāʿ who "had recourse to Islam".[121] The typically Jewish name Silsila b. Barhām/Abrāhām suggests that he was a non-Najjārī Jewish client of the Najjār.

Yahūd Banī l-Aws

The lists of participants are asymmetrical with regard to the Aws. While there are Banū l-Aws and Yahūd Banī l-Aws, there are no Jewish counterparts for the Arab subdivisions ʿAmr b. ʿAwf and the Nabīt, both of whom belonged to the Aws. One could argue that there were simply no Yahūd Banī ʿAmr b. ʿAwf and Yahūd Banī l-Nabīt, but this argument can be refuted easily: since the Ḥāritha were part of the Nabīt, the Yahūd Banī Ḥāritha could also be considered Yahūd Banī l-Nabīt. (Admittedly, such a group is not attested in the sources.) Moreover, the Yahūd Banī ʿAmr b. ʿAwf are specifically mentioned; Qardam b. ʿAmr of the Yahūd Banī ʿAmr b. ʿAwf is listed among the Prophet's Jewish adversaries.[122] For whatever reason, the Yahūd Banī ʿAmr b. ʿAwf and the Yahūd Banī l-Nabīt (including the sizeable Yahūd Banī Ḥāritha) did not take part in the Kitāb.

Compared to the Yahūd Banī Ḥāritha, the Yahūd of the other Nabīt sections appear to have been less numerous. Another clan of the Nabīt, the ʿAbd al-Ashhal, reportedly had in its midst only one Jewish client (*jār*) called Yūshaʿ al-Yahūdī, who is said to have announced Muḥammad's appearance.[123] Since Yūshaʿ is a typical Jewish name, he could not have been one of the ʿAbd al-Ashhal themselves. The apologetic statement

[121] Ibn Hishām, II, 174–75. The name Silsila is very uncommon. For a Silsila in the genealogy of the Ṭayʾ see e.g. Ibn Mākūlā, V, 170.

[122] The name Qardam is not typically Jewish. It is seldom attested among the Arabs (cf. Ibn Mākūlā, VI, 158) and is probably a variant of Kardam that is rather common. There were converts to Judaism among the ʿAmr b. ʿAwf; Lecker, *Muslims, Jews and Pagans*, 52–55. However, Qardam may have been a client of the ʿAmr b. ʿAwf.

[123] *Ibid.*, 23n; Lecker, "King Ibn Ubayy and the *Quṣṣāṣ*", 53–54; Abū Nuʿaym, *Dalāʾil*, 74–75 no. 34 (*kāna lanā jār yahūdī fī banī ʿabdi l-ashhal...*); see also *ibid.*, 79 no. 40; Ibn Kathīr, *Bidāya*, II, 309:20 (quoting Abū Nuʿaym, *Dalāʾil*): *lam yakun fī banī ʿabdi l-ashhal illā yahūdī wāḥid yuqālu lahu yūshaʿ*. The source is Muḥammad b. Maslama (printed: ...Salama; Salama was in fact Muḥammad's grandfather). For an *isnād* ending with Maḥmūd b. Labīd ← Muḥammad b. Maslama, see Ṭabarānī, *Kabīr*, XIX, 230. Muḥammad b. Maslama belonged to a subdivision of the Ḥāritha called Majdaʿa b. Ḥāritha (cf. above, 69n) and was a client (*ḥalīf*) of the ʿAbd al-Ashhal; *Iṣāba*, VI, 33 no. 7811. With one exception there were no hypocrites, male or female, among the ʿAbd al-Ashhal; Ibn Hishām, II, 172.

(*lam yakun fī banī ʿabdi l-ashhal illā yahūdī wāḥid...*) is not necessarily accurate,[124] but is unlikely to be detached from historical fact. In other words, shortly after the *hijra* the number of individual Jewish clients among the ʿAbd al-Ashhal, not to mention the number of Ashhalī converts to Judaism (if there were any such converts at all) was negligible.

We now arrive at the Yahūd Banī l-Aws, who do have an Arab counterpart. This Aws is not identical with the Aws who was Khazraj's brother for two reasons. First, this would disturb the symmetry since the name Khazraj does not appear in the Kitāb. Second, since two subdivisions of the Aws, namely the ʿAmr b. ʿAwf and the Nabīt, are listed in the Kitāb, the mention of Aws who was Khazraj's brother would mean an overlapping. Therefore Wellhausen's suggestion (68) that the Aws correspond to the Aws Allāh should be adopted.[125] Symmetry is thus retained: all five subdivisions of the Khazraj are mentioned, and this is also the case with the five Aws subdivisions: Aws Allāh (Wāʾil, Khaṭma and Wāqif), ʿAmr b. ʿAwf and Nabīt.

Since the evidence of Jewish converts among the Aws Allāh is meagre,[126] it follows that Yahūd Banī l-Aws mainly included client groups and individuals. One such group was the judaised Murīd (or Murayd) that belonged to the Balī.[127]

Precisely what components of the Aws Allāh participated in the Kitāb is another question. Since the main body of the Aws Allāh only embraced Islam after the battle of the Ditch,[128] it seems unlikely that all of them participated in the Kitāb. The Aws or Aws Allāh groups referred to in the Kitāb were probably the Salm and the Saʿīd b. Murra, who left the Aws Allāh territory and settled in Qubāʾ and in the Sāfila, respectively. Consequently, they embraced Islam before the *hijra* and shortly after it, several years earlier than the rest of the Aws Allāh. Politically they ceased

[124] On the incorporation of the Jewish clan Zaʿūrāʾ into the ʿAbd al-Ashhal as clients see Lecker, *Muslims, Jews and Pagans*, 21–22. However, they may have embraced Islam with the rest of the ʿAbd al-Ashhal before the conclusion of the Kitāb.

[125] There is no difficulty regarding the omission of the latter part of their name, namely Allāh (originally Allāt); the Zayd Allāt for example could simply become Zayd; above, 66.

[126] Lecker, *Muslims, Jews and Pagans*, 41–45.

[127] *Ibid.*, 45–48.

[128] *Ibid.*, 19–49.

to be part of the Aws Allāh, but kept their genealogy,[129] and hence could still be referred to as al-Aws.[130]

The Last Three Groups

The Kitāb itself indicates that the Yahūd Banī Thaʿlaba begin a new sub-list of Jewish clans: the formula found in the clause opening in the list of Jewish participants (§28... *illā man ẓalama wa-athima fa-innahu lā yūtighu illā nafsahu wa-ahl baytihi*) is reiterated in the clause on the Yahūd Banī Thaʿlaba (§34).

Yahūd Banī Thaʿlaba

The name Thaʿlaba appears three times: *wa-inna li-yahūd banī thaʿlaba mithl mā li-yahūd banī ʿawf* (§34); *wa-inna jafna baṭn min thaʿlaba* (§35); and *wa-inna mawāliya thaʿlaba ka-anfusihim* (§38). The three clauses refer to one and the same group. The first refers to them by their full name, Yahūd Banī Thaʿlaba, while the other two simply have Thaʿlaba.

There is a variety of opinions concerning the identity of the Thaʿlaba referred to in these clauses. Wellhausen (70f) thought that there was more than one group called Thaʿlaba: the second and third clauses refer to the Jewish clan Thaʿlaba, whereas the first clause refers to the nameless Jewish clients of the ʿAmr b. ʿAwf subdivision called Thaʿlaba b. ʿAmr b. ʿAwf. Wensinck[131] linked all three clauses to the same Jewish group. In Serjeant's division of the Kitāb (27–30) the first two clauses are in the document marked C, while the third is in document D. For the first clause Serjeant followed Wellhausen, suggesting that the Thaʿlaba of Yahūd Banī Thaʿlaba were the Banū Thaʿlaba b. ʿAmr b. ʿAwf. Regarding the second clause Serjeant wrote:

> Jafnah is the leading house of G͟hassān. Jafnah and T͟haʿlabah were both reckoned sons of ʿAmr (Muzayqiyāʾ) whose son was the father of Aws and K͟hazraj. It looks as if a small section of Jafnah was attached to T͟haʿlabah b. ʿAmr. It is not suggested that they were Jews.

[129] At least at this early stage; cf. *ibid.*, 35 n. 49.
[130] *Ibid.*, 28–35.
[131] 56 n. 5; 57 n. 5.

Elsewhere in his study Serjeant said:

> Banū Thaʿlabah in document C/2g [the first clause — M. L.] are presumably the Aws tribe of Thaʿlabah b. ʿAmr b. ʿAwf, but the question arises as to whether Thaʿlabah in C/3 [the second clause] are Arabs or the Jewish tribe of Banū Thaʿlabah b. al-Fiṭyawn. The evidence seems to point out to their being the Arab tribe, but then, in D/1 [the third clause] (where Thaʿlabah as in C/3 has no 'Banū' prefixed to the name), I feel unable to come to a decisive opinion.

Gil (62) suggested that the Banū Thaʿlaba were "at least partly Judaised", adding:

> While speaking about the estate al-Dilāl, said to have been one of the properties of the famous Jewish convert Mukhayrīq, Samhūdī states that it belonged to Banū Thaʿlaba whom he describes as *min yahūda*.[132]

The assumption that the Thaʿlaba mentioned in the three clauses stand for more than one tribal group is unfounded. All of them relate to the Thaʿlaba b. al-Fiṭyawn, who descended from a branch of Azd called al-Ḥārith *al-muḥarriq* b. ʿAmr Muzayqiyāʾ.[133]

For the purpose of identifying the last three groups the geographical evidence is crucial. The Thaʿlaba b. al-Fiṭyawn lived in the village or town of Zuhra.[134] They are probably identical with the Banū Thaʿlaba who joined the Naḍīr, the Qurayẓa and the Aws in the battle of Buʿāth and are said to have been "from Ghassān";[135] being the descendants of al-Ḥārith *al-*

[132]Gil mentions Mukhayrīq's estates in his "The Origin of the Jews of Yathrib", 209 n. 18 = Ibn Sayyid al-Nās, I, 208 (instead of Maythab, read al-Mīthab and instead of Ḍiyāfa, read al-Ṣāfiya; see Samhūdī, III, 988–94 and Yāqūt, V, 241a, s.v. Mīthab). See also Watt, 226–27.

[133]Ibn al-Kalbī, *Jamhara*, 617, 619–20; Ibn Ḥazm, *Ansāb*, 373. Cf. Caskel, II, 547b, s.v. Taʿlaba b. ʿĀmir (al-Fiṭyaun). Al-Fiṭyawn and his descendants are still awaiting a thorough study.

[134]Lecker, "Muḥammad at Medina", passim; Lecker, *Jews and Arabs*, Index; Samhūdī, I, 161, 164; IV, 1229–30, s.v. Zuhra. In Gil, "The Origin of the Jews of Yathrib", 211, read instead of Zahra: Zuhra.

[135]*Aghānī*, XV, 162:15; *Aghānī* (Dār al-Kutub), XVII, 120: ... *wa-dakhalat maʿahum qabāʾil min ahli l-madīna, minhum banū thaʿlaba, wa-hum min ghassān, wa-banū zaʿūrāʾ, wa-hum min ghassān.* On the latter see Lecker, "Muḥammad at Medina", 44–46. Cf. Ibn al-Athīr, *Kāmil*, I, 680: *thumma inna qurayẓa wa-l-naḍīr jaddadū l-ʿuhūd maʿa l-aws... wa-dakhala maʿahum qabāʾil mina l-yahūd ghayr man dhakarnā.*

muḥarriq b. ʿAmr Muzayqiyāʾ they belonged to the federation of Azdī tribes called Ghassān.[136]

There is no contradiction between Ghassānī affiliation and Jewish origin: the Jewish Banū Zaʿūrāʾ who fought in Buʿāth with the Jewish–Awsī coalition were also "from Ghassān". Yaʿqūbī probably had these and other groups of Ghassān in mind when he mentioned people from Ghassān who converted to Judaism.[137] The Jewish king of Taymāʾ, al-Samawʾal b. ʿĀdiyā, descended from Kaʿb b. ʿAmr Muzayqiyāʾ whose descendants also belonged to Ghassān.[138] Masʿūdī calls al-Samawʾal "al-Ghassānī".[139]

The Thaʿlaba, who were Arab converts to Judaism, were the only Jewish tribe of some weight included in the Kitāb. Winning over the Thaʿlaba was for Muḥammad a major breakthrough. In AH 3 the Thaʿlaba were expelled from Medina "without a fight" and went to Syria (which perhaps suggests their place of origin). They were given the choice between war and exile and chose the latter option.[140]

As in the case of other Jewish tribes expelled by Muḥammad, not all of the Thaʿlaba went into exile; those who chose to stay probably converted to Islam and attached themselves as clients to an Arab clan. One of the Thaʿlaba who remained was Abū l-Ḥakam Rāfiʿ b. Sinān, whose offspring included several intellectuals, most notably his great-great-grandson, the

---

[136]Cf. Lecker, "The Levying of Taxes for the Sassanians", 115–20.

[137]Gil, "The Origin of the Jews of Yathrib", 210; Lecker, "Judaism Among Kinda and the *Ridda* of Kinda", 635; Yaʿqūbī, *Taʾrīkh*, I, 257.

[138]Ibn al-Kalbī, *Jamhara*, 618–19. Cf. on him *EI*², s.v. al-Samawʾal b. ʿĀdiyā (Th. Bauer).

[139]Masʿūdī, *Tanbīh*, 243:4. It was said that al-Samawʾal's mother was from Ghassān; *Aghānī*, XIX, 98:22; *Aghānī* (Dār al-Kutub), XXII, 117. Yaʿqūbī mentions al-Samawʾal's father, ʿĀdiyā, in his unique report on the origin of the Qurayẓa: the Qurayẓa, a clan (*fakhidh*) of the Judhām, converted to Judaism in the days of ʿĀdiyā; Yaʿqūbī, *Taʾrīkh*, II, 52; Gil, "The Origin of the Jews of Yathrib", 212. Taymāʾ is close to the territory of the Judhām and some substantial evidence may be behind Yaʿqūbī's report. Cf. *Kashf al-ẓunūn*, I, 793: *dīwān al-samawʾal b. ʿadiyā al-ghassānī al-yahūdī.*

[140]Lecker, "Muḥammad at Medina", 41 n. 87 = Ibn Ḥabīb, *Muḥabbar*, 112: *thumma sanat thalāth. Fīhā ajlā rasūlu llāh ṣ banī l-fiṭyawn ʿan ghayr qitāl fa-laḥiqū bi-l-shām.* See also Qayrawānī, *Jāmiʿ*, 276: *wa-fīhā* [AH 3] *ghazwat banī fiṭyawn, wa-ādhanahumu l-nabī ʿalayhi l-salām bi-l-ḥarb aw bi-l-jalāʾ fa-jalaw min ghayr qitāl ilā l-shām.* This formula is different from the one common in reports about the *ridda*, where the rebels are given a choice between *silm mukhziya*, i.e. an ignominious agreement or rather submission, and *ḥarb mujliya*, i.e. a war leading to the rebels' expulsion from their territory; *Iṣāba*, II, 222–23; Ibn al-Athīr, *Nihāya*, I, 290–91, s.v. *j-l-w*; Zamakhsharī, *Fāʾiq*, I, 225, s.v. In Ṭabarī, *Tafsīr*, VI, 183:15, interpretation of Qurʾān 5,54, the rebels were given a choice between *khuṭṭa mukhziya* and *ḥarb mujliya*.

ḥadīth transmitter ʿAbd al-Ḥamīd b. Jaʿfar (d. 153/770) who took part in the rebellion of al-Nafs al-Zakiyya.[141] Rāfiʿ's conversion to Islam became famous because of the legal precedent it established: his wife refused to convert to Islam (remaining Jewish), and their baby daughter had to choose between her parents.[142]

Descent from Thaʿlaba b. al-Fiṭyawn was probably not a great honour in early Islam, and hence this pedigree was often omitted; the *nisba* al-Fiṭyawnī, which is distinctive and quite useful, is employed to refer to Jews who lived at the time of Muḥammad but not to their Muslim offspring. A book specializing in Anṣārī genealogies mentions Rāfiʿ b. Sinān twice: once on the list of Quraẓīs who were clients (*ḥulafāʾ*) of the Aws, and again in the chapter on Anṣār whose specific Anṣārī tribe was unknown.[143]

The association between al-Fiṭyawn and Zuhra was still remembered in the Islamic period, as is shown by a case brought before Muḥammad b. ʿAbd al-ʿAzīz al-Zuhrī,[144] the *qāḍī* of Medina at the time of the ʿAbbāsid caliph

[141]Ibn al-Kalbī, *Jamhara*, 620–21; *Tahdhīb al-kamāl*, XVI, 416–17 no. 3709: *...al-Awsī... wa-yuqālu innahum min wuldi l-fiṭyawn ḥulafāʾi l-aws*. The same appears in the entry on ʿUmar b. al-Ḥakam b. Rāfiʿ b. Sinān, the brother of ʿAbd al-Ḥamīd's grandfather (*wa-yuqālu innahu min wuldi l-fiṭyawn ḥulafāʾi l-aws*); *Tahdhīb al-kamāl*, XXI, 309 no. 4220. ʿAbd al-Ḥamīd is often quoted by Wāqidī; Wāqidī, III, 1200, Index; Ibn Saʿd, *al-Ṭabaqa al-rābiʿa*, II, 921, Index. On his role in the said rebellion see Ṭabarī, VII, 553 [III, 190]; 555 [193]; 559 [199]; Ibn al-Athīr, *Kāmil*, V, 529, 531. ʿAbd al-Ḥamīd's son, Saʿd (d. 219/834) lived in Baghdad and was one of those who transmitted Mālik's *Muwaṭṭaʾ*. He was one of Ibn Abī Khaythama's teachers; Ibn Qudāma, *Istibṣār*, 346; *Tahdh.*, III, 477 no. 887; *Tahdhīb al-kamāl*, X, 285–87 no. 2218. See Rāfiʿ's pedigree in Caskel, I, Taf. 195; also that of Abū l-Muqshaʿirr (see below). Caskel has: al-Muqshaʿarr, read: Abū l-Muqshaʿirr; see also *ibid.*, II, 196b; Ibn al-Kalbī, *Jamhara*, 621.

[142]See e.g. *Iṣāba*, VIII, 36, s.v. ʿUmayra bint Abī l-Ḥakam Rāfiʿ b. Sinān. Given the family's background, special attention should be given to a *ḥadīth* of Rāfiʿ b. Sinān's grandson, ʿUthmān b. al-Ḥakam b. Rāfiʿ, on the authority of one of his paternal uncles and "his fathers": they had a leaf (*waraqa*) that was transmitted from father to son. When the Prophet came to Medina, they brought it to him. It foretold the appearance of an *umma* at the end of time whose people will wet the extremities of their body (*la-yabullūna aṭrāfahum*, i.e. wash them after relieving themselves), put an *izār* or loin-cloth around their waists (*wa-yūtirūna ʿalā awsāṭihim*, read: *wa-yaʾtazirūna...*) and sail the sea to fight their enemies; Ibn Kathīr, *Bidāya*, II, 327–28. Cf. *Kanz al-ʿummāl*, XIV, 43 no. 37885, where the source is the above-mentioned grandson of Rāfiʿ, ʿUmar b. al-Ḥakam b. Rāfiʿ (*ḥaddathanī baʿḍ ʿumūmatī wa-ābāʾī annahu kānat ʿindahum waraqa...*).

[143]Ibn Qudāma, *Istibṣār*, 337–38, 346.

[144]A member of the Qurashī Banū Zuhra, not an inhabitant of Zuhra.

al-Manṣūr.[145] The descendants of a stranger of unknown descent (*atāwī*) claimed to have been of "the people of Zuhra" and said more specifically: "We are the offspring of al-Fiṭyawn" (*iddaʿaw fī āl zuhra fa-qālū: naḥnu banū l-fiṭyawn*). Some Anṣār testified in their favour and one of the witnesses confirmed that they were descendants of ʿAmr b. ʿĀmir (i.e. ʿAmr Muzayqiyāʾ), and hence had the right of inheritance (*wārithūna muwarrathūna*, i.e. from their kin). The said *qāḍī* gave this claim official recognition.[146] The report shows that by the early ʿAbbāsid period the negative connotations associated with al-Fiṭyawn had lost their sharp edge. Al-Fiṭyawn's descendants were no longer available for testimony, and one assumes that long before this case was looked into they had attached themselves to other tribal groups. The *āl zuhra* appear as *ahl zuhra* on the list of the Jewish tribes of Medina.[147]

Jafna

Jafna b. ʿAmr Muzayqiyāʾ was, like al-Ḥārith *al-muḥarriq*, the "uncle" of the Aws and Khazraj. Gil does not seem to identify Jafna with the famous kings of Ghassān:

> It should be noted, however, that the document does include some names of clans whose Jewish identity is presumable. It speaks about Jafna, who are a *baṭn* of Thaʿlaba.... Jafna therefore seems to have been a Jewish family, clients of Thaʿlaba. Samhūdī quotes a tradition that they were part of Ghassān, and had been "Kings" in Palestine (Shām).[148]

[145] Muṣʿab, *Nasab*, 271:8. For his involvement in genealogical matters see also Ibn Ḥabīb, *Munammaq*, 260–61 (a tribal group claiming descent from the Lakhm present to him a letter from a *qāḍī* in Shām including their pedigree).

[146] Wakīʿ, *Akhbār al-quḍāt*, I, 214. The *qāḍī* and the Anṣārī witnesses are criticized for incompetence and perjury, respectively.

[147] Samhūdī, I, 164: *wa-minhā banū thaʿlaba wa-ahl zuhra bi-zuhra wa-hum rahṭu l-fiṭyawn.*

[148] Gil, 61–62; also *idem*, "The Origin of the Jews of Yathrib", 211. Samhūdī (I, 179:4) says: *wa-qāla baʿḍuhum: kāna abū jubayla min wuld jafna b. ʿamr b. ʿāmir qad aṣāba mulkan bi-l-shām wa-sharafan. Qultu* (= Samhūdī): *qad taqaddama anna abnāʾ jafna min ghassān, wa-kānū bi-l-shām mulūkan.* This passage unmistakably refers to the ruling house of Ghassān, not to some Jewish family. Shām in this context means Syria, not Palestine.

As we shall see, the detailed evidence available on Medina makes it possible to identify the Jafna with a specific group of Jafnī descent living in Medina.[149]

Banū l-Shuṭayba or al-Shaṭba

Although the clause dealing with the Shaṭba (§36) has the same formula as the clauses dealing with the Jewish groups (*wa-inna li-... mithl mā li-...*), they are Banū l-Shaṭba (or al-Shuṭayba), not Yahūd Banī l-Shaṭba, which means that they were not Jewish.[150] Yet they are mentioned here because of their association with the Jews. They did not belong to the Banū Isrāʾīl but were among the Arab clans that "were with the Jews", i.e. were their clients.[151]

Shaṭba's pedigree can be traced in the genealogy of the Jafna b. ʿAmr Muzayqiyāʾ. Jafna begot Thaʿlaba and Thaʿlaba begot al-Akhtham whose mother was al-Shaṭba. Al-Akhtham's descendants were known after their mother (i.e. as Banū l-Shaṭba). They were in Medina, among the Anṣār.[152]

The Prophet's Territorial Basis

The Thaʿlaba b. al-Fiṭyawn, the Jafna and the Shaṭba lived close to each other, near the Prophet's territorial basis; the geographical realities account for their participation in the Kitāb.

[149]Below, 85f.

[150]Wellhausen, 12 n. 2 (al-Shaṭba are the same as al-Shuṭayba), 70–71; Nöldeke, *Ǧafna*, 6, 62 (al-Shaṭba; Nöldeke expressed doubts regarding the accuracy of the reading); Wensinck (57) vocalizes: al-Shuṭba and remarks (n. 2) on the authority of Nöldeke that the spelling al-Shuṭayba is wrong; Wensinck adds: "Most of the Shuṭbah were probably Jewish proselytes"; Watt, 224 n. 1. Gil, 61–62, adduces valuable source material from Samhūdī linking the Shuṭayba to Rātij; the evidence is also found in Caskel, II, 529. Serjeant, 28 no. 4, recommends Caskel's reading al-Shaṭiba as authoritative. See also Robin, "Le royaume", 698.

[151]*Aghānī*, XIX, 95:13; *Aghānī* (Dār al-Kutub), XXII, 109: ... *wa-kāna maʿahum min ghayr banī isrāʾīl buṭūn mina l-ʿarab... wa-banū l-shaẓiyya* [read: *al-shaṭba/al-shuṭayba*; Wellhausen, 12 n. 2] *ḥayy min ghassān*. Cf. Ibn Rusta, 61–62; Samhūdī, I, 162. Gil, 61–62, thinks that the Jewish identity of Shuṭayba and the other two groups is presumable, but this is not borne out by the evidence. For this sense of the preposition *maʿa* see Ibn Ḥazm, *Ansāb*, 249:9.

[152]*Fa-walada thaʿlaba al-akhtham* [printed: *al-akhtam*], *wa-ummuhu l-shaṭba* [vocalized: al-shaṭaba], *bihā yuʿrafūna, wa-ʿidāduhum fī l-anṣār bi-l-madīna*; Ibn al-Kalbī, *Jamhara*, 617. Ibn al-Kalbī, *Nasab Maʿadd*, I, 433, has correctly: al-Akhtham. Ibn Ḥazm, *Ansāb*, 372, has instead of al-Shaṭba: al-Nabaṭiyya.

The Prophet's territorial basis included the land he reportedly "found" in Zuhra. It belonged to the people of Rātij and Ḥusayka who had been expelled before the Prophet's arrival, leaving behind them a large tract of land.[153] An update on this matter would be in place here, since it sheds some light on conditions in Medina shortly after the *hijra*.

The report on the territorial basis is quoted by Samhūdī[154] from Ibn Shabba's history of Medina.[155] A slightly more informative version of the same report is found in a book by the Andalusian Ibn al-Ṭallāʿ (d. 497/1104). Here we find that the former owners of the land "found" by the Prophet were expelled *shortly* before the Prophet's arrival. Ibn al-Ṭallāʿ continues: "And some of them relinquished their land *after* the Prophet's arrival".[156] The expulsion of unspecified people after the *hijra* should possibly be linked to one or more of the lesser expulsions carried out by Muḥammad. As has been mentioned, the Thaʿlaba b. al-Fiṭyawn who lived in Zuhra were expelled in AH 3, whereas the Yahūd Banī Ḥāritha were expelled at an unknown time.[157] The *hijra* must have increased the pressure on Muḥammad's neighbours to embrace Islam or go to exile.

We owe what we know about the Prophet's territorial basis to the dispute between the Anṣār and the Muhājirūn over the first *ṣadaqa* or charitable endowment in Islam.[158] The former said that it was Muḥammad's *ṣadaqa*, while the latter said that it was ʿUmar's. The reference to the land that the Prophet "found" shortly after his arrival at Medina[159] is adduced as an

---

[153] Lecker, "Muḥammad at Medina", 29–30, 39–42.

[154] Samhūdī, IV, 1166, s.v. Thamgh.

[155] Part of it was found and edited; see Jāsir, "Mu'allafāt fī ta'rīkh al-madīna", no. 3, 328.

[156] *Wa-qad kānū jalaw ʿani l-madīna qabla maqdami l-nabī ṣ al-madīna* BI-YASĪR, WA-MINHUM MANI NJALĀ ʿAN ARḌIHI BAʿDA MAQDAMI L-NABĪ Ṣ, *wa-tarakū arḍan wāsiʿa*; Ibn al-Ṭallāʿ, *Aqḍiya*, 498 (the edition is of poor quality). Cf. the parallel text in al-Khaṣṣāf (d. 261/874; *GAS*, I, 436), *Aḥkām al-awqāf*, 5: *kānū jalaw ʿani l-madīna qabla maqdam rasūli llāh ṣ l-madīna wa-baʿda maqdamihi. Jalaw* in Ibn al-Ṭallāʿ and al-Khaṣṣāf means the same as *ujlū* in Samhūdī (that may be the result of dittography: *kānū ujlū*): "they were expelled". Cf. the report on Salima's attack against the Jews of Ḥusayka in Lecker, "Muḥammad at Medina", 40; Samhūdī, III, 972, 975; IV, 1190–91, s.v. Ḥusayka; Ibn Shabba, *Ta'rīkh al-madīna*, I, 158–59. The expulsion of some of them after the *hijra* is not mentioned in Samhūdī's abridged report. It may have been omitted due to the fact that the words *maqdami l-nabī ṣ* appear twice.

[157] On the expulsion of Jews and Christians cf. Ward, "A Fragment from an Unknown Work"; al-Tāzī, (ed.), "al-Nuṣūṣ al-ẓāhira".

[158] Above, 71.

[159] *Awwal mā qadima l-madīna*; Samhūdī, IV, 1166:9. Ibn al-Ṭallāʿ, 498 has: *lammā qadima l-madīna*.

argument in favour of the claim of the Muhājirūn that the first charitable endowment was ʿUmar's: the Prophet had given ʿUmar part of the land, namely Thamgh. ʿUmar bought an adjacent plot of land from some Jews and the Prophet told him to declare it a charitable endowment.

There is yet another report on the same matter, similarly quoted by Samhūdī from Ibn Shabba.[160] In this report the claims of both sides are curiously represented by two scholars who descended from Quraẓī survivors. When Muḥammad b. Kaʿb al-Quraẓī (d. 118/736) declared that the first *ṣadaqa* in Islam was the Prophet's (as the Anṣārī claim went), he was interrupted by his younger contemporary al-Miswar al-Quraẓī (d. 138/755),[161] who said: "But the people say [that it is] ʿUmar's *ṣadaqa*". Ibn Kaʿb retorted that 22 months after the *hijra* the Prophet seized the estates that Mukhayrīq had bequeathed to him and declared them charitable endowments, while ʿUmar declared Thamgh a charitable endowment when he returned from Khaybar in AH 7.[162] The claim of the Muhājirūn is attributed elsewhere to ʿUmar's son, ʿAbdallāh b. ʿUmar, who said: "Thamgh was the first estate in Islam to be declared *ṣadaqa*".[163]

One expects to find this claim above all among ʿUmar's descendants, many of whom played leading roles in early Islamic society; the dispute over the first *ṣadaqa* must have started many years before the cases of both sides were presented by Ibn Kaʿb and al-Miswar. But a closer look at the sources for the claim in ʿUmar's favour that includes the report on the territorial basis (in Samhūdī and Ibn al-Ṭallāʿ) reveals that in the pre-literary phase it was transmitted by a leading Anṣārī family. There are differences between the two sources, but as we shall see they are insignificant. Samhūdī (← Ibn Shabba) has a report on the authority of ʿAmr, the son of the famous Companion Saʿd b. Muʿādh (of the ʿAbd al-Ashhal).[164] According to some, ʿAmr was a Companion.[165] He was the first-born son of Saʿd whose *kunya*

[160]Samhūdī, II, 1166:18.

[161]Miswar's father, Rifāʿa, should be added to Abū Mālik's two sons mentioned in Lecker, "Abū Mālik ʿAbdallāh b. Sām of Kinda". Among those who transmitted from Miswar were both Mālik b. Anas and Ibn Isḥāq; *Tahdhīb al-kamāl*, XXVII, 580 no. 5966. Mālik's accusation that Ibn Isḥāq transmitted from the descendants of Jewish converts (Kister, "The Massacre of the Banū Qurayẓa", 76) is rather curious.

[162]Cf. Ibn Saʿd, I, 501, 503 (al-Miswar [printed erroneously: al-Maysūr] b. Rifāʿa ← Ibn Kaʿb, regarding Mukhayrīq and the Prophet's charitable endowments).

[163]Samhūdī, IV, 1166, s.v. Thamgh; Ibn Saʿd, III, 358.

[164]Samhūdī has erroneously Saʿīd instead of Saʿd.

[165]*Iṣāba*, IV, 635.

was Abū ʿAmr.[166] But ʿAmr's Companion status (as well as that of his brother, ʿAbdallāh) and ʿAmr's claim to have been Saʿd's eldest son were probably disputed, or Saʿd would not have had to appear in a dream and testify that the two took part in the "pledge of consent" (*bayʿat al-riḍwān*) and that ʿAmr was his eldest son.[167] This is not the only *ḥadīth* going back to ʿAmr. Two dictionaries of Companions[168] have a *ḥadīth* in praise of Saʿd b. Muʿādh that goes back to Saʿd's grandson, Wāqid b. ʿAmr b. Saʿd b. Muʿādh (d. 120/738)[169] ← his father, ʿAmr. The theme (Saʿd's handkerchiefs in Paradise, *manādīl Saʿd*) is quite widespread in Islamic literature, though not in this particular form and from these sources. We have here evidence that ʿAmr was involved in *ḥadīth* transmission, though perhaps on a small scale.

Another component of Ibn Shabba's *isnād* can be obtained from Ibn Ḥajar's *Fatḥ al-bārī*.[170] Having adduced a summary of Ibn Shabba's report,[171] Ibn Ḥajar adds: *wa-fī isnādihi l-wāqidī*. Wāqidī links us to Ibn Ṭallāʿ's version of the same report.[172] Ibn Ṭallāʿ quotes the *Wāḍiḥa*, i.e. ʿAbd al-Malik b. Ḥabīb's (d. 238/852) *K. al-wāḍiḥa fī l-sunna wa-l-fiqh*,[173] which in turn quotes Wāqidī ← al-Ḥuṣayn b. ʿAbd al-Raḥmān [b. ʿAmr][174] b. Saʿd b. Muʿādh (d. 126/744). Now Wāqidī could not have transmitted this *ḥadīth* directly from al-Ḥuṣayn, and one transmitter (ʿUtba b. Jabīra of the ʿAbd al-Ashhal) is missing between them.[175]

These data suggest that the crucial report on ʿUmar's *ṣadaqa* and the Prophet's territorial basis was transmitted by the descendants of Saʿd b.

---

[166] Ibn Saʿd, III, 420.

[167] *Iṣāba*, IV, 635 no. 5845. ʿAmr was married to Muḥammad b. Maslama's niece, Hind bint Maḥmūd b. Maslama; Ibn Saʿd, VIII, 332.

[168] Quoted in *Iṣāba*, IV, 635.

[169] *Tahdhīb al-kamāl*, XXX, 412–13 no. 6669.

[170] V, 301:23.

[171] Ibn Shabba (...) ← ʿAmr b. Saʿd b. Muʿādh: *saʾalnā ʿan awwal ḥabs fī l-islām, fa-qāla l-muhājirūna: ṣadaqat ʿumar, wa-qāla l-anṣār: ṣadaqat rasūli llāh ṣ.*

[172] Ibn al-Ṭallāʿ, *Aqḍiya*, 498.

[173] See *GAS*, I, 362; Muranyi, "Fiqh", 315; *idem*, *Beiträge zur Geschichte der Ḥadīṯ- und Rechtsgelehrsamkeit der Mālikiyya*, 472–73; ʿAbd al-Malik b. Ḥabīb, *Taʾrīkh*, Introduction, 58; Fierro, "La *Fahrasa* de Ibn al-Ṭallāʿ", 291–92; Ossendorf-Conrad, *Das "K. al-Wāḍiḥa"*.

[174] ʿAmr is missing in Ibn al-Ṭallāʿ. He is also missing in al-Ḥuṣayn's pedigree in Ibn Ḥazm, *Ansāb*, 339:6.

[175] See for example the references in Wāqidī, III, 1158, Index, s.v. al-Ḥuṣayn b. ʿAbd al-Raḥmān b. ʿAmr b. Saʿd. For an entry on (al-)Ḥuṣayn see e.g. *Tahdhīb al-kamāl*, VI, 517–19 no. 1357. Ibn Isḥāq is mentioned among his pupils. For a *ḥadīth* that Ibn Isḥāq quoted from him see Ibn Kathīr, *Bidāya*, IV, 37:2 (printed ʿUmar instead of ʿAmr). It concerns al-Uṣayrim, on whom see Lecker, *Muslims, Jews and Pagans*, 22.

Muʿādh. More specifically, al-Ḥuṣayn b. ʿAbd al-Raḥmān b. ʿAmr b. Saʿd b. Muʿādh reported it on the authority of his father ← his grandfather, or directly from his grandfather. It can be shown that the latter possibility is the correct one. An *awāʾil* book has an abridged version of the report with a full *isnād* going back to Abū Zayd, i.e. Ibn Shabba ← Muḥammad b. Yaḥyā, i.e. Abū Ghassān al-Kinānī al-Madanī[176] ← Wāqidī ← ʿUtba b. Jabīra (d. 154/771)[177] ← al-Ḥuṣayn b. ʿAbd al-Raḥmān ←[178] ʿAmr b. Saʿd b. Muʿādh.[179] This abridged version does not include the details of the territorial basis, but it does fill in the gaps regarding the sources of this pro-Muhājirī report. Ibn Ḥajar[180] draws our attention to the fact that Wāqidī reports in his *Maghāzī* that the first *ṣadaqa mawqūfa* in Islam included the estates that Mukhayrīq bequeathed to the Prophet.[181] But it appears that the rival claim, namely the one with the territorial basis and Thamgh, was more successful.

An episode from the Qurayẓa affair probably reveals a pro-Muhājirī attitude of the Anṣārī family in question. It was probably Saʿd b. Muʿādh who decreed that the lands of the Qurayẓa be allotted to the Muhājirūn, and his decree was met with opposition among the other Anṣār.[182]

Having discussed in some detail the transmission of the report on Muḥammad's territorial basis, let us return to the three groups that concern us here. All of them lived in the adjacent places Zuhra and Rātij, which are associated, together with a place called Ḥusayka, with Muḥammad's territo-

---

[176] Jāsir, "Muʾallafāt fī taʾrīkh al-madīna", no. 2, 262–63; no. 3, 328 (Jāsir argues that Abū Ghassān's knowledge was not transmitted orally, as claimed by Ṣāliḥ Aḥmad al-ʿAlī, and that he compiled a book).

[177] Ibn Saʿd, *Qism mutammim*, 427; Wāqidī, III, 1206, Index, s.v.

[178] "ʿ*An*" can of course be read as "*b.*" and still be correct; but in Samhūdī and *Fatḥ al-bārī* ʿAmr b. Saʿd b. Muʿādh is the source of this report, and hence the "ʿ*an*" should be left in place. See also Ibn Qudāma, *Istibṣār*, 212, who says about ʿAmr: *aḥad ʿulamāʾi l-anṣāri l-fuqahāʾi l-fuḍalāʾ*.

[179] ʿAskarī, *Awāʾil*, I, 256–57 (read ʿAmr instead of ʿUmar and Saʿd instead of Saʿīd). The title of the item is: *awwal māl ḥtubisa fī l-islām ṣadaqat ʿumar raḍiya llāh ʿanhu.* Cf. al-Khaṣṣāf, *Aḥkām al-awqāf*, 4, who attaches to the report on the first *ṣadaqa* the following *isnād*: Wāqidī ← ʿUtba b. Jabīra ← al-Ḥuṣayn b. ʿAbd al-Raḥmān b. (*sic*) ʿAmr b. Saʿd b. Muʿādh.

[180] *Fatḥ al-bārī*, V, 301:25.

[181] This statement could not be found in the *Maghāzī*; cf. I, 262–63, 378.

[182] Kister, "The Massacre of the Banū Qurayẓa", 95–96.

rial basis. These geographical realities played a decisive role in the inclusion of these groups in the Kitāb.[183]

The Banū Thaʿlaba b. al-Fiṭyawn lived in Zuhra itself.[184] As to the Jafna, they are identical with a group of Jafnī descent that was among the people of Rātij. The Jafnīs were the descendants of ʿUlba b. Jafna.[185] The Shaṭba too lived in Rātij. Before they settled there they had lived in two other places in the Medina area. When they came from Shām, they settled at Mayṭān (a mountain southeast of Medina), but it did not agree with them so they moved to a place near Judhmān.[186] Finally they settled in Rātij, where they lived with two other clans. Samhūdī quotes these details from Ibn Zabāla in whose book they close the section on the territories of the Anṣār. The details regarding the Shaṭba appear at the end of the section because the Shaṭba, being of Jafnī extraction and former clients of the Jews, formed a special case.[187] When the Prophet arrived at Medina, he apparently found them in Rātij.[188]

The Shaṭba/Shuṭayba were close to one of the Prophet's *ṣadaqāt*, namely al-Aʿwāf. Ibn Zabāla mentions a rock (perhaps a landmark) placed between

---

[183]Khāzin, *Tafsīr*, VII, 47:21, interpretation of Qur'ān 59,2, says in the context of Muḥammad's siege of the Naḍīr that they were in a village called Zuhra. *Sīra ḥalabiyya*, II, 263:11, says that their village was called Zuhra; Lecker, "Muḥammad at Medina", 33. Still, the much larger Naḍīr were not in the Kitāb.

[184]Above, 76.

[185]Ibn Saʿd (d. 230/845) reports that in his time their offspring lived in al-Ṣafrā' (west of Medina) and claimed descent from the Nabīt (Aws): *... illā anna fī ahl rātij qawman min ghassān min wuld ʿulba b. jafna ḥulafā'uhum* (printed: *khulafā'uhum*)...; Ibn Saʿd, III, 446; Lecker, "Muḥammad at Medina", 46 n. 120 (where the page number 449 appears twice; but its first occurrence is wrong, read: 446); Watt, 160. See also Ibn Hishām, *Tījān*, 274:15 (ʿUlba was one of ʿAmr Muzayqiyā''s eleven sons), 289:10, 296:-2; 300:16 (when the father of the Aws and Khazraj, Ḥāritha b. Thaʿlaba, came from Shām to Yathrib, he was joined by Thaʿlaba [read: ʿUlba] b. Jafna, ʿAmr b. Jafna's brother); ʿAwtabī, *Ansāb*, II, 53: *... wa-thaʿlaba* [read: *wa-ʿulba*] *b. jafna wa-hum ahl rābiḥ* [read: *rātij*] *wa-hum fī l-anṣār.*

[186]In Medina itself. A verse of Qays b. al-Khaṭīm of the Ẓafar (Nabīt) indicates that it was in his clan's territory; Wellhausen, 53–54, mentions Shaṭba's settlement there; Yāqūt, II, 116a, s.v. Judhmān. Bakrī, II, 372, s.v. Judhmān, gives the following popular etymology, possibly indicating the former owners of Judhmān: at that place Tubbaʿ cut off (*jadhama*) in their middle palm trees belonging to the Ḥārith b. al-Khazraj.

[187]Samhūdī, I, 214:14: *qāla bn zabāla ʿaqiba dhikr jamīʿ manāzili l-anṣāri l-mutaqaddima: wa-nazala banū l-shaṭba ḥīna qadimū mina l-shām mayṭān, fa-lam yuwāfiqhum, fa-taḥawwalū qarīban min judhmān, thumma taḥawwalū fa-nazalū bi-rātij, fa-hum aḥad* [*sic*] *qabā'il rātij al-thalāth.*

[188]Rubin's remark (9 n. 23) that the identification of Thaʿlaba, Jafna and Shuṭayba is "quite problematic" is too pessimistic.

al-Aʿwāf and al-Shuṭayba. A thief fleeing from Muḥammad was bruised by it and was consequently caught by Muḥammad. The latter blessed it and it was later visited by the people who drew blessing from it.[189] In Samhūdī's days al-Aʿwāf was the name of "a large winding of a valley" (*jizʿ kabīr*) including many wells, but it was no longer clear which of them was the well of al-Aʿwāf. The place-name al-Shuṭayba and the rock were no longer known in Samhūdī's time.[190] Ibn Zabāla's report identified al-Shuṭayba with the *māl* or estate of a certain Ibn ʿUtba, who owned al-Shuṭayba at one time. Samhūdī credibly suggests to identify *māl* Ibn ʿUtba with the place known in his time as al-ʿUtbī, close to al-Aʿwāf.[191]

Let us sum up this discussion of the Jewish participation in the Kitāb. The list of participants found at the beginning of the treaty of the Jews includes nine groups two of which, the Jafna and the Shaṭba/Shuṭayba, are not Jewish but closely associated with the Jews. The remaining seven are of the "Yahūd Banī so-and-so" type. Six of the Yahūd Banī so-and-so groups have a counterpart in the list of participants found in the treaty of the Muʾminūn, while the seventh, namely the Yahūd Banī Thaʿlaba, has no such counterpart. The Yahūd of the first six groups are either Jewish clans in client status, or individual Jewish clients, or Arab converts to Judaism who were free-born members of the relevant clans, or any combination of these categories.

The Yahūd Banī Thaʿlaba or the Jewish Banū Thaʿlaba were the Arab Jewish tribe of Thaʿlaba b. al-Fiṭyawn. They share two common features with the Jafna and Shaṭba. First, they were of Ghassānī origin. Second,

---

[189] Samhūdī, III, 949–50: *ṭalaba rasūlu llāhi ṣ sāriqan fa-haraba minhu fa-nakabahu l-ḥajaru lladhī wuḍiʿa bayna l-aʿwāf ṣadaqati l-nabī ṣ wa-bayna l-shuṭayba* [printed here and below: *al-sh.ṭ.b.ya*] *māli bn ʿutba, fa-waqaʿa l-sāriq fa-akhadhahu rasūlu llāh ṣ wa-barraka rasūlu llāh ṣ fī l-ḥajar wa-massahu wa-daʿā lahu, fa-huwa l-ḥajaru lladhī fīmā bayna l-aʿwāf wa-l-shuṭayba yaṭlaʿu ṭarafuhu yamassuhu l-nās.*

[190] Al-Shuṭayba (printed erroneously: al-Sh.ṭ.b.ya) is also mentioned in Samhūdī, IV, 1140–41, s.v. Biʾr Midrā.

[191] Al-Shuṭayba appears in a verse by a Quraẓī (Samhūdī, IV, 1243, s.v. al-Shuṭayba), which may suggest that it was in the territory of the Qurayẓa. This is supported by a detail concerning the nearby al-Aʿwāf: Ibn Zabāla reports (Samhūdī, III, 950) that al-Aʿwāf belonged to Khunāfa the Jew, the ancestor of the Prophet's Jewish wife or mistress Rayḥāna, who is usually said to have been of the Qurayẓa. Cf. perhaps the court of Ibn ʿUtba in the territory of the Banū Zurayq (Khazraj) who were also among the inhabitants of Rātij; Lecker, "Muḥammad at Medina", 55; Samhūdī, II, 743 (... *ilā dāri bni ʿUtba bi-Banī Zurayq*). The court of Nāfiʿ b. ʿUtba b. Abī Waqqāṣ could be meant here; it is mentioned in Samhūdī, II, 741, 743.

they lived in the Zuhra–Rātij area, in or near the Prophet's territorial basis in the Sāfila of Medina that was his first foothold there.

The identity of the Jewish participants in the Kitāb leads to the conclusion that its significance with regard to the relationship between the Prophet and the Jews of Medina is rather limited. Most of the Jews of Medina, including the main tribes Naḍīr, Qurayẓa and Qaynuqāʿ, were not part of it; the main tribes concluded less binding treaties with the Prophet.[192]

[192] Lecker, "Did Muḥammad Conclude Treaties with the Jewish Tribes". Goto (12–13) argues correctly that the treaties with the three main Jewish tribes are not related to the Kitāb. He says that apart from the Kitāb, "Muḥammad wrote a document or documents to the Jews who had formed their own tribes". The relevant part of the Kitāb (which Goto marks as document III) "might concern the Jews other than those of the three tribes".

Chapter 4

The Treaty of the Muʾminūn

§1. *hādhā kitāb min muḥammad al-nabī bayna l-muʾminīna wa-l-muslimīna min quraysh wa-yathrib wa-man tabiʿahum fa-laḥiqa bihim wa-jāhada maʿahum*

THIS IS A COMPACT FROM MUḤAMMAD THE PROPHET BETWEEN THE MUʾMINŪN AND MUSLIMŪN OF QURAYSH AND YATHRIB AND THOSE WHO JOIN THEM AS CLIENTS, ATTACH THEMSELVES TO THEM AND FIGHT THE HOLY WAR WITH THEM.

§2. *innahum umma wāḥida min dūni l-nās*[1]

THEY FORM ONE PEOPLE TO THE EXCLUSION OF OTHERS.

§3. *al-muhājirūn min quraysh ʿalā ribāʿatihim,*[2] *yataʿāqalūna baynahum wa-hum yafdūna ʿāniyahum bi-l-maʿrūf wa-l-qisṭ bayna l-muʾminīna*

THE MUHĀJIRŪN FROM QURAYSH KEEP TO THEIR TRIBAL ORGANIZATION AND LEADERSHIP, CO-OPERATING WITH EACH OTHER REGARDING BLOOD MONEY [and related matters] AND RANSOMING THEIR CAPTIVES ACCORDING TO WHAT IS CUSTOMARY AND EQUITABLE AMONG THE MUʾMINŪN.

§4. *wa-banū ʿawf ʿalā ribāʿatihim, yataʿāqalūna maʿāqilahumu l-ʾūlā, wa-kull ṭāʾifa minhum tafdī ʿāniyahā bi-l-maʿrūf wa-l-qisṭ bayna l-muʾminīna*

§§5–11. *wa-banū l-ḥārith ʿalā ribāʿatihim, yataʿāqalūna maʿāqilahumu l-ʾūlā, wa-kull ṭāʾifa minhum tafdī ʿāniyahā bi-l-maʿrūf wa-l-qisṭ bayna l-*

[1] Abū ʿUbayd's recension and some versions of Ibn Isḥāq's recension have: … *dūna l-nās.*

[2] Written *r.b.ʿ.tihim.*

mu'minīna, wa-banū sā'ida... wa-banū jusham... wa-banu l-najjār... wa-banū 'amr ibn 'awf... wa-banū l-nabīt... wa-banū l-aws...

THE BANŪ 'AWF KEEP TO THEIR TRIBAL ORGANIZATION AND LEADERSHIP, CONTINUING TO CO-OPERATE WITH EACH OTHER IN ACCORDANCE WITH THEIR FORMER MUTUAL AID AGREEMENTS REGARDING BLOOD MONEY [and related matters], AND EVERY SUB-GROUP RANSOMS ITS CAPTIVES ACCORDING TO WHAT IS CUSTOMARY AND EQUITABLE AMONG THE MU'MINŪN.

THE BANŪ L-ḤĀRITH KEEP TO THEIR TRIBAL ORGANIZATION AND LEADERSHIP. . . .

THE BANŪ SĀ'IDA KEEP TO THEIR TRIBAL ORGANIZATION AND LEADERSHIP. . . .

THE BANŪ JUSHAM KEEP TO THEIR TRIBAL ORGANIZATION AND LEADERSHIP. . . .

THE BANŪ L-NAJJĀR KEEP TO THEIR TRIBAL ORGANIZATION AND LEADERSHIP. . .

THE BANŪ 'AMR IBN 'AWF KEEP TO THEIR TRIBAL ORGANIZATION AND LEADERSHIP. . . .

THE BANŪ L-NABĪT KEEP TO THEIR TRIBAL ORGANIZATION AND LEADERSHIP. . . .

THE BANŪ L-AWS KEEP TO THEIR TRIBAL ORGANIZATION AND LEADERSHIP. . . .

umma

Rubin (12–13) argues that *umma* in the Kitāb should be understood in the light of its usage in the Qur'ān, where we find no less than nine occurrences of *umma wāḥida*, all of which have a religious orientation. He concludes:

> This article declares that the Muslims of Quraysh and Yathrib, as well as the Jews,[3] constitute one unity, sharing the same religious orientation, thus being distinct from all the rest of the people who adhere to other kinds of faith. It is thereby clear that the

[3]Cf. below, 139.

> new unity is designed to be based not only on common sacred territory but also on common faith.[4]

But §1 does not mention the Jews who appear elsewhere in the Kitāb 20 times. The *umma* included the Mu'minūn, the Muslimūn and the lesser unspecified participants (*wa-man tabiʿahum* etc.).

Considering the character of the Kitāb one wishes to relate the term *umma* to concrete matters such as tribal alliances and blood money arrangements rather than abstract concepts. However, very little could be found in this direction, perhaps due to the prevailing Qur'ānic use of *umma*. *Umma* appears to have the sense of tribe in a report concerning Najrān. When the people of Najrān were informed about the Prophet's death — at that time they numbered 40,000 warriors from the Banū l-Afʿā, the *umma* that was in Najrān before the Ḥārith (i.e. al-Ḥārith b. Kaʿb) — they sent to Abū Bakr a delegation in order to renew their treaty with the Muslim state.[5] Admittedly, the *umma* called Afʿā was made of Christians and became extinct, which could link it to the Qur'ānic *umma* (*wa-li-kulli ummatin ajalun*; Qur'ān 7,34; also 10,49; 15,5; 23,43). But an *umma* that preceded the Ḥārith b. Kaʿb tribe was probably a tribe. Elsewhere *umma* is interpreted as *qabīla*, which is as close as one could get to a concrete interpretation of the term.[6]

---

[4]There is a sizeable secondary literature on the term *umma*. See, for example, Paret, "Ummah"; Denny, "The Meaning of *Ummah* in the Qur'ān"; *idem*, "*Ummah* in the Constitution of Medina"; *idem*, *EI*², s.v. *umma*, and the bibliography quoted there; Massignon, "L'*Umma*"; Giannakis, "The Concept of Ummah"; van Nieuwenhuijze, "The Ummah"; Lichtenstaedter, "From Particularism to Unity", 260–63.

[5]Ṭabarī, III, 321:9 [I, 1987]. Cf. *The History of al-Ṭabarī*, X, trans. Donner, 163 (who renders *umma*: "community"). The Banū l-Afʿā were probably called after al-Afʿā al-Jurhumī of Najrān, the ancestor of the Najrān bishops al-Sayyid and al-ʿĀqib who was the first of the *ḥukkām al-ʿarab* or "the arbiters of the Arabs"; Ibn Ḥabīb, *Muḥabbar*, 132. See also Ibn Durayd, *Ishtiqāq*, 362 (he was of the Ruhm, from the Zayd b. Kahlān); Caskel, I, 142b, s.v. al-Afʿā b. al-Ḥuṣain. He was a descendant of Ruhm b. Murra b. Udad all of whose descendants disappeared; Ibn Ḥazm, *Ansāb*, 417; Balādhurī, *Ansāb*, I, 29–30, quoting Ibn al-Kalbī.

[6]See Qurṭubī, *Tafsīr*, X, 171, interpretation of Qur'ān 16,92 (... *an takūna ummatun hiya arbā min ummatin*): *nazalat hādhihi l-āya fī l-ʿarabi lladhīna kānati* L-QABĪLA *minhum idhā ḥālafat ukhrā thumma jā'at iḥdāhumā* QABĪLA *kathīra qawiyya fa-dākhalathā, ghadari l-'ūlā wa-naqaḍat ʿahdahā wa-rajaʿat ilā hādhihi l-kubrā, qālahu mujāhid.* See also Ṭabarī, *Tafsīr*, XIV, 112, quoting Mujāhid's interpretation on this verse: *kānū yuḥālifūna l-ḥulafā' fa-yajidūna akthar minhum wa-aʿazz fa-yanquḍūna ḥilf hā'ulā'i wa-yuḥālifūna hā'ulā'i lladhīna hum aʿazz minhum fa-nuhū ʿan dhālika.* *Umma* and *qabīla* interchange, for example, in a *ḥadīth*; *Majmaʿ al-zawā'id*, X, 243: ... *qawm ya'tūna min baʿdikum yuʿṭā l-rajul minhum mā yakfī l-qabīla awi l-umma thumma lā yashbaʿu.* On a Qur'ānic

Admittedly, the evidence is not very impressive, and hence *umma* was rendered by the general term "people".

min dūni l-nās

TO THE EXCLUSION OF OTHERS

Wellhausen (67): "Sie bilden eine einizige Gemeinde, gegenüber den Menschen".[7]
Wensinck (52): "They are one community to the exclusion of [other] people".
Watt (221): "They are a single community distinct from (other) people". He adds: "The literal translation of the last phrase is 'from the people', which might refer to the Jews; but on the whole this is unlikely".
Serjeant (18, 21): "They are a single confederation set apart from the people".[8] Regarding the expression *min dūni* he remarks that sometimes it has the sense of "to the exclusion of".
Gil's article includes (49–50) a section entitled "The New Unity", where he says:

> The title of the document speaks of it as a pact between the *Muhājirūn*, the *Anṣār*, and those who follow them. Henceforth they are a party, a community, and not clans. This is obviously the right way to understand *min dūni 'l-nāsi. Dūna* is used several times in the document; every time it gives the clear impression of an idiomatic use, putting it instead of the simple negation. The most correct way to translate *dūna* in this document, therefore, seems to be to invert the two elements of the sentence: (The parties so-and-so) are not individuals (any more), but (they are) an *umma.*

But elsewhere Gil (50 n. 41) says:

---

umma in the sense of tribe see also Lichtenstaedter, "From Particularism to Unity", 262 (Qur'ān 28,23).

[7] Cf. Lichtenstaedter, "From Particularism to Unity", 259: "... the Prophet conceived of his *ummat al-Islām* as a body over against 'the rest of mankind,' *min duna-n-nāsi*, namely all those who did not, (or not yet) belong to it".

[8] Donner, "From Believers to Muslims", 30, has: "They are a single people (*umma*) set apart from [the rest of] mankind".

> When the B. Qurayẓa tell Abū Lubāba, Wāqidī, II, 506: *naḥnu mawālīka dūna 'l-nāsi kullihim*, the meaning is: "We are not the clients of anybody in the world, but yours".[9]

Sa'd b. 'Ubāda concluded his speech at the Saqīfa by calling upon the Anṣār to rule exclusively of the others, since authority belonged to them alone to the exclusion of others (*istabiddū bi-hādhā l-amr fa-innahu lakum dūna l-nās*).[10] The Ḥawāriyyūn or Apostles supported Jesus and were his party and helpers to the exclusion of others (*fa-kānū shī'atahu wa-anṣārahu dūna l-nās*).[11]

More relevant for us here is the expression *min dūni l-nās* in a prophetic *ḥadīth* declaring Quraysh, the Anṣār and several small tribes living in the vicinity of Medina the *mawālī* of the Prophet and of Allāh;[12] they are the Prophet's *mawālī* to the exclusion of others.

yata'āqalūna baynahum

CO-OPERATING WITH EACH OTHER REGARDING BLOOD MONEY [and related matters].

Wellhausen (67): "...zahlen gemeinsam für sich das Sühngeld...."
Wensinck (52): "They pay jointly blood-wite...."
Watt (221): "...pay jointly the blood-money between them".
Serjeant (18): "...paying jointly among themselves their blood-money".

The preposition *baynahum* appears in §3 but not in §4–§11. The Muhājirūn undertook to handle matters of *ma'āqil* among themselves, while each of the Anṣār clans continued its previous arrangements. The Muhājirūn did not have such arrangements and relied on their internal solidarity. According to Ya'qūbī, the writing of Medina's *ma'āqil* — this may be a reference to the

[9]This is comparable to §17, *wa-inna l-mu'minīna ba'ḍuhum mawālī ba'ḍ dūna l-nās*, since it also includes the word *mawālī*.

[10]Ṭabarī, III, 218:-6 [I, 1838]; *The History of al-Ṭabarī*, X, trans. Donner, 2: "[So] keep [control of] this matter to yourselves, to the exclusion of others, for it is yours and yours alone". See also Ibn Ḥabīb, *Munammaq*, 191: 'Abbās was the only person allowed to stay in Mecca during the nights of Minā because of the *siqāya* for which he was responsible, *uṭliqa dhālika lahu dūna l-nās min ajli l-siqāya*.

[11]Abū 'Ubayd, *Gharīb*, II, 16, s.v. *ḥ-w-r*.

[12]*Quraysh wa-l-anṣār wa-aslam wa-ghifār wa-juhayna wa-muzayna wa-ashja' mawāliyya min dūni l-nās, laysa lahum min dūni llāh mawlan*; *Ma'rifa wa-ta'rīkh*, I, 316–17.

Kitāb — took place after the Prophet had moved from Qubā' to the Sāfila of Medina.[13]

Elsewhere it is reported that the Prophet recorded in writing for each tribal group (*baṭn*) its obligations in the case of a blood feud.[14] This is not a reference to the Kitāb, since it is unlikely that the Muhājirūn were referred to as a *baṭn*.[15] Moreover, the Prophet is reported to have established agreements of limited mutual assistance between Quraysh and the Anṣār with regard to blood money. The parties undertook to assist each other in the case of injuries the indemnity for which did not exceed one third of the *diya*, i.e. the blood money due in the case of death.[16] Another report on this matter is more informative. A man of the Salima (Khazraj) reported that in the Jāhiliyya the tribesmen were supposed to pay immediate indemnities of up to one third of the *diya*. If they could not pay, the sum due from them was considered a debt. After the advent of Islam the Prophet established mutual assistance between Quraysh and the Anṣār regarding injuries the compensation for which amounted to one third of the *diya*.[17] None of this is related to the Kitāb, in which there is no evidence of such co-operation.[18]

§3 and the following clauses are reflected in the following report (Miqsam ← Ibn ʿAbbās): *kataba rasūlu llāhi ṣ kitāban bayna l-muhājirīna wa-l-anṣār an yaʿqilū maʿāqilahum wa-an yafdū ʿāniyahum bi-l-maʿrūf wa-l-iṣlāḥ bayna l-muslimīna.*[19] The next report in the same source (← al-Shaʿbī) includes Quraysh at this point: the Prophet imposed the payment of blood money

[13] *Thumma ntaqala ilā l-madīna fa-kataba maʿāqilahā*; Yaʿqūbī, *Buldān*, 313; quoted in the *Glossarium* of Ṭabarī (Leiden), s.v. *ʿ-q-l*.

[14] Aḥmad, III, 321:29: *kataba l-nabī ṣ ʿalā kull baṭn ʿuqūlahu* [printed erroneously with a *tā' marbūṭa*; this is followed by a clause from the Kitāb; below, 203:] *thumma innahu kataba: innahu lā yaḥillu an yatawālā* [var. *yatawallā*] *mawlā rajul muslim bi-ghayr idhnihi* (Jābir b. ʿAbdallāh). Also *Majmaʿ al-zawā'id*, VI, 301, has a *tā' marbūṭa* here.

[15] One *ḥadīth* (←ʿAlī) has it that the Prophet wrote for each *baṭn* its *ʿuqūl*, which are provisions concerning the duties of the *ʿāqila* or the agnatic relatives (see below) in matters of blood money; *Lisān al-ʿarab*, XIII, 54, s.v. *b-ṭ-n*: *kataba ʿalā kull baṭn ʿuqūlahu... ay kataba ʿalayhim mā taghramuhu l-ʿāqila mina l-diyāti fa-bayyana mā ʿalā kull qawm minhā.* Cf. below, 195n.

[16] Ibn Ḥazm, *Muḥallā*, XI, 53: *ʿāqala rasūlu llāh ṣ bayna quraysh wa-l-anṣār fa-jaʿala l-ʿaql baynahum ilā thulthi l-diya.*

[17] *Ibid.*: *kunnā fī jāhiliyyatinā wa-innamā naḥmilu mina l-ʿaql mā balagha thultha l-diya wa-nu'khadhu bihi ḥālan, fa-in lam yūjad ʿindanā kāna bi-manzilati lladhī yutajāzā. Fa-lammā jā'a llāh taʿālā bi-l-islām kunnā fīman sanna* (the word *fīhim* appears to be missing here) *rasūlu llāh ṣ mina l-maʿāqil bayna quraysh wa-l-anṣār thultha l-diya.*

[18] Cf. the report in Ṭabarī to the effect that the Prophet "wrote the *maʿāqil*" in AH 2; below, 195n.

[19] The Kitāb has: ... *wa-l-qisṭ bayna l-mu'minīna.*

for Quraysh on Quraysh and for the Anṣār on the Anṣār (*jaʿala rasūlu llāhi ṣ ʿaql quraysh ʿalā quraysh wa-ʿaqla l-anṣār ʿalā l-anṣār*).[20]

The singular of *maʿāqil*, *maʿqula*, is said to mean blood money (*diya*).[21] The verb *ʿaqala* also covers indemnity for injury,[22] but the third-form *ʿāqala* is more relevant for us here.

The association of *maʿāqil* and *ribāʿa* in §§3–11 suggests a close link between the terms. In fact, Abū ʿUbayd interprets *ribāʿa* as *maʿāqil*. Qasṭallānī renders *maʿāqil* as *diyāt*, but his interpretation of *yataʿāqalūna...* conveys a broader meaning: "That is to say, they will be in the same position as before concerning the collection and payment of blood money". He adds: "It is said: *banū fulān ʿalā maʿāqilihimi llatī kānū ʿalayhā*, i.e. their positions and condition (*ay marātibihim wa-ḥālatihim*).[23] The word *marātib* or "positions" suggests that *ʿalā maʿāqilihim* relates to status with regard to blood money; as is well known, there is a big difference in this respect between a free-born individual and a slave. *ʿĀqala* can also mean "to be equal with regard to the compensation for injuries": ... *inna l-marʾa tuʿāqilu l-rajul ilā thulthi l-diya, fa-idhā balaghati l-thulth rajaʿat ilā l-niṣf*, "a woman receives the same compensation for injuries as a man up to [an injury compensated by] one third of the amount of blood money due in the case of death. Beyond that point compensation is relegated to one half of the compensation paid for a man".[24] *Muʿāqala* is also the execution of *qiṣāṣ* or retaliation (by slaying, wounding or mutilating).[25] *Maʿqula* and *maʿāqil* can be found in a variety of contexts, all of which are related to the matters just mentioned. *Maʿqula* is the overall responsibility of a master to pay com-

---

[20]Ibn Abī Shayba, *Muṣannaf*, IX, 318, 319 nos. 7627, 7628.

[21]Suhaylī, II, 251; Zurqānī, IV, 169:19. For *maʿāqil* and *ʿaql* in the sense of blood money see Marzūqī, *Sharḥ dīwān al-ḥamāsa*, I, 215: *fa-lā taʾkhudhū ʿaqlan mina l-qawmi innanī arā l-ʿāra yabqā wa-l-maʿāqilu tadhhabu*. Aṣmaʿī is supposed to have interpreted the expression *ṣāra damuhu maʿqula ʿalā qawmihi*, as *ṣārū yadūnahu*. See also above, 42n.

[22]In Samhūdī, I, 164, a man whose hand was cut off demanded to be given an estate called Khunāfa by way of compensation for his hand (*aʿṭinī khunāfa ʿaqlan bi-yadī*). See also Azraqī, II, 240: a *dār* or court became the property of Umayya b. ʿAbd Shams as a compensation for a stroke on his behind (*ʿaqlan fī ḍarb alyatihi*); Balādhurī, *Ansāb*, V (Sāʾir furūʿ Quraysh), 331–32.

[23]Qasṭallānī, II, 270.

[24]Ṭūsī, *Tahdhīb al-aḥkām*, X, 184.

[25]*Ibid.*, 170–71: *laysa bayna ahli l-dhimma muʿāqala fīmā yajnūna min qatl aw jirāḥa, innamā yuʾkhadhu dhālika min amwālihim.*

pensation in the case of injury or death incurred by his client; the obligation is linked to the master's right to the client's inheritance.[26]

These references are complementary rather than contradictory, and in the tribal context they refer to different aspects of the commitments undertaken by tribal groups towards their members. The term *maʿāqil* appears to relate to a group rather than to an individual.

The basic group with regard to blood money and related matters is the *ʿāqila* or *ʿaṣaba*, i.e. the agnates or relations on the father's side: one's father, grandfather, brothers, paternal uncles and paternal cousins.[27] But aid from the *ʿāqila* is not always granted. Essentially it is withheld in the case of a premeditated crime. In some cases, when the burden of compensation is relatively light, the offender himself pays indemnity from his own property.

The verb *taʿāqala* appears in a *ḥadīth* of ʿUmar b. al-Khaṭṭāb: *innā lā nataʿāqalu l-muḍagh baynanā*, "We do not compensate each other for 'pieces of flesh'" (i.e. small injuries). A man informed him that his paternal cousin had received a blow that laid bare his bone (*shujja mūḍiḥa*). ʿUmar wished to know if the victim was from among the settled (*ahl al-qurā*) or the nomads (*ahl al-bādiya*). Having been informed that he belonged to the latter, ʿUmar uttered these words. Some explained it as a ruling that the settled and the nomads do not indemnify each other in such cases, while others interpreted it as relating to minor injuries not covered by the *ʿāqila*.[28]

We now return to the Kitāb. Conditions within the participating groups probably concerned the Prophet less than their links with other groups, similarly referred to by the verb *taʿāqala*. Muḥammad refrained from slaying in retaliation a Muslim of the Kaʿb (Khuzāʿa; "were I to kill a believer for an unbeliever", he said, "I would have killed him"). Instead, he ordered his clan to pay the blood money, which the Kaʿb did with assistance from

[26] *Ibid.*, 175 (Abū ʿAbdallāh): *man lajaʾa ilā qawm fa-aqarrū bi-wilāyatihi kāna lahum mīrāthuhu wa-ʿalayhim maʿqulatuhu*; see also *ibid.*, IX, 396 (Abū ʿAbdallāh): *idhā wālā l-rajul l-rajul fa-lahu mīrāthuhu wa-ʿalayhi maʿqulatuhu.* And see *ibid.*, IX, 274: *inna l-marʾa laysa ʿalayhā jihād wa-lā nafaqa wa-lā ʿalayhā maʿqula innamā dhālika ʿalā l-rijāl.*

[27] The *ʿāqila* is "the group of persons upon whom devolves, as the result of a natural joint liability with the person who has committed homicide or inflicted bodily harm, the payment of compensation in cash or in kind"; *EI*², s.v. *ʿāḳila* (R. Brunschwig).

[28] Abū ʿUbayd, *Gharīb*, III, 347–48. Another source has a slightly different wording. ʿUmar told a nomad who came to him with regard to a wound that exposed the bone: *innā maʿāshir ahli l-qurā lā nataʿāqalu l-muḍagh baynanā*; Ibn Ḥajar, *Maṭālib*, II, 129. The son of a man from the Ghifār who received a wound in the head that laid bare the bone (*shujja*) heard from ʿUmar the same answer: the settled did not indemnify each other for such a wound: *inna hādhihi lā yataʿāqaluhā ahlu l-qurā*; Ibn Abī Shayba, *Muṣannaf*, IX, 375.

their allies (*ḥulafā'*), the Mudlij;[29] the agreement between the two tribes is described by the third and sixth forms of *ʿ-q-l*.[30] The sixth-form of the verb also describes mutual aid in connection with ransom.[31]

The Kitāb prescribes regarding the Anṣār (§§4–11) that the former *maʿāqil* or mutual aid agreements between the Anṣārī clans and other groups remain unchanged. This relates above all to co-operation in the payment of blood money and the ransoming of captives. At the background of this co-operation is the huge burden of blood money and ransom for the tribal economy.[32]

On the margin of the Qurayẓa affair it is reported that when the Prophet came to Medina, he made an agreement with the Qurayẓa, the Naḍīr and the other Jews of Medina to the effect that they would be neither with nor against him; and some said that they would assist him against whomever of them would attack him,[33] *wa-yuqīmū ʿalā maʿāqilihimi l-'ūlā llatī bayna l-aws wa-l-khazraj*,[34] "... and they would retain their former *maʿāqil* agreements between the Aws and Khazraj". This is comparable to *yataʿāqalūna maʿāqilahumu l-'ūlā* of the Kitāb. Some Jewish tribes probably had such agreements with the Aws, while other Jewish tribes had similar agreements with the Khazraj.

The preservation of the Jews' former links with the Aws and Khazraj seems to be behind another passage dealing with the agreements between the Jews and the Prophet.[35] The following appears in the story of the Qaynuqāʿ: "When the Messenger of God arrived at Medina, all the Jews made a non-belligerency agreement with him and he wrote a treaty between them and himself. He left each clan in its former alliances" (*lammā qadima rasūlu llāhi ṣ l-madīna wādaʿathu yahūd kulluhā, wa-kataba baynahu wa-baynahā kitāban wa-alḥaqa rasūlu llāhi ṣ kull qawm bi-ḥulafā'ihim*).[36] *Maʿāqil ūlā bayna l-*

[29] *Iṣāba*, VI, 547 no. 8985.

[30] Wāqidī, II, 845–46: *wa-kānū yuʿāqilūnahā fī l-jāhiliyya, thumma shaddahu l-islām*. In other words, Islam strengthened this alliance. Also: *wa-kānū yataʿāqalūna fī l-jāhiliyya*; Azraqī, II, 124.

[31] *Wa-kānū yataʿāqalūna*; *Iṣāba*, VII, 608 no. 11092, s.v. Khirnīq bint al-Ḥuṣayn.

[32] Gil (51) suggests another reading: "Every clan enumerated is said to have the obligation of paying the blood-money first of all for its own people. This is how *al-awlā* is to be understood, meaning "with priority", not "previous". However, Gil's suggestion does not conform to Arabic usage.

[33] *Man dahamahu minhum*; cf. below, 175.

[34] Wāqidī, II, 454–55.

[35] Wāqidī, I, 176, quoting Muḥammad b. Kaʿb al-Quraẓī.

[36] Wellhausen (73) correctly interpreted *qawm* as a reference to the Jewish clans: "... und er schrieb... eine Schrift, darin liess er jede Judenschaft zusammen mit ihren Eidgenossen",

aws wa-l-khazraj in the former report is the equivalent of *wa-alḥaqa... bi-ḥulafā'ihim* in the latter. In other words, in this specific case the alliances involved *maʿāqil*. The main Jewish tribes were not part of the Kitāb and the agreements with them were supplementary to the *maʿāqil* section of the Kitāb. At this early stage in the Prophet's activity in Medina both the Arab clans that participated in the Kitāb and the Jewish clans that did not retained their former *maʿāqil* agreements.

Some say that the Prophet himself had a similar agreement with the Naḍīr. After the battle of Bi'r Maʿūna he came to the Naḍīr to ask for their assistance in paying the blood money for two men of the Kilāb; there was between them (i.e. the Prophet and the Naḍīr) an agreement prescribing co-operation in *maʿāqil*.[37] Other sources speak of a treaty between the Naḍīr and the ʿĀmir b. Ṣaʿṣaʿa, the larger tribe to which the Kilāb belonged.[38] But this makes little sense in the given context and may be an apologetic attempt to avoid an inconvenient account on the mutual aid agreement between Muḥammad and the Naḍīr.[39] Muḥammad's agreement with the

---

i.e. from among the Anṣār. But Gil (59) rendered: "He confirmed the alliances between the Jews and each tribe (*qawm*)". See similarly Serjeant (25), according to whom Wāqidī speaks here of "... the affiliation of each tribe (*qawm*) to it allies (*ḥulafā'*)... — the *ḥulafā* meaning the Jews". Wellhausen's opinion that *qawm* refers to the Jewish tribes is supported by a text from *Bahjat al-maḥāfil*, I, 167: *fa-fī l-sanati l-'ūlā* (see below, 182) *banā ṣalla llāhu taʿālā ʿalayhi wa-ālihi wa-sallama masjidahu wa-masākinahu wa-kataba l-kitāb bayna l-muhājirīna wa-l-anṣār...*; 168: *wa-fīhā* (AH 1) *wādaʿa yahūd wa-sharaṭa ʿalayhim wa-lahum wa-alḥaqa kull qabīla minhum bi-ḥulafā'ihim mina l-anṣār, thumma ākhā....*

[37]Samarqandī, *Bustān*, 228:25 (*ghazwat banī l-naḍīr*): *...yastaʿīnu ʿalā diyati l-kilābiyyayni, wa-qad kāna baynahum ʿahd an yuʿīnū ʿalā maʿāqilihim.* One expects here the sixth-form *yataʿāwanū*, since such agreements were normally reciprocal. Rāzī, *Tafsīr*, XI, 182–83, interpretation of Qur'ān 5,11 (← Ibn ʿAbbās, al-Kalbī and Muqātil): *wa-qad kānū ʿāhadū l-nabī ṣ ʿalā tarki l-qitāl wa-ʿalā an yuʿīnūhu fī l-diyāt.* See more accurately *Bad'*, IV, 212 (*ghazāt banī l-naḍīr*): *wa-kāna fī l-ʿahdi lladhī baynahum wa-bayna rasūli llāh ṣ an yataghāwathū wa-yataḥammala mā yanūbu baʿḍuhum ʿan baʿḍ.* The MS has *yataʿāwathū*, which should perhaps be read *yataʿāwanū*.

[38]Ṭabarī, III, 551 [I, 1448]: *wa-kāna bayna banī l-naḍīr wa-bayna banī ʿāmir ḥilf wa-ʿaqd*; Wāqidī, I, 364: *wa-kānat banū l-naḍīr ḥulafā' li-banī ʿāmir.*

[39]Most unusual is the story in Ibn al-Ḍiyā', *Ta'rīkh Makka*, 260: it was the Prophet who concluded the treaty between the Naḍīr and the ʿĀmir; ʿAmr b. Umayya who killed the two ʿĀmirīs (i.e. the above-mentioned Kilābīs) was from the Naḍīr: *iʿlam anna l-nabī ṣ qad ʿaqada ḥilfan bayna banī l-naḍīr mina l-yahūd wa-bayna banī ʿāmir fa-ʿadā ʿamr b. umayya l-ḍamrī min banī l-naḍīr ʿalā rajulayni min banī ʿāmir....* See the same in Ibn al-Najjār, *Durra*, 350. *Mawrid al-ẓam'ān*, 218b, combines elements from different sources: the Prophet came to inquire the Naḍīr about the blood money (*li-yas'alahum kayfa l-diya fīhim*) "so that they would help him pay the blood money of the two persons killed by ʿAmr b. Umayya on his return from Bi'r Maʿūna. The Messenger of God had concluded

Naḍīr may have been an extension of an existing agreement between the Naḍīr and some Arab clans in Medina, probably belonging to the Khazraj.[40]

In sum, the Anṣār retain their agreements with other parties, including the Jews, regarding the payment of blood money and related matters.[41]

ʿalā ribāʿatihim

KEEP TO THEIR TRIBAL ORGANIZATION AND LEADERSHIP

Wellhausen (67, 68): "Die Emigranten von Quraisch bleiben wie sind", to which he remarks: "Im ersten Satz lässt sich *ʿalā ribʿatihim* nicht lokal auffassen; den die Emigranten hatten in Medina kein gemeinsames Quartier abgesondert für sich, sondern sie wohnten zerstreut unter den Ançār. Es kann nur heissen: sie sollen für sich bleiben, ebenso wie jedes Geschlecht der Ançār für sich bleibt..., unbeschadet der Einheit der Gemeinde".

Wensinck (52): "The *muhājirūn* of Quraysh [remain] in their condition". He rejects the rendering of *ʿalā ribʿatihim* by Krehl, "nach ihren Wohnsitzen":[42] "On the contrary, the meaning is that all the *muhājirūn* together, irrespective of where they were living, must pay blood-wite as they had been doing until then".

Watt (221): "The Emigrants of Quraysh, according to their former condition...". He quotes from Lane's *Arabic-English Lexicon* the translation of *ʿalā ribʿati-him* as "according to their former or good condition". Watt adds: "There is no reason to suppose any reference to 'quarter'. The interpretation is either that each group remains distinct or that it follows its previous practice".

---

with them an agreement prescribing that they should help him pay blood money; the more so since there was an alliance and agreement between them and the tribe of the slain men" (*wa-kāna rasūlu llāhi ṣ qad akhadha l-ʿahd ʿalayhim an yuʿāwinūhu fī l-diyāt siyyamā wa-qad kāna baynahum wa-bayna ahli l-qatīlayni ḥilf wa-ʿaqd*).

[40]On the alliance between the Naḍīr and the Khazraj that was reinstated after the battle of Buʿāth, see Lecker, "King Ibn Ubayy and the *Quṣṣāṣ*", 41–44.

[41]Gil's concluding notes (65) are: "The document... was a formal statement of intent to disengage the Arab clans of Medina from the Jewish neighbours they had been allied with up to that time". However, the Kitāb was concluded during Muḥammad's first year in Medina, whereas such policies could only have been adopted by him after he had established himself. Besides, when the Kitāb was concluded, there were still peaceful relations with the main Jewish tribes; see Lecker "Did Muḥammad Conclude Treaties with the Jewish Tribes".

[42]Krehl, *Das Leben Muhammed*, 143. (Krehl has: Wohnplätzen.)

Serjeant (18, 21): "The *Muhājirūn* of Quraysh are in charge of the management of their affairs". He quotes without further comment several interpretations of the expression.

The use of *rab*ʿ, or *rab*ʿ*a*, pl. *ribā*ʿ, in the sense of "quarters" is common.[43] In the description of the boundaries of the market of Medina, *rab*ʿ*a* includes at least one *dār* or court.[44] ʿUthmān bought a *rab*ʿ*a* and added it to the Prophet's mosque.[45] Also *ribā*ʿ*a* appears in the same sense.[46]

The correct reading is *ribā*ʿ*a*, which is the one preferred by Abū ʿUbayd. At one point Abū ʿUbayd records a partial recension of the Kitāb going back to Zuhrī via ʿAbdallāh b. Ṣāliḥ (← al-Layth b. Saʿd ← ʿUqyal b. Khālid ← Zuhrī): ...ʿ*alā r.b*ʿ*ātihim*.... The following passage in his book refers to another recension of Zuhrī that reached Abū ʿUbayd via Yaḥyā b. ʿAbdallāh b. Bukayr (← al-Layth ← ʿUqayl ← Zuhrī). There is only one difference between the two recensions: the latter has *ribā*ʿ*atihim* instead of *r.b*ʿ*ātihim*, and Abū ʿUbayd remarks that *ribā*ʿ*a* is the correct reading.[47] Indeed, throughout the Kitāb Abū ʿUbayd has *ribā*ʿ*atihim*. The reading *ribā*ʿ*a* appears also in Abū ʿUbayd's commentary on the Kitāb (264), where it is said to mean *ma*ʿ*āqil*; one who is in charge of his clan's *ribā*ʿ*a* handles their affairs and represents them before the authorities when calamities befall them.[48] Suhaylī quotes the versions found in Abū ʿUbayd in reverse order: he refers *r.b*ʿ*ātihim* to Abū ʿUbayd ← Ibn Bukayr ← ʿUqayl ← Zuhrī, while referring *ribā*ʿ*atihim* to Abū ʿUbayd ← ʿAbdallāh b. Ṣāliḥ etc. Suhaylī adds

[43] On the *ribā*ʿ of Mecca see Fākihī, *Akhbār makka*, VI, Index, 244–45. When the Prophet came from Qubā' to Medina, Ḥāritha b. al-Nuʿmān of the Najjār is supposed to have told him: ... *qad* ʿ*alimati l-khazraj annahu laysa rab*ʿ *awsa*ʿ *min rab*ʿ*ī*; Samhūdī, I, 260.

[44] See Samhūdī, II, 752: *thumma wajhu l-rab*ʿ*a llatī fīhā dār āl abī* ʿ*uthmān ḥulafā' azhar b.* ʿ*abd* ʿ*awf*.

[45] Ibn Abī Shayba, *Muṣannaf*, XII, 53 no. 12104.

[46] *Ayyumā qawm kānat baynahum ribā*ʿ*a aw dār*; Aḥmad, III, 310:8.

[47] Abū ʿUbayd, *Amwāl*, 166 nos. 328–29: *wa-ḥaddathanī yaḥyā... mithl dhālika bi-ṭūlihi, illā annahu qāla*: ʿ*alā ribā*ʿ*atihim. Qāla abū* ʿ*ubayd*: *wa-hādhā* ʿ*indī huwa l-maḥfūẓ*.

[48] *Qawluhu*: *banū fulān* ʿ*alā ribā*ʿ*atihim, al-ribā*ʿ*a hiya l-ma*ʿ*āqil. Wa-qad yuqālu*: *fulān* ʿ*alā ribā*ʿ*at qawmihi idhā kāna l-mutaqallid li-umūrihim wa-l-wāfid* ʿ*alā l-umarā' fīmā yanūbuhum*. A slightly different interpretation appears in Khushanī, 135: ʿ*alā rib*ʿ*atihim*: *al-rib*ʿ*a wa-l-ribā*ʿ*a* (printed *wa-l-rabā*ʿ*a*) *l-ḥālu llatī jā'a l-islām wa-hum* ʿ*alayhā, wa-yuqālu fulān yaqūmu bi-ribā*ʿ*at ahlihi idhā kāna yaqūmu bi-amrihim wa-sha'nihim*. Cf. the expression *ḍā*ʿ*at ribā*ʿ*atuhum* used by an Umayyad poet; *Aghānī*, XI, 165:2; *Aghānī* (Dār al-Kutub), XIII, 89.

that there are two possibilities of vocalizing the word, *ribāʿa* and *rabāʿa*.[49] Zamakhsharī interprets *ribāʿatu l-rajul*: *sha'nuhu wa-ḥāluhu lladhī huwa rābiʿ ʿalayhā, ay thābit muqīm*; to which he attaches a *ḥadīth*: one of the signs of the Day of Resurrection disclosed by the Prophet to ʿUmar b. al-Khaṭṭāb is that sin (*fāḥisha*) will become the norm (*ribāʿa*). Zamakhsharī adds another interpretation, according to which *ribāʿa* refers to good condition only (*wa-lā yakūnu fī ghayr ḥusni l-ḥāl*). One says: "Among the Banū so-and-so there is no person capable of effectively managing his *ribāʿa* except so-and-so" (*mā fī banī fulān man yaḍbiṭu ribāʿatahu ghayr fulān*).[50] Akhṭal's eulogy of Maṣqala b. Hubayra al-Shaybānī refers to the latter's guarantee for the full payment of blood money owed by his tribe: "Nobody among the Maʿadd [but him] can make his *ribāʿa* free from want...".[51] Ibn Sayyid al-Nās (I, 199) quotes the following interpretation from *kitāb al-muzanī*, i.e. the recension of the Kitāb by al-Muzanī:[52] *al-r.b.ʿa*: *al-ḥālatu llatī jā'a l-islām wa-hum ʿalayhā*.

The term *ribāʿa* repeated separately regarding each of the participating groups covers vital areas of tribal organization. The *ribāʿa* belongs to the whole tribal group. Some of the passages quoted above interpret the term in very general terms, while elsewhere it is given a more specific meaning. The terms *naqīb* and *wāfid* associated with *ribāʿa* indicate that it is connected to the leadership of the tribal group as well as its relations with others. The right to one fourth of the spoils (*mirbāʿ*) and the roles associated with

[49] Suhaylī, II, 251, quoting Abū ʿUbayd: *thumma qāla abū ʿubayd: yuqālu fulān ʿalā ribāʿat qawmihi idhā kāna naqībahum wa-wāfidahum.* Suhaylī explains: *bi-kasri l-rā' fīhi l-qiyās ʿalā hādhā l-maʿnā li-annahā wilāya, wa-in jaʿala l-rabāʿa maṣdaran fa-l-qiyās fatḥu l-rā' ay ʿalā sha'nihim wa-ʿādatihim min aḥkāmi l-diyāti wa-l-dimā'*. Serjeant (10–11), with reference to Suhaylī, has: "He was their *naqīb* and the one of them over their affairs and custom consisting of the judgements of blood-wits and blood(shed)". But *wa-wāḥidahum* in Suhaylī's edition used by Serjeant is an error; read *wa-wāfidahum*. A man of the Saʿd b. Bakr came to the Prophet and introduced himself: *innī wāfid qawmī wa-sayyiduhum*; Abū ʿUbayd, *Amwāl*, 298 no. 568. Serjeant also refers to Ibn al-Athīr's *Nihāya*, II, 189, s.v. *r-b-ʿ*: *wa-fī kitābi l-muhājirīna wa-l-anṣār: ...ʿalā ribāʿatihim, yuqālu l-qawm ʿalā ribāʿatihim wa-ribāʿihim, ay ʿalā stiqāmatihim, yurīdu annahum ʿalā amrihimi lladhī kānū ʿalayhi.*

[50] Zamakhsharī, *Fā'iq*, II, 25, s.v. *r-b-ʿ*.

[51] Bakrī, *Simṭ al-la'ālī*, I, 394: *mā fī maʿaddin fatan yughnī ribāʿatahu....* The reading *tughnī ribāʿatuhu* in *Lisān al-ʿarab*, VIII, 108, is wrong. See also Akhṭal, *Dīwān*, I, 159–60 no. 13, verses 51, 52 (*yughnī ribāʿatahu*).

[52] Below, 200.

the *ribāʿa*, such as the handling of blood vengeance, typically belong to the tribal leader.[53]

As has been mentioned, Abū ʿUbayd interprets *ribāʿa* as *maʿāqil*. Indeed, the following phrase (*yataʿāqalūna* etc.) is complementary. *Ribāʿa* is an undertaking to pay blood money. Al-Aʿshā says: *wa-āsi sarāta l-ḥayyi ḥaythu laqītahum wa-lā taku ʿan ḥamli l-ribāʿati wāniya*, "Carry the burden along with the leaders of the tribe when you come together with them, and do not falter in bearing the *ribāʿa*". The link between the roots *r-b-ʿ* and *ḥ-m-l* is significant.[54]

The limits of the obligation to pay blood money are also the limits of the tribal group, and hence *r(i/a)bāʿa* also means *qabīla*.[55] The responsibility for settling blood feuds was one of the *sayyid*'s major functions. The expression *wa-huwa ʿalā ribāʿat qawmihi* means *huwa sayyiduhum*.[56]

Blood money was usually divided into three annual installments, and hence a guarantor was often required to facilitate the conclusion of a settlement. In Kaʿb b. al-Ashraf's elegy dedicated to the Meccan pagans killed at Badr he mentioned those among the dead who carried heavy burdens (*ḥammāl athqāl*), were leaders of their tribe and undertook to pay the blood

[53] A Khawlānī poet boasts: *naḥnu min ḥimyara fī dhirwatihā wa-lanā l-mirbāʿu minhā wa-l-ribāʿa*; Nashwān, *Shams al-ʿulūm*, 40.

[54] According to Abū ʿUbayda, *rabʿ* means the lifting of a (heavy) stone as a means of testing one's strength; Abū ʿUbayd, *Gharīb*, I, 16: *al-rabʿ an yushāla l-ḥajar bi-l-yad, yufʿalu dhālika li-tuʿrafa bihi shiddatu l-rajul.* Abū ʿUbayd comments that this is specifically used with regard to stones. A *rabīʿa* is a stone lifted and carried by hand; Ibn Durayd, *Ishtiqāq*, 312: *al-ṣakhratu llatī turbaʿu wa-tuḥmalu bi-l-yad.* Carrying and strength are also conveyed by other derivatives of the same root: *tarabbaʿa* means to carry; *Lisān al-ʿarab*, VIII, 111, s.v. *r-b-ʿ*: *wa-tarabbaʿati l-nāqa sanāman ṭawīlan, ay ḥamalathu. Istarbaʿa* means *aṭāqa*, or to be able to accomplish or endure something; *ibid.*, VIII, 108, 110–11. The expression *inna fulānan qadi rtabaʿa amra l-qawm* means that he expects to become their leader; *ibid.*, VIII, 108: ... *ay yantaẓiru an yu'ammara ʿalayhim.* Akhṭal's verse quoted above is followed in the *Lisān al-ʿarab* by the remark: *wa-l-ribāʿa ayḍan naḥw mina l-ḥamāla*; *Lisān al-ʿarab*, VIII, 108. *Rabaʿa* also means "to accept blood money"; see the elegy on Kulayb Wā'il by his brother, Muhalhil, in *ʿIqd*, V, 220: *qatalū kulayban thumma qālū rbaʿū* ....

[55] *Lisān al-ʿarab*, 108. Also Akhṭal, *Dīwān*, II, 414 no. 45, verse 15, where the commentator says that the word *usra* in the verse is the same as *al-faṣīla, al-ṭāriqa, al-rahṭ, al-nafar, al-ʿashīra, al-ribāʿa* and *al-ʿimāra*, all of which mean *al-qabīla*. The pre-Islamic Tamīmī poet al-Aswad b. Yaʿfur (*GAS*, II, 182–83) replied to his daughter's accusations that he had wasted his wealth (naturally in the form of camels) on blood money owed by his tribe (*fīmā yanūbu qawmahu min ḥamāla*) and on gifts to their poor: ... *wa-qad yughnī ribāʿatahu l-waḥīdu*, "A single man can possibly render his *ribāʿa* free from want"; *Aghānī*, XI, 138:-1; *Aghānī* (Dār al-Kutub), XIII, 26.

[56] *Lisān al-ʿarab*, VIII, 108.

money owed by it.[57] The expression *ḥammāl athqāl* refers to *ḥamāla*, namely the burden of a tribal leader who undertook to cover the blood money agreed upon with another tribe, or guaranteed the payment at his own risk. In the Second Fijār war between Quraysh and the Hawāzin there was some fighting followed by limited claims of blood money that Ḥarb b. Umayya, who made an agreement between the parties, undertook to defray.[58] It is legitimate to ask people for money (*mas'ala*) for one who guarantees the payment of blood money in order to achieve a settlement between two tribes.[59] This is confirmed by a *ḥadīth* going back to Qabīṣa b. al-Mukhāriq, who relates how he came to Muḥammad to ask for help;[60] Qabīṣa was his tribe's *sayyid*.[61]

The pre-Islamic tribal concepts were still valid in the Umayyad period. When the poet of the Ṭay', Ḥurayth b. ʿAnnāb, was jailed in Medina and his own subdivision, the Nabhān, refused to help him, he was assisted by *ʿurafā'* or appointed tribal chiefs of the Buḥtur subdivision who had arrived at Medina with their tribal taxes (*ṣadaqāt*); they assisted him under the principle of *ribāʿa*. A verse by the grateful poet includes the term *ribāʿa*: *li-kulli banī ʿamri bni ghawthin ribāʿatun wa-khayruhum fī l-sharri wa-l-khayri buḥturu*, "All of the ʿAmr b. Ghawth share one *ribāʿa*, and the best of them in happiness and misfortune is Buḥtur".[62] ʿAmr b. Ghawth b. Ṭay' is the eponym of almost the whole of Ṭay',[63] and the poet claimed that they formed one solidarity group. In this specific case the solidarity was behind his release from jail.[64]

In sum, the expression *ʿalā ribāʿatihim* reiterated nine times in the Kitāb prescribes that the participating groups from Quraysh and the Anṣār preserve their tribal organization and leadership. At this early stage

---

[57] *Kam qad uṣība bihā min abyaḍa mājidin dhī bahjatin ya'wī ilayhi l-ḍuyyaʿu ṭalqi l-yadayni idhā l-kawākibu akhlafat ḥammāli athqālin yasūdu wa-yarbaʿu*; Wāqidī, I, 185–86. See also Ibn Hishām, III, 55. Guillaume, *The Life of Muhammad*, 365, renders: "How many noble handsome men, The refuge of the homeless were slain; Liberal when the stars gave no rain, Who bore others' burdens, ruling and taking their due fourth". But *wa-yarbaʿu* in this context relates to *ribāʿa*, not to *mirbāʿ* or the leader's share in the booty.

[58] *ʿIqd*, V, 252:10: ...*wa-kāna baynahum qitāl wa-dimā' yasīra fa-ḥamalahā ḥarb b. umayya wa-aṣlaḥa baynahum*.

[59] Abū ʿUbayd, *Gharīb*, II, 61: *rajul taḥammala bi-ḥamāla min* [var. *bayna*] *qawm*.

[60] *Ataytu rasūla llāhi fī ḥamāla* etc.; Abū ʿUbayd, *Amwāl*, 293–94 no. 564.

[61] *Ibid.*, 657 no. 1723.

[62] *Aghānī*, XIII, 103; *Aghānī* (Dār al-Kutub), XIV, 384–85.

[63] Ibn Ḥazm, *Ansāb*, 398–404.

[64] Cf. Marzūqī, *Sharḥ dīwān al-ḥamāsa*, II, 633–34.

Muḥammad was not strong enough to support tribal leaders who were more sympathetic to his cause than the established ones.

wa-hum yafdūna ʿāniyahum... wa-kull ṭāʾifa minhum tafdī ʿāniyahā

RANSOMING THEIR CAPTIVES..., EVERY SUB-GROUP RANSOMS ITS CAPTIVES.

Wellhausen (67–68): "...und lösen selber ihre Gefangenen. ...und jeder Verband löst seine Gefangenen". He remarks: "Was ich mit Verband übersetzt habe, ist eine Unterabteilung der Gruppe, welche vielleicht der *Dār* oder auch dem Geschlechte entspricht. Also während für das Sühngeld die ganze Gruppe aufkommt, wird das Lösegeld nur von dem nächstbeteiligten Verwandtenkreise aufgebracht".
Wensinck (52): "...and ransom their captives. ...Every group ransoms their captives". He adds: "It is not quite apparent what is meant by *ṭāʾifah.* But the meaning of the section is clear: the entire clan mentioned sees to it that the blood-wite is paid. Ransom money, which amounts to considerably less, is raised by the clan to which the captive belongs. *Ṭāʾifah* is possibly a territorial as well as geographical unit".
Watt (221–22): "...and they (as a group) ransom their captive(s)...and each sub-clan ransoms its captive(s)".
Serjeant (18): "...and they will ransom a prisoner of them...and each group/section will ransom a prisoner of them ...". He remarks (21): "It is possible that prisoners, other than those captured in war, might be persons held for some offence".
Gil (51) has another opinion:

> Each of the clans thus considered by Muḥammad to be confederated publicly took a solemn pledge to be responsible for blood ransoms, while the redemption of its prisoners was to be dealt with by the community of the believers. The two elements are not appended to one another, as has been generally understood. They rather express an antinomy. Whereas blood money was to be paid separately and intimately by each clan, ransoming of captives was to become a joint affair of the whole party.

But his opinion does not tally with the wording of the clauses: *wa-banū ʿawf ʿalaʿ ribāʿatihim... wa-kullu ṭāʾifa* minhum *tafdī...*.

As we have just seen, the term *maʿāqil* also includes the ransoming of captives. It can be shown that after the battle of Badr the ʿAmr b. ʿAwf as a whole (cf. §9), and not a *ṭā'ifa* or sub-group from among them, were involved in the release of one of them. But perhaps the Kitāb was no longer in force after Badr; besides, the Kitāb speaks of payment and not of intercession. The details are as follows. In the battle of Badr a son of Abū Sufyān was captured by the Prophet, but the former refused to ransom him. Instead, he captured Saʿd b. al-Nuʿmān b. Akkāl of the ʿAmr b. ʿAwf, more precisely of the Muʿāwiya, who had arrived at Mecca for the "lesser pilgrimage". Verses by Abū Sufyān specify the ʿAmr, i.e. ʿAmr b. ʿAwf, as those responsible for the release of his hostage. The ʿAmr b. ʿAwf actually received Abū Sufyān's captured son from Muḥammad and sent him to his father in Mecca, thus obtaining Saʿd's release.[65]

A fragment of the Kitāb found in Abū ʿUbayd[66] has *yafukkūna* instead of *yafdūna*. This could be considered the *lectio difficilior*, but it is somewhat inconsistent in Abū ʿUbayd's recension, and the full text of the Kitāb elsewhere in Abū ʿUbayd's book has *yafdūna*, followed by *tafdī* in each of the successive clauses. In addition, later in the Kitāb (§12) we find ... *fī fidā' aw ʿaql*. A comment of Abū ʿUbayd[67] makes it clear that for him the *fidā' al-ʿānī* means the ransoming of captives. The version *yafukkūna ʿāniyahum* is also found in Zurqānī,[68] who offers two interpretations: first, the ransoming of captives; second, the rescuing of one inflicted by weariness or hardship, in which case everyone participated according to his capability.[69]

The expression *yafukku ʿāniyahu* does appear in the context of ransom,[70] but it is also found in a different context. According to some, the maternal uncle inherits from one who has no heirs on his father's side. The right to the inheritance is accompanied by an obligation: *yafukku ʿānahu/ʿāniyahu/ʿuniyyahu*, i.e. the maternal uncle has to pay debts normally covered by the *ʿāqila*, such as blood money and the compensation for

---

[65] Ṭabarī, II, 466–67 [I, 1345–46] (← Ibn Isḥāq ← ʿAbdallāh b. Abī Bakr b. Muḥammad b. ʿAmr b. Ḥazm).

[66] *Amwāl*, 166 no. 328.

[67] *Ibid.*, no. 327.

[68] IV, 168:21 (erroneously printed: ... *ʿāfiyahum*).

[69] *Wa-kadhā yukhalliṣūna man aṣābahu taʿab aw mashaqqa bi-ḥasbi l-ṭāqa.* Similarly Ibn al-Aʿrābī glosses *ʿanā ʿalayhi l-amr*: *shaqqa ʿalayhi*; *Lisān al-ʿarab*, XV, 104, s.v. *ʿ-n-y*. See also Khushanī, 135: *wa-l-ʿānī l-asīr wa-l-makhdhūlu lladhī tarakahu qawmuhu wa-lam yuwāsūhu.*

[70] A governor of ʿAlī b. Abī Ṭālib who bought captured Christian rebels and released them from captivity was referred to by the captives as *fakkāk al-ʿunāt*; Thaqafī, *Ghārāt*, I, 362–64.

injuries left unpaid by the deceased.[71] In other words, when, in the absence of an *ʿāqila*, the maternal uncle inherits from his nephew, he is also responsible for the debts of the deceased. "Captivity" is used here figuratively. A parallel tradition has instead of *yafukku ʿāniyahu*: *yaʿqilu ʿanhu*.[72]

Considering the context of this clause it is rather tempting to argue that *ʿānin* here is not a captive but one burdened by a debt of blood money; he should be "released", viz. his debt should be paid according to tribal law. In this case *ṭāʾifa* means *ʿāqila* or the agnatic relatives. But there is not enough evidence to support this interpretation. In addition, *fidāʾ* in §12 can only mean "ransom".

bi-l-maʿrūf wa-l-qisṭ bayna l-muʾminīna

ACCORDING TO WHAT IS CUSTOMARY AND EQUITABLE AMONG THE MUʾMINŪN.

Wellhausen (68): "Die Mitwirkung der (übrigen) Gläubigen dabei ist Sache der Freundlichkeit und Billigkeit".
Wensinck (53): "[This is carried out] in an upright and just [manner] among the believers".
Watt (222): "... with uprightness and justice between the believers".
Serjeant (18, 21): "... in accordance with what is customary and by fair sharing among the *Muʾminūn*". He remarks: "I understand *maʿrūf* in this context to mean *sharʿ*, a word still in use in south-west Arabia for customary laws".

In Qurʾān 2,178, *fa-ttibāʿun bi-l-maʿrūfi* relates to the person who receives the blood money and not to those who pay it, as in the Kitāb. The exegetes interpret this verse as an injunction not to distress the person who has to

[71] *Al-khāl wārith man lā wārith lahu, yafukku ʿānahu, ay ʿāniyahu fa-ḥadhafa l-yāʾ. Wa-fī riwāya: yafukku ʿuniyyahu ..., yuqālu ʿanā yaʿnū ʿunuwwan wa-ʿuniyyan. Wa-maʿnā l-asr fī hādhā l-ḥadīth mā yalzamuhu wa-yataʿallaqu bihi bi-sababi l-jināyāti llatī sabīluhā an yataḥammalahā* [*sic*] *l-ʿāqila, hādhā ʿinda man yuwarrithu l-khāl. Wa-man lā yuwarrithuhu yakūnu maʿnāhu annahā ṭuʿma yuṭʿamahā l-khāl lā an yakūna wārithan*; *Lisān al-ʿarab*, XV, 102, s.v. *ʿ-n-y*, quoting *ḥadīth al-miqdām*; see the following footnote.

[72] Abū ʿUbayd, *Amwāl*, 282 no. 542 (← al-Miqdām b. Maʿdīkarib): ... *wa-l-khāl wārith man lā wārith lahu, yarithuhu wa-yaʿqilu ʿanhu, wa-anā wārith man lā wārith lahu, arithuhu wa-aʿqilu ʿanhu.*

pay (*wa-lā yuʿsirahu*); *maʿrūf* is said to mean "leniency" (*an yarfuqa bihi wa-lā yuʿsirahu*).[73] But it is doubtful that this is relevant for us here.

In Zurqānī's opinion (IV, 168:25) *qisṭ* means equity (*ʿadl*). Equity in this case does not mean equal shares, since everyone was expected to participate according to his wealth.[74]

§12. *wa-inna l-mu'minīna lā yatrukūna mufraḥan baynahum an yuʿṭūhu bi-l-maʿrūf fī fidā' aw ʿaql*

THE MU'MINŪN SHALL NOT NEGLECT TO GIVE [aid] TO A DEBTOR AMONGST THEM [who is not entitled to support according to tribal law, but will aid him] ACCORDING TO WHAT IS CUSTOMARY IN MATTERS OF RANSOM OR BLOOD MONEY.

Wellhausen (68): "Denn die Gläubigen lassen keinen Belasteten im stich, sondern unterstützen ihn freundwillig bei der Aufbringung des Lösegeldes und des Sühngeldes".
Wensinck (53): "The believers shall not fail to give just assistance to a debtor among them for redemption money or blood-wite".
Watt (222): "The believers do not forsake a debtor among them, but give him (help), according to what is fair, for ransom or blood-wit".
Serjeant (19, 21): "The *Mu'minūn* will not leave a *mufraj* (one turned Muslim among a people to whom he does not belong) among them without giving him what is (established by) custom for ransom or blood money". He remarks with regard to this clause: "... The alternative reading, *mufraḥ*, loaded with debts and with many dependents, seems to fit a little less well, as also its synonym, *mafdūḥ*. If, however, it be understood in this last sense,

---

[73] Ṭūsī, *Tahdhīb al-aḥkām*, X, 178–79. Cf. Zurqānī, IV, 168:23: (*bi-l-maʿrūf*) *bi-ḥaythu lā yartakibūna fī dhālika muḥarraman bal yuḥāfiẓūna ʿalā izālat taʿab man aṣābahu muṣība maʿa riʿāyat qawānīni l-sharʿ*.

[74] For uneven *qisṭs* of meat divided among the people of Ṣanʿā' in AH 11, see Ṭabarī, III, 233 [I, 1859–60]: *wa-jaʿaltu āmuru li-l-rahṭ bi-l-jazūr wa-l-ahli l-bayt bi-l-baqara wa-li-ahli l-khalla* [var. *l-ḥilla*] *bi-ʿ.dda ḥattā akhadha ahl kull nāḥiya bi-qisṭihim*; *The History of al-Ṭabarī*, X, trans. Donner, 29: "... I began to order that the slaughtered camels be given to the clan, the cows to the family, and the equipment to the needy, until the people of each district had taken their share". A parallel text in Ibn ʿAsākir, XLIX, 487, confirms the reading *ḥilla*, which means a collection of *buyūt*, or 100 and more of them; Lane, I, 621b, s.v. In other words, a *ḥilla* is a small quarter. The text moves from the small to the large: first the *rahṭ* or a family, more precisely a man's nearer kinfolk, then the *ahl al-bayt* or a man's *ʿāqila* (§28; below, 148), and finally the quarter. In this case the reading *ʿidda* or "several (cows)" instead of *ʿudda* is preferable.

it might have something to do with the setting up of the brotherhood to assist the poor *Muhājirs*".

This clause signals a shift from clauses relating to specific tribal groups to general clauses relating to the Muʾminūn in general. One expects this clause, like the preceding ones, to be linked to *maʿāqil*.

Mufraḥ is the correct reading, because it is attested in most versions of the Kitāb.[75] Abū ʿUbayd, probably using the Kitāb outside its original context, interprets this clause as referring to the duty to ransom captives. He adduces two fragmentary recensions of the Kitāb in a chapter of his *Kitāb al-amwāl* dedicated to enemy captives (*bābu l-ḥukm fī riqāb ahli l-ʿanwa mina l-asārā wa-l-saby*). Muslim women and children count as men with regard to their ransoming and it is the duty of the leader (*imām*) and the Muslims to release and rescue them by freeing captives held by the Muslims or by paying the ransom, "and this was imposed by the Messenger of God on the Muhājirūn and Anṣār" (*wa-huwa sharṭ rasūli llāhi ṣ ʿalā l-muhājirīna wa-l-anṣār*).[76] The fragment of the Kitāb quoted by Abū ʿUbayd from Zuhrī (166 no. 328) ends with the clause discussed here: *wa-hum yafukkūna* [*sic*] *ʿāniyahum bi-l-maʿrūf wa-l-qisṭ bayna l-muʾminīna*, followed by the words *thumma dhakara ḥadīthan ṭawīlan fī l-maʿāqil*. Later (no. 330) Abū ʿUbayd quotes a small fragment of the Kitāb going back to Ibn Jurayj that ends with the words: *inna l-muʾminīna lā yatrukūna mafdūḥan* [*sic*] *minhum an yuʿṭūhu bi-l-maʿrūf fī fidāʾ aw ʿaql*. Abū ʿUbayd remarks that sources other than Ibn Jurayj have *mufraḥ*, but that the meaning remains the same: one burdened by debt (*al-muthqal bi-l-dayn*). The reading *mafdūḥ* is attested in the dictionaries, but it is wrong nonetheless. *Fadaḥahu*, said of a debt, an affair and a load, means: it burdened him, or burdened him heavily, and *mafdūḥ* means: one burdened, or heavily burdened, by debt.[77]

[75] It is also attested in this fragment or rather paraphrased version of some clauses from the Kitāb: ← Jābir al-Juʿfī ← Shaʿbī: *qaraʾtu fī jafn* [sheath] *sayf rasūli llāh ṣ dhī l-faqār: al-ʿaql ʿalā l-muʾminīna, wa-lā yutraku mufraḥ fī l-islām — wa-l-mufraḥ yakūnu fī l-qawm lā yuʿlamu lahu mawlan* [= a gloss] — *wa-lā yuqtalu muslim bi-kāfir*; Ibn Saʿd, I, 486.

[76] *Amwāl*, 165–67 nos. 327–30.

[77] Lane, II, 2351, s.v. Aṣmaʿī interprets *mufraḥ*: *huwa lladhī qad afraḥahu l-dayn, yaʿnī athqalahu, qāla yaqūlu: yuqḍā ʿanhu daynuhu min bayti l-māl wa-lā yutraku madīnan, wa-ankara qawlahum mufraj bi-l-jīm*; Abū ʿUbayd, *Gharīb*, I, 30–31. Another source (Quṭrub, *Aḍdād*, 80–81) says that *mufraḥ* is one of the *aḍdād*, meaning both *masrūr* or cheerful and *al-muthqal bi-l-dayn* or one burdened with debt. In his interpretations on the Kitāb, Ibn Sayyid al-Nās (I, 199) quotes from Ibn Jurayj another version: *wa-l-mufraḥ, rawāhu bn jurayj mufrajan. Qāla abū ʿubayd: wa-maʿnāhumā wāḥid.* But as we have just seen,

In his commentary on the full text of the Kitāb Abū ʿUbayd says that the *mufraḥ* or one burdened by debt should be aided: if he is a captive he should be released, and if he unintentionally committed an offence, blood money should be paid for him.[78] Among other versions Abū ʿUbayd[79] has *mufraj*, a man living amidst a group to which he does not belong; they have to pay blood money for him (... *fa-ḥaqq ʿalayhim an yaʿqilū ʿanhu*). In any case, the clause under discussion prescribes help rather than full responsibility, with the main burden remaining the *mufraḥ*'s.

Mufraj is also interpreted as a dead man found in a desert (*falāt*) far from a settlement (*qarya*). His blood money should be paid from the treasury and not be forfeited.[80] *Mufraj* is "one who has no clan" (*lladhī lā ʿashīra lahu*).[81] Ṭabarānī has: *lā yutraku mufraj fī l-islām*. He adds that one version of this *ḥadīth* includes the words *ḥattā yuḍamma ilā qabīla*, "until he is attached to a tribe".[82] The addition indicates that a *mufraj* is a man without a tribal affiliation. Abū ʿUbayda says that a *mufraj* is a man who embraces Islam without becoming someone's *mawlā* (... *an yuslima l-rajul fa-lā yuwālī aḥadan*). A crime committed by him that requires retaliation (*jināya*) is to be covered by the treasury because he has no *ʿāqila* or agnates. An unspecified scholar says that a *mufraj* is one who is not registered in the *dīwān*,[83] viz. one who is not entitled to an annual salary.

These interpretations are irrelevant for us here. The verb *afraḥahu* is attested in the sense of "it [the burden of blood money] became too heavy for him to carry". When Khufāf b. Nudba al-Sulamī found out that his rival ʿAbbās b. Mirdās wished to end their dispute, he said: ... *al'āna lammā aqdaḥathu* [read: *afraḥathu*] *l-ḥarb wa-ḥtamala thiqala l-dimā' ansha'a yuẓhiru l-nadāma*, "Now that war has put upon him a burden too heavy for him to carry and he had to pay large amounts in blood money, he composed verses feigning regret".[84] ʿAbd al-Razzāq, who quotes a *ḥadīth*

---

the fragment of the Kitāb quoted by Abū ʿUbayd from Ibn Jurayj has *mafdūḥ*; *Amwāl*, 166–67 no. 330.

[78] *Ibid.*, 264 no. 518: ... *in kāna asīran fukka min isārihi wa-in kāna janā jināyat khaṭa' ʿaqalū ʿanhu.*

[79] *Gharīb*, I, 30.

[80] *Ibid.*, 31.

[81] Ibn Sayyid al-Nās, I, 199, quoting Thaʿlab.

[82] *Kabīr*, XVII, 24 (← Kathīr b. ʿAbdallāh b. ʿAmr b. ʿAwf al-Muzanī ← his father ← his grandfather). Cf. below, 200f.

[83] Abū ʿUbayd, *Gharīb*, I, 31.

[84] Ibn ʿAsākir, XXVI, 43–32. The following verse is quoted with regard to Khufāf's words: *idhā lam tazal yawman tu'addī amānatan wa-taḥmilu ukhrā aqdaḥatka* [read

that reflects a clause of the Kitāb, glosses *mufraḥ* as "one who has to pay blood money from his own property".[85] The wording implies that the person who committed a crime could not rely on tribal solidarity either because his crime was premeditated or for another reason.[86] Alternatively, a *mufraḥ* could have been one burdened by an amount of blood money that was less than one third of the *diya*, in which case he was not entitled to his clan's aid.

The Banū Sāʿida (§6) had a *maʿqula* of their own.[87] (This may well have been true for all the groups listed here.) They only supported their members when the blood money amounted to one third or more of the *diya*; lesser injuries were paid for by the offender himself.[88] It is unlikely that the Sāʿida as a whole functioned as one *ʿāqila*, and hence the report deals with the *ʿāqila*s amidst the Sāʿida. Their practice regarding blood money could not have been different from that of the other Anṣārī clans.

---

afraḥatka] l-maghārimu. Mufdaḥ [!] means *lladhī qadaḥahu* [!] *l-dayn wa-athqalahu.* In another version *mufdaj* [!] is one who has nobody from his family to pay (blood money) for him (*lā aḥad yu'addī ʿanhu min ahlihi*); or one who committed a crime who has neither a clan nor agnates to pay the blood money and compensation for his offence (*al-jānī lladhī lā ʿashīra lahu wa-lā ʿāqila taʿqiluhu fa-tu'addī ʿanhu ʿaql jināyatihi wa-arsh jarīratihi*).

[85]Abū Dāwūd, *Marāsīl*, 29 (*bāb diyat al-dhimmī*; ← Zuhrī): *lammā* [*sic*] *balaghanā anna rasūla llāh ṣ qāla fī l-kitābi lladhī katabahu bayna quraysh wa-l-anṣār*: *lā yatrukūna muqraḥan* [!], *yuʿīnūnahu fī fikāk aw ʿaql. Qāla ʿabd al-razzāq*: *al-muqraḥu* [!] *lladhī yaqaʿu ʿalayhi l-ʿaql fī mālihi.* It is not clear why Zuhrī's report is included in the section dealing with the blood money of a *dhimmī*. The Arnāwūṭ edition of the *Marāsīl* (1988) does not have this tradition in the said section (215–17).

[86]The cases in which the *ʿāqila* was not held responsible are listed in a *ḥadīth* (← Shaʿbī); Abū ʿUbayd, *Gharīb*, IV, 445–46: *lā taʿqilu l-ʿāqila ʿamdan wa-lā ʿabdan wa-lā ṣulḥan wa-lā ʿtirāfan*; see *EI*², s.v. *ʿāḳila* (R. Brunschvig). In his interpretation Abū ʿUbayd uses an expression similar to ʿAbd al-Razzāq's: the compensation in such cases is paid for *fī māli l-jānī khāṣṣa*. Abū ʿUbayd goes on to explain: *ʿamdan* means that a deliberate offence that cannot be considered unintentional (*jināyat ʿamd laysat bi-khaṭa'*) is covered from the property of the offender himself; *ṣulḥ* means unintentional crimes (*al-jināyāt fī l-khaṭa'*) regarding which a settlement was reached between the parties; *iʿtirāf* means admitting, i.e. when a man admits to having committed a *jināya* without decisive proof being brought against him (*min ghayri bayyina taqūmu ʿalayhi*). Abū ʿUbayd adds: *wa-ini ddaʿā annahā khaṭa' lā yuṣaddaqu l-rajul ʿalā l-ʿāqila*. Finally, there is a dispute concerning the *ʿabd* category. One opinion has it that it relates to a *jināya* committed by a slave, while according to another opinion it concerns an offence committed against a slave. Although these cases are found in a legal context in the Umayyad period, they no doubt reflect tribal practice and hence are relevant for us here.

[87]Cf. the *maʿqula* of Quraysh, above, 42.

[88]Ibn Ḥazm, *Muḥallā*, XI, 53: *inna rasūla llāh ṣ allafa bayna l-nās fī maʿāqilihim fa-kānat banū sāʿida furādā ʿalā maʿqula yataʿāqalūna thultha l-diya fa-ṣāʿidan wa-yakūnu mā dūna dhālika ʿalā mani ktsaba wa-janā.*

In sum, the clause relates to offenders burdened by blood money that was to be paid from their own property, since for some reason they were not entitled to receive aid from their *ʿāqila*. The Mu'minūn are obliged to help such offenders. The clause introduces a novelty. Many Mu'minūn could no longer rely on their *ʿāqila*, especially when many of its members were still polytheists; the risk of being sold into slavery after causing a relatively minor injury was not a theoretical one.

§13. *wa-lā yuḥālifu mu'min mawlā mu'min dūnahu*

NO MU'MIN SHALL MAKE AN ALLIANCE WITH AN ALLY OF ANOTHER MU'MIN TO THE EXCLUSION OF THE LATTER.

Wellhausen (68): "Kein Gläubiger darf mit dem Beisassen eines anderen Gläubigen, ihm zuwider, eine Eidgenossenschaft eingehen". In a footnote Wellhausen renders *dūnahu*: "...so dass er sich dazwischen drängt, *ʿal panav*..."
Wensinck (53): "No believer shall enter into alliance with the client of a believer without the latter's consent".
Watt (222): "The believer does not take as confederate (*ḥalīf*) the client of a believer without his (the latter's) consent".
Serjeant (19): "A *Mu'min* will not make an alliance with the client/ally of a *Mu'min*, intervening between him/the latter".

The plural of *mawlā*, *mawālin*, appears later in the Kitāb four times (§§17, 28, 38 and 57). *Mawlā* in the Kitāb means an ally.

The clause appears to be connected to the *maʿāqil*: regarding blood feuds and related matters a Mu'min should not make an alliance with an ally of another Mu'min to the exclusion of that Mu'min.

The clause does not appear in Abū ʿUbayd's recension but is perhaps echoed in *ḥadīth*. Abū l-Zubayr[89] asked Jābir b. ʿAbdallāh about a man who makes an alliance (*yatawallā*) with an ally (*mawlā*) of another without the latter's consent, and Jābir referred to the Kitāb that forbade it.[90]

§14. *wa-inna l-mu'minīna l-muttaqīna ʿalā man baghā minhum awi btaghā dasīʿat ẓulm aw ithm aw ʿudwān aw fasād bayna l-mu'minīna wa-inna aydiyahum ʿalayhi jamīʿan wa-law kāna walad aḥadihim*

[89] Al-Makkī Muḥammad b. Muslim; *Tahdhīb al-kamāl*, XXVI, 402–11 no. 5602.

[90] Aḥmad, III, 342:18: *sa'altu jābiran ʿani l-rajul yatawallā mawlā l-rajul bi-ghayr idhnihi, fa-qāla: kataba rasūlu llāh ṣ ʿalā kull baṭn ʿuqūlahum, thumma kataba: innahu lā yaḥillu an yatawallā mawlā rajul muslim bi-ghayr idhnihi.*

THE GOD-FEARING MUʾMINŪN ARE AGAINST WHOSOEVER OF THEM DEMANDS AN EXCESSIVE SUM OF BLOOD MONEY OR DESIRES A GIFT OF INJUSTICE, SIN, TRANSGRESSION, OR EVIL AMONG THE MUʾMINŪN. THEY SHALL ALL UNITE AGAINST HIM EVEN IF HE IS THE SON OF ONE OF THEM.

Wellhausen (68): "Die Gläubigen, die Frommen, stehen wider den, der frevelt unter ihnen, oder einen Akt der Gewalt oder des Truges begeht, oder Feindschaft oder Unheil zwischen den Gläubigen stiftet; sie stehen mit vereinten Kräften insgesamt wider ihn, wäre er auch der Sohne eines von ihnen".
Wensinck (53–54): "The God-fearing believers [act] against those of them who cause an act of injustice or fraud or hostility or harm among the believers. Their hands are all against him even if he is the son of one of them".
Watt (222): "The God-fearing believers are against whoever of them acts wrongfully or seeks (? plans) an act that is unjust or treacherous or hostile or corrupt among the believers; their hands are all against him, even if he is the son of one of them".
Serjeant (19, 21–22): "The *Muʾminūn* who keep free of dishonourable acts are against (any) one of them who acts oppressively or/and (any one of them who) demands an unjust (i.e. forced) gift or (commits) crime/treachery, or an act of aggression, or (stirs) dissension among the *Muʾminūn*...".

The word *al-muttaqīna* also appears in §22 as an epithet of the Muʾminūn. The verb *ittaqā* appears in §63.[91]

This sanctions clause concludes a section dedicated to matters of blood money, and hence should be interpreted against this background.

The reading *baghā minhum* in Ibn Isḥāq seems superior to *baghā ʿalayhim* in some versions of Abū ʿUbayd's recension, since the clause concerns an action of the Muʾminūn against one of them who commits a transgression. This is borne out by the concluding passage of the clause, *wa-law kāna walad aḥadihim*, "even if he is the son of one of them".

Baghā has a specific meaning in the context of blood money. Zurqānī (IV, 168:27) correctly glosses *baghā* as *taʿaddā*, "went beyond what was right, acted unjustly". Before Yawm Sumayḥa, Mālik b. al-ʿAjlān (Khazraj),

[91]Only a Muʾmin who is also a *muttaqin* would act against his own son; an observation made by the student Hillel Wexler. In his commentary Zurqānī (IV, 168:27) refers to the seemingly superfluous *al-muttaqīna*. The clause, he says, refers to the condition of those who achieved perfection, because people who only attained *īmān* might commit a forbidden act: *wa-qayyada bi-l-muttaqīna ishāra ilā anna hādhihi ḥālatu l-kāmilīna fa-mani ttaṣafa bi-aṣli l-ʾīmān qad yartakibu l-ḥarām fa-yabghī wa-yukhālifu l-ḥudūd fa-yumnaʿu min dhālika.*

the then *sayyid* of the Aws and Khazraj, demanded that a free-born man (*ṣarīḥ*) from the ʿAmr b. ʿAwf be killed in retaliation for his client who had been killed by that free-born man. When this demand was turned down, he demanded ample compensation (i.e. a compensation due for a free-born man).[92] The ʿAmr b. ʿAwf agreed to give him what they regarded satisfactory compensation and asked him not to make excessive demands beyond what had been agreed upon between them (*innā nuʿṭīka l-riḍā min mawlāka... fa-khudh minnā ʿaqlahu wa-lā tabghi minnā ghayr mā kunnā ʿalayhi naḥnu wa-antum mina l-ḥaqq*). A free-born man could not be killed in retaliation for a client and the client's blood money was half that of a free-born man, they argued. When Mālik insisted, they blamed him for attempting to humiliate them and for making an excessive demand (*inna hādhā tadhallul minka lanā wa-baghy ʿalaynā*). In other words, *baghy* in the context of blood feuds means an excessive demand regarding blood money or retaliation.

Dasīʿa is "a wrongful, or tyrannical, pushing, or thrusting, or the like".[93] But *dasīʿa* also means a gift or a large gift, as in the phrase *ḍakhmu l-dasīʿa*, "one who grants generously" (said of the Prophet).[94] According to Zamakhsharī, *dasīʿat ẓulm* means *dasīʿa mina l-ẓulm*, a gift demanded from a party because it is being wronged or because of the oppressor's wrongdoing.[95]

Although the term could not be linked to blood money or a related matter, it seems that a compensation for death or injury larger than what was customary is meant here.

Derivatives of *ẓ-l-m* and *'-th-m* are also found in this order in the latter part of the Kitāb: *illā man ẓalama wa-athima* (§§28, 34 and 42); *wa-innahu lā yaḥūlu hādhā l-kitāb dūna ẓālim wa-āthim* (§61).[96]

ʿUdwān has a specific sense in the context of blood feuds. Both *ʿadā* and *iʿtadā* mean "to murder (the offender himself or a member of his *ʿāqila*) after having settled the affair peacefully", hence *ʿudwān* means a transgression of

---

[92]Ḥassān, *Dīwān*, II, 36–37: *...fa-innī ghayr tārikihi ḥatta aqtulahu aw arḍā min mawlāya.*

[93]Lane, I, 879c, s.v. *d-s-ʿ*.

[94]*Usd al-ghāba*, I, 101:4 (in a verse), s.v. Aṣyad b. Salama al-Sulamī.

[95]Zamakhsharī, *Fā'iq*, II, 26: *... ayi btaghā minhum an yadfaʿū ilayhi ʿaṭiyya ʿalā wajh ẓulmihim, ay kawnihim maẓlūmīna, aw aḍāfahā ilā ẓulmihi li-annahu sabab dafʿihim lahā.* See also Khushanī, 135: *wa-l-dasīʿa l-ʿaṭiyya wa-hiya mā yakhruju min ḥalqi l-baʿīr idhā raghā fa-staʿārahu hunā li-l-ʿaṭiyya wa-arāda bihi hunā mā yunālu ʿanhum* [read: *minhum*] *min ẓulm.*

[96]Cf. *wa-innahu lan ya'thama mru' bi-ḥalīfihi wa-inna l-naṣr li-l-maẓlūm* (§48).

tribal law or an excessive retaliation. One who suffers the death of a person from his *ʿāqila* or the amputation of a limb can either exact vengeance, or accept blood money, or forgive. If he wants to act differently (opting for "a fourth alternative"), he must be prevented from doing so. If he chooses one of the peaceful options and then transgresses the proper limit (*ʿadā*), i.e. kills the offender in retaliation, he will be in Hellfire forever.[97]

§15. *wa-lā yaqtulu muʾmin muʾminan fī kāfir wa-lā yanṣuru kāfiran ʿalā muʾmin*

A MUʾMIN WILL NOT KILL A MUʾMIN IN RETALIATION FOR A NON-BELIEVER AND WILL NOT AID A NON-BELIEVER AGAINST A MUʾMIN.[98]

Wellhausen (69): "Kein Gläubiger darf einen Gläubigen töten wegen eines Ungläubigen, noch einem Ungläubigen beistehen gegen einen Gläubigen".
Wensinck (54): "No believer shall kill a believer on account of an unbeliever; neither shall he help an unbeliever against a believer".
Watt (222): "A believer does not kill a believer because of an unbeliever, and does not help an unbeliever against a believer".
Serjeant (18, 22): "A *Muʾmin* will not slay a *Muʾmin* in (retaliation for) a *Kāfir* (disacknowledger, one who declares himself quit or free of), nor will he support a *Kāfir* against a *Muʾmin*". Regarding *kāfir* he refers to Abraham's address to his people, Qurʾān 60,4. "This of course is exactly the situation between Muḥammad and Quraysh of Mecca — his membership of their tribal group has been dissolved and he is at enmity with them".

The clause aimed at stopping the vicious cycle of killings in Medinan society by assuring the participating parties that the old accounts were sealed: every new slaying would be the killing of a fellow Mu'min for a *kāfir*, since those killed before Islam were of course *kuffār*. More significantly, the clause fur-

[97]See the prophetic *ḥadīth* in Aḥmad, IV, 31:-12: *man uṣība bi-dam aw khabal — al-khabalu l-jirāḥ — fa-huwa bi-l-khayār bayna iḥdā thalāth: immā an yaqtaṣṣa, aw yaʾkhudha l-ʿaql, aw yaʿfuwa, fa-in arāda rābiʿa fa-khudhū ʿalā yadayhi, fa-in faʿala shayʾan min dhālika, thumma ʿadā baʿdu fa-qatala, fa-lahu l-nār khālidan fīhā mukhalladan.* At the time of the Prophet a man killed the person who had murdered his brother after having received blood money for his brother: *... thumma ʿadā ʿalā qātil akhīhi fa-qatalahu*; Wāqidī, I, 407–408; Yāqūt, IV, 228b, s.v. Fāriʿ. See also *Fākhir*, 223:5: *biʾsa mā faʿaltum bi-qawmikum, qabiltumu l-diya wa-raḍītum, thumma ʿadawtum ʿalā bn ʿammikum wa-ṣihrikum wa-jārikum fa-qataltumūhu wa-ghadartum.* For the verb *iʿtadā* in this sense see Bakrī, I, 80: *wa-qālū lahum: iʿtadaytum yā qawmanā, akhadhtumu l-amwāl wa-qataltumu l-anfus.* The same is true of Qurʾān 2,178: *... kutiba ʿalaykumu l-qiṣāṣu fī l-qatlā... fa-mani ʿtadaā baʿdu fa-lahu ʿadhābun alīmun.* See also Ṭūsī, *Tahdhīb al-aḥkām*, X, 178–79.

[98]E.g. in exacting retaliation from a Mu'min.

ther strengthened the ties among the Mu'minūn themselves at the expense of their family members who had not yet become Mu'minūn. Muḥammad's goal was no doubt the unification of Medinan society, but during the interim period between the conclusion of the Kitāb and the full Islamization of Medina his tactics enhanced division rather than accord. If a Mu'min killed a *kāfir* whose brother was a Mu'min, the other Mu'min could no longer exact blood vengeance. This was a novelty in Medinan society; there was a total separation between Mu'minūn and *kuffār* with regard to blood vengeance.

The latter part of the clause prescribes that a Mu'min will not support a *kāfir* against a Mu'min, viz. he will not help him exact any form of retaliation against another Mu'min. Muḥammad was consistent in demanding physical separation between Mu'minūn and *kuffār*; the clause states this policy in terms of blood vengeance. In case of a dispute with a Mu'min, a *kāfir* could no longer rely on his relatives who were Mu'minūn. If the *ʿāqila* included many Mu'minūn, those who were still *kuffār* lost some of the guarantees for their physical security. There was no question of including the *kuffār*, still a strong element in Medinan society, in the *umma*.[99]

Beside *kāfir* we also find the term *mushrik* in §23. While the former is the opposite of Mu'min, be he Jewish, Christian or polytheist, the latter is strictly a polytheist.

§16. *wa-inna dhimmata llāh wāḥida, yujīru ʿalayhim adnāhum*[100]

THE PROTECTION OF ALLĀH [as extended by the Mu'minūn] IS UNVARYING, [and hence] THE LEAST OF THEM IS ENTITLED TO GRANT PROTECTION THAT IS BINDING FOR ALL OF THEM.

Wellhausen (69): "Die Schutzgemeinschaft Gottes ist eine einzige und allgemeine, die Schutzgewähr des Geringsten verpflichtet alle". He remarks: "Die dhimmat Allah (Schutzgemeinschaft Gottes) ist eine solidarische Einheit, in der Allah für jeden, und folgerecht jeder für den anderen eintritt".[101]
Wensinck (54): "The protection of Allah is one; the protection granted by the least of them is binding on all". He remarks that this relates to the least of the believers.
Watt (222): "The security of God is one; the granting of 'neighbourly protection' by the least of them (the believers) is binding on them".

[99] Cf. above, 49n.

[100] The clause does not exist in Abū ʿUbayd's recension.

[101] Similarly, Lichtenstaedter, "From Particularism to Unity", 259, renders: "The protection of Allāh is one and even the lowliest man by granting protection obliges every member to keep this obligation".

Serjeant (19): "The security of Allāh (for life and property) is one — the lowliest/least of them (the *Muʾminūn*, etc.) being (competent) to give protection on behalf of them (all)".
Gil (53–54) proposes another interpretation of this clause:

> The believers become each other's clients, and are the warrantors for the safety of any of them against the unbelievers. The new union of mutual responsibility is considered to be under the absolute protection of God, who makes no distinctions. The ambiguous formulation of this principle brought about some misinterpretations in modern translations. On the other hand, it is echoed in the *ḥadīth* sources in modified versions....
>
> The phrase *yujīru ʿalayhim* has Allāh as the subject. Weil's translation: *Und erstreckt sich über den geringsten* renders the meaning though it is not correct grammatically, taking *dhimmatu ʾllāhi* as the subject.

According to Gil, Watt's translation "is not correct, though inspired by the later well-known principle that every Muslim could grant protection to a *kāfir*". As to the "modified versions" in which the *ḥadīth* is echoed, they are the following: *dhimmatu l-muslimīna wāḥida* in Bukhārī "is obviously an alteration of the primary source, which is our document"; two sources add *yasʿā bihā adnāhum*; and in one source the phrase becomes: *yujīru ʿalā l-muslimīna adnāhum wa-yaruddu ʿalā l-muslimīna aqṣāhum.*

Gil concludes:

> *Dhimmatu ʾllāhi* should therefore be understood, as indeed it was, in the sense of a solidary union, protected by Allāh, who intervenes for the sake of everyone, and so does every man concerning his fellow. The old obligation of the clan to avenge the blood of its members is transferred to the new community, provided the blood was spilled for the sake of Allāh. Hence the obligation of the believers to pursue the killer of one of them, and no excuse could free them from this obligation. Later tradition has explained it as a statement of the solidarity of all Muslims against non-Muslims, and the reciprocal equality of blood and property: *yad al-muslimīna ʿalā man siwāhum, tatakāfaʾu dimāʾuhum wa-amwāluhum.*

Wāḥida means "the same".[102] When Shaʿbī heard that al-Ḥasan al-Baṣrī declared that the blood money for a slain Zoroastrian was 800 (*dirhams*), while that of a slain Jew or Christian was 4,000, he objected: *diyatuhumā wāḥida*.[103]

Adnāhum, and not Allāh, is the subject of *yujīru*. *Adnāhum* (plural *adānin* and *dawānin*), "the least of them" could mean a client.[104] *Ḥalīfuhumu l-adnā wa-jāru buyūtihim* (in a verse) is a man who attached himself as a client (*jāwara*) to a tribe that was not his own after having shed the blood of a fellow tribesman.[105]

An expression similar to *yujīru ʿalayhim adnāhum* appears in the story of the Prophet's return to Mecca after his fruitless attempt to win the Thaqīf over for the cause of Islam. He asked a Thaqafī living in Mecca, al-Akhnas b. Sharīq, to grant him protection, but the latter replied that a client of Quraysh could not grant security that was binding for the Quraysh themselves who, unlike their client al-Akhnas, were "of pure lineage". Then the Prophet asked Suhayl b. ʿAmr to protect him, but the latter replied that the Quraysh branch to which he belonged, the ʿĀmir b. Lu'ayy, could not grant security that was binding for the other Quraysh branch, namely the Kaʿb b. Lu'ayy. In both answers given to Muḥammad, *ajāra ʿalā* has exactly the same meaning as in the Kitāb: *inna ḥalīf quraysh lā yujīru ʿalā ṣamīmihā... inna banī ʿāmir b. lu'ayy lā tujīru ʿalā banī kaʿb b. lu'ayy*.[106] *Ajāra ʿalā banī fulān* means: he granted security in the name of the Banū so-and-so, that is to say, he granted security that was binding for them. It follows that *adnāhum* is the subject in the latter part of the clause.[107]

---

[102]Blau, "Arabic Lexicographical Miscellanies", 186.

[103]Ṭabarī, *Tafsīr*, V, 134:-6, interpretation of Qur'ān 4,92. *Qarābatuhum wāḥida* is said of one's daughters and one's brother's son, i.e. with regard to their entitlement to an inheritance they have the same relationship with the deceased; Ṭūsī, *Tahdhīb al-aḥkām*, IX, 323.

[104]It could also mean "the nearest to them", i.e. the one living next to them who enjoys their protection.

[105]*Aghānī*, X, 148:-6; *Aghānī* (Dār al-Kutub), XII, 17.

[106]Ibn Kathīr, *Bidāya*, III, 137 (← the *Maghāzī* of al-Umawī). Cf. Kister, "On Strangers and Allies in Mecca", 129. In another version to the same effect al-Akhnas said: *inna l-ḥalīf lā yujīru ʿalā l-ṣarīḥ*; Ibn al-Jawzī, *Muntaẓam*, III, 15. Al-Akhnas was a client (*ḥalīf mulḥaq*) of the Qurashī subdivision of Zuhra, and hence he was called *zanīm*, "one adopted among a people to whom he does not belong"; Qurṭubī, *Tafsīr*, XVIII, 235, interpretation of Qur'ān 68,14; Lane, I, 1259c, s.v. *z-n-m*.

[107]*Ajāra ʿalā* appears in Qur'ān, 23,88: ...*wa-huwa yujīru wa-lā yujāru ʿalayhi*, but *ʿalayhi* here means "from him"; see Harawī, *Gharībayni*, I, 418: *ay yu'amminu man akhāfahu ghayruhu, wa-man akhāfahu huwa lam yu'amminhu aḥad*.

The clause is extraordinary in that it comprises two seemingly disassociated parts, each having a different subject: Allāh, followed by *adnāhum*. However, the link between *dhimma* and *yujīru* is clear. Admittedly, *dhimmatu l-muʾminīna* instead of *dhimmatu llāhi* would have made for a smoother clause;[108] in addition, in the *ḥadīth* literature we find *dhimmatu l-muslimīna*. But all the versions of the Kitāb checked so far have *dhimmatu llāhi*.

It is noteworthy that in versions of a certain prophetic *ḥadīth* that includes the latter part of the clause, *adnāhum* is replaced by *aḥaduhum* or *baʿḍuhum* or *al-rajul minhum*.[109] These versions avoid the somewhat difficult *adnāhum*.

§17. *wa-inna l-muʾminīna baʿḍuhum mawālī baʿḍ dūna l-nās*

THE MUʾMINŪN ARE EACH OTHER'S ALLIES TO THE EXCLUSION OF OTHER PEOPLE.

Wellhausen (69): "Die Gläubigen sind sich gegenseitig zu Schutz verpflichtet gegen die Menschen".
Wensinck (54): "The believers protect each other to the exclusion of [other] people".
Watt (222): "The believers are patrons (or clients — *mawālī*) of one another to the exclusion of (other) people".
Serjeant (19): "The *Muʾminūn*, some are allies/clients of others to the exclusion of the people (i.e. other people)".

Mawlā in the Kitāb is an ally.[110] *Walī* (§24) means a member of one's *ʿāqila* or an agnate. *Mawālin* are not agnates — the Mu'minūn did not form one big *ʿāqila*. §21 demands the Mu'minūn to secure full retaliation for one of them, but this does not turn them into an *ʿāqila*. *Mawālin* also appears in the second part of the Kitāb or the treaty of the Jews: *wa-inna yahūd*

[108] Cf. §19: *wa-inna silma l-muʾminīna wāḥida, lā yusālimu muʾmin dūna muʾmin....* *Silm... wāḥida* is comparable to *dhimma ... wāḥida*, but of course in §19 *al-muʾminīna...* is followed by *muʾmin... muʾmin.*

[109] *Majmaʿ al-zawāʾid*, V, 329; Ibn Abī Shayba, *Muṣannaf*, XII, 451–52, 455 nos. 15234-36, 15244; Aḥmad, V, 250:28.

[110] A possible echo of this clause can be found in a saying ascribed to the Prophet (← Jarīr b. ʿAbdallāh): *al-muhājirūn wa-l-anṣār baʿḍuhum awliyāʾ baʿḍ fī l-dunyā wa-l-ākhira wa-l-ṭulaqāʾ min quraysh wa-l-ʿutaqāʾ min thaqīf baʿḍuhum awliyāʾ baʿḍ fī l-dunyā wa-l-ākhira*; Ṭabarānī, *Kabīr*, II, 309 no. 2284. In another version of this saying (313 no. 2302, 314 no. 2310) the Anṣār are missing. The late conversion of most of the Qurashīs and all of the Thaqafīs was a blemish that could never be removed.

banī ʿawf mawāliyahum wa-anfusahum (§28); *wa-inna mawāliya thaʿlaba ka-anfusihim* (§38); obviously, these *mawālī* cannot be agnates.[111]

§18. *wa-innahu man tabiʿanā min yahūd fa-inna lahu l-naṣr wa-l-uswa, ghayr maẓlūmīna wa-lā mutanāṣar ʿalayhim*

THE JEWS WHO JOIN US AS CLIENTS WILL RECEIVE AID AND EQUAL RIGHTS; THEY WILL NOT BE WRONGED, NOR WILL THEIR ENEMIES BE AIDED AGAINST THEM.

Wellhausen (69): "Die Juden, die uns folgen, bekommen Hilfe und Beistand; es geschieht ihnen kein Unrecht und ihre Feinde werden nicht unterstützt".
Wensinck (54): "Whoever of the Jews follow us [receive] help and support without being wronged and without the one helping the other against them". Regarding the word "follow" he remarks: "I.e., follow our policy", and regarding "support" (*uswa*) he mentions that it actually means consolation. He adds with reference to the Qurʾān: "The word is also used in the meaning of example. Muhammad is a good example for the community, *uswa ḥasana*".
Watt (222): "Whoever of the Jews follows us has the (same) help and support (as the believers), so long as they are not wronged (by him) and he does not help (others) against them".
Serjeant (19, 22): "Whoever of the Jews (Yahūd) follows us shall have support/what is customary, and parity, not undergoing injustice and no mutual support being given against them". He remarks: "To 'follow' indicates that the Jews were in a subordinate position to the Yathrib tribes, but it does not necessarily indicate inferiority. They are indeed to have parity".
Gil (63) remarks:

> The Jews are first mentioned in the clauses which proclaim the *dhimmatu ʾllāhi* and the community of believers. Here we read

[111] *Mawlā* in the sense of ally is attested in interpretations of Qurʾān, 4,33: ... *wa-li-kullin jaʿalnā mawāliya*. For many meanings of the word (including *ḥalīf* in the sense of ally) see *Fatḥ al-bārī*, VIII, 186, in connection with this verse. (Ibn Ḥajar shows that this is one of the cases in which "Maʿmar" mentioned in Bukhārī is Abū ʿUbayda Maʿmar b. al-Muthannā and not Maʿmar b. Rāshid; see also Lecker, "Biographical Notes on Abū ʿUbayda Maʿmar b. al-Muthannā", 92 n. 83.) With reference to the same verse the exegete Ibn Zayd explains how the non-Arabs who attached themselves to Muslims became known by the term which before Islam (but not in the Kitāb!) denoted members of the *ʿaṣaba*. It was inspired, he says, by the Qurʾān: *al-mawālī l-ʿaṣaba, hum kānū fī l-jāhiliyya l-mawālī, fa-lammā dakhalati l-ʿajam ʿalā l-ʿarab lam yajidū lahumu sman, fa-qāla llāh: fa-in lam taʿlamū ābāʾahum fa-ikhwānukum fī l-dīn wa-mawālīkum* (Qurʾān 33,5), *fa-summū l-mawāliya....*

> a general promise of concern for the welfare of those Jews "who will follow us" (*man tabiʿanā*). We have seen that the document is addressed to "those who follow, adhere to, and strive with" the Muslims. There is no reason why we should understand it in any meaning but the plain one. Those among the Jews who will accept Islam will enjoy the Prophet's "help and favour". It can by no means be considered a promise of safety to Jews who wish to keep their faith. The document makes no special promise regarding the Jews, and therefore no change for the worse in Muḥammad's attitude towards the Jews can be alleged.

As already argued,[112] *tabiʿa* means "he became someone's client". The clause relates to Jews who choose to become clients. For this reason it is located amidst clauses dealing with the Mu'minūn and not in the second part of the Kitāb or the treaty of the Jews. The Jews who were to become clients were not expected to embrace Islam, since there was no need for a separate clause dealing with Muslims who were former Jews.

As in §20 we have here the first-person plural (*tabiʿanā*, not *tabiʿa l-mu'minīna*). The main contracting parties, namely the Mu'minūn and Muslimūn, are meant here with reference to their relations with foreign elements.[113] Although the clause mentions Jews, it does not signal the beginning of the treaty of the Jews, and hence the mention of Jews at this place cannot be used as an argument against the unity of the Kitāb.

Naṣr and *uswa* that are guaranteed to the potential Jewish clients correspond to *ghayr maẓlūmīna wa-lā mutanāṣar ʿalayhim*, in reverse order.[114]

Naṣr in agreements between masters and clients signifies the securing of the client's rights in connection with revenge and blood money. This is also the context of *naṣr* in §15: *wa-lā yaqtulu mu'min mu'minan fī kāfir wa-lā yanṣuru kāfiran ʿalā mu'min*, where *naṣr* is linked to the *kāfir*'s claims regarding blood vengeance. *Nuṣra* is the mutual help among the members

---

[112] Above, 45.

[113] Above, 41.

[114] On this parallelism see above, 43. *Naṣr* and *maẓlūm* can be found in §48 that also deals with clients.

of the *ʿāqila* in carrying the burden of blood money.[115] Sometimes *uswa* means parity.[116]

In sum, the terms *naṣr* and *uswa* typically appear in agreements between clients and their masters and are also used regarding alliances between groups.

§19. *wa-inna silma l-mu'minīna wāḥida lā yusālimu mu'min dūna mu'min fī qitāl fī sabīli llāh illā ʿalā sawāʾ wa-ʿadl baynahum*

THE PEACE OF THE MU'MINŪN IS UNVARYING, [and hence] A MU'MIN WILL NOT MAKE PEACE TO THE EXCLUSION OF ANOTHER MU'MIN IN FIGHTING IN THE CAUSE OF ALLĀH, EXCEPT ON THE BASIS OF EQUALITY AND EQUITY BETWEEN THEM.

Wellhausen (69): "Der Friede der Gläubigen ist ein einziger und allgemeiner; kein Gläubiger kann für sich, mit Ausschluss eines anderen Gläubigen, Friede schliessen im Kampfe für Gottes Sache; sondern die Bedingungen müssen für alle gleich sein".

Wensinck (54–55): "The peace of the believers is one. No peace shall be made with a believer apart from an[other] believer when there is fighting

[115] Qurṭubī, *Tafsīr*, V, 321:2, interpretation of Qur'ān 4,92: *wa-ajmaʿa ahlu l-siyar wa-l-ʿilm anna l-diya kānat fī l-jāhiliyya taḥmiluhā l-ʿāqila fa-aqarrahā rasūlu llāhi ṣ fī l-islām, wa-kānū yataʿāqalūna bi-l-nuṣra, thumma jā'a l-islām fa-jarā l-amr ʿalā dhālika ḥattā jaʿala ʿumaru l-dīwān.*

[116] See ʿUmar b. al-Khaṭṭāb's instructions to his governors in Syria concerning the new Persian recruits (*al-ḥamrā'*): ... *fa-jʿalūhum uswatakum fī l-ʿaṭā' wa-l-maʿrūf*; Abū ʿUbayd, *Amwāl*, 300–36 no. 572. Cf. Abū ʿUbayd, *Gharīb*, III, 485. See also Yaʿqūbī, *Ta'rīkh*, II, 175: ʿUthmān lowered ʿĀ'isha's allowance, *wa-ṣayyarahā uswat ghayrihā min nisā' rasūli llāh.* It is comparable with another derivative of the same root, *mu'āsāt*, or the sharing with another, the making of another to share with one in the means of subsistence; also the being, or becoming, equal with another; Lane, I, 60b, s.v. *'-s-w*. *Mu'āsāt* and *nuṣra* are attested in the context of a pre-Islamic clientage: *wa-lladhīna ʿaqadat aymānukum fa-'ātūhum naṣībahum* (Qur'ān 4,33): *ammā ʿāqadat aymānukum fa-l-ḥilf, kāna l-rajul fī l-jāhiliyya yanzilu fī l-qawm fa-yuḥālifūnahu ʿalā annahu minhum yuwāsūnahu bi-anfusihim, fa-idhā kāna lahum ḥaqq aw qitāl kāna mithlahum, wa-idhā kāna lahu ḥaqq aw nuṣra khadhalūhu. Fa-lammā jā'a l-islām sa'alū ʿanhu wa-abā llāhu illā an yushaddidahu. Wa-qāla rasūlu llāhi ṣ: lam yazidi l-islāmu l-ḥulafā' illā shidda*; Ṭabarī, *Tafsīr*, V, 35:23 (← al-Suddī). *Tanāṣur* and *mu'āsāt* appear in connection with the treaty between the Prophet's grandfather ʿAbd al-Muṭṭalib and the Khuzāʿa: ... *taḥālafū ʿalā l-tanāṣur wa-l-muwāsāt...*; *Wath.*, 274 no. 171 (later in that document we find *ʿalā ʿabdi l-muṭṭalibi l-nuṣra lahum... wa-ʿalā khuzāʿa l-nuṣra li-ʿabdi l-muṭṭalib...*). See also Ḥassān, *Dīwān*, II, 18.

in the way of Allah. However, [peace must be concluded] on the basis of mutual equality and justice".[117]
Watt (222): "The peace of the believers is one; no believer makes peace apart from another believer, where there is fighting in the way of God, except in so far as equality and justice between them (is maintained)".
Serjeant (19): "The peace that the *Mu'minūn* make is one. No *Mu'min* will make peace to the exclusion of/separately from a *Mu'min* in fighting in the path of Allāh, if it be not on the basis of equity and justice/fair dealing between them".

The expression *ʿalā sawāʾ* is connected elsewhere to the termination of a treaty. When one party wishes to end it, it must not attack the other party before informing it that the treaty is no longer in force. It is done *ʿalā sawāʾ* or "on the basis of equality", that is to say, both parties should be on equal grounds regarding their knowledge of the fact that the treaty has been terminated.[118] This should prevent one party from assaulting the other while the latter still believes that the treaty is valid. Muʿāwiya intended to attack the Byzantines, with whom he had a treaty (*ʿahd*). While he was advancing in their territory, a Companion of the Prophet protested, quoting the Prophet's saying: "He who has a treaty with some party must not terminate it (literally: untie a knot) until he renounces it (literally: casts it off), so that both parties to the treaty are equal to each other" (*ʿalā sawāʾ*, i.e. in the knowledge that the treaty is no longer valid).[119]

The Kitāb takes into account the possibility that a Mu'min will make peace to the exclusion of another Mu'min while they are engaged in fighting in the cause of Allāh; he is allowed to make peace (and cease fighting) provided he abides by certain generally acknowledged rules.

---

[117] Lichtenstaedter, "From Particularism to Unity", 259, renders: "The conclusion of peace is binding upon all the believers; no believer may conclude peace for himself excluding the other believers who are fighting for the cause of Allāh".

[118] *Zād al-maʿād*, IV, 20: ...*lā yanhaḍu ilayhim wa-yuḥāribuhum ḥattā yuʿlimahum ʿalā sawāʾ, li-yastawū hum wa-huwa fī l-ʿilm bi-naqḍi l-ʿahd.*

[119] Abū ʿUbayd, *Amwāl*, 212 no. 448: *man kāna baynahu wa-bayna qawm ʿahd fa-lā yaḥullu ʿuqda ḥattā yanbidha ilayhim ʿalā sawāʾ*. For another version of this report see Abū Dāwūd, *Sunan*, II, 75–76. A clause in the treaty of the Nubians (in 31/652) refers to its breach by them, in which case *fa-qad bariʾat minkum hādhihi l-hudna wa-l-amān wa-naḥnu wa-antum ʿalā sawāʾ ḥattā yaḥkuma llāh baynanā wa-huwa khayru l-ḥākimīna*; *Wath.*, 531 no. 369. See also Qur'ān 8,58: ...*fa-nbidh ilayhim ʿalā sawāʾin.*

§20. *wa-inna kull ghāziya ghazat maʿanā yaʿqubu baʿḍuhā baʿḍan*

EACH RAIDING PARTY THAT RAIDS WITH US WILL TAKE TURNS WITH EACH OTHER.

Wellhausen (69): "Bei jeder Truppe, die mit uns zu Felde zieht, lässt einer den andern wechseln", to which he remarks, referring to Ibn Hishām: "Nämlich im Reiten, wenn nicht jeder ein Reittier hat; s. das Verzeichnis der Leute, die bei Badr sich in je ein Kamel teilen mussten".
Wensinck (55): "In every expedition made with us the parties shall take turns with one another".
Watt (222): "In every expedition made with us the parties take turns with one another". He adds: "This may apply to taking turns at riding a camel, or to all military duties".
Serjeant (19, 22): "Each raiding party which raids along with us — one shall succeed another". He remarks: "One patrol is to relieve another by turns so that none is on duty permanently". He refers to the interpretation found in a *ḥadīth* dictionary (which, however, quotes the clause without the preposition *maʿanā* — it is also missing in Abū ʿUbayd's recension): *ay yakūnu l-ghazw baynahum nuwaban fa-idhā kharajat ṭā'ifa thumma ʿādat lam tukallaf an taʿūda thāniyatan ḥattā taʿqubahā ukhrā ghayruhā.*[120]

Zamakhsharī says that the feminine noun *ghāziya* indicates the horses while referring to their riders.[121] The clause, he says, decrees that the raiders should take turns; he who returns will not have to set out again until his next turn arrives.[122] The same tactic was practiced by ʿUmar b. al-Khaṭṭāb, who would send out raiders in turns.[123]

The first-form plural in *maʿanā* shows that the clause concerns the relations between the main contracting parties and foreign elements. The clause

[120]Ibn al-Athīr, *Nihāya*, III, 267, s.v. *ʿ-q-b*.

[121]Hence *baʿḍuhum* in Abū ʿUbayd; Ibn Isḥāq has *baʿḍuhā*.

[122]*Fā'iq*, II, 26: *inna ʿalā l-ghuzāt an yatanāwabū wa-lā yukallafu man yaqfulu l-khurūj ilā an tajī'a nawbatuhu.*

[123]*Kāna yuʿqibu bayna l-ghuzāt...*; Ibn Saʿd, III, 306. Similarly, *Lisān al-ʿarab*, I, 614, s.v. *ʿ-q-b*: *wa-minhu ḥadīth ʿumar annahu kāna yuʿaqqibu l-juyūsh fī kull ʿām.* Both the second and the fourth forms have the same meaning; *Manāl al-ṭālib*, 231: *wa-l-taʿqīb wa-l-iʿqāb min ʿaqqabtu l-ghuzāt wa-aʿqabtuhum idhā jaʿaltu l-ghazw baynahum nuwaban mutaʿāqiba qawman baʿda qawm.* For *ʿuqba* in the sense of taking turns on a riding beast see *Usd al-ghāba*, V, 77:11, s.v. Wāthila b. al-Asqaʿ: in the expedition of Tabūk a warrior without a beast received from another an equal share in his beast in return for the former's share in the spoils: *anā aḥmiluka ʿuqba bi-l-layl wa-yaduka uswat yadī wa-lī sahmuka.* This, however, is irrelevant for us here.

assures these unspecified groups that the military burden of raiding "with us" will not be assigned unequally.

§21. *wa-inna l-muʾminīna yubīʾu baʿḍuhum ʿan baʿḍ bi-mā nāla dimāʾahum fī sabīli llāh*

THE MUʾMINŪN WILL FULLY RETALIATE ON EACH OTHER'S BEHALF IN THE CASE OF DEATH OR INJURY INCURRED WHILE FIGHTING IN THE CAUSE OF ALLĀH.[124]

Wellhausen (69): "Die Gläubigen sind einer des anderen Bluträcher in betreff ihres für Gottes Sache vergossen Blutes".
Wensinck (55): "The believers exact vengeance for the blood of one another [that is shed] in the way of Allah".
Watt (222–23): "The believers exact vengeance for one another where a man gives his blood in the way of God".
Serjeant (19, 22): "The *Muʾminūn* — one of them will slay on behalf of another in retaliation for what harms their blood in the path of Allāh". He comments: "The whole *ummah* confederation is responsible for avenging any of its members killed by parties outside it".

Abāʾa appears with the prepositions *ʿan* and *ʿalā*, but the former seems preferable, in the sense of "on behalf" (of another Muʾmin). The root *b-w-ʾ* denotes "parity, equity". *Bawāʾ* means *sawāʾ*. The shares in the booty of the Qurayẓa were *bawāʾ*, i.e. equal.[125] Tribal custom demanded that retaliation for a murder be exacted against one who is of the same status as the victim. The killing of a slave was not considered full retaliation for the murder of a free-born man. Sometimes even the slaying of a free-born man was not considered full retaliation; many were killed in retaliation for several. Ṭufayl al-Ghanawī boasted: "We have fully avenged our dead by killing double their number from the enemy tribe in addition to capturing innumerable tied up captives".[126] A man who avenged his brother's murder by killing the murderer declared that it was not a satisfactory revenge: "I said to him: 'May your death be a compensation for the death of a man

[124]The clause is not found in Abū ʿUbayd.

[125]Wāqidī, II, 522: *wa-kānati l-suhmān yawmaʾidhin bawāʾan.* Surprisingly, Khushanī, 135, has at this point: *wa-yubīʾu: yamnaʿu wa-yakuffu.*

[126]*Abaʾnā bi-qatlānā mina l-qawmi ḍiʿfahum wa-mā lā yuʿaddu min asīrin mukallabi*; Abū ʿUbayd, *Gharīb*, II, 252. Caskel renders the expression *buʾ bi-dam fulān*: "sei gleichwertig dem Blute des..."; see his review of H. Lammens, *L'Arabie occidentale avant l'Hégire*, in *Orientalische Literaturzeitung* 1931, 970.

like whom you are not although the taking of your life is [otherwise] sufficient for one seeking revenge' ".[127] "The appeasing revenge" (*al-tha'ru l-munīm*) is a sufficient one or, according to another version, a revenge following which one sleeps peacefully.[128] The Qurayẓa and Naḍīr wanted Muḥammad to arbitrate between them according to the differences in status (*tafāḍul*) between their dead. The Prophet refused, declaring *al-qatlā bawā'*, glossed as *sawā'*.[129]

All this leads to the conclusion that *abā'a* is not merely "to retaliate" but "to exact full retaliation" by killing a man who is of the same status as the slain one.

Alternatively, the clause could indicate that the Mu'minūn have the same status with regard to retaliation or blood money.[130] But it appears that in the context of the Kitāb the free-born Mu'min is assured that full revenge will be exacted for him should he be killed while fighting in the cause of Allāh.

The retaliation for one's death is usually the duty of his *ʿāqila*. The Kitāb does not abolish the *ʿāqila* and the Mu'minūn do not form one *ʿāqila*. But some Mu'minūn whose *ʿāqila* still included many polytheists needed to be assured that should their blood be shed in the cause of Allāh, full retaliation would be exacted by their fellow Mu'minūn.

§22. *wa-inna l-mu'minīna l-muttaqīna ʿalā aḥsan hādhā*[131] *wa-aqwamihi*

THE GOD-FEARING MU'MINŪN GUARANTEE THE BEST AND MOST UPRIGHT FULFILMENT OF THIS [treaty].

---

[127] Abū 'Ubayd, *Gharīb*, II, 251–52: *fa-qultu lahu bu' bi-mri'in lasta mithlahu wa-in kunta qunʿānan li-man yaṭlubu l-damā*. Abū 'Ubayd comments on this: *yaqūlu*: *anta, wa-in kunta fī ḥasabika maqnaʿan li-kull man ṭalabaka bi-tha'rihi fa-lasta mithl akhī*.

[128] *Lisān al-ʿarab*, IV, 98–99, s.v. *th-'-r*: *wa-l-tha'ru l-munīmu*: *lladhī yakūnu kufu'an li-dam waliyyika*; ... *al-tha'ru l-munīmu*: *lladhī idhā aṣābahu l-ṭālib raḍiya bihi fa-nāma baʿdahu*.

[129] *Gharā'ib al-qur'ān*, VI, 159 (← Muqātil), interpretation of Qur'ān 5,50. See the same expression in Ḥassān, *Dīwān*, II, 42; also 46 (it is said of the dead: *fa-bāwa'ū bihim*, or they considered them equal).

[130] *Nūr al-Nibrās*, I, 649, says regarding this clause: *yaʿnī anna dimā'ahum mutakāfi'a, yuqālu mā fulān bi-bawā' li-fulān ay bi-kuf' lahu*.

[131] *Hudan* in some versions is erroneous: the expression *aḥsan hudan* is suspect since it suggests that there are grades of *hudan*. Abū 'Ubayd's recension and some versions of Ibn Isḥāq's recension have here *hādhā*. Unlike the proposition *ʿalā* in §14, this *ʿalā* is similar to the one in §§43, 53 and 60.

Wellhausen (69): "Die Gläubigen, die Frommen, folgen der besten und richtigsten Leitung".
Wensinck (55): "The God-fearing believers are under the best and most correct guidance".
Watt (223): "The God-fearing believers are under the best and most correct guidance".
Serjeant (19): "The *Mu'minūn* who keep free of dishonourable acts and offences are (following) the best and truest guidance/way".

§23. *wa-innahu lā yujīru mushrik mālan li-quraysh wa-lā nafsan wa-lā yaḥūlu dūnahu ʿalā muʾmin*

A POLYTHEIST WILL NOT GRANT PROTECTION TO ANY PROPERTY[132] OR TO ANY PERSON OF QURAYSH, NOR WILL HE INTERVENE BETWEEN THEM [viz. the property or person] AND A MUʾMIN.[133]

Wellhausen (69): "Kein Heide darf weder die Habe noch die Person eines Quraischiten in Schutz nehmen und nicht seinetwegen einem Gläubingen entgegentreten". He adds: "Das Beste wäre, die Mediner wären alle gläubig; leider gibt es aber noch Heiden unter ihnen. Diese werden nun nicht aus ihren Geschlechtern und aus der Gemeinde exkommunicirt, sondern bleiben darin und behalten ihre Rechte. Aber das Recht der Igâra, das ihnen übrigens nicht genommen wird, dürfen sie nicht ausüben in bezug auf die Quraisch, die erklärten Feinde Gottes und der Gemeinde".
Wensinck (55): "No polytheist may grant protection to the property or person of Quraysh, neither shall he protect him against a believer".
Watt (223): "No idolator gives 'neighbourly protection' for goods or person of Quraysh, nor intervenes in his (a Qurashī's) favour against a believer".
Serjeant (24): "No Polytheist will grant protection to property belonging to Quraysh, or person; nor will he intervene between him against a *Muʾmin*". He adds: "Quraysh means the *Muhājirūn* and *Mushrik* means those Polytheists at Yathrib — who are forbidden to mediate in a dispute between Quraysh *Muhājirūn* and Yathrib *Muʾminūn*".

This is the only mention of *mushrik* in the Kitāb. Elsewhere there is mention of *kāfir* in the sense of non-believer, be he Jewish, Christian or polytheist. The *mushrikūn* or polytheists, precisely like the *kuffār*, were not part of the Kitāb.

---

[132] *Māl* is usually translated in this monograph "orchard".
[133] Abū ʿUbayd's recension differs considerably: ... *wa-lā yuʿīnuhā ʿalā muʾmin.*

Quraysh were mentioned above twice (§§1, 3) as participants. However, in this clause and in §54 where the tone is hostile to Quraysh, the Quraysh of Mecca are referred to.[134]

The clause warns the polytheists that the Mu'minūn will not respect the guarantee of security they grant to the Qurashīs and their goods. A polytheist granting such protection risks confiscation or capture by a Mu'min (who might be the polytheist's brother or cousin).[135] The property in question is probably merchandise; there were close trading links between Mecca and Medina before the advent of Islam.[136] This further weakens the family ties between the Mu'minūn and their polytheist relatives: should a polytheist do business with a Qurashī, his Mu'min relative (and indeed any Mu'min) was at liberty to seize the property and capture the person involved. According to §54, not only the *mushrikūn* were prohibited from sheltering Quraysh, but also the Jews.

The phrase *ḥāla dūna* (see also §61) means to intervene between something or someone and one who wants to take or harm it or him.

§24. *wa-innahu mani ʿtabaṭa muʾminan qatlan ʿan bayyina fa-innahu qawad yad*[137] *illā an yarḍā waliyyu l-maqtūl wa-inna l-muʾminīna ʿalayhi kāffa wa-lā yaḥillu lahum illā qiyām ʿalayhi*

SHOULD ANYONE MURDER A MUʾMIN ARBITRARILY, AND SHOULD UNDISPUTED EVIDENCE OF THIS MURDER EXIST, HE WILL BE SLAIN IN RETALIATION, UNLESS THE AGNATIC KIN OF THE DECEASED IS APPEASED [with blood money]. ALL THE MUʾMINŪN ARE [united] AGAINST HIM AND IT IS NOT PERMISSIBLE TO THEM NOT TO ACT AGAINST HIM.

Wellhausen (70): "Wenn jemand einen Gläubigen mordet und überführt wird, so findet Talio statt, es sei denn, dass sich der Anwalt des Getöteten (mit Sühngeld) zufrieden gibt. Die sämtlichen Gläubigen müssen wider den Mörder stehen, sie dürfen nicht anders als gegen ihn Partei nehmen".[138]

---

[134] Abū ʿUbayd has at this point: ... *wa-lā yuʿīnuhā ʿalā muʾmin.*

[135] Cf. Denny, "*Ummah* in the Constitution of Medina", 43: "'Quraysh' designates the Emigrants.... Later [i.e. later in the Kitāb], however, Quraysh means the enemies of Muḥammad from Mecca..., who are not to receive 'neighbourly protection.'

[136] Lecker, "*Yahūd/ʿUhūd*", 175–76, 178–81.

[137] Some versions have *bihi.*

[138] Wellhausen's considered this clause an important step towards the transfer of criminal retribution from the family to the state, but his argument was criticized by Bravmann, *Spiritual Background*, 315–34. Bravmann wrote (332–33): "The person convicted of a crime (especially of the crime of homicide) is, according to early Arab consuetudinary law, surrendered by the community, even by his own kin, to the rightful avengers of the

Wensinck (55): "When evidence has been given that someone killed a believer then he is killed in retaliation for him unless the person entitled to revenge is satisfied [with blood-wite]. The believers are against him as one man. They must take action only against him".
Watt (223): "When anyone wrongfully kills a believer, the evidence being clear, then he is liable to be killed in retaliation for him, unless the representative of the murdered man is satisfied (with a payment). The believers are against him (the murderer) entirely; nothing is permissible to them except to oppose him".
Serjeant (24): "Whosoever kills a *Mu'min* without any transgression on the part of the latter, proof (against the murderer) being shown, shall be slain in retaliation for him, unless the next of kin to the murdered man consent to (accept) the blood money".[139]
Gil (54) remarks: "The root *ʿbṭ*... contains the idea of unrestrained and arbitrary force, as in Ethiopic".[140]

---

crime, so that they may 'lead' him away in order to kill him". — But of course the involvement of the Mu'minūn as a unified body is a novelty introduced by Muḥammad — M. L. The expression *bi-ghayr bayyina* appears in connection with one of the Aws and Khazraj wars, namely the Sumayr war. Wellhausen doubted that blood feuds of the kind involved in that war were submitted to juridical procedures in Medina ("Der Beweis setzt ein Gericht voraus, wenn auch nur ein frei vereinbartes Schiedsgericht. Aber schwerlich wurde im alten Medina solch ein Fall vor Gericht gebracht und der überwiesene Mörder ausgeliefet"). But his claim was refuted by Bravmann, who showed that the story specifically mentions arbiters, and observed: "The participation of judges in the solution of talio-cases however necessarily implies a juridical procedure based on evidence, in agreement with what is expressly stated in the report concerning the Sumayr-affair.... [T]he application of... *qiṣāṣ* (or *qawad*) was also in pre-Islamic time basically dependent on juridical evidence, which in cases of complicated, or unclear character — as in the Sumayr-feud — was normally (or in any case: frequently) supervised by an arbiter (we may also say: judge, Arabic *ḥakam*), who passed his judgment... on the basis of evidence"; *ibid.*, 326–39.

[139]Serjeant quotes Abū ʿUbayd's interpretation of *iʿtibāṭ*: *an yaqtulahu bariyyan muḥarrama l-dam*; *Amwāl*, 264 no. 518. The opposite of *ʿan bayyina* is *ʿan shakk*; *Aghānī*, XX, 69; *Aghānī* (Dār al-Kutub), XXIII, 147:17. "The burden of proof (by testimony) lies upon the one who makes the allegation and the oath belongs to him who denies"; Wāqidī, II, 837:2 (*wa-l-bayyina ʿalā mani ddaʿā wa-l-yamīn ʿalā man ankara* — from the Prophet's speech at the Farewell Pilgrimage); EI^2, s.v. *bayyina* (R. Brunschwig).

[140]Schacht (EI^2, s.v. *ḳiṣāṣ*) writes: "In the so-called constitution of the community at Medina, which belongs to the early Medinan period, it is laid down that if any one slays a believer and is convicted (proof of guilt in a trial before the authority — Muḥammad — is therefore required as a condition for the carrying out of *ḳiṣāṣ*), talion takes place *even if* [italics added — M. L.] the avenger of the blood of the slain man declares himself satisfied; all believers must be against the murderer and must take an active part against

Iʿtabaṭa means to slaughter a sheep or a camel that do not suffer from any disease.[141] The slaughter of a healthy or young animal was considered an act of lavish generosity; a host did it to feed his guests and poets would sing his praise.[142]

The clause attempts to prevent the settlement of accounts left open from the Jāhilī period. The victim is one killed *bi-lā jināya* or without having committed a crime requiring retaliation.[143]

Although *qawad bihi* is attested,[144] the obscure *qawad yad* is preferable, being the *lectio difficilior*. Furthermore, an almost identical clause is found in a letter of the Prophet. Dārimī adduces this clause from the Prophet's letter to the people of Yemen (... Zuhrī ← Abū Bakr b. Muḥammad b. ʿAmr b. Ḥazm ← his father ← his grandfather): *anna rasūla llāhi kataba ilā ahli l-yaman, wa-kāna fī kitābihi: inna mani ʿtabaṭa mu'minan qatlan ʿan bayyina*[145] *fa-innahu qawad yadayhi, illā an yarḍā awliyā'u l-maqtūl.*[146] The phrases *qawadu l-yad* and *qawad yadayhi*, respectively, appear in two *ḥadīths* in which they are linked to *ʿamd* as opposed to *khaṭa'*.[147] The phrase

him. Here the *kiṣāṣ* is brought from the sphere of tribal life into that of the religious-political community (*umma*), which finds an echo in the law, not however to be taken literally, that believers are one another's blood-avengers for their blood spilt for the sake of Allāh; but it is also throughout recognized as a personal vengeance, as is also laid down in the case of the Medina Jews, and no-one is to be prevented from avenging a wound [cf. below, 157]. A limitation of *kiṣāṣ*, logical from the standpoint of the *umma*, lies in the fact that the believer is forbidden in the ordinance of the community to kill a Muslim on account of an unbeliever".

[141] Abū ʿUbayd, *Gharīb*, IV, 374: *yuqālu ʿtubiṭati l-ghanam wa-l-ibl idhā dhubiḥat aw nuḥirat min ghayr dā', wa-li-hādhā qīla li-l-dami l-khāliṣ ʿabīṭ; wa-l-ʿabīṭu lladhī dhubiḥa min ghayr ʿilla.* See also Ibn Qutayba, *Mushkil al-qur'ān*, 467: *wa-ẓulmu l-jazūr an yuʿtabaṭa ay yunḥara min ghayr ʿilla.*

[142] Cf. *Naqā'iḍ*, II, 563:3 (*bi-maʿbūṭin: nanḥaru li-l-aḍyāf min iblinā l-ṣaḥīḥāti llatī lā ʿayb bihā min maraḍ wa-lā ghayrihi*). When they are served meat, the Arabs inquire whether it came from a healthy or a diseased animal: *a-ʿabīṭ am ʿāriḍa?*; *Lisān al-ʿarab*, VII, 178, s.v. *ʿ-r-ḍ*.

[143] Zurqānī, IV, 168:-2. Or *bi-lā jināya kānat minhu wa-lā jarīra tūjibu qatlahu*; Ibn al-Athīr, *Nihāya*, III, 172, s.v. *ʿ-b-ṭ*.

[144] Cf. in particular the analogy found by Bravmann between this clause and the story of the Sumayr war; *Spiritual Background*, 328 (*in kāna sumayr qatala ṣarīḥan mina l-qawm fa-huwa bihi qawad*).

[145] Printed: *b.t.y.r.*

[146] Dārimī, II, 188, *bāb al-diya fī qatli l-ʿamd.* See also the Prophet's letter to Shuraḥbīl b. ʿAbd Kulāl and others from the *aqyāl* of Yemen: *wa-inna mani ʿtabaṭa mu'minan qatlan ʿan bayyina fa-innahu qawad illā an yarḍā awliyā'u l-maqtūl*; *Wath.*, 228 no. 110/j.

[147] *Al-ʿamd qawadu l-yad wa-l-khaṭa' ʿaql lā qawad fīhi, wa-man qutila fī ʿimmiyya bi-ḥajar aw ʿaṣan aw sawṭ fa-huwa diya mughallaẓa fī asnāni l-ibl*; Qurṭubī, *Tafsīr*, V, 329–30,

qawad yadihi is also found in a prophetic *ḥadīth* that is rather similar to this clause.[148]

Zurqānī (IV, 169:9), quoting *al-Nūr*, i.e. *Nūr al-nibrās* (I, 649) says regarding the verb *y.r.ḍ.y.* that it can either be vocalized *yurḍiya* with the murderer as subject and the *walī* or agnate as object, or *yarḍā* with the *walī* as subject. *Walī* is a member of one's *'āqila* or *'aṣaba*. *Mawlā* sometimes has this sense, but *mawlā* in the Kitāb means "ally". According to Abū 'Ubayd, many believe that one's *mawlā* (or a member of one's *'āqila*) is one's paternal cousin, but it is not so; every *walī* of a person is his *mawlā*, namely his father, brother, nephew, paternal uncle, paternal cousin and the rest of the *'aṣaba*.[149]

§25. *wa-innahu lā yaḥillu li-mu'min aqarra bi-mā fī hādhihi l-ṣaḥīfa wa-āmana bi-llāh wa-l-yawmi l-ākhir an yanṣura muḥdithan wa-lā yu'wiyahu wa-innahu man naṣarahu aw āwāhu fa-inna 'alayhi la'nata llāhi wa-ghaḍabahu yawma l-qiyāma wa-lā yu'khadhu minhu ṣarf wa-lā 'adl*

IT IS NOT PERMISSIBLE TO A MU'MIN WHO ACKNOWLEDGES WHAT IS IN THIS TREATY AND BELIEVES IN ALLĀH AND THE LAST DAY TO SUPPORT A MURDERER OR GIVE HIM SHELTER. UPON WHOEVER SUPPORTS HIM OR GIVES HIM SHELTER IS THE CURSE OF ALLĀH AND HIS WRATH ON THE DAY OF RESURRECTION, AND NEITHER REPENTANCE NOR RANSOM WILL BE ACCEPTED FROM HIM.

Wellhausen (70): "Kein Gläubiger, der den Inhalt dieser Schrift anerkennt und an Gott und den jüngsten Tag glaubt, darf einem Störenfried beistehen oder Zuflucht gewähren; sonst trifft ihn der Fluch Gottes und sein Zorn am

---

interpretation of Qur'ān 4,93 (← Ibn 'Abbās ← the Prophet). Regarding the importance of the ages of camels see Kennett, *Bedouin Justice*, 50–51. Also: *man qutila fī 'aṣabiyya, fī ramy yakūnu minhum bi-ḥijāra aw jald bi-l-siyāṭ aw ḍarb bi-l-'aṣī fa-huwa khaṭa', diyatuhu diyatu l-khaṭa', wa-man qatala 'amdan fa-huwa qawadu yadayhi*; Ṭabarī, *Tafsīr*, V, 136:20, interpretation of Qur'ān, 4,93 (← Sufyān b. 'Uyayna ← 'Amr b. Dīnār ← Ṭāwūs). A prophetic *ḥadīth* has: *man qutila fī 'immiyyā aw rimmiyyā bi-ḥajar aw 'aṣan fa-inna diyatahu mughallaẓa 'alā 'āqilatihi, wa-man qatala bi-yadihi fa-huwa qawad yadihi, wa-man ḥāla dūnahu fa-'alayhi la'natu llāh wa-l-malā'ika wa-l-nās ajma'īna, lā yuqbalu minhu ṣarf wa-lā 'adl*; Ṭabarānī, *Kabīr*, XI, 52 no. 11017 (← Ṭāwūs ← Ibn 'Abbās.)

[148] *Mani ghtabaṭa* [!] *mu'minan qatlan fa-huwa qawad yadihi wa-l-mu'minūna 'alayhi kāffa, lā yaḥillu li-rajul yu'minu bi-llāh wa-l-yawmi l-ākhir an yu'wiyahu aw yanṣurahu, fa-man āwāhu aw naṣarahu fa-'alayhi la'natu llāh wa-l-malā'ika wa-l-nās ajma'īna, lā yuqbalu minhu ṣarf wa-lā 'adl*; *Ḥilyat al-awliyā'*, VII, 98 (← 'Aṭā' b. Abī Rabāḥ ← Zayd b. Khālid al-Juhanī).

[149] Abū 'Ubayd, *Gharīb*, III, 141–42.

Tage der Auferstehung, wo kein Geld oder Ersatz von ihm angenommen wird". He goes on to explain that *muḥdith* is "wer Anstoss gibt, Skandal macht, das Wasser aufrührt; durch Verletzung von Anstand, Sitte und Recht, durch Frevel und eigenmächtiges Gebahren".
Wensinck (55–56): "No believer who understands what is said in this document and who believes in Allah and the last day shall give assistance to a wrong-doer or give him shelter. If anyone helps him or shelters such a person, upon him be the curse and wrath of Allah on the day of resurrection. No price or substitute shall be accepted from him". With regard to *aqarra*, which he renders "understands", Wensinck comments, following an observation of Wellhausen (83, the Kitāb was an edict of Muḥammad, not a negotiated agreement):[150] "This does not imply that the believers officially recognized the constitution; as far as we know, this was never done".
Watt (223): "It is not permissible for a believer who has agreed to what is in this document and believed in God and the last day to help a wrong-doer or give him lodging. If anyone helps him or gives him lodging, then upon this man is the curse of God and His wrath on the day of resurrection, and from him nothing will be accepted to make up for it or take its place". He comments on *muḥdith* that while literally it means "innovator", it means here one who disturbs the existing state of affairs in any way.
Ḥamīdullāh suggests that *ḥadath* means murder, *muḥdith* is a murderer *wa-kull man atā ḥaddan mina l-ḥudūd*.[151]
Serjeant (24; he divides the clause in two): "It is not lawful to (any) *Mu'min* who has affirmed what is on this sheet and/or trusts (*āmana*) in Allāh and the Last Day, to support or shelter an aggressor/innovator. Whosoever supports him or shelters him shall have upon him the curse of Allāh and His wrath on the Day of Resurrection. No intercession or propitiatory gift will be accepted from him". Regarding *aqarra* Serjeant remarks: "In south Arabian documents today this wording, *aqarra bi-mā fī*... is the formula used by signatories to an agreement. It is likely to have been employed by signatories to the eight documents here".[152] Serjeant's translation of *āmana* follows that of Bravmann; "but perhaps one should go further and render it 'finds security in'", Serjeant observes.[153] According to him, "*Muḥdith* is

[150] See also Wellhausen, *The Arab Kingdom*, 11 (it was a decree).
[151] Ḥamīdullāh, "Aqdam dustūr", 123.
[152] On Serjeant's theory that the Kitāb is made of eight separate documents see below, 185.
[153] Bravmann, *Spiritual Background*, 28, argued that *āmana* and *amina* mean "be (or: feel) secure (from danger)".

somebody who introduces a new element into a situation, which is therefore bad". Serjeant considers *ṣarf wa-ʿadl* "a cliché of quite frequent occurrence. *Ṣarf* is said to mean *tawbah*, repentance, and further sense given it is a voluntary gift (*nāfilah*), while *ʿadl* is assigned the sense of *fidyah*, ransom". He suggests that the phrase should be understood in the light of practices in Ḥadramawt: "A murderer's clan will give the Manṣab of a *ḥawṭah*, if he has committed the murder in it, a propitiatory gift called *suqṭān*, say a sheep. Later a pledge, known as *ʿadl* will be placed in the Manṣab's hand in earnest of the tribe's wish to have the case come to judgement. In so serious a case as clause 3b [= the first half of the clause discussed here — M. L.] it looks as if the offender would be outlawed and/or slain".

Following the conquest of Mecca Muḥammad restated its inviolability, adding: *lā yaḥillu li-mu'min bi-llāh wa-l-yawmi l-ākhir an yasfika fīhā daman wa-lā yaʿḍida fīhā shajaran.*[154] In the Prophet's letter to the Nahd, *abā* is the antonym of *aqarra*: *man aqarra bi-mā fī hādhā l-kitāb fa-lahu min rasūli llāh l-wafā' bi-l-ʿahd wa-l-dhimma, wa-man abā fa-ʿalayhi l-rabwa.*[155] The Prophet's letter to Khālid b. Ḍimād al-Azdī who converted to Islam stipulates: ... *wa-lā yu'wiya muḥdithan.*[156] A prophetic *ḥadīth* transmitted by the Companion ʿAmr b. ʿAwf al-Muzanī[157] includes a prohibition to change the boundaries of one's land at the expense of others: *man ghayyara tukhūma l-arḍ fa-ʿalayhi laʿnatu llāhi wa-ghaḍabuhu yawma l-qiyāma, lā yaqbalu llāhu minhu ṣarfan wa-lā ʿadlan.*[158]

The verb *aḥdatha* is found several times in Muḥammad's letters. Possibly relevant for us here is its occurrence at the beginning of his letter to the ʿAbd

[154]Wāqidī, II, 843–44. A similar formula appears in the *waṣiyya* or will of ʿAlī b. Abī Ṭālib at the end of its main section that deals with his estates: *hādhā mā qaḍā bihi ʿalī b. abī ṭālib fī amwālihi hādhihi l-ghad min yawm qadima maskin btighā' wajhi llāh wa-l-dāri l-ākhira, wa-llāhu l-mustaʿānu ʿalā kull ḥāl. Wa-lā yaḥillu li-mri' muslim yu'minu bi-llāhi wa-l-yawni l-ākhir an yughayyira shay'an mimmā awṣaytu bihi fī mālī wa-lā yukhālifu fīhi amrī min qarīb wa-lā baʿīd*; Ṭūsī, *Tahdhīb al-aḥkām*, IX, 148.

[155]Zurqānī, IV, 163:25; *Manāl al-ṭālib*, 8. *R(a/i/u)bwa* means "increase, excess, addition", i.e. those who do not comply will be punished by paying more than those who do; *ibid*, 24.

[156]Ibn Saʿd, I, 267; Wellhausen, 107–108 no. 17 ("... und keinem Frevler oder Rebellen aufnahme gewähre"). No entry on this man was found in the dictionaries of Companions.

[157]On whom see below, 200.

[158]Ṭabarānī, *Kabīr*, XVII, 23. Another prophetic *ḥadīth* has it that [on the Day of Resurrection] God will accept neither *ṣarf* nor *ʿadl* from a *ṣaqqūr*, i.e. one who pimps for his own wife; Ṭabarānī, *Kabīr*, XIX, 294; *Lisān al-ʿarab*, IV, 467, s.v.

al-Qays.[159] *Aḥdatha* has a wide range of meanings,[160] but in the present context a *muḥdith* is a murderer; *mani ʿtabaṭa* of §24 and *muḥdith* refer to the same crime. §24 prescribes that the perpetrator of *iʿtibāṭ* will be killed in retaliation for his crime, unless the victim's agnatic kin is satisfied with a compensation; in other words, he will be handed over to the relatives of the slain man. §25 prohibits helping the *muḥdith* or giving him shelter. There were still many unsettled accounts and the flaring up of old tensions could jeopardize Muḥammad's project.[161]

More evidence can be adduced in support of this interpretation. *Ḥadath* and *aḥdatha* refer to the murder of a fellow tribesman.[162] Abū Bakr's governor in the Yemen, Abān b. Saʿīd, was not prepared to take action against Qays b. Makshūḥ who had murdered Dādhawayh during the *ridda*. He declared that the Prophet had voided the blood feuds of the Jāhiliyya and threatened to punish everyone who would shed blood under Islam (*aḥdatha... ḥadathan*).[163] The guarantee of security that al-Mukhtār granted ʿUmar b. Saʿd b. Abī Waqqāṣ assured the latter that he would not be punished for his past crimes (*lā tuʾākhadhu bi-ḥadath kāna minka qadīman*). The *amān* would be in power provided ʿUmar did not commit a crime (*illā an yuḥditha ḥadathan*).[164] A member of the Ḥanīfa who wanted to assassinate Khālid b. al-Walīd was detained by his fellow tribesmen. In return for his release he was prepared to pledge *allā yuḥditha ḥadathan*. The Ḥanīfa did not trust him, but he escaped and killed himself after having tried to in-

[159] *Innahum āminūna bi-amāni llāhi wa-amān rasūlihi ʿalā mā aḥdathū fī l-jāhiliyya mina l-quḥam*; *Wath.*, 71 no. 72. *Quḥma*, pl. *quḥam*, means *al-umūr al-ʿaẓīma l-shāqqa*; Ibn al-Athīr, *Nihāya*, IV, 19, s.v. *q-ḥ-m*.

[160] Cf. *Futūḥ miṣr*, Glossary, 34, s.v. *ḥ-d-th*, IV, "to 'sin,' 'do wrong,' in the most general sense".

[161] Suwayd b. al-Ṣāmit was murdered by al-Mujadhdhar b. Dhiyād (above, 60) on the eve of the battle of Buʿāth, and during the battle of Uḥud Suwayd's son, al-Ḥārith, killed his father's murderer; Wāqidī, I, 303–305; Ibn Qudāma, *Istibṣār*, 327–28.

[162] Sijistānī, *Waṣāyā*, 123 (*aṣāba daman fī qawmihi*). On his deathbed a murderer enjoined his sons to compensate the victim's tribe (i.e. his *ʿāqila*): *wa-amarahum an yuʿṭū qawmahu l-niṣf* [read: *al-naṣaf*] *min ḥadathihi lladhī aḥdatha fīhim*.

[163] *Iṣāba*, I, 17 no. 2: *inna rasūla llāh ṣ qad waḍaʿa kull dam kāna fī l-jāhiliyya, fa-man aḥdatha fī islām ḥadathan akhadhnāhu bihi*.

[164] Abū Jaʿfar Muḥammad b. ʿAlī (the fifth *imām* of the Twelver Shīʿa) commented sarcastically that the provision regarding *ḥadath* meant: provided he did not defecate (*dakhala l-khalāʾ fa-aḥdatha*); Ṭabarī, VI, 60–61 [II, 672]. See also Ibn Kathīr, *Bidāya*, VIII, 273:8: *mā lam yuḥdith ḥadathan, wa-arāda l-mukhtār mā lam yaʾti l-khalāʾ fa-yabūlu aw yaghūṭu*. On the fifth *imām* see EI^2, s.v. Muḥammad b. ʿAlī al-Bāḳir (E. Kohlberg).

filtrate Khālid's camp;[165] *aḥdatha ḥadathan* refers to the taking of a human life.

Ṣarf and *ʿadl* belong to the proceedings of the Day of Resurrection. One version of Ibn Isḥāq's recension has *ilā yawmi l-qiyāma*, and the preposition *ilā* also appears in almost all the versions of the Abū ʿUbayd recension;[166] still, it is superfluous. Retaliation for betraying one's vow to grant security will take place on the Day of Resurrection.[167]

According to Abū ʿUbayd,[168] *ṣarf* means *tawba* (repentance) or *nāfila* (supererogatory prayer), but the first interpretation seems to him more likely. He interprets *ʿadl* as *fidya* (ransom) or *farīḍa* ("an obligatory ordinance of God"), but prefers the former.

§26. *wa-innakum mahmā khtalaftum fīhi min shayʾ fa-inna maraddahu ilā llāh wa-ilā muḥammad*[169]

WHATEVER YOU DIFFER ABOUT SHOULD BE BROUGHT BEFORE ALLĀH AND MUḤAMMAD.

Wellhausen (70): "Wenn ihr über irgend eine Sache im Streit seid, so muss sie vor Gott und vor Muhammad gebracht werden".
Wensinck (56): "Whenever you differ about anything it is to be referred to Allah and Muhammad".
Watt (223): "Wherever there is anything about which you differ, it is to be referred to God and to Muḥammad (peace be upon him)".
Serjeant (24, 25): "In whatever thing you are at variance, its reference back (*maradd*) is to Allāh, Great and Glorious, and to Muḥammad, Allāh bless

[165] Ṭabarī, III, 299–300 [I, 1956]; cf. *The History of al-Ṭabarī*, X, trans. Donner, 132: "Salamah promised them that he would do nothing else if they would forgive him".

[166] The expression *ilā yawmi l-qiyāma*, "until the Day of Resurrection", appears in different contexts. Aḥmad, IV, 32:17: *fa-hiya* (i.e. Mecca) *ḥarām min ḥarāmi llāhi taʿālā ilā yawmi l-qiyāma*. See also Wāqidī, III, 1006:-3; *ibid*, II, 514:-1; *ʿIqd*, I, 152:8. The following prophetic *ḥadīth* includes *ilā* and is particularly relevant for us here, being a reflection of the Kitāb: *man aḥdatha fīhā ḥadathan aw āwā muḥdithan fa-ʿalayhi laʿnatu llāh ilā yawmi l-qiyāma, lā yuqbalu minhu ṣarf wa-lā ʿadl*; Abū ʿUbayd, *Gharīb*, III, 167.

[167] Ṭūsī, *Tahdhīb al-aḥkām*, VI, 139: ...*fa-innakum in tukhfirū dhimamakum wa-dhimam ābāʾikum wa-ikhwānikum kāna aysar ʿalaykum yawma l-qiyāma min an tukhfirū dhimmata llāh wa-dhimmat rasūli llāh ṣ wa-ālihi*. If the retaliation does not occur in this world, it takes place on the Day of Resurrection; Ibn Ḥajar, *Maṭālib*, II, 124: *bāb man lam yuqtaṣṣa minhu fī l-dunyā qtuṣṣa minhu fī l-ākhira*. One of the two *ḥadīth*s quoted here goes back to the Prophet's wife Umm Salama: *daʿā rasūlu llāhi ṣ waṣīfa lahu fa-abṭaʾat fa-qāla*: *lawlā makhāfatu l-qawad yawma l-qiyāma la-awjaʿtuki bi-hādhā l-siwāk*.

[168] *Gharīb*, III, 167–68.

[169] Abū ʿUbayd has *ḥukmahu* instead of *maraddahu*.

and honour him". According to him, this is the final clause of document B. He comments on the resemblance between it and the first half of Qur'ān 42,10: *wa-mā khtalaftum fīhi min shay' fa-ḥukmuhu ilā llāhi*, and remarks that a little earlier in the Sūra there is mention of *umma wāḥida*.

This is the only occurrence in the Kitāb of the second-person plural.[170] While the wording implies that all disputes should be brought before Muḥammad, considering the character of the Kitāb one assumes that this clause relates above all to disputes concerning blood feuds.

The office of arbiter[171] is closely linked to tribal leadership.[172] Arbitration (*ḥukūma*), command in the battlefield (*ri'āsa*), the right to carry the banner (*liwā'*) and the right to one fourth of the booty belonged to the prerogatives of the tribe's leading family (*bayt*).[173] Arbitration involved prestige and power, which is possibly as far as authority can go in a tribal environment. Al-Walīd b. al-Mughīra al-Makhzūmī, who was at some point *ḥakam quraysh*, was asked to arbitrate in a blood feud between two clans of Quraysh.[174] Quraysh prepared a crown for al-Walīd in order to crown him with it, but the advent of Islam foiled their plan.[175]

---

[170]See above, 41.

[171]Cf. *EI*², s.v. *ḥakam* (E. Tyan).

[172]It was said of ʿĀmir al-Ḍaḥyān of the Namir b. Qāsiṭ: *kāna sayyid qawmihi wa-ḥākimahum*; *Aghānī*, XII, 16:-3; *Aghānī* (Dār al-Kutub), XIII, 140.

[173]Ibn ʿAbd al-Barr, *al-Inbāh*, 97–98, quoting Ibn al-Kalbī: *awwal bayt kāna fī rabīʿa b. nizār kānat fīhi l-ri'āsa wa-l-ḥukūma wa-l-liwā' wa-l-mirbāʿ, yakūnu dhālika kābiran ʿan kābir wa-yatawārathūnahu lā yunāzaʿūna fīhi — ḍubayʿa b. rabīʿa b. nizār....*

[174]ʿAskarī, *Awā'il*, I, 54.

[175]*Ibid.*, 57; Lecker, "King Ibn Ubayy and the *Quṣṣāṣ*", 57.

Chapter 5

The Treaty of the Jews

§27. *wa-inna l-yahūd yunfiqūna maʿa l-muʾminīna mā dāmū muḥāribīna*

THE JEWS SHARE EXPENDITURE WITH THE MUʾMINŪN AS LONG AS THEY ARE AT WAR.[1]

Wellhausen (70, 71): "Die Juden sollen zu den Kriegskosten beisteuern mit den Gläubigen, so lange dieselben in Kriege sind". He remarks that the clause is repeated later in the Kitāb[2] and is better located in the latter place.

Wensinck (56): "The Jews pay a share of the expenses of the believers so long as they are at war".

Watt (223): "The Jews bear expenses along with the believers so long as they continue at war".

Serjeant (27): "The Jews will pay the *nafaqah* along with the *Muʾminūn* while they continue at war". He comments: "*Nafaqah* is a tax; it is sometimes synonymous with *ṣadaqah*.... After al-Ṭāʾif joined Muḥammad it paid him *nafaqah*.... Some tribal Arabs around Medina disliked paying it. *Wa-min al-Aʿrābi man yunfiqu maghram-an* 'There are some of the tribal Arabs who take what they pay as *maghram*/impost/levy (Qurʾān IX, 99)' ".[3]

---

[1]Cf. §44.

[2]See the variant readings to §48.

[3]The correct wording of the Qurʾān verse (9,98) is: *wa-mina l-aʿrābi man yattakhidhu mā yunfiqu maghraman*. As to the *nafaqa* of Ṭāʾif, Serjeant refers to a passage found in the entry on ʿUthmān b. Abī l-ʿĀṣ al-Thaqafī in a dictionary of Companions comparing him to the other members of the Thaqīf delegation: *kāna aḥraṣahum ʿalā l-n.f.q.h. fī l-islām wa-taʿlīmi l-qurʾān*; *Usd al-ghāba*, III, 373:6. But *n.f.q.h.* should be read *tafaqquh*, "He was the most eager of them to obtain knowledge in Islam". Elsewhere we read: *kāna*

The clause begins the treaty of the Jews. As one can expect, the expression *fī sabīl allāh* or "in the cause of Allāh" only occurs in the treaty of the Mu'minūn, while in the treaty of the Jews we find *man ḥāraba fī l-dīn*. Abū ʿUbayd, in his interpretation of the Kitāb, makes an apologetic comment regarding the Jews' right to a share of the booty. He says that the *nafaqa* specifically relates to war, and that the Prophet made it obligatory for them to aid him against his enemy. He only granted the Jews a share in the booty (*yushimu*, i.e. a share equal to that of the Muslims) when they raided with the Muslims because of this *nafaqa* stipulation, otherwise they would not have had a share in the booty of the Muslims.[4]

§28. *wa-inna yahūd banī ʿawf umma maʿa [amana mina] l-muʾminīna, li-l-yahūd dīnuhum wa-li-l-muslimīna dīnuhum, mawālīhim wa-anfusihim, illā man ẓalama wa-athima fa-innahu lā yūtighu illā nafsahu wa-ahl baytihi*

THE JEWS OF BANŪ ʿAWF ARE SECURE FROM THE MUʾMINŪN. THE JEWS HAVE THEIR RELIGION AND THE MUSLIMŪN HAVE THEIRS. [This applies to] THEIR ALLIES AND THEIR PERSONS. BUT WHOEVER ACTS UNJUSTLY AND SINS WILL ONLY DESTROY HIMSELF AND HIS AGNATES.

§§29–33. *wa-inna li-yahūd banī l-najjār mithl mā li-yahūd banī ʿawf... wa-inna li-yahūd banī l-ḥārith... wa-inna li-yahūd banī sāʿida... wa-inna li-yahūd banī jusham... wa-inna li-yahūd banī l-aws...*

THE JEWS OF THE BANŪ L-NAJJĀR RECEIVE THE SAME RIGHTS AS THE JEWS OF BANŪ ʿAWF.

THE JEWS OF BANŪ L-ḤĀRITH RECEIVE THE SAME RIGHTS AS THE JEWS OF BANŪ ʿAWF.

THE JEWS OF BANŪ SĀʿIDA RECEIVE THE SAME RIGHTS AS THE JEWS OF BANŪ ʿAWF.

THE JEWS OF BANŪ JUSHAM RECEIVE THE SAME RIGHTS AS THE JEWS OF BANŪ ʿAWF.

THE JEWS OF BANŪ L-AWS RECEIVE THE SAME RIGHTS AS THE JEWS OF BANŪ ʿAWF.

---

aḥraṣahum ʿalā l-tafaqquh fī l-islām wa-taʿallumi l-qurʾān; Ṭabarī, III, 99 [I, 1691]; *The History of al-Ṭabarī*, IX, trans. Poonawala, 45: "...he was the most zealous in his desire to study Islam and to learn the Qurʾān".

[4] *Amwāl*, 266 no. 518.

§34. *wa-inna li-yahūd banī thaʿlaba mithl mā li-yahūd banī ʿawf, illā man ẓalama wa-athima fa-innahu lā yūtighu illā nafsahu wa-ahl baytihi*

THE JEWS OF BANŪ THAʿLABA HAVE THE SAME [rights] AS THE JEWS OF BANŪ ʿAWF. BUT WHOEVER ACTS UNJUSTLY AND SINS WILL ONLY DESTROY HIMSELF AND HIS AGNATES.

Wellhausen (70): "Die Juden der Banu ʿAuf... behalten zwar ihre Religion, bilden aber eine Gemeinde mit den Gläubigen, sowol sie selber als ihre Beisassen; ausgenommen wer Gewalt oder Trug begeht: ein solcher aber stürzt sich selbst und seine Familie in das Unglück".
Wensinck (56): "The Jews of the Banū ʿAwf are one community with the believers. To the Jews their religion and to the Muslims their religion. [This applies] to their clients and to themselves with the exception of anyone who has done wrong or committed treachery, for he harms only himself and his family".
Watt (223): "The Jews of Banū ʿAwf are a community along with the believers. To the Jews their religion and to the Muslims their religion. (This applies) both to their clients and to themselves, with the exception of anyone who has done wrong or acted treacherously; he brings evil only on himself and on his household".
Serjeant (27): "The Jews of Banū ʿAwf are a confederation with the *Muʾminūn*, the Jews having their religion/law and the *Muslimūn/Muʾminūn* having their religion/law, their clients and their persons, excepting anyone who acts wrongfully and commits crime/acts treacherously/breaks an agreement, for he but slays himself and the people of his house".

The status of the Jews vis-à-vis the *umma* was conceived of in two ways. Some thought that Yahūd Banī ʿAwf were an *umma* on their own "with" (*umma maʿa*) the Muʾminūn, i.e. in alliance with them;[5] but most scholars believed that they were part of the general *umma*.[6]

[5]See Khadduri, *War and Peace in the Law of Islam*, 209: "Each Jewish tribe constituted a 'nation with the believers'; but the Jewish tribes as a whole do not form a nation by themselves".

[6]See Sprenger, *Leben*, III, 23 ("Die Juden der Banû ʿAwf gehören wie die Gläubigen zur Staats-Gesellschaft"); Wellhausen, 74–75; Buhl, *Leben*, 210; Gil, 63 ("The Jews belong to the *umma*, since they are the clients of Muslim clans"). The following prophetic *ḥadīth* suggests that "this *umma*" includes Jews and Christians: *wa-lladhī nafs Muḥammad bi-yadihi lā yasmaʿu bī aḥad min hādhihi l-umma yahūdī wa-lā naṣrānī thumma yamūtu wa-lam yuʾmin bi-lladhī ursiltu bihi illā kāna min aṣḥābi l-nār*; Qurṭubī, *Tafsīr*, IX, 18, interpretation of Qurʾān 11,18. However, this is irrelevant to the Kitāb.

M. Ḥamīdullāh says:

> And the Jews of Banū ʿAwf shall be considered as one political community along with the believers" (*ummatun maʿa l-muʾminīna*).... This is the version transmitted by Ibn Isḥāq (Ibn Hishām), which one tries to render as "a separate community yet allied to the Muslims"; this in order to avoid embarrassment. Yet the text of this clause transmitted by Abū ʿUbayd (in his *Kitāb al-Amwāl*, f. 517) does not give even this much of latitude, the term employed there being *ummat min al-muʾminīna* (a community forming part of the Believers, i.e. Muslims).[7]

Denny writes:

> The *ummah* of the Constitution is made up of believers and Muslims, and quite possibly Jews as well (although they may constitute a separate *ummah* "alongside").... Serjeant's position that the Jews constitute an *ummah* "alongside" is more likely. This satisfies the religious stipulations of the term's meaning at this time, which are reflected in those Qurʾānic instances which refer exclusively either to the Muslims as an *ummah* or to other *ummahs*, especially the Jews and Christians.[8]

Rubin (14–15, 20) rejects Serjeant's interpretation: the correct reading is *umma min*, as in Abū ʿUbayd's version (which Serjeant calls "defective"), not *umma maʿa* as in Ibn Isḥāq's version. The former conforms to Qurʾānic usage and means "an *umma* of believers" (the *min* being *min li-l-bayān*). Their recognition as "believers" goes back to the first Medinan period, during which the Prophet was willing to make concessions in order to reconcile the Jews who were given a special position within the *umma wāḥida* of Medina.[9]

---

[7] Ḥamīdullāh, "Sources of Islamic Law", 207.

[8] Denny employs the term "sub-*ummah*" to describe the position of the Jews; Denny, "*Ummah* in the Constitution of Medina", 43, 44.

[9] See also Lichtenstaedter, "From Particularism to Unity", 259: "From the very outset he [the Prophet] received the Jews into this commonwealth; they were to be an integral factor and a component of its constituency". She renders the clause as follows: "The Jews of the Banū ʿAuf...form one *ummah* with the believers; however, the Jews have their faith (*dīn*), their clients (*mawālī*) as well as they themselves". Rubin's conclusions were adopted by Friedmann, *Tolerance and Coercion*, 33 ("certain Jewish groups are recognized as 'a community belonging to the believers'"). See also Hoyland, "Sebeos, the

The presumed recognition of the Yahūd Banī ʿAwf in §28 as an *umma* similar to the general *umma* — not to mention the inclusion of these Yahūd in this *umma* — was probably problematic for some Muslim scholars of later times. It follows that when the word *umma* in §28 is replaced in certain versions by more "convenient" words, one could suspect a deliberate change aimed at removing the difficulty. But there are cogent reasons for maintaining one of the alternative readings of *umma*.

umma/amana

I argue that *umma maʿa l-muʾminīna* should be replaced by *amana mina l-muʾminīna*. There are arguments for and against the adoption of this variant reading, but on a balance the latter is the better reading.

The unique variant *ʾ.m.na* is found in one of the editions of the *Fāʾiq* (II, 25); this source includes a partial text of the Kitāb that belongs to Abū ʿUbayd's recension.[10] *ʾ.m.na* can be read as *amana/āmina/amina*, henceforth it will be vocalized *amana*.

Let us look into the arguments for rejecting the variant reading *amana* and then discuss the more cogent arguments for keeping it.

First, the reading is only attested in one manuscript of the *Fāʾiq*. In the 1971 edition of the *Fāʾiq* the editors, al-Bijāwī and Ibrāhīm, remark regarding *amana* that the fine manuscript on which their edition is based[11] has at this point: *umma*. The reading *amana*, which they preferred to *umma*, was taken from the Indian edition of the *Fāʾiq*.[12] It is not clear whence the reading *amana* reached the Indian edition, because no details

Jews and the Rise of Islam", 95 (the *min* in *umma min al-muʾminīn* is partative rather than explicative, "a community forming part of the believers"). Donner, "From Believers to Muslims", 30–31, renders: "The Jews of Banū ʿAwf are a people (*umma*) with the *Muʾminūn*, the Jews having their law (*dīn*) and the *Muslimūn* having their law". He continues: "From this passage it is patently obvious that at least some Jews were included in the *umma*". According to him (32): "Document C may reflect a time when the Jews of B. ʿAwf etc. had just joined the *umma*".

[10]The text is mentioned in the *Glossarium* of Ṭabarī (Leiden), s.v. *ʿ-q-l*.

[11]Dār al-Kutub 25, *shīn*.

[12]Hyderabad 1924, I, 221. The date and place in which the Indian edition appeared were specified in the older edition of the *Fāʾiq* by al-Bijāwī and Ibrāhīm: Cairo: Dār Iḥyāʾ al-Kutub al-ʿArabiyya and ʿĪsā al-Bābī al-Ḥalabī, 1364/1945–1366/1947, I, *jīm*. The two editors remark in the 1971 edition that the Indian edition is inaccurate, but since it is based on manuscripts it was also consulted; *ibid.*, I, 5: *kamā rajaʿnā ilā maṭbūʿati l-hind wa-hiya khāliya mina l-ḍabṭ wa-lakinnahā ʿalā kull ḥāl tuʿaddu aṣlan li-annahā ṭubiʿat min uṣūl khaṭṭiyya*. The older edition was based on the Hyderabad 1924 edition.

are given in it regarding the manuscript or manuscripts consulted. Yet one assumes that it is from a manuscript of the *Fāʾiq* found in Hyderabad, more precisely in the Āṣafiyya library;[13] *al-aṣl* that is often mentioned in the Indian edition may well be a reference to this manuscript. The variant reading given in the Indian edition, *umma* (*wa-fī nuskha: umma mina l-muʾminīna*) is probably taken from another manuscript of the *Fāʾiq* found in Hyderabad, more precisely in the Osmaniya University library.[14] The answer to this argument would be that a correct reading is sometimes attested in one source only.

Second, for some *amana* was a more convenient reading than *umma*. Asked about a *ḥadīth* declaring the Jews and Christians part of *ummat Muḥammad*, Aḥmad b. Ḥanbal said that it was a filthy idea which should not be discussed.[15] But it can be argued that for others *umma* was more convenient than *amana*.[16]

Third, one could argue that the reading *amana* should be rejected because it does not conform to one of the interpretive comments of *Fāʾiq*'s author, Zamakhsharī. This is a relatively strong argument, since the interpretation refers to the clause as if it included *umma min* rather than *amana min*.[17] The answer would be that Zamakhsharī (538/1144) actually copied the interpretive comment from an earlier source without paying much attention to the presumed contradiction between his interpretation and the clause itself: an almost identical comment is found in Harawī's (d. 401/1010)

---

[13] *GAL S*, I, 511.

[14] On the two libraries see *World Survey of Islamic Manuscripts*, I, 400–403.

[15] Friedmann, *Tolerance and Coercion*, 32–33, links this *ḥadīth* to the Kitāb.

[16] Ibn Taymiyya, for example (below, 146n), wrongly assumed that Yahūd Banī ʿAwf of the Kitāb were in fact the Qaynuqāʿ. In AH 3 the Thaʿlaba b. al-Fiṭyawn, i.e. the Thaʿlaba of the Kitāb, were expelled from Medina (above, 77). It is true that the sources systematically put the blame for the Jews' mishaps on the Jews themselves; still, an explicit *amān* clause may have been regarded as more problematic than the recognition of the Jews as an *umma* on its own, or as part of the *umma* created by Muḥammad.

[17] *Yahūd banī ʿawf, bi-sababi l-ṣulḥi l-wāqiʿ baynahum wa-bayna l-muʾminīna ka-umma minhum fī anna kalimatahum wāḥida ʿalā ʿaduwwihim, fa-ammā l-dīn fa-kull firqa minhum ʿalā ḥiyālihā.* The *ka-* of *ka-umma* is of course meaningful.

Gharībayni.[18] Hence Zamakhsharī's version of the clause should probably be detached from the comment that was not in fact his own.

There are stronger arguments for sustaining the reading *amana*. First, in Arabia an *amān* was not a luxury, and in the turbulence of the post-*hijra* period small Jewish tribal groups or individuals living amidst the growing community of Muʾminūn must have feared for their lives and property. Events in Medina on the eve of the *hijra* demonstrated the precarious position of Jewish groups in certain parts of Medina,[19] and events following the *hijra* indicated that their presumed fears were not unfounded. The Yahūd Banī ʿAwf, for example, were associated with the ʿAwf, who were of the Khazraj. They needed a guarantee security against possible attacks by members of the Aws who were now among the Mu'minūn. In the light of §15 it is doubtful that a Muʾmin of the Banū ʿAwf would have retaliated for an attack by a Muʾmin of the Aws on a *kāfir* of the Yahūd Banī ʿAwf.

Second, Ibn Isḥāq's introduction to the Kitāb indicates that an *amān* was granted to the Jews. He states that in the Kitāb between the Muhājirūn and the Anṣār the Prophet made an agreement of non-belligerency and a pact with the Jews, permitting them to remain in their former religion and keep their orchards intact (*wādaʿa fīhi yahūd wa-ʿāhadahum wa-aqarrahum ʿalā dīnihim wa-amwālihim*).[20] Simonsen translates Ibn Isḥāq's introduction as follows:

> Thus, ibn isḥâq interprets the Constitution as an agreement entered into between the Muslims (here defined as *al-muhâdjirûn* and *al-anṣâr* and not, as in the Constitution, *al-muhâdjirûn* and *al-muʾminûn*) and the Jews.[21]

[18]I, 89: *yurīdu annahum bi-l-ṣulḥi lladhī waqaʿa baynahum wa-bayna l-muʾminīna ka-umma mina l-muʾminīna, kalimatuhum wa-aydīhim wāḥida.* Cf. the interpretation found in yet another *gharīb* dictionary the author of which died shortly after Zamakhsharī: Ibn al-Athīr (d. 606/1209), *Nihāya*, I, 68, s.v. *umma* has: *inna yahūd banī ʿawf umma mina l-muʾminīna, yurīdu annahum bi-l-ṣulḥi lladhī waqaʿa baynahum wa-bayna l-muʾminīna ka-jamāʿa minhum, kalimatuhum wa-aydīhim wāḥida.* Another treatise by the same author, *Manāl al-ṭālib*, 232, has: *yurīdu annahum bi-l-ṣulḥi lladhī waqaʿa baynahum wa-bayna l-muʾminīna fa-ṣārat aydīhim wa-ʾaydī mawālīhim maʿa l-muʾminīna wāḥida ʿalā ʿaduwwi l-muʾminīna ka-umma mina l-muʾminīna illā anna li-hāʾulāʾi dīnahum wa-li-hāʾulāʾi dīnahum, illā man ẓalama wa-athima bi-naqḍi l-ʿahd wa-l-nakth.*

[19]Above, 81.

[20]Ibn Hishām, II, 147.

[21]Simonsen, *Studies in the Genesis and Early Development of the Caliphal Taxation System*, 45. He adds: "By his interpretation of the Constitution as a pact between the Jews and the Muslims ibn isḥâq anticipates the later conflicts between Muhammad and

Gil says (58):

> The document is described by Ibn Isḥāq as an agreement between the Prophet and the Jews, stating their rights and duties.

Serjeant (15) is of another opinion:

> The vital point is that, as Ibn Isḥāq presents it, *this is not a treaty with the Jews* [the italics are Serjeant's — M. L.] and his attitude is confirmed by the internal evidence of the documents themselves. The treaty is between the Muhājirūn and the Anṣār. The text has *yahūd* not *al-yahūd*, i.e., Jews considered as a group, a tribe even.

But the distinction between *yahūd* and *al-yahūd* is insignificant. It is true that the Kitāb was in the first place a treaty between the Muhājirūn and the Anṣār; however, it included a treaty with the Jews of the type called *muwādaʿa* (*wādaʿa fīhi yahūd*).

A comparable relationship existed several years later between the Prophet and the tribe of Khuzāʿa, as reflected in a report on the Ḥudaybiyya treaty. Wāqidī says:

> When the Messenger of God settled in Ḥudaybiyya, Budayl b. Warqāʾ and a party of riders from Khuzāʿa came to him. They were confident and sincere advisers of the Messenger of God in Tihāma. Part of them were Muslims and part were in a state of *muwādaʿa*. They would reveal to him everything that occurred in Tihāma.[22]

A *muwādaʿa* is by definition a treaty with non-Muslims, and hence we find elsewhere that *muwādiʿ* in this context is replaced by *mushrik*.[23] At the time of Ḥudaybiyya the Khuzāʿa were divided into Muslims and polytheists and the latter had a *muwādaʿa* with Muḥammad. This is comparable though not identical to the situation in Medina upon the conclusion of the Kitāb. The Anṣār included converts to Islam and polytheists (who were not part of

---

the big Jewish tribes of Medina. Their expulsion becomes logical because they broke the pact signed with Muhammad in 622".

[22]Wāqidī, II, 593: *qālū*: *fa-lammā ṭmaʾanna rasūlu llāh ṣ bi-l-ḥudaybiyya jāʾahu budayl b. warqāʾ wa-rakb min khuzāʿa wa-hum ʿayba nuṣḥ li-rasūli llāh bi-tihāma, minhumu l-muslim wa-minhum l-muwādiʿ*.

[23]Ibn Hishām, III, 326: *wa-kānat khuzāʿa... muslimuhā wa-mushrikuhā...*; *Fatḥ al-bārī*, V, 246:2: *wa-kānat khuzāʿa ʿaybat rasūli llāh ṣ muslimuhā wa-mushrikuhā*.

the Kitāb); in their midst lived Jews (whatever their relationship with the Anṣār) with whom a *muwāda'a* was concluded.

Let us return to *amana*. The verb *wāda'a* in itself suffices as evidence that the Kitāb included an *amān* for the Jews, since a *muwāda'a* is in the first place a reciprocal *amān* or guarantee of security.[24] That *muwāda'a* and *amān* are near-synonyms is shown by the following reports. After the battle of Bi'r Ma'ūna two members of a tribe that had a *muwāda'a* treaty with Muḥammad were slain by one of the Prophet's Companions;[25] elsewhere the same tribesmen are said to have had an *amān* from the Prophet.[26]

Still with regard to Ibn Isḥāq's introduction, the case for *amana* is corroborated by the verb *aqarra* or "made someone remain, left him in his place": *wa-aqarrahum 'alā dīnihim wa-amwālihim* is the equivalent of an *amān* granted to the *dīn* or religion and *amwāl* or orchards of the Jews.[27] Where in the Kitāb is there a reference to *amān*? It is true that §62 refers to *amān*, but it is a clause one expects to find at the end of a treaty and not a general declaration of *amān*.

We know where to look for the *amān*. The *iqrār 'alā dīn* of Ibn Isḥāq's introduction corresponds to *li-l-yahūd dīnuhum* of §28. The *amān* granted to the *amwāl* or orchards should also be found in the same clause, although the *amwāl* are not specifically mentioned in it. All this leads to the conclusion that *amana* is the correct reading.

Third, the granting of *amān* explains the formula used with regard to the other Jewish groups: *wa-inna li-yahūd banī... mithl mā li-yahūd banī 'awf*. The *amān* granted to the Yahūd Banī 'Awf — obviously the most important Yahūd group — was extended to the other groups. The preposition *li-* in Muḥammad's treaties (and in a similar context elsewhere) indicates the granting of a right.[28] The same formula can also be found in connection

[24]Below, 204.

[25]Ṭabarī, *Tafsīr*, VI, 93:-5, interpretation of Qur'ān 5,11.

[26]Rāzī, *Tafsīr*, XI, 182:-2, interpretation of the same verse. A passage similar to Ibn Isḥāq's introduction is found in Suhaylī (II, 250). (However, Suhaylī inaccurately introduces the Kitāb as including only a treaty between the Prophet and the Jews.) According to him, the *amān* was also granted to the Jews' families: *kitāb rasūli llāh ṣ fīmā baynahu wa-bayna l-yahūd, sharaṭa lahum fīhi wa-sharaṭa 'alayhim, wa-ammanahum fīhi 'alā anfusihim wa-ahlīhim wa-amwālihim*.

[27]Cf. e.g. 'Abd al-Jabbār, *Tathbīt*, II, 327 (regarding the Persians who came under Muslim rule): *fa-inna 'umar ḥīna malakahum aqarrahum 'alā adyānihim wa-amwālihim wa-akhadha l-jizya minhum....* For *iqrār* that is the opposite of *ṭard* see Jāḥiẓ, *Bayān*, III, 372.

[28]See e.g. Ibn Sa'd, I, 269 (where it is found with *amān*); 266 (with *jiwār*); 270 (with *dhimma*, with *naṣr*).

with the *muwāda'a* treaty that the Prophet concluded with the nomadic leader Hilāl b. 'Uwaymir al-Aslamī: the *jiwār* or safe conduct promised to Hilāl was extended to others who would join him.[29]

Fourth, the granting of a right in §28 and the following clauses is also indicated by the stipulation at the end of §28 that excludes certain individuals: *illā man ẓalama wa-athima....* In other words, the *amān* is not granted to those who act unjustly and sin. This concept can also be found in §61, *wa-innahu lā yaḥūlu hādhā l-kitāb dūna ẓālim wa-āthim*, where the Kitāb itself figures as a kind of *amān*. Also §62 includes a conditional *amān*: *wa-innahu man kharaja āmin wa-man qa'ada āmin, illā man ẓalama wa-athima*. As in §§28 and 61, wrongdoers are excluded. Finally, the Yahūd Banī Tha'laba enjoy the same rights as the Yahūd Banī 'Awf with the usual exception: *illā man ẓalama wa-athima* (§34).

Fifth, one expects an *amān* at or near the beginning of the treaty of the Jews because it is common in Muḥammad's treaties with non-Muslims. Those who had not yet converted to Islam needed an *amān*. In Muḥammad's letter to the Juhayna, for example, we find: *wa-kataba rasūlu llāhi ṣ li-banī zur'a wa-banī l-rab'a min juhayna annahum āminūna 'alā anfusihim wa-amwālihim*.[30] Kister says about the treaty with the Juhayna:

> When the Prophet settled in Medina, he was, of course, concerned to establish peaceful relations with its neighbours, D̲j̲uhayna. D̲j̲uhayna, making a careful assessment of the fundamental change in the situation in Medina with the advent of the Prophet, were eager to secure their position in the new structure of power. According to some traditions, a delegation of D̲j̲uhayna came to the Prophet in Medina, pointed out that the Prophet alighted 'among them' (*bayna aẓhurinā*, i.e. in the area controlled by them) and requested him to conclude with them an agreement of mutual security (*fa-awthiq lanā ḥattā na'manaka wa-ta'mananā*). This treaty was indeed agreed upon between the Prophet and D̲j̲uhayna. A peculiar aspect of this treaty was the tacit agreement by the Prophet for D̲j̲uhayna not to convert

---

[29]... *Wāda'a waqt khurūjihi ilā makka hilāl b. 'uwaymir al-aslamī 'alā an lā ya'ṣiyahu wa-lā yu'īna 'alayhi wa-'alā anna kull man waṣala ilā hilāl wa-laja'a ilayhi fa-lahu mina l-jiwār mithl mā li-hilāl*; Rāzī, *Tafsīr*, X, 222, interpretation of Qur'ān 4,90.

[30]The letter continues: *wa-anna lahumu l-naṣr 'alā man ẓalamahum aw ḥārabahum, illā fī l-dīn, wa-li-ahl bādiyatihim man barra minhum wa-ttaqā mā li-ḥāḍiratihim wa-llāhu l-musta'ānu*; Ibn Sa'd, I, 270; Wellhausen no. 27 (= 11 of the Arabic section, 112 of the German section); *Wath.*, 262 no. 151; Watt, 355.

> to Islam; this is clearly indicated in the account about the treaty, *wa-lam yuslimū*.[31]

In other words, as in the case of the Jews of the Kitāb, the Juhanīs remained polytheists, and hence needed an *amān*. In the letter of the Ḍamra we find: *wa-kataba rasūlu llāhi ṣ li-banī ḍamra... annahum āminūna ʿalā amwālihim wa-anfusihim*.[32] Conversion to Islam made an *amān* superfluous. Several nomadic tribes declared that they believed (i.e. converted to Islam) in order to safeguard themselves and their properties (*qālū: āmannā, li-yaʾmanū ʿalā anfusihim wa-amwālihim*).[33]

Sixth, in a strange coincidence the *nūn* of *amana* was also omitted from the treaty that the Thaqīf concluded with Muḥammad several years after the conclusion of the Kitāb. One of its clauses grants the Thaqīf freedom of movement in Muslim territory: *wa-hum umma* [read: *amana*] *mina l-muslimīna yatawallajūna mina l-muslimīna ḥaythu mā shāʾū wa-ayna tawallajū walajū*.[34] *Umma* is a corruption of *amana* that conforms to the freedom of movement granted to the Thaqīf. There is further evidence of *amān* in the Thaqīf treaty: the *amān* granted to the lives and property of those present was extended to those who were not. In addition, the *amān* granted to the Wādī of Ṭāʾif, Wajj, was extended to their other Wādī, Liyya:[35] *wa-mā kāna li-thaqīf min nafs ghāʾiba aw māl fa-inna lahu mina l-ʾ.m.n.* [read probably: *l-amān*] *mā li-shāhidihim*;[36] *wa-mā kāna lahum min māl bi-liyya fa-inna lahu mina l-ʾ.m.n. mā lahum* [read probably: *mā li-mālihim*] *bi-wajj*.[37] The *amān* of Wajj was in the form of its declaration as *ḥaram* or sacred territory, while the *amān* granted to those present was their declaration as *amana* [written: *umma*] *mina l-muslimīna*. The Thaqīf treaty is

[31] *EI*[2], s.v. Ḳuḍāʿa, 315b–316a (M.J. Kister); *idem*, *Concepts and Ideas at the Dawn of Islam*, III, 3.

[32] Ibn Saʿd, I, 274–75.

[33] Qurṭubī, *Tafsīr*, XVI, 348, interpretation of Qurʾān 49,14.

[34] Abū ʿUbayd, *Amwāl*, 248 no. 507; *Wath.*, 285 no. 181. The wording of this clause in Ibn Zanjawayh, *Amwāl*, II, 453 no. 735, is: *wa-hum umma* [read: *amana*] *mina l-muslimīna yatawallajūna mina l-muslimīna ḥaythu mā shāʾū wa-ayna mā tawallajū*. The clause was not reciprocal, since the Thaqīf could prevent the entrance of unwanted people into their territory: *wa-man karihū an yalija ʿalayhim mina l-nās fa-innahu lā yaliju ʿalayhim*.

[35] Kister, "Some Reports Concerning al-Ṭāʾif", 14–15, 17.

[36] Indeed, the Thaqīf delegation requested "to conclude a treaty concerning the rest of their tribe as well as their lands" (*wa-yaktubūna kitāban ʿalā man warāʾahum min qawmihim wa-bilādihim*); Wāqidī, III, 964:10.

[37] Abū ʿUbayd, *Amwāl*, 248 no. 507; *Wath.*, 285 no. 181. Ibn Zanjawayh, *Amwāl*, II, 454 no. 735, has in both places *l-amr* instead of *l-ʾ.m.n.* which should be considered the *lectio facilior*.

comparable to the Ḥudaybiyya treaty in that they ended the sieges of Ṭāʾif and Mecca, respectively.[38]

Seventh, the variant reading *amana* can possibly be supported by another variant, *dhimma*, that belongs to the same semantic sphere: *wa-inna* LI-*yahūd banī ʿawf dhimma mina l-muʾminīna....* This variant appears in the versions of Ibn Isḥāq's recension found in books by Ibn Taymiyya (d. 728/1328) and his student, Ibn Qayyim al-Jawziyya (d. 751/1350). The reading *dhimma* is repeated in Ibn Taymiyya's comments on the Kitāb (*thumma bayyana anna li-yahūd kull baṭn mina l-anṣār dhimma mina l-muʾminīna*). He goes on to explain that all the Jews of Medina had alliances with either the Aws or one of the *buṭūn* of the Khazraj. According to him, the Qaynuqāʿ were the allies of the ʿAwf b. al-Khazraj, the *baṭn* listed first in the document.[39] It seems unlikely that Ibn Taymiyya forged the clause by replacing *yahūd... umma...* with *li-yahūd... dhimma...*, although *dhimma* may have been more convenient from his point of view. Perhaps a scribe copying one of the sources employed by Ibn Taymiyya considered *amana* to be too obscure and replaced it with the more common *dhimma*.

Eighth, it seems improbable that the Yahūd with whom a *muwādaʿa* treaty was concluded were part of the *umma* declared in §2. It is even less

[38]In the latter treaty the *amān* exchanged by the parties is followed by a clause similar to the *tawallaja/walaja* clause of the Thaqīf treaty. The non-belligerency treaty is indicated by the verb *hādana* which is synonymous with *wādaʿa*: *fa-hādanat quraysh rasūla llāhi ṣ wa-ṣālaḥathu ʿalā sinīna arbaʿ an yaʾmana baʿḍuhum baʿḍan ...fa-man qadima ḥājjan aw muʿtamiran aw mujtāzan ilā l-yaman aw ilā l-ṭāʾif fa-huwa āmin, wa-man qadima l-madīna mina l-mushrikīna ʿāmidan ilā l-shām aw ilā l-mashriq fa-huwa āmin*; Abū ʿUbayd, *Amwāl*, 207. Ibn Shahrāshūb, I, 175, has only: *wa-ṣṭalaḥā ʿalā waḍʿi l-ḥarb ʿani l-nās sabʿ sinīna yaʾmanu fīhinna l-nās wa-yakuffu baʿḍuhum ʿan baʿḍ wa-yaʾmanu l-mujtāzīna* [!] *mina l-farīqayni*. See also Ṭabarī, *Tafsīr*, XXVI, 61:4, interpretation of Qurʾān, 48,25. The treaty with the Nubians concluded at the time of ʿUthmān was a non-belligerency treaty (*amān wa-hudna*) and prescribed free movement for each party in the other party's territory; *Wath.*, 530–31 no. 369: *ʿalā an tadkhulū baladanā mujtāzīna ghayr muqīmīna fīhi wa-nadkhula baladakum mujtāzīna ghayr muqīmīna fīhi*. See also Ayalon, "The Nubian Dam".

[39]*Wa-lam yakun bi-l-madīna aḥad mina l-yahūd illā wa-lahu ḥilf, immā maʿa l-aws aw maʿa baʿḍ buṭūni l-khazraj. Wa-kāna banū Qaynuqāʿ ḥulafāʾ banī ʿAwf b. al-Khazraj... l-baṭni lladhīna* [*sic*] *budiʾa bihim fī hādhihi l-ṣaḥīfa*. He also mentions that the Qaynuqāʿ and the Naḍīr were the allies of the Khazraj, while the Qurayẓa were allied with the Aws; Ibn Taymiyya, *Ṣārim*, 62–64; Ibn Qayyim, *Aḥkām*, II, 837–38. Regarding the participation of the Qaynuqāʿ in the Kitāb cf. above, 57f. Cf. the saying (referring to the people of Egypt) ...*fa-man aslama minhum fa-umma wa-man aqāma minhum fa-dhimma*; *Futūḥ miṣr*, 89:15 and Glossary, 30.

likely that the Yahūd Banī ʿAwf, whatever their significance, were an *umma* on their own.

wa-inna yahūd banī ʿawf anfusahum wa-amwālahum...

> *Fāʾiq* has: *wa-inna yahūd banī ʿawf* ANFUSAHUM WA-AMWĀLAHUM *amana mina l-muʾminīna, li-l-yahūd dīnuhum wa-li-l-muʾminīna dīnuhum.*
>
> Abū ʿUbayd's *Amwāl* has: *wa-inna yahūd banī ʿawf* WA-MAWĀLIYAHUM WA-ANFUSAHUM *umma mina l-muʾminīna, li-l-yahūd dīnuhum wa-li-l-muʾminīna dīnuhum.*
>
> Ibn Zanjawayh has: *wa-inna yahūd banī ʿawf umma mina l-muʾminīna, li-l-yahūd dīnuhum wa-li-l-muʾminīna dīnuhum* WA-MAWĀLĪHIM WA-ANFUSIHIM. . . .

Should Ibn Isḥāq's *mawālīhim* be replaced by *Fāʾiq*'s *amwālahum*?[40] The common association of *amwāl* with *amān* in the early treaties of Muḥammad can be used as an argument in favour of *Fāʾiq*'s version; this could be further corroborated by the occurrence of *māl* and *nafs* in §23. But *mawālin* and *anfus* appear twice in the Kitāb itself, in §§38: *wa-inna mawāliya thaʿlaba ka-anfusihim*,[41] and 57: *wa-inna yahūda l-aws mawāliyahum wa-anfusahum ʿalā mithl mā li-ahl hādhihi l-ṣaḥīfa....*

dīn/dayn

Gil (63–64) suggests to read in §28 *dayn* instead of *dīn*:

> The real and practical result of the new status for the *mawālī* [i.e., according to Gil, the Jews who participated in the Kitāb — M. L.] is indicated by the statement that the Muslims are responsible for the debts of their Jewish clients. In the phrase: *Wa-li-l-muslimīna daynuhum mawālīhim wa-anfusihim* one has probably to understand *dyn* as *dayn*, rather than *dīn*. If *dīn* is meant here, the phrase is very inaccurate indeed, both logically and grammatically. It does not seem to be a proclamation of

[40] As to *Fāʾiq*'s *wa-li-l-muʾminīna dīnuhum*, Ibn Isḥāq's *wa-li-l-muslimīna dīnuhum* is more difficult, and hence preferable.

[41] Comparing §28 to §34 one expects to find *mawālin* in the latter clause. However, the *mawāli Thaʿlaba* appear in §38 that fills the gap. The clause is not found in Abū ʿUbayd.

> religious tolerance, rather it proclaims the responsibility of the Muslims for debts, both those of their *mawālī*, and their own. ...In other words, the *Anṣār* will have to pay if their Jewish clients do not....

The reading *dayn* is unfounded.[42] That Abū ʿUbayd read here *dīn* is demonstrated by his somewhat apologetic interpretation of the *umma/amana* clause.[43] *Dīn* reappears in §56 that concerns mutual military aid. It stipulates that the Muʾminūn will provide aid to the Jews with one exception: ... *illā man ḥāraba fī l-dīn*.[44] This is parallel to the fighting *fī sabīli llāh* in the first part of the Kitāb, namely in §§19 and 21; for the Jews it was not war in the path of Allāh but fighting *fī l-dīn*. Finally, *dayn* would have required the preposition *ʿalā* rather than *li-*.[45]

yūtighu

The context in which the verb *yūtighu* is usually employed suggests that §28 refers to punishment on the Day of Resurrection rather than retaliation in this world. The verb appears in a stern warning, in the garb of a prophetic *ḥadīth*, addressed to all men of authority.[46] §28 is comparable at this point to §25: ... *fa-inna ʿalayhi laʿnata llāhi wa-ghaḍabahu yawma l-qiyāma*.

ahl baytihi

The phrase is also found in §§34 and 42. With regard to §42 Serjeant (31) remarks: "By 'the people of his house' (*ahl bayti-hi*) only the males are intended". He is probably right: *ahl bayt* in the Kitāb means *ʿāqila*.[47]

---

[42] It was also rejected by Donner, "From Believers to Muslims", 31–32.

[43] *Innamā arāda naṣrahumu l-muʾminīna wa-muʿāwanatahum iyyāhum ʿalā ʿaduwwihim bi-l-nafaqati llatī sharaṭahā ʿalayhim, fa-ammā l-dīn fa-laysū minhu fī shayʾ. Alā tarāhu qad bayyana dhālika fa-qāla: li-l-yahūd dīnuhum wa-li-l-muʾminīna dīnuhum?*; *Amwāl*, 266 no. 519.

[44] Cf. *mā dāmū muḥāribīna* in §27.

[45] As has been pointed out by Rubin, 16 n. 44. See also above, 143n.

[46] *Mā min amīr ʿashara illā wa-huwa yajīʾu yawma l-qiyāma maghlūla yadāhu ilā ʿunuqihi ḥattā yakūna ʿamaluhu huwa lladhī yuṭliquhu aw yūtighuhu*; Abū ʿUbayd, *Gharīb*, III, 170; Abū ʿUbayd interprets *yuṭliquhu*: *yunjīhi*, and *yūtighuhu*: *yuhlikuhu*.

[47] Cf. Madelung, *The Succession to Muḥammad*, 15: "The *ahl al-bayt* of Muḥammad meant, as was consistent with the general usage of the term at the time, primarily his blood relations, the same Banū Hāshim who were forbidden to receive alms in order that their state of purity not be soiled and, in second place, the wives".

Muḥammad's *ahl bayt* were gathered by him when Qur'ān 26,214 (*wa-andhir ʿashīrataka l-aqrabīna*) was revealed; they included 30 men.[48] Those gathered were Muḥammad's *ʿāqila*: another *ḥadīth* describing a similar gathering has it that Muḥammad addressed the Banū ʿAbd al-Muṭṭalib.[49] The Prophet reportedly foretold in resignation the ascension to the throne of the descendants of al-Ḥakam b. Abī l-ʿĀṣ when their number would reach 30 or 40.[50] The numbers 30 and 40 also appear in prophetic *ḥadīth*s clearly hostile to this family's ascension to the throne.[51] Marwān b. al-Ḥakam supposedly asked the caliph Muʿāwiya for support because he (the former) was the father of ten (males), the paternal uncle of ten and the brother of ten.[52] Marwān and *āl marwān*, or the family or *ʿāqila* of Marwān, were *ahl bayt min qays*.[53] This refers to the fact that al-Ḥakam b. Abī l-ʿĀṣ was married over the years to three wives from the Qays who bore him children.[54]

The Kitāb provides us at this point a valuable extra-Qur'ānic occurrence of the expression *ahl al-bayt* in its original environment of genealogy and blood vengeance.[55]

---

[48]Ṭabarī, *Tahdhīb al-āthār* (Musnad ʿAlī), 60–61: *jamaʿa rasūlu llāh ṣ ʿalayhi ahl baytihi fa-jtamaʿū thalāthīna rajulan.*

[49]*Ibid.*, 62–63.

[50]*Iṣāba*, II, 105 no. 1783.

[51]Ibn Kathīr, *Bidāya*, VI, 242; VIII, 258–59.

[52]*Ibid.*, VI, 242:20. In Ṭabarī, V, 536 [II, 475], read instead of *ʿashīra*: *ʿashara*; Ibn ʿAsākir, LVII, 262; Ibn Saʿd, V, 41; cf. *The History of al-Ṭabarī*, XX, trans. Hawting, 57: "Marwān is the father of a clan, the brother of a clan and the uncle of a clan ...". Cf. *ʿIqd*, V, 216: a pre-Islamic tribal leader that was the father of ten, the brother of ten and the paternal uncle of ten, all of whom were the cavalrymen of their tribe.

[53]Ṭabarī, V, 536 [II, 475]; Ibn ʿAsākir, LVII, 262.

[54]One was from the Murra b. ʿAwf and two from the Thaqīf. Marwān's mother was, however, of the Kināna; Muṣʿab, *Nasab*, 159–60.

[55]For rich evidence regarding the term *ahl al-bayt* in the sense of agnates see now Orthmann, *Stamm und Macht*, 249–54. Sharon, "*Ahl al-bayt* — People of the House", 179, argues that "the meaning of the term before its Islamization by the Prophet was the tribe of Quraysh in general"; alternatively, "the term could have even a wider meaning, which includes all those who venerated the *kaʿbah*", 180. His assumptions are untenable. If, as argued here, one's *ahl bayt* were one's *ʿāqila*, then the expression did not have its origin in *al-bayt* in the sense of "the ruling family of a tribe", as argued in *EI*², s.v. Ahl al-Bayt (I. Goldziher – C. van Arendonk and A.S. Tritton). Sharon, *ibid.*, 180, says: "...Ibn al-Kalbī, when speaking about Yarbūʿ and Qumayr, two brother families in the clan of Māzin (Ghaṭafān), says that they were '*ahl bayt fī Dimashq* — a leading family in Damascus'". He continues: "The indication of the *place* in which the family's leadership was recognized can be well understood, in view of the fact that with the growth and subdivision of the tribes, particularly after the conquests, leading families emerged in many tribal communities". But Ibn al-Kalbī, *Jamhara*, 441, refers to the Qumayr alone

§35. *wa-inna jafna baṭn min thaʿlaba ka-anfusihim*

THE JAFNA[56] ARE A TRIBAL GROUP OF THE THAʿLABA AND ARE ON A PAR WITH THEM.

Wellhausen (70, 71): "Die Gafna, eine zu den Thaʿlaba gehörige Familie, stehen diesen selber gleich".
Wensinck (57): "Jafnah are a subdivision of Thaʿlabah. They are like them".
Watt (223): "Jafnah, a subdivision of Thaʿlabah, are like them".
Serjeant (27): "Jafnah is a sept of Thaʿlabah like themselves".

The recensions of Ibn Isḥāq and Abū ʿUbayd differ considerably with regard to Jafna. In Ibn Isḥāq's recension Jafna is a *baṭn* or tribal group of the Thaʿlaba and the clause is located after a clause dealing with the Thaʿlaba. (The word *ka-anfusihim* does not appear in some versions.) In Abū ʿUbayd's recension, Banū al-Shaṭba (sometimes referred to as al-Shuṭayba) are a *baṭn* of Jafna and the clause is located towards the end of the Kitāb (without *ka-anfusihim*).

Gil (61) writes regarding the term *baṭn*: "*Baṭn* (further: *biṭāna*) is the equivalent of *ḥayy, qabīla*, and *fakhidh*, and fell into desuetude in the early Islamic period. It probably designated the smallest unit within a tribe". However, *biṭāna* (§39) is irrelevant here and has another meaning; and *baṭn* is not the equivalent of the other terms.[57]

The *ʿāqila* (or *ʿaṣaba*) that was the smallest tribal group was smaller, sometimes much smaller, than a *baṭn*. This can be demonstrated by a passage from Ibn Ḥazm's *Muḥallā* on the responsibility for blood money, which in his opinion should start with the *ʿaṣaba* and not go beyond the *baṭn*.[58]

---

when he says that they are *ahl bayt bi-Dimashq*; moreover, living in Damascus they could not have been a leading family of the nomadic ʿAbs to which they belonged, but merely "a family" or alternatively "an *ʿāqila*". Instead of Khālid b. Burd (Sharon, *ibid.*, 181) read: Khālid b. Barz; see Elad, "The Southern Golan in the Early Muslim Period", 60–62. In Sharon, *ibid.*, 181 n. 37, where there is reference to Ibn Durayd, *Ishtiqāq*, 359, read instead of Abū al-Jiddayh: Dhū l-Jaddayni. This was the nickname of Qays b. Masʿūd's great-grandfather. See also above, 106n.

[56] On their identity see above, 79, 85.

[57] Cf. *Lisān al-ʿarab*, XIII, 54b, s.v. *b-ṭ-n*: *wa-l-baṭn dūna l-qabīla, wa-qīla huwa dūna l-fakhidh wa-fawqa l-ʿimāra*; ... *al-baṭn mā dūna l-qabīla wa-fawqa l-fakhidh.* See also Abū ʿUbayd, *al-Gharīb al-muṣannaf*, I, 110 (Ibn al-Kalbī ← his father): *al-shaʿb akthar* [read: *akbar*?] *mina l-qabīla thumma l-qabīla thumma l-ʿimāra thumma l-baṭn thumma l-fakhidh.*

[58] *Fa-wajaba an nabdaʾa fī l-ʿaql bi-l-ʿaṣaba kamā amara rasūlu llāh ṣ, wa-an lā natajāwaza l-baṭn kamā ḥadda rasūlu llāh ṣ ... yukallafu* [*sic*] *dhālika l-ʿaṣaba ḥaythu kānū ilā l-baṭn...*; Ibn Ḥazm, *Muḥallā*, XI, 48. That a *baṭn* is larger than an *ʿāqila* may also

The term *baṭn* was in use at least to the early ʿAbbāsid period, as can be demonstrated by the story of the Ghirāra, a *baṭn* belonging to the Jusham (who participated in the Kitāb). Their eponym is removed from Jusham by three generations: Ghirāra b. Mālik b. Ghaḍb b. Jusham. The Ghirāra were the smallest *baṭn* among the Banū Mālik b. Ghaḍb. When one of them killed a member of another *baṭn* of the Mālik b. Ghaḍb, the Ghirāra offered to pay blood money. But the victim's agnates (*ahl al-qatīl*) demanded an eye-for-an-eye retaliation. When the Bayāḍa intervened in favour of the victims, the Ghirāra chose to leave the court (*dār*) of the Bayāḍa (who were probably the strongest group in the court) and go to Qubāʾ, where they made an alliance and intermarried with the ʿAmr b. ʿAwf (Aws). On the eve of Islam they tried in vain to return to their kin — they wanted to join Bayāḍa's brothers, the Zurayq — but had to remain with their "maternal uncles", the ʿAmr b. ʿAwf. They were still there at the time of the ʿAbbāsid caliph al-Mahdī, who in 160/177 included the Anṣār among the recipients of the annual *ʿaṭāʾ* (*faraḍa... li-l-anṣār*); at that time they transferred their registration to the Bayāḍa (*fa-ntaqalū bi-dīwānihim ilā banī bayāḍa*).[59] It appears that the reference to the Ghirāra as a *baṭn* reflects a living usage in Medina at the time of Muḥammad as well as much later. The settlement of the blood feud took place at the level of the Ghirāra *baṭn*: the offer of blood money, the negotiations with the Bayāḍa and finally the exile. This small tribal group preserved its tribal identity at least to the time of al-Mahdī and perhaps much later. For them and for the rest of the Anṣār the intricacies of tribal genealogy were not a matter of academic indulgence; they were basic facts of life.

§36. *wa-inna li-banī l-shuṭayba mithl mā li-yahūd banī ʿawf*.

THE BANŪ L-SHUṬAYBA[60] HAVE THE SAME [rights] AS THE JEWS OF BANŪ ʿAWF.

§37. *wa-inna l-barr dūna l-āthim*

THE RIGHTEOUS MAN WILL RESTRAIN THE SINNER.

---

be suggested by the fact that three *baṭns* from Kinda had mosques of their own in Kūfa; Lecker, "Kinda on the Eve of Islam and During the *Ridda*", 344–45, 347.

[59]Samhūdī, I, 207–208. They are called here ʿAdhāra instead of Ghirāra; but I follow Caskel, s.v., II, 275.

[60]On whom see above, 80.

Wellhausen (70):[61] "Lauterkeit steht vor Trug", to which he adds: "Der letzte Satz... scheint unter der Hülle der sehr allgemeinen Wahrheit, dass Lauterkeit vor Trug schütze oder Trug hindere, einen sanften Ausdruck des Mistrauens zu erhalten".
Wensinck (57): "Honesty without treachery [is demanded]". He adds: "It is doubtful that these words express assurance or admonition".
Watt (224): "[H]onourable dealing (comes) before treachery". He adds this alternative: "Or 'honourable dealing without treachery (is demanded)'".
Serjeant (27, 28): "Observation of one's undertakings eliminates treachery/breaking of treaties". He adds: "This is one of the commonest terminal formulae[62] in these engagements... the terminal formula is an injunction to the signatories and those whom they represent to adhere to the undertakings which they swore to observe".

The above clause appears in the Kitāb three times. Both medieval and modern scholars assumed that it includes two abstract nouns.[63] But the widely accepted vocalization of these nouns appears to be wrong. Instead of *birr* read: *barr/bārr*, and instead of *ithm* read: *āthim*. §57 probably includes the expression *al-barr al-muḥsin*, as in §64.[64] §37 stipulates that those of the Jews who observe the fulfillment of the Kitāb will restrain those who would violate it; literally, they have to intervene between them and their perfidy.[65]

[61] At the end of the clause on the Shuṭayba.

[62] On which see below, 185f.

[63] See, for example, Zamakhsharī, *Fā'iq*, II, 26, s.v. *r-b-ʿ*: *al-birr dūna l-ithm*: *ayi l-wafā' bi-l-ʿahdi lladhī maʿahu l-sukūn wa-l-ṭum'anīna ahwan mina l-nakthi l-mu'addī ilā l-ḥurūb wa-l-matāʿibi l-jamma.*

[64] §64 is missing in Serjeant (39). Suhaylī's interpretation of the preposition *dūna* (II, 252) is accurate: *al-birru wa-l-wafā' yanbaghī an yakūnā ḥājizan ʿani l-ithm*, the righteous should form a barrier. The expression *yaḥūlu dūnahu* (above, 125f) has the same meaning.

[65] Serjeant (28) renders the expression *abarra llāhu qasamahu*: "Allāh verified his oath", but one expects here: "May Allāh render his oath fulfilled". Serjeant quotes from Bukhārī the expression *man law aqsama ʿalā llāh la-abarrahu*, which he renders: "Of the servants of Allāh is he who, should he swear by Allāh, would fulfil it". But the subject of the verb *abarra* is Allāh, not His servant. Cf. Samhūdī, I, 126: Yazīd b. Muʿāwiya took an oath to have Ibn al-Zubayr brought before him in shackles. Someone thought of an ingenious way of fulfilling the oath without humiliating Ibn al-Zubayr, but the latter refused, saying: "May God not fulfil his oath" (... *fa-aqsama lā yu'tā illā maghlūlan... wa-tubirra qasamahu...*, *qāla fa-lā abarra llāh qasamahu*). Regarding the meaning of *birr* cf. Kister, "*al-Taḥannuth*", 234–35. For verses including oaths with derivatives of *b-r-r* see Kowalski, "Zu dem Eid bei den altern Arabern", 69 (*yamīn ṣidq barra*), 72 (*aliyyat barr ṣādiq*), 79 (*yamīn mri' barr*).

§38. *wa-inna mawāliya thaʿlaba ka-anfusihim*

THE ALLIES OF THE THAʿLABA ARE ON A PAR WITH THEM.

Wellhausen (70): "Die Beisassen der Thaʿlaba stehen ihnen selber gleich". Wensinck (57) and Watt (224): "The clients of the Thaʿlabah are like them". Serjeant (29): "The clients/allies of Thaʿlaba are as themselves".

§39. *wa-inna biṭānat yahūd ka-anfusihim*

THE NOMADIC ALLIES OF THE JEWS ARE ON A PAR WITH THEM.

Wellhausen (71): "Die Freundschaft der Juden steht ihnen selber gleich".[66] Wensinck (57, 58n): "The friends of the Jews are like them". He comments: "These friends of the Jews were probably Arab proselytes not belonging to the Banū Qaylah who had been associated with the Jews for a long time". Watt (224): "The *biṭānah* of (particular) Jews are as themselves".[67] Serjeant (29, 30): "Those associated with Jews (with alliance and bonds of mutual protection) are as themselves". His interpretation is along the lines suggested by Wensinck. He adds: "What is meant by the *biṭānah* of Jews (Yahūd, as if a tribe) is... not certain. The clue perhaps lies in *Aghānī*, XIX, 95, where it is stated that the Banū M.rānah (Samhūdī, I, 152, Banū M.rābah, the vocalization being uncertain) who used to live in the place of Banū Ḥārithah, the Khazraj tribe[68] had septs of Arabs (*buṭūn min al-ʿArab*), i.e. Arab sedentaries as opposed to tribal Arabs (Aʿrāb), living alongside them.... It may have been for some economic reason that these Arab septs were associated with the Jews, as merchants, or camel-hirers, or possibly... as sharecroppers, and indeed such a possibility is not to be entirely excluded".

Serjeant's interpretation of the *Aghānī* passage is questionable: although the M.rāna are mentioned just before the sentence *wa-kāna maʿahum min*

[66]He refers to the Qur'ānic *biṭāna* (Qur'ān 3,118) that means "Leute, die eigentlich der Gemeinde fremd und nur durch Freundschaft und Wahl ihr zugehörig sind". Like the Jafna, the Shuṭayba and the *mawālī thaʿlaba* of the preceding clauses, this clause deals with non-Jews who were closely connected to the Jews, "Nichtjuden... die sich aber zu den Juden halten". He continues: "Vielleicht ist das Wort zu einem halben Eigennamen für eine ganz bestimmte Gruppe von Familien geworden, die durch ihr Verhältnis zu den Juden eine Sonderstellung einnahmen. Ein staatsrechtlicher Begriff, wie *Mavālī*, scheint *Bitâna* nicht zu sein".

[67]Referring to the sources employed by Wellhausen he interprets the term as "those who were closely connected with some Medinan Jews by ties of friendship, not of blood".

[68]In fact the Ḥāritha were of the Aws; see above, 71.

ghayr banī isrāʾīl buṭūn mina l-ʿarab, it does not mean that the M.rāna "had septs of Arabs... living alongside them". The preposition *maʿahum* refers to the Jews of Medina as a whole, as is shown by the parallel text in Samhūdī (I, 162): ... *mimman kāna mina l-ʿarab maʿa yahūd qabla l-anṣār, banū unayf*....

The meaning of *biṭāna* is close to that suggested by Ḥamīdullāh: *lladhīna khārija l-qarya wa-l-madīna*.[69] *Biṭāna* appears in *ḥadīth al-istisqāʾ*: "And the people of the *biṭāna* clamoured, asking for aid" (*wa-jāʾa ahlu l-biṭāna yaḍijjūna*). *Biṭāna* is interpreted as "those living outside Medina" (or outside the area inhabited by the settled community, *al-khārij mina l-madīna*).[70] The *biṭāna* are the nomadic (or semi-nomadic) groups living outside the sedentary community and maintaining close contacts with it. During the hot season they are sheltered by the settled population, and the same occurs at times of drought. The events during *ʿām al-ramāda* or "the year of drought" at the time of ʿUmar demonstrate how this relationship functioned.[71]

Istabṭanahu, literally: "he put him in his belly", is used figuratively of one of the settled population who grants protection to a nomad. A black camel shepherd returned to Baṣra after a long grazing period in the vicinity of Yamāma, where he only met Persian-speaking peasants with whom he could not communicate. He was much relieved to be among Arabs again, and made this observation: "In my opinion, compared to the rest of mankind, the Arabs are like a wound on a horse's skin. Had God not had mercy upon them and had he not 'put them in his belly' (*jaʿalahum fī ḥashāhu*), these Persians would have blotted out all trace of them". The phrase *jaʿalahum fī ḥashāhu*, i.e. *istabṭanahum*, means: he gave them shelter; a man would say to a nomad to whom he gave shelter: "I hid you in my belly".[72]

---

[69]Ḥamīdullāh, "Aqdam dustūr", 123. Cf. *Wath.*, 585: *ayi l-yahūdu lladhīna khārija l-Madīna*, "the Jews living outside Medina".

[70]Ibn al-Athīr, *Nihāya*, I, 136, s.v.; *Lisān al-ʿarab*, XIII, 55a, s.v. *b-ṭ-n*. Harawī, *Gharībayni*, I, 182, interprets *al-biṭāna* in connection with *wa-jāʾa ahlu l-biṭāna yaḍijjūna*: *al-biṭāna — khārij al-madīna*. *Biṭāna* and *ẓihāra* belong to the *aḍdād* or "the words that have two opposite meanings"; Anbārī, *Aḍdād*, 342 no. 228.

[71]Ibn ʿAsākir, XLIV, 348 (when it finally rained, ʿUmar hastened to send them back to their respective tribal territories, *ilā bādiyatihim*); Lecker, "Muḥammad at Medina", 31.

[72]*ʿIqd*, III, 325-26: *wa-mā raʾaytu hādhihi l-ʿarab fī jamīʿi l-nās illā miqdāra l-qarḥa fī jildi l-faras. Wa-lawlā anna llāha raqqa ʿalayhim fa-jaʿalahum fī ḥashāhu la-ṭamasat hādhihi l-ʿujmān āthārahum... wa-qawluhu: jaʿalahum fī ḥashāhu, ayi stabṭanahum, yaqūlu l-rajul li-l-ʿarabī idhā stabṭanahu: khabaʾtuka fī ḥashāya.* See also the expression *wa-ḍammatka li-l-aḥshāʾ*, referring to Bakr b. Wāʾil's protection of Farazdaq; Jumaḥī, I, 358 no. 470.

The *biṭāna* of the Jews were the bedouin who allied themselves with them and sometimes converted to Judaism.[73]

This clause is comparable though not identical to clauses in Muḥammad's treaties that extend the rights of the settled to the nomads. In his treaty with the Juhayna we find: *wa-li-ahl bādiyatihim man barra minhum wa-ttaqā mā li-ḥāḍiratihim.*[74] The treaty of Najrān is addressed to the people of Najrān and their *ḥāshiya*, viz. the nomads (or semi-nomads) living in the vicinity of Najrān and maintaining close connections with its people.[75]

§40. *wa-innahu lā yakhruju minhum aḥad illā bi-idhn muḥammad*

NO-ONE OF THEM [viz. of the Jews' nomadic allies] MAY GO OUT [of Medina] WITHOUT MUḤAMMAD'S PERMISSION.

Wellhausen (71): "Es darf keiner von ihnen[76] zu Felde ziehen ohne Erlaubnis Muhammads". He connects it to §62, *wa-innahu man kharaja āmin...* which he renders: "Wer zu Felde zieht...".
Wensinck (58): "No one of them (Wensinck explains: "The people of this document") shall go out [to war] without Muhammad's consent".
Watt (224): "No one of them (? those belonging to the *ummah*) may go out (to war) without the permission of Muḥammad (peace be upon him)".
Serjeant (29, 30): "No one will come out from them, except by permission from Muḥammad, Allāh bless and honour him". He remarks: "*Kharaja* means 'to disassociate from'.

Thus Serjeant interprets the verb *kharaja* in a report found in Hamdānī, *Iklīl*, X, 179, but there is no need to abandon the common meaning of the verb. Hamdānī's report concerns a murderer who, having been sheltered by his

---

[73] Cf. Lecker, "On Arabs of the Banū Kilāb Executed Together with the Jewish Banū Qurayẓa".

[74] Above, 144. See also the treaty of the Aslam: *wa-li-ahl bādiyatihim mā li-ahl ḥāḍiratihim wa-innahum muhājirūna ḥaythu kānū*; Ibn Saʿd, I, 271.

[75] Ibn Saʿd, I, 288:8: *wa-li-najrān wa-ḥāshiyatihim jiwāru llāhi wa-dhimmat muḥammad...*; Abū ʿUbayd, *Amwāl*, 244 no. 503. Balādhurī, *Futūḥ*, Glossarium, 28, s.v., has *territorium adjacens urbi*; but the extension appears to relate to the people of Najrān's *bādiya*, not to their land. The treaty that Suwayd b. Muqarrin concluded with the people of Qūmis was addressed to *ahl qūmis wa-man ḥashaw*; Ṭabarī, IV, 152 [I, 2657]. Elsewhere it is possible to understand *ḥāshiya* as "suburbs" or "the *territory adjoining* a city or town"; *Futūḥ miṣr*, Glossary, 35*. Cf. the phrase *ahl ḥawāshī arḍika* in Suwayd b. Muqarrin's treaty with Ṭabaristān; Ṭabarī, IV, 153 [I, 2659]: ...*ʿalā an takuffa luṣūtaka wa-ahl ḥawāshī arḍika*; cf. *The History of al-Ṭabarī*, XIV, trans. Rex Smith, 30–31: "...on condition that you restrain your robbers and the people on the borders of your territory".

[76] According to Wellhausen, this refers to the Jews.

"maternal uncles", shed blood again, went out (*kharaja*) and was sheltered by the Madhḥij: ...*fa-ajārathu akhwāluhu...thumma aḥdatha fīhim wa-kharaja fa-jāwara fī madhḥij*. Serjeant remarks: "The Ḥaḍramī tribes have the expression *mutakharrī mutabarrī* = *mutakharrij mutabarri'* in the sense of 'disassociating oneself from', and of course this is the meaning of the Khawārij — those who disassociated themselves from ʿAlī b. Abī Ṭālib".

A prohibition to leave Medina is included in the following saying:[77] "[All of] the towns were conquered by the sword except Medina, which was conquered by the Qur'ān. Shortly after his arrival at Medina the pledge of allegiance given to the Messenger [of God] prescribed that no one would leave it and whoever left it would be committing an act of disobedience".[78] It is not clear which pledge of allegiance is meant here, but in any case it is unrelated to the Kitāb. Perhaps it belongs to the *ḥadīth*s created in the Umayyad period that prohibited the people of Medina from leaving it. Their background must have been a sharp fall in the number of the town's inhabitants.[79]

The clause is linked to the preceding one: the *biṭāna* of the Jews or their nomadic allies are hereby prohibited from leaving Medina or its vicinity without Muḥammad's permission. Muḥammad sought to limit the freedom of movement of these mobile and potentially dangerous elements.[80]

---

[77] Possibly attributed to Mālik b. Anas; but perhaps the two following sentences should not be lumped together.

[78] Ḥimyarī, *Rawḍ*, 401b:6, s.v. Ṭayba: *uftutiḥati l-qurā bi-l-sayf wa-ftutiḥati l-madīna bi-l-qur'ān. Wa-kānat bayʿat rasūli llāhi ṣ fī awwal qudūmihi l-madīna allā yakhruja aḥad ʿanhā, fa-man kharaja kāna ʿāṣiyan.*

[79] Cf. the saying attributed to the caliph ʿUmar b. ʿAbd al-ʿAzīz: *samiʿtu bi-l-madīna wa-l-nās yawma'idhin bihā kathīr...*; Ibn ʿAsākir, X, 229. See also Arazi, "Matériaux pour l'étude du conflit de préséance entre la Mekke et Médine", 180. (On 182 read *khabath al-ḥadīd* instead of *khubth al-ḥadīd*; Muʿādh b. Jabal instead of Maʿādh b. Jabal.)

[80] Some comparable evidence concerns unspecified bedouins who had embraced Islam and then asked for the Prophet's permission to go out to their tribal territory. They proceeded farther and farther from Medina until they joined the polytheists; Rāzī, *Tafsīr*, X, 218, interpretation of Qur'ān, 4,88: ...*nazalat fī qawm qadimū ʿalā l-nabī ṣ wa-ālihi muslimīna fa-aqāmū bi-l-madīna mā shā'a llāh, thumma qālū: yā rasūla llāhi, nurīdu an nakhruja ilā l-ṣaḥrā' fa-'dhan lanā fīhi. Fa-adhina lahum. Fa-lammā kharajū lam yazālū yarḥalūna marḥala marḥala ḥattā laḥiqū bi-l-mushrikīna.* See also the interpretation of the same verse in Suyūṭī, *Durr*, II, 190:17, 191:3.

Even if we assume that the Jews as a whole are addressed here rather than their *biṭāna*, this clause is a prohibition to leave Medina and not a prohibition to go out to war.[81]

§41. *wa-innahu lā yunḥajazu ʿalā thaʾr jurḥ*[82]

THERE IS NO REFRAINING FROM RETALIATION FOR A WOUND.

Wellhausen (71):[83] "Es soll freilich niemand verhindert werden eine Wunde zu rächen".
Wensinck (58): "But no one shall be prevented from taking vengeance for wounds".
Watt (224): "... but he is not restrained from taking vengeance for wounds".
Serjeant (29, 30–31): "A wound will not be restricted to retaliation". He remarks: "This difficult clause is to be explained in the light of Qurʾān V, 45, which states 'We (Allāh) prescribed for the Jews in the Torah, a soul for a soul, an eye for an eye, etc. and *al-jurūḥa qiṣāṣ-un*, glossed by al-Bayḍāwī... as *dhātu qiṣāṣ-in.* That is — wounds will be avenged by retaliation on the wounder". Referring to Ibn al-Athīr, *Nihāya*, I, 345, s.v. *ḥ-j-z*, where *inḥajaza* has the sense of "refraining from blood vengeance", Serjeant argues that "it might be possible to understand the clause as, 'Blood revenge for a wound will not be refrained from', i.e. it *must* be exacted. This however seems out of line with the Prophet's policy". Serjeant quotes M.A. al-Ghul's suggested rendering: "He cannot be detained because of a claim for an injury/wound only".

The *ḥadīth* quoted by Ibn al-Athīr under *ḥ-j-z* deals with a murder following which the victim's family, both men and women — or, according to another view, only his agnates — have the right to refrain from retaliating by killing the murderer: *wa-li-ahli l-qatīl an yanḥajizū l-adnā fa-l-adnā, wa-in kānati mraʾa*, i.e. starting from the nearest of kin, even if it were a woman.[84]

[81]Cf. in *Manāqib mazyadiyya*, I, 318, the agreement between Quṣayy and the Khuzāʿa forbidding the latter to leave the *ḥaram* of Mecca: ... *wa-l-ḥaram li-quṣayy wa-qawmihi wa-khuzāʿa jīrān fīhi wa-lā yakhrujūna ʿanhu.*

[82]Abū ʿUbayd does not have this clause.

[83]As we have just seen he understood the preceding clause as a prohibition to go to war.

[84]Ibn al-Athīr, *Nihāya*, I, 345, s.v. *ḥ-j-z.* Also Abū ʿUbayd, *Gharīb*, II, 160–61, s.v. The liberal approach was the Iraqī one, while the Ḥijāzīs, probably following Arabian practice, gave the right to the agnates alone. Abū ʿUbayd himself inclined to the former opinion.

Jurm would seem to be a better reading than *jurḥ*, but none of the variants of Ibn Isḥāq's recension has a *mīm* instead of a *ḥā'*.[85] As we have just seen, the verb *yanḥajizu* was found in the context of murder rather than injury; *tha'r* is associated with murder, not with wounds.[86] Besides, why should the clause deal with injuries rather than with murder? One must not refrain from retaliating for a wound, but may refrain from retaliating for a murder? Finally, the following clause §42 that obviously deals with murder is probably connected to this one.

Jurm, "crime", "transgression", often relates to murder. A polytheist who *aḥdatha ḥadathan ʿaẓīman*[87] by brutally killing a Muslim acknowledged his *jurm* and fled from Muḥammad.[88] After the assassination of Kaʿb b. al-Ashraf, the Naḍīr complained to Muḥammad that he had been murdered treacherously without having committed any *jurm* or *ḥadath* of which they had knowledge.[89] The two terms designate a crime such as murder that could have been used to justify the assassination.

The clause stipulates (assuming that *jurm* is the correct reading) that the Jews must retaliate for a murder by slaying the murderer or his agnate. An obscure account (← Shaʿbī) concerns a Jew who, having killed another Jew, wished to find out through his Muslim allies (*ḥulafā'*) what Muḥammad's verdict was going to be. Should Muḥammad decree blood money, the parties would bring their case before him. But should he have in mind retaliation, they would not do it.[90] More concrete reports mention in this context the Naḍīr and Qurayẓa.[91] When a man from the former killed a man from the latter, there was usually no talion but only blood money because of the

---

[85] Admittedly, also *jurḥ* is found in the context of retaliation; cf. the expression *waliyyu l-dam wa-l-jurḥ*, i.e. a member of the *ʿāqila* who must retaliate for the murder or wounding of one of its members; Ṭabarī, *Tafsīr*, VI, 136:10, interpretation of Qur'ān 5,33.

[86] Lane, I, 328a, s.v. *tha'r*: "Blood-revenge; or retaliation of murder or homicide; or a seeking to revenge, or avenge, or retaliate, blood; or a desire, or seeking, for retaliation of a crime or of enmity", etc. In *ʿIqd*, V, 133:-1, *ṣāḥib tha'rihim* is the murderer who should be slain in retaliation for his crime. *Thā'ir* is the person who should retaliate for a murder; Wāqidī, II, 655; *Lisān al-ʿarab*, IV, 99, s.v. *th-'-r*: ...*al-mawtūru l-thā'ir, ay ṭālibu l-tha'r, wa-huwa ṭalabu l-dam*; see also Wāqidī, I, 408.

[87] Cf. on *muḥdith* above, 129f.

[88] Wāqidī, III, 913.

[89] *Ibid.*, I, 192: *qutila ghīla bi-lā jurm wa-lā ḥadath ʿalimnāhu.*

[90] ... *Fa-in kāna yaqḍī bi-l-diya khtaṣamnā ilayhi, wa-in kāna ya'murunā bi-l-qatl lam na'tihi*; Ṭabari, *Tafsīr*, VI, 150:3, interpretation of Qur'ān, 5,41.

[91] Cf. Ṭabarī, *Tafsīr*, VI, 157:12 (← Ibn Isḥāq ← 'Ikrima): the Naḍīr were entitled to a full *diya* (*diya kāmila*), while the Qurayẓa were only entitled to a half; the Prophet made the *diya* equal.

superiority of the former to the latter (*li-faḍlihim ʿalayhim*). But when one of the latter killed one of the former, the victim's tribe would only agree to talion because of their conceited conviction that they were superior to them (*li-faḍlihim ʿalayhim fī anfusihim taʿazzuzan*). When the Prophet came to Medina, they were in this state. They (viz. the Naḍīr) wanted to bring the matter to the Prophet, but one of the *munāfiqūn* told them that since it was a case of premeditated murder, he feared that Muḥammad would order talion. If he agreed to blood money — accept it, he added, and if not, beware of him.[92] Whatever its historicity, the account marks retaliation for a murder as an area of dispute between Muḥammad and the Jews of Medina. This is probably the context of this obscure clause that makes retaliation obligatory. The Jews who participated in the Kitāb (not including the Naḍīr and Qurayẓa) committed themselves to the standards known from elsewhere to have been demanded by Muḥammad.

§42. *wa-innahu man fataka fa-bi-nafsihi wa-ahl baytihi, illā man ẓalama*

HE WHO KILLS [someone entitled to security] KILLS HIMSELF AND HIS AGNATES, UNLESS HE [viz. his victim] ACTED UNJUSTLY.

Wellhausen (71): "...doch wer mutwillig den Frieden bricht, tut es auf kosten seiner Person und seiner Familie; es sei denn, dass ihm Unrecht geschah...".
Wensinck (58): "...Whoever acts on his own account [involves] himself and his family, except him who has been wronged".[93]
Watt (224): "Whoever acts rashly, it (involves) only himself and his household, except where a man has been wronged".
Serjeant (29, 31): "Whosoever assassinates, assassinates himself and the people of his house, except if (he assassinate) one who acts wrongfully (*ẓalama*)". He comments: "By 'the people of his house' only the males are intended. Among the noble tribes there was a code of honour about womenfolk, at least those of tribal standing". He goes on to give an example from the Yemen. Regarding *fataka* he quotes a prophetic *ḥadīth*: *qayyada l-īmānu l-fatk, lā yaftiku muʾmin.*

[92]... *Fa-in qabila minkumu l-diya fa-khudhūhu* [*sic*], *wa-illā fa-kūnū minhu ʿalā ḥadhar*; Ṭabarī, *Tafsīr*, VI, 154:1 (← Qatāda), interpretation of Qurʾān, 5,46.

[93]He remarks: "The meaning of the last two regulations seems to be that the offender himself was responsible for a careless criminal act. If the deed was committed to exact vengeance, he was assured of the assistance of the *ummah*".

The source quoted by Serjeant does provide some details on the type of murder called *fatk*: it is the murder of one who is inattentive (*ghārr*) and does not know that the murderer wants to kill him; or it occurs when the murderer lies in ambush at night or in daytime and assassinates the victim when he finds him unprepared. Then *fatk* became so widely used that the accomplishment of any major undertaking became known as *fatk*.[94] The victim feels secure because it is a sacred month (in which no bloodshed is permitted),[95] or he is at home or in the territory of his own clan, or he is protected by a covenant.[96]

The expression *illā man ẓalama*[97] is obscure, since one expects *fatk* to be forbidden under all circumstances.

§43. *wa-inna llāh ʿalā abarr hādhā*

ALLĀH GUARANTEES THE MOST RIGHTEOUS FULFILMENT OF THIS [treaty].

Wellhausen (71): "Gott wacht über die billigste Ausführung dieser Schrift". (He renders the similar clauses §§53 and 60 in the same manner.)
Wensinck (58): "Allah is the truest [fulfiller] of this [document]". He remarks: "The meaning of these words is somewhat uncertain".
Watt (224): "God is the truest (fulfiller) of this (document)". He adds that this "might mean 'God is very far from this'".
Serjeant (29, 31–32, 35, 37): "Allāh is (surety) for the most observing of this undertaking". §§53 and 60 are rendered by him: "Allāh is (surety) for what is most avoided of covenant breaking and what is most honoured in the observance of what is contained in this sheet"; "Allāh is (surety) for the truest (of oaths) and most honoured in the observance of what is on this sheet".

Serjeant quotes without further comment Suhaylī's interpretation of this clause: *inna llāh wa-ḥizbahu li-l-muʾminīna ʿalā l-riḍā bihi*, "God and his company guarantee its approval".[98] Serjeant refers here to Ḥuyayy b. Akhṭab's pact with Muḥammad in which Allāh was made *kafīl* or guar-

---

[94] *Fākhir*, 254 no. 385. See also Abū ʿUbayd, *Gharīb*, III, 301–302; also *ibid.*, IV, 6–7, where it is said that in a *fatk*-murder the murderer knows his victim beforehand.

[95] *Ibid.*

[96] Thaʿālibī, *Thimār*, 128–30 no. 184 (*fatkat al-Barrāḍ*) lists the three most famous *fatakāt* of the Jāhiliyya and the two most famous ones of Islam; *ʿIqd*, V, 254:3. On *ahl al-bayt* see above, 148f.

[97] Followed by *wa-athima* in §§28, 34 and 62.

[98] Suhaylī, II, 252. The same reading is found in the edition used by Serjeant, namely Cairo 1332/1914, II, 17.

antor. When, after the surrender of the Qurayẓa, Ḥuyayy and his son were captured and beheaded, the Prophet said: "The guarantor has paid in full" (*awfā l-kafīl*).[99]

§§43, 53 and 60 have Allāh as the subject and follow the same pattern.[100] They resemble §22 in the first part of the Kitāb: *wa-inna l-muʾminīna l-muttaqīna ʿalā aḥsan hādhā wa-aqwamihi*. In §§43, 53 and 60, however, the formulation is not *wa-inna l-yahūd ʿalā abarr hādhā* etc.; the guarantor is Allāh.[101] The treaty with Jarbā and Adhruḥ includes the following clause: *wa-llāh kafīl ʿalayhim bi-l-nuṣḥ wa-l-iḥsān ilā l-muslimīna....*[102]

In the treaty between Muḥammad's grandfather and the Khuzāʿa, *kafīl* and *ḥamīl* are synonyms: *wa-jaʿalū llāha ʿalā dhālika kafīlan, wa-kafā bihi ḥamīlan.*[103] Other pre-Islamic treaties must have referred to the relevant idols instead of Allāh. This is suggested by the following exchange of guarantees or oaths in a contest of distinction between two tribal leaders. One of them asked: ...*man lī bi-l-wafāʾ*? The reply was: *kafīlī allāt wa-l-ʿuzzā wa-isāf wa-nāʾila wa-shams wa-yaʿūq wa-l-khalaṣa wa-nasr. Fa-man ʿalayka bi-l-wafāʾ*? The reply was: *wadd wa-manāt wa-fals wa-ruḍan.*[104]

§44. *wa-inna ʿalā l-yahūd nafaqatahum wa-ʿalā l-muslimīna nafaqatahum*

INCUMBENT UPON THE JEWS IS THEIR EXPENDITURE AND UPON THE MUSLIMŪN THEIRS.

---

[99]Abū ʿUbayd, *Amwāl*, 217–18 no. 461. See the report also in Balādhurī, *Futūḥ*, 22. For a similar expression in which the verb is in second-form see Ṭabarī, III, 468 [I, 2195]: *fa-waffā llāhu kafālatī*; *The History of al-Ṭabarī*, XI, trans. Blankinship, 208: "...so that God fulfilled my promise". The context is an oath taken by a warrior during the conquest of Iraq, that if the troops withstand two Persian onslaughts, they will be victorious in the third: ...*wa-anā zaʿīm lakum bi-l-ẓafar fī l-thālitha*. For *zaʿīm* in the sense of guarantor see the prophetic *ḥadīth* in *Futūḥ miṣr*, 278: *anā l-zaʿīm li-man āmana bī wa-aslama bi-bayt fī rabaḍi l-janna....*

[100]Cf. §63: *wa-inna llāha jār....*

[101]Allāh appears as a guarantor in the Qurʾān (16,91): *wa-qad jaʿaltumu llāha ʿalaykum kafīlan*. The verse is quoted in a letter sent in the early ʿAbbāsid period by the governor of Egypt to the king of Nubia; Hinds and Sakkout, "A Letter from the Governor of Egypt", 218, 226. On 210, 214–15, "one of the shaykhs of yore", or in abbreviated form "SY", is the translation of *baʿḍ al-mashāʾikhi l-mutaqaddimīna*; *Futūḥ miṣr*, 189:3. But the correct rendering is "one of the above-mentioned shaykhs", referring to *baʿḍ mashāʾikh ahl miṣr* mentioned in 188:18.

[102]Zurqānī, III, 360:-5; Wāqidī, III, 1032 (*li-l-muslimīna* instead of *ilā l-muslimīna*).

[103]Balādhurī, *Ansāb*, I, 72. Cf. Wāqidī, II, 781:-5: *bi-smika llahumma. Hādhā ḥilf ʿabdi l-muṭṭalib b. hāshim li-khuzāʿa.... Inna baynanā wa-baynakum ʿuhūda llāhi wa-ʿuqūdahu....*

[104]*Naqāʾiḍ*, I, 141:3 (printed: Wudd, Fils).

Wellhausen (71): "Die Juden bezahlen ihre Ausgaben und die Muslime bezahlen ihre Ausgaben".
Wensinck (58): "The Jews must bear their expenses and the Muslims must bear their expenses". He remarks: "Evidently taxes in general".
Watt (224): "It is for the Jews to bear their expenses and for the Muslims to bear their expenses".
Serjeant (33): "The Jews are responsible (for paying) their *nafaqah*, and the *Muslimūn* are responsible (for paying) their *nafaqah*".

While §27 mentions Mu'minūn, this clause relates to Muslimūn whose expenditure is separate from that of the Jews; the Jews and the Muslimūn are not responsible for each other's expenditure.[105]

§45. *wa-inna baynahumu l-naṣr ʿalā man ḥāraba ahl hādhihi l-ṣaḥīfa*

THEY WILL AID EACH OTHER AGAINST WHOSOEVER IS AT WAR WITH THE PEOPLE OF THIS TREATY.

Wellheusen (71): "...sie leisten sich aber gegenseitige Hilfe gegen jeden, der die Genossen dieser Schrift bekriegt".
Wensinck (58–59): "They help one another against those who make war against the people of this document".
Watt (224): "Between them (that is, to one another) there is help against whoever wars against the people of this document".
Serjeant (33): "There is support between them against anyone who goes to war with the people of this sheet".

The preposition *baynahum* should perhaps be linked to *ahl hādhihi l-ṣaḥīfa*: all the participating parties, Jews, Mu'minūn and Muslimūn undertake to co-operate with each other against anyone declaring war on any of the parties. There are two problems with this argument. First, *ahl hādhihi l-ṣaḥīfa* are only mentioned for the first time later in this clause, whereas one expects *baynahum* to refer to those mentioned earlier. Second, it has a near-parallel in §55. It is more plausible that the clause relates to those mentioned in §44, namely the Yahūd and the Muslimūn who should cooperate against whosoever attacks the *ahl hādhihi l-ṣaḥīfa*.

[105] *Nafaqa* also appears in connection with the ʿAqaba meeting: when the Anṣār pledged their allegiance, they reportedly undertook to pay *nafaqa* at good and evil times; *Majmaʿ al-zawā'id*, V, 226 (ʿUbāda b. al-Ṣāmit reminded Abū Hurayra that he had not been with the Anṣār... *idh bāyaʿnā rasūla llāh... wa-ʿalā l-nafaqa fī l-ʿusr wa-l-yusr*). See also Fākihī, *Akhbār makka*, IV, 232 no. 2539.

§46. *wa-inna baynahumu l-nuṣḥ wa-l-naṣīḥa*

THERE IS AMONG THEM SINCERE ADVICE AND COUNSEL.

Wellhausen (71): "... und es herrscht zwischen ihnen ehrliche Freundschaft".
Wensinck (59): "Between them is good understanding, honourable dealing...".
Watt (224): "Between them is sincere friendship and honourable dealing".
Serjeant (33, 34): "There is good will and sincerity of intention between them". According to him, *nuṣḥ wa-naṣīḥa* is a "technical cliché".

Like §§44 and 45, the clause possibly relates to the Yahūd and the Muslimūn. A combination of *nuṣḥ* and *iḥsān* is found in the Prophet's treaty with Jarbā and Adhruḥ,[106] while *nuṣḥ* and *iṣlāḥ* conclude Abū Bakr's treaty with the Christians of Najrān.[107] *Naṣr* and *naṣīḥa* are the nucleus of Muḥammad's treaty with Nuʿaym b. Masʿūd b. Rukhayla al-Ashjaʿī.[108] In all of these cases *nuṣḥ* was not linked to conversion to Islam. But *nuṣḥ* is not necessarily linked with non-Muslims. It describes the relationship between Muḥammad and the Khuzāʿa who at the time of Ḥudaybiyya included both Muslims and polytheists and were spying for Muḥammad in Tihāma.[109] *Nuṣḥ* also appears in the Prophet's treaty with Ḥāritha b. Qaṭan and the Kalbīs of Dūmat al-Jandal who embraced Islam.[110] Jarīr b. ʿAbdallāh al-Bajalī converted to Islam and pledged his allegiance to Muḥammad, undertaking *al-nuṣḥ* [var. *al-naṣīḥa*] *li-kull muslim*.[111] Consequently, when he put up merchandise for sale he prepared an inventory of its faults.[112]

§47. *wa-l-barr dūna l-āthim*

THE RIGHTEOUS MAN WILL RESTRAIN THE SINNER.

---

[106] Above, 161.

[107] *Wa-ʿalayhimi l-nuṣḥ wa-l-iṣlāḥ fīmā ʿalayhim mina l-ḥaqq*; Ṭabarī, III, 322 [I, 1988]; *The History of al-Ṭabarī*, X, trans. Donner, 164: "They owe [the Muslims] advice and righteousness in those just duties that are incumbent upon them".

[108] *Ḥālafahu ʿalā l-naṣr wa-l-naṣīḥa*; Ibn Saʿd, I, 274.

[109] Above, 142; Wāqidī, II, 593: *wa-hum ʿayba nuṣḥ rasūli llāh ṣ bi-tihāma, minhumu l-muslim wa-minhumu l-muwādiʿ, lā yukhfūna ʿalayhi bi-tihāma shayʾan.* The expression *huwa ʿaybat fulān* means: "He is the depository of the secret (or secrets) of such a one"; Lane, II, 2206c, s.v. *Fatḥ al-bārī*, V, 245:-3, explains: *al-ʿayba... mā tūḍaʿu fīhi l-thiyāb li-ḥifẓihā, ay annahum mawḍiʿu l-nuṣḥ lahu wa-l-amāna ʿalā sirrihi.*

[110] *Lakum bi-dhālika l-ʿahd wa-l-mīthāq, wa-lanā ʿalaykumu l-nuṣḥ wa-l-wafāʾ wa-dhimmatu llāh wa-rasūlihi, shahida llāhu wa-man ḥaḍara mina l-muslimīna*; Ibn Saʿd, I, 333.

[111] Ṭabarānī, *Kabīr*, II, 348–51, 352, 358.

[112] *Ibid.*, II, 359.

§48. *wa-innahu lan ya'thama mru' bi-ḥalīfihi wa-inna l-naṣr li-l-maẓlūm*

A MAN WILL NOT ACT UNJUSTLY TOWARDS HIS CLIENT; AID WILL BE PROVIDED TO HIM WHO HAS BEEN WRONGED.

Wellhausen (71): "...und keiner pflegt seinen Eidgenossen treulos zu behandeln".
Wensinck (59): "No one is responsible for his confederate. Help [is to be given] to whomever is wronged".
Watt (224): "A man is not guilty of treachery through (the act of) his confederate. There is help for (or, help is to be given to) the person wronged".
Serjeant (32–35) prefers the reading *lam ya'tham*, which is found in most versions. He renders: "A man did not deal treacherously with his ally". What follows belongs, according to Serjeant, in a separate clause: "Support is due to the person wronged". Serjeant's argument is somewhat hard to follow at this point because he starts with the massacre of the Qurayẓa and continues with the assassination of Kaʿb b. Ashraf several years earlier:

> This clause poses a problem of identification of the unexpected phrase, 'A man did not...'. It may be a formal indirect manner of alluding to the Prophet. Saʿd b. ʿUbādah [read: Saʿd b. Muʿādh — M. L.], for example, when asking the Prophet to promise to accept his verdict on Banū Qurayẓah, asks him, '(And is it binding) on one who is here (*ʿalā man hāhunā*)?'[113] Saʿd employed this form of address out of veneration (*ijlāl-an*) for the Prophet. So if the allusion is in fact to Muḥammad, then he may be formally absolving himself from the assassination of Kaʿb [*sic* — M. L.]. The texts on the contrary show that Muḥammad had no compunction about the murder of Kaʿb, and publicly declared that he considered Kaʿb had only met with his deserts.

Serjeant goes on to suggest another possible historical background, namely the assassination of Ibn Sunayna by Muḥayyiṣa:[114] "A Jewish ally (*ḥalīf*), a merchant who had already accepted Islam of a Banū Ḥari<u>th</u>ah tribesman was murdered, quite wantonly, by his Ḥāri<u>th</u>ī protector". (In fact, Ibn Sunayna was the Ḥārithī's client, not his ally.) It is with Ibn Sunayna that Serjeant finally suggests to link this clause: "What is more likely is that Muḥammad is repudiating any part in the Ḥāri<u>th</u>ī's murder of his *ḥalīf*, who would be

---

[113] Ṭabarī, II, 587–88 [I, 1492–93].
[114] Above, 70.

also a *ḥalīf* of Muḥammad in a secondary way. Clause 2 [= the latter part of §48, *wa-inna l-naṣr li-l-maẓlūm*] could then be interpreted as requiring amends to be made to the family of the murdered *ḥalīf*". Serjeant proposes yet another possibility regarding the latter sentence: "On the other hand one could understand the clause to be a general application to 'a person wronged', in which case it is only a reaffirmation of such principles as that laid down in document A/8 [= §18], etc".

Although *lam ya'tham* seems to be more widespread than *lan ya'thama*, one does not expect this clause or indeed any clause to refer to past events. It is also untenable that the Prophet should be referred to as *imru'*, "a man".

Athima bi- can either mean "to act unjustly towards" or "to bear the burden of someone's guilt". The former should be preferred here. According to a report (← 'Alī) on al-Walīd b. 'Uqba's violent treatment of his wife, the Prophet tried in vain to provide shelter to the battered woman. He even gave her a piece from the border (*hudba*) of his garment and told her to inform her husband that the Prophet had given her shelter (*ajāranī*). In the end the Prophet cursed the aggressor, raising his hands: *allahumma 'alayka [bi-]l-walīd, athima bī marratayni.*[115] This rather suspicious account is particularly relevant for us here since the expression *athima bi-* appears in it in the context of protection: "he acted unjustly towards me", i.e. "he violated my protection". The expression appears in the Kitāb in the same context.[116]

The second part of the clause, *wa-inna l-naṣr li-l-maẓlūm*, is comparable to §18; the latter part of both clauses secures the rights of clients. Should one act unjustly towards one's client, the wronged client will receive succour.

§49. *wa-inna yathrib ḥarām jawfuhā li-ahl hādhihi l-ṣaḥīfa*

THE JAWF OF YATHRIB IS A ḤARAM FOR THE PEOPLE OF THIS TREATY.

Wellhausen (72): "Das Tal von Jathrib ist heilig für die Genossen dieser Schrift".[117]

---

[115] *Majma' al-zawā'id*, IV, 332.

[116] The 'Abd al-Qays leader, al-Jārūd, testified before the caliph 'Umar that the governor of Baḥrayn, Qudāma b. Maẓ'ūn, had drunk wine, and demanded loudly that Qudāma be flogged. He told the caliph's son 'Abdallāh: "By God, your maternal uncle will be flogged or your father will be acting unjustly towards (or committing a crime against) God" (*yujladu wa-llāhi khāluka aw ya'thamu abūka bi-rabbihi*); Ibn Sa'd, V, 561. Qudāma was 'Abdallāh's maternal uncle; *Iṣāba*, V, 424 no. 7092.

[117] He suggests to read here *ḥaram* instead of *ḥarām*: "Für das Adjectiv *harâm* wird man vielleicht das Substantiv *haram* herstellen dürfen, da die alte Schrift kein langes

Wensinck (59): "The valley of Yathrib is sacred for the people of this document". He adds: "This regulation, which is of purely political tendency, created a sacred territory around Medina similar to that around Mecca".
Watt (224): "The valley of Yathrib is sacred for the people of this document".
Serjeant (34–35, 38–39): "The Jawf of Ya<u>th</u>rib is inviolate/a sacred enclave, for the people of this sheet". Serjeant explains: "The Jawf is the flat area of Ya<u>th</u>rib lying between the mountains and lava-tracts, its boundaries being variously named in the Traditions which allege that the actual names of these boundaries figure in the *taḥrīm*-document — but they evidently do not, and the delimitation should probably be regarded as a later accretion".

The clause refers to *ahl hādhihi l-ṣaḥīfa*, i.e. all the participants of the Kitāb. The declaration of the *ḥaram* of Medina is comparable to the declaration of Wajj, the Wādī of Ṭā'if, as *ḥaram*.[118]

For several years after the *hijra* Muḥammad's power base was located in the Sāfila of Medina,[119] and hence one expects his *ḥaram* to have been located in the same area. Indeed, the *ḥaram* can be linked to the market of the Prophet (the former cemetery of the Sāʿida) that was situated, in terms of Islamic Medina, between the court of the Prophet's Companion Zayd b. Thābit[120] and that of the traditionist Ibn Abī Dhi'b (d. 158/775 or 159/776).[121] Now Zayd's *ṣadaqa* or charitable endowment that presumably included his court was in the *ḥaram* of Medina. In Yāqūt's geographical

---

a schreibt und also beide Lesungen offen lässt". But this is unnecessary: the account of Muḥammad's reconfirmation of Mecca's status during "the Farewell Pilgrimage" (Wāqidī, II, 836) has: *alā inna llāh ḥarrama makka yawm khalaqa l-samawāt wa-l-arḍ, fa-hiya ḥarām bi-ḥurmati llāh...*; also 844: *...fa-hiya ḥarām ilā yawmi l-qiyāma.* Cf. Wellhausen, *The Arab Kingdom*, 12: "The Umma embraces a wide area, — the whole precincts of Medina are to be a district of inviolable peace".

[118]The felling of its (acacia) trees, the hunting of its wildlife and any illegal action there were forbidden; Abū ʿUbayd, *Amwāl*, 247 no. 507: *inna wādiyahum ḥarām muḥarram li-llāh kullahu, ʿiḍāhuhu wa-ṣayduhu wa-ẓulm fīhi wa-sarq fīhi aw isā'a. Wa-thaqīf aḥaqqu l-nāsi bi-wajj.* Thaqīf's properties in Wādī Liyya were given the same *amān* as the estates in Wajj; above, 145. He who fells trees or hunts in Wajj will be flogged and stripped of his clothes; *ibid.*, 250–51 no. 508, has: *inna ʿiḍāh wajj* [*wa-ṣaydahu* is superfluous] *lā yuʿḍadu wa-lā yuqtalu ṣayduhu, fa-man wujida yafʿalu shay'an min dhālika fa-innahu yujladu wa-tunzaʿu thiyābuhu, wa-man taʿaddā dhālika fa-innahu yu'khadhu fa-yublaghu muḥammadan rasūla llāhi ṣ.*

[119]Above, 80f.

[120]On whom see *EI*[2], s.v. Zayd b. <u>Th</u>ābit (M. Lecker).

[121]On whom see *Tahdhīb al-kamāl*, XXV, 642–43 no. 5408. On the location of the market see Lecker, "Muḥammad at Medina", 53; *idem*, "On the Markets of Medina", 141, 144.

dictionary we find that al-Aswāf is the name of the *ḥaram* of Medina or, according to another version, of a specific place in the area of the Baqīʿ.[122] The Baqīʿ in question is not the famous Baqīʿ al-Gharqad but another Baqīʿ, namely Baqīʿ al-Khayl.[123] Yāqūt also quotes a *ḥadīth* involving both Zayd and Ibn Abī Dhiʾb. The latter reported on the authority of Shuraḥbīl b. Saʿd (d. 123/741):[124] "I was with Zayd b. Thābit in al-Aswāf when a bird was captured (*fa-akhadhū ṭayran*). Zayd entered[125] and they (i.e. the poachers) put it in my hands and fled. Zayd took the bird and released it. Then he tapped me on the nape of my neck and said: 'You son of a slavegirl (*lā umma laka*, literally: you do not have a free-born mother), did you not know that the Messenger of God declared as *ḥaram* what is between the two tracts of land covered with black stones (*mā bayna lābatayhā*)?"[126]

As we shall see, the word *jawf* indicates a specific area in Medina, which does not conform to the *ḥaram*'s definition as the area between the two *lāba*s or *ḥarra*s of Medina. The wider definition is not necessarily a forgery and may belong to a later extension of the original *ḥaram*.[127]

Serjeant dates the declaration of the *ḥaram* to "round about Year 7". He remarks that "the authorities are at variance about the date of the setting up of the sacred enclave (*taḥrīm*), al-Samhūdī placing it so late as ensuing upon Muḥammad's return from Khaybar". But the declaration of the *ḥaram* upon Muḥammad's return from the expedition of Khaybar uses the formula *mā bayna lābatayhā*,[128] while §49 mentions a specific and much smaller area.

Beside the place-name al-Aswāf there is another point of reference with regard to the early *ḥaram* of Medina, namely the mosque of the Khazraj subdivision of Sāʿida (whose cemetery has just been mentioned in connection with the Prophet's market).[129] Among the mosques in which the Prophet is

---

[122] *Wa-huwa sm ḥarami l-madīna, wa-qīla: mawḍiʿ bi-ʿaynihi bi-nāḥiyati l-baqīʿ wa-huwa mawḍiʿ ṣadaqat zayd b. thābit l-anṣārī wa-huwa min ḥarami l-madīna*; Yāqūt, s.v. al-Aswāf.

[123] Lecker, "On the Markets of Medina", 144.

[124] *Tahdhīb al-kamāl*, XII, 417 no. 2714.

[125] This occurred in an orchard surrounded by a wall.

[126] For a variant of this story see Bakrī, I, 151, s.v. al-Aswāf. See also *Majmaʿ al-zawāʾid*, III, 303; Ṭabarānī, *Kabīr*, V, 126–27 no. 4830 (Zayd b. Thābit releases a hunted fox). In Dāraquṭnī, *Sunan*, IV, 78, we find Khārija b. Zayd b. Thābit's grandmother (i.e. Zayd b. Thābit's mother) who lived in al-Aswāf.

[127] See also below, 201.

[128] See e.g. *Fatḥ al-bārī*, VI, 64:19 (*bāb man ghazā bi-ṣabī li-l-khidma*).

[129] It will be recalled that the Sāʿida and "the Jews of the Sāʿida" appear in the two lists of participants in the Kitāb. At least one member of the Ḥārith b. al-Khazraj who appear in the Kitāb had land in al-Aswāf: the house (*manzil*) of Saʿd b. al-Rabīʿ was in al-Aswāf;

said to have prayed there was one belonging to the Sāʿida that is described as *al-khārij min buyūti l-madīna* or "the one that is beyond the houses of Medina". The description differentiates between this specific mosque of the Sāʿida and another mosque belonging to them. The report that immediately follows in the source quoted here defines the location of the former mosque in other terms: it was *fī jawfi l-madīna*.[130] Obviously, "the *jawf* of Medina" is not identical to *mā bayna lābatayhā* but is an area outside the inhabited zone of Medina, probably north of the town.[131] The mosque of the Sāʿida that concerns us here was beyond the houses of Medina, "in their other territory" (*manzil*) north of Jirār Saʿd, near Dhubāb.[132] The mosque near Dhubāb was the one located in *jawf al-madīna*.

It appears that the parties to the Kitāb agreed in this clause to declare a certain area in Medina, namely its *jawf*, as a *ḥaram* because they had vital interests there, be they agricultural (as in the case of Wādī Wajj and Wādī Liyya), or commercial (as in the case of Mecca), or both.[133] On the eve of Islam there were major shifts in the population of that area[134] and the parties may have wanted to ensure that no one party, be it settled or nomadic, would appropriate it.

Majmaʿ al-zawāʾid, IX, 57. This is a marginal detail in a prophetic *ḥadīth* stating that the first caliphs were in Paradise (*yaṭlaʿu ʿalaykum rajul min ahli l-janna*...). Saʿd was, more precisely, of the Mālik al-Agharr; Ibn Qudāma, *Istibṣār*, 114. Cf. Lecker, "Muḥammad at Medina", 50. He was killed in the battle of Uḥud, which took place not far from his house.

[130]Ibn Shabba, *Taʾrīkh al-madīna*, I, 64.

[131]In the early days of Islam this area must have been devoid of houses, as is suggested by the fact that the Egyptians who murdered the caliph ʿUthmān pitched their tents in al-Aswāf; Ṭabarī, IV, 373 [I, 2992], 378 [2999].

[132]*ʿUmdat al-akhbār*, 179:-6, quoting Ibn Shabba who in his turn quotes Saʿd b. Isḥāq: *...l-khārij min buyūti l-madīna, ay bi-manzilihimi l-ākhar, shāmiyya jirār saʿd qurb dhubāb*. On Dhubāb see Lecker, *Jews and Arabs*, Index. Elsewhere we are told that the Prophet prayed in the mosque of the Sāʿida inside (*dākhil*) Medina east of its market, near the Saqīfa (i.e. the famous Saqīfat Banī Sāʿida). They had another mosque outside of it (i.e. outside Medina), near Dhubāb; Qalyūbī, 116. See also Lecker, "Muḥammad at Medina", 51 n. 149 (the Sāʿida seem to have been the owners of a fortress called al-Shawṭ in the same area); Samhūdī, I, 210 (the Sāʿida owned a territory north of Masjid al-Rāya).

[133]Simonsen, *Studies in the Genesis and Early Development of the Caliphal Taxation System*, 43–44, ascribes the establishment of the *ḥaram* to trade interests: "If Mecca's commercial position was to be undermined, then Medina of necessity had to obtain *ḥarâm* status. Only in this way would it be possible for Medina to achieve a place in the local and eventually in the international trade. Accordingly, the person Muhammad is attributed with special powers as to possible future disputes arising in connection with the oasis' position as *ḥarâm*. He alone was to solve such disputes". Cf. §26.

[134]Lecker, "Muḥammad at Medina", 39–42.

Upon Muḥammad's return from the expedition of Khaybar a renewal of this initial declaration took place, with the newly defined *ḥaram* occupying *mā bayna lābatayhā*. Later even more generous definitions of the boundaries of the *ḥaram* were adopted.[135]

§50. *wa-inna l-jār ka-l-nafs ghayr muḍārr wa-lā āthim*

THE PROTECTED NEIGHBOUR IS LIKE ONE'S SELF, AS LONG AS HE DOES NOT CAUSE DAMAGE OR ACT SINFULLY.

Wellhausen (72): "Der Beisasse ist gleichberechtigt, so lange er nicht schädigt noch trügt".
Wensinck (59): "The guest is as his host except he who causes harm or acts treacherously". He remarks that *jār* means a guest for a limited time.
Watt (224): "The 'protected neighbour' is as the man himself so long as he does no harm and does not act treacherously".
Serjeant (35): "The protected person is like (one's) self, neither molested nor committing an unlawful act". He remarks with regard to *muḍārr*: "The Arabic is ambiguous in form, and could be understood also as 'molesting'. The sense is that a stranger, visiting or resident presumably, will be secure in the sacred enclave from aggression but must himself behave properly".
Gil (62–63) says that the words *al-jāru ka-l-nafs* are of "tremendous importance in understanding Muḥammad's policy concerning the Jews of Medina...." He continues:

> The statement means that the patron is responsible for the deeds of his client. If one conceives the position of such a client to be that of a freedman, one will have to compare this new regulation to the controversial position of this clause in the different parts of ancient society. In this particular case we obviously have a deterioration in the status of the Jews in Medina, who were the *jiwār* [*sic* — M. L.] par excellence. In other words, the Jews were no longer allowed to engage either in inter-tribal politics, such as concluding new treaties, or in warfare. Assuming that the previous situation was the opposite of the new one, this means that the Jews formerly had the right to handle affairs themselves (including warfare) and were, on the other hand, themselves responsible for any damage inflicted or debts incurred by them.

[135]Cf. below, 201. The existence of the Prophet's *ḥaram* in Medina was not overlooked by local scholars engaging in the collection of the *faḍā'il* or "praises" of Medina.

This clause is comparable with three other clauses in the latter part of the Kitāb or the treaty of the Jews that include the plural of *nafs* with the preposition *ka-*, namely §§35, 38 and 39: *wa-inna jafna baṭn min thaʿlaba ka-anfusihim*; *wa-inna mawāliya thaʿlaba ka-anfusihim*; *wa-inna biṭānat yahūd ka-anfusihim*.

The Jafna, the *mawālī* and the *biṭāna* share a common denominator with the *jār*: they are all secondary groups attached to the main contracting Jewish parties that are granted the rights of the main parties. The main right granted to the participating Jewish groups was that of *amān*. However, this right was conditional: ... *illā man ẓalama wa-athima* (§§28, 34). A similar condition is found in §62, where it is again a matter of *amān*: *illā man ẓalama wa-athima*.[136] *Ghayr muḍārr wa-lā āthim* is a condition, although it does not conform to the *illā man ẓalama wa-athima* formula. Still, a derivative of the root *ʾ-th-m* is used here, while *ẓ-l-m* is replaced by *ḍ-r-r*.

The expression *ghayr muḍārr* is found in the Qurʾān, 4,12.[137] The Qurʾānic verse addresses a damage caused by a testator to his heirs; he should not bequeath a debt that does not exist in order to incur losses on the heirs, nor may he admit such debt.[138] *Ḍirār* can mean something that brings one no benefit while harming one's neighbour (*lladhī laysa laka fīhi manfaʿa wa-ʿalā jārika fīhi l-maḍarra*).[139] A telling case of *ḍirār* is one of a *ḥalīf* or client who owned part of a palm grove most of which belonged to a certain Anṣārī. The client turned down the Prophet's suggestions that he sell his part to the Anṣārī, or give it to him as a present, or exchange it for a similar property elsewhere. The Prophet told him: *anta muḍārruhu*.[140]

---

[136] Cf. §61, where the Kitāb figures as an *amān*.

[137] See Powers, *Studies in Qurʾān and* Ḥadīth, Index, s.v. Q. 4:12.

[138] See e.g. Qurṭubī, *Tafsīr*, V, 80, interpretation of Qurʾān 4,12: *ay yūṣī bihā ghayra muḍārr, ay ghayr mudkhili l-ḍarar ʿalā l-waratha, ay lā yanbaghī an yūṣiya bi-dayn laysa ʿalayhi li-yuḍirra bi-l-waratha wa-lā yuqirra bi-dayn, fa-l-iḍrār rājiʿ ilā l-waṣiyya wa-l-dayn.* See also Suyūṭī, *Durr*, II, 128:1: *min ghayr ḍirār, lā yuqirru bi-ḥaqq laysa ʿalayhi wa-lā yūṣī bi-akthar mina l-thulth muḍārra li-l-waratha.*

[139] Qurṭubī, *Tafsīr*, VIII, 254.

[140] Lecker, *Muslims, Jews and Pagans*, 99 (where other examples of *ḍirār* are given). This specific one is from Zamakhsharī, *Fāʾiq*, II, 442, s.v. *ʿ-ḍ-d*. The *ḥalīf* in question was Samura b. Jundab al-Fazārī whose widowed mother married an Anṣārī in Medina. At the time of Muḥammad Samura was a young lad; see his entry in *Iṣāba*, III, 178–79 no. 3477. The report in the *Fāʾiq* suggests that the Anṣārī who wanted to stop Samura's visits to his palm trees was concerned about chastity (*wa-maʿa l-rajul ahluhu*). Still, one wonders whether the Anṣārī was not Samura's adoptive father.

§51. *wa-innahu lā tujāru ḥurma illā bi-idhn ahlihā*

NO PROTECTION WILL BE GRANTED WITHOUT THE PERMISSION OF THE PARTIES TO THIS TREATY.

Wellhausen (72): "Eine Frau wird nicht als Beisassin aufgenommen, ausser mit Erlaubnis ihrer Familie".
Wensinck (59): "No woman can be treated as a guest except with the consent of her family".
Watt (224): "No woman is given 'neighbourly protection' without the consent of her people".
Serjeant (35): "A woman shall not be accorded protection except by permission of her people". He remarks: "Her people would be her male next of kin".
Gil (57) observes, in a section of his article entitled "Restrictions regarding women":

> Another clause whose aim was to promote safety among the clans and abolish an eternal source of bloody disputes, was the interdiction against giving protection to a woman belonging to another clan, without the permission of the latter. This apparently aimed at the abolition of the remnants of ancient matriarchate which persisted in the form of a certain amount of sexual freedom for women, outside their paternal clans. The tendency now was towards the consolidation of patriarchal institutions, and Muḥammad seems to have readily adopted this new view, which may have already been his own in his Meccan period.

Ḥamīdullāh is the only scholar who does not refer to women in the context of this clause. He links it to the preceding one that is among the clauses referring to the relatives and allies of the Jews, those called *mawālī, baṭn and biṭāna.* These groups share with the Jews the same rights and duties; but — and here comes Ḥamīdullāh's reference to this clause — the man given protection is not allowed to grant security to another without the consent of his protector.[141]

Ḥamīdullāh is right in establishing a link between the two clauses, although it would seem that at stake here is not the *jār*'s freedom to grant security but that of the participating Jewish parties. A version of the *kitāb ʿAlī*[142] in a

[141]Ḥamīdullāh, "Aqdam dustūr", 111: *illā anna l-mujār lā yusmaḥu lahu an yujīra ghayrahu illā bi-idhn mujīrihi.*
[142]Cf. below, 194.

Shīʿī source includes this clause and the preceding one in reverse order. Then there follows another clause that is not found in the Kitāb and includes the expression *ḥurmatu l-jār*;[143] it lends some support to the assumption that the *ḥurma* in the Kitāb has nothing to do with women. *Ḥurma, amn* (or *amān*) and *jiwār* appear elsewhere as synonyms.[144] *Ḥurmatī ḥurmatukum*, glossing *al-hadamu l-hadam*, appears in the agreement concluded between the Anṣār and the Prophet at the ʿAqaba meeting.[145] In order to save his life, Rifāʿa b. Samawʾal of the Qurayẓa asked Salmā bint Qays of the Najjār to intervene on his behalf with Muḥammad because of his long-standing relationship with her, with her brother and with the rest of the people in the court; they were obliged to protect him, and he was entitled to *ḥurma* from them.[146] *Ḥurma* is also synonymous with *dhimma* and means security, safety, protection etc.[147]

The clause prescribes that an obligation to protect someone's safety should only be undertaken with the permission of *ahlihā*. The possessive pronoun does not go back to *ḥurma* but to the *ṣaḥīfa* mentioned several times in the treaty of the Jews. *Ahl hādhihi l-ṣaḥīfa* appear, for instance, in §49.[148] The clause does not state that *ahl hādhihi l-ṣaḥīfa* are responsible for an obligation undertaken by one of the participants, but merely that prior consent is necessary before extending such obligation. This clause limits the political freedom of the participating Jewish individuals or groups.

§52. *wa-innahu mā kāna bayna ahl hādhihi l-ṣaḥīfa min ḥadath awi shtijār yukhāfu fasāduhu, fa-inna maraddahu ilā llāh wa-ilā muḥammad*

---

[143] *Qaraʾtu fī kitābi ʿalī ʿalayhi l-salām anna rasūla llāhi ṣallā llāhu ʿalayhi wa-ālihi kataba kitāban bayna l-muhājirīna wa-l-anṣār wa-man laḥiqa bihim min ahl yathrib: inna kull ghāziya ghazat maʿanā yaʿqubu baʿḍuhā baʿḍan bi-l-maʿrūf wa-l-qisṭ mā bayna l-muslimīna, wa-innahu lā yujāru* [*sic*] *ḥurma illā bi-idhn ahlihā, wa-inna l-jār ka-l-nafs ghayr muḍārr wa-lā āthim, wa-ḥurmatu l-jār ka-ḥurmat ummihi wa-abīhi, lā yusālimu muʾmin dūna muʾmin fī qitāl fī sabīli llāh illā ʿalā ʿadl wa-sawāʾ*; Ṭūsī, *Tahdhīb al-aḥkām*, VI, 140–41 (*bāb iʿṭāʾi l-amān*; Aḥmad b. Muḥammad ← Muḥammad b. Yaḥyā ← Ṭalḥa b. Zayd ← Abū ʿAbdallāh ← his father).

[144] Suyūṭī, *Durr*, IV, 350:-2, interpretation of Qurʾān XXII, 25: *sawāʾ fī jiwārihi wa-amnihi/wa-amānihi wa-ḥurmatihi l-ʿākif fīhi — ahl makka, wa-l-bād — man yaʿtakifuhu min ahli l-āfāq*.

[145] Lecker, "*Yahūd/ʿUhūd*", 171n.

[146] Wāqidī, II, 514: *wa-kāna... lahu nqiṭāʿ ilayhā wa-ilā akhīhā... wa-ahli l-dār wa-kāna ḥīna ḥubisa arsala ilayhā an kallimī muḥammadan fī tarkī fa-inna lī bikum ḥurma.* She told the Prophet (515): *kāna yaghshānā wa-lahu binā ḥurma fa-habhu lī.*

[147] Lane, I, 555b.

[148] The other combination including *ahl*, *ahl baytihi*, is irrelevant for us here because *bayt* is masculine while *ṣaḥīfa* is feminine.

EVERY MURDER [or another major crime] OR DISPUTE BETWEEN THE PEOPLE OF THIS TREATY FROM WHICH EVIL IS TO BE FEARED SHOULD BE BROUGHT BEFORE ALLĀH AND MUḤAMMAD.

Wellhausen (72): "Wenn zwischen den Genossen dieser Schrift etwas vorkommt oder ein Zank entsteht, voraus Unheil zu befürchten ist, so soll die Sache vor Gott und Muhammad gebracht werden".
Wensinck (59): "Whenever there is disagreement among the people of this document and trouble is to be anticipated, the matter is to be referred to Allah and Muhammad".
Watt (224): "Whenever among the people of this document there occurs any incident (disturbance) or quarrel from which disaster for it (the people) is to be feared, it is to be referred to God and to Muḥammad, the Messenger of God (God bless and preserve him)".
Serjeant (35): "Whatsoever aggression/misdemeanour or quarrel there is between the people of this sheet, which it is feared may cause dissension, will be referred to Allāh, Great and Glorious, and to Muḥammad the Apostle of Allāh, Allāh bless and honour him". Regarding "the people of this sheet" he observes: "This can only mean the signatories to the document".

The *ahl hādhihi l-ṣaḥīfa* are the parties to the Kitāb. This is an arbitration clause having a partial parallel in §26. §52 is less comprehensive: not every matter should be brought before Muḥammad, but only cases of *ḥadath* and *ishtijār* occurring between the parties to the Kitāb. It is doubtful that at this early stage Muḥammad was involved in internal disputes among the Jews themselves; the Jews accepted his arbitration only in their disputes with the other parties.

Muḥdith in the Kitāb is a murderer,[149] and hence *ḥadath* is murder (or another major crime). *Ishtijār*[150] is found in a variety of context. The one most relevant for us here is probably the dispute between the Banū Hāshim and Banū Umayya over the compensation for the foetus lost by the Prophet's daughter, Zaynab, while she was escaping from Mecca: *fa-shtajara fīhā banū hāshim wa-banū umayya*; the Umayya demanded the blood money because Zaynab's husband was one of them.[151] Blood money is closely linked to

[149]Above, 132.
[150]The sixth form, *tashājur*, appears more frequently.
[151]Bayhaqī, *Dalā'il*, III, 156.

inheritance, and it is not surprising that *ishtijār* can also mean a dispute over an inheritance.[152]

§53. *wa-inna llāh ʿalā atqā mā fī hādhihi l-ṣaḥīfa wa-abarrihi*

ALLĀH GUARANTEES THE TRUEST AND MOST RIGHTEOUS FULFILMENT OF THE CLAUSES OF THIS TREATY.

§54. *wa-innahu lā tujāru quraysh wa-lā man naṣarahā*

NO PROTECTION WILL BE GRANTED TO QURAYSH NOR TO WHOEVER SUPPORTS THEM.

Wellhausen (74): "Die Quraischiten dürfen nicht in Schutz genommen werden, noch wer ihnen beisteht".
Wensinck (59): "No protection is to be given to the Quraysh or to those who help them".
Watt (224): "No 'neighbourly protection' is given to Quraysh and those who help them".
Serjeant (37): "Quraysh will not be accorded protection, nor will whosoever supports them".

This clause has a partial parallel in §23. According to the pattern of §23 one expects here: *wa-innahu lā yujīru yahūdī qurayshan...*; but only the plural Yahūd is used in the Kitāb.

§55. *wa-inna baynahumu l-naṣr ʿalā man dah(a/i)ma yathrib*

THEY [viz. the participating parties] UNDERTAKE TO AID EACH OTHER AGAINST WHOSOEVER ATTACKS YATHRIB.

Wellhausen (72): "Man ist verpflichtet zu gegenseitigem Beistand gegen die welche Jathrib angreifen".
Wensinck (59): "They help one another against those who attack Yathrib". He explains that "they" relates to the people of this document.
Watt (225): "Between them (? the people of this document) is help against whoever suddenly attacks Yathrib".

[152] Samhūdī, I, 208. It was said about two *baṭns* from the Bayāḍa (Khazraj): *kāna baynahum mīrāth fī l-jāhiliyya fa-shtajarū fīhi.* They decided to settle the dispute by fighting each other in an orchard; their mutual destruction in the orchard gave it the name *ḥadīqat al-mawt* or "the orchard of death". The name was later given to an orchard in Yamāma that was the scene of fierce fighting during the *ridda*; see Lecker, *People, Tribes and Society*, no. XI. For *tashājur* in the sense of a dispute over the blood money of people who fell into a lion's pit, see Ṭūsī, *Tahdhīb al-aḥkām*, X, 239.

Serjeant (37, 38): "There is support between them against any who makes an unexpected treacherous attack on Ya<u>th</u>rib". Serjeant repeats this translation of the verb *dahama* (or *dahima*) with reference to Wāqidī, II, 503–504, where we find, according to Serjeant, "a Jew of Qurayẓah who accuses his tribe, or parts of it, of breaking the alliance they had made (*ḥālafa*) with Muḥammad, 'that you would not support anyone of his foes against him, and that you would support him against anyone who made an unexpected treacherous attack upon him' ".[153]

The verb *dah(a/i)ma* is sometimes associated with a surprise attack,[154] but in this case one expects an unrestricted obligation rather than a limited one that only covers sudden or surprise attacks. *Dahama* signifies an attack by a large army.[155] A pertinent *ḥadīth* is the following: *man arāda l-madīna bi-dahm adhābahu llāh kamā yadhūbu l-milḥ fī l-mā'*, "He who intends to attack Medina with a large army, God will dissolve him as salt dissolves in water".[156]

§56. *wa-idhā duʿū ilā ṣulḥ yuṣāliḥūnahu wa-yalbasūnahu, fa-innahum yuṣāliḥūnahu wa-yalbasūnahu; wa-innahum idhā daʿaw ilā mithl dhālika fa-innahu lahum ʿalā l-mu'minīna, illā man ḥāraba fī l-dīn; ʿalā kull unās ḥiṣṣatuhum min jānibihimu lladhī qibalahum*

---

[153] *Allā tanṣurū ʿalayhi aḥadan min ʿaduwwihi* [these two words were omitted by Serjeant] *wa-an tanṣurūhu mimman dahamahu.*

[154] See, for example, Khushanī, 135–36, who associates the verb with a cavalry attack: *man dahima: yurīdu man fāja'ahum, yuqālu dahimathumu l-khayl tadhamuhum.*

[155] *Wa-dahmin ka-junḥi l-layli zurnā bihi l-ʿidā*, in a verse by Farazdaq is commented upon by Abū ʿUbayda: *qawluhu: wa-dahmin ka-junḥi l-layli, yaʿnī jayshan kathīra l-ʿadad, yuqālu min dhālika: qad dah(a/i)mahum jamʿ kathīr, wa-dhālika idhā jā'ahum; Naqā'iḍ*, II, 648–49.

[156] Zamakhsharī, *Fā'iq*, I, 448, s.v. *d-h-m.* Also: *man arāda ahl hādhihi l-balda bi-d(a/u)hm aw bi-sū'...*; *ʿUmdat al-akhbār*, 70:15. In Muḥammad's treaty with the Aslam, *dahama* is combined with *ẓulm*: *wa-inna amranā wa-amrakum wāḥid ʿalā man dahamanā mina l-nās bi-ẓulm, al-yad wāḥida wa-l-naṣr wāḥid*; Wāqidī, II, 782. The following clause in the Aslam treaty prescribes that both the sedentary and nomadic or semi-nomadic Aslamīs were included in the treaty; *wa-li-ahl bādiyatihim mithl mā li-ahl qarārihim.* No such co-operation could have taken place in the case of a surprise attack. The same is true of the alleged initial agreement between the Ghassān and the Byzantines after the former's victory over the Salīḥ, where *dahamakum d(a/u)hm* means "you will be attacked by a large army". The Byzantine emperor suggested these terms: *in dahamakum d(a/u)hm mina l-ʿarab amdadtukum bi-arbaʿīna alf muqātil mina l-rūm bi-adātihim, wa-in dahamanā d(a/u)hm mina l-ʿarab fa-ʿalaykum ʿishrūna alf muqātil ʿalā an lā tadkhulū baynanā wa-bayna fāris* (i.e. you will not be involved in our war against the Persians, you will only provide aid against other Arabs); Ibn Ḥabīb, *Muḥabbar*, 371.

IF THEY [the Jews] ARE CALLED [by the other parties to the treaty] TO CONCLUDE AND ACCEPT (?) AN AGREEMENT, THEY WILL CONCLUDE AND ACCEPT (?) IT; AND IF THEY [the Jews] CALL FOR THE SAME, IT IS INCUMBENT UPON THE MU'MINŪN TO GIVE IT THEM, WITH THE EXCEPTION OF THOSE FIGHTING FOR RELIGION. EVERYBODY SHOULD PAY THEIR SHARE AT THEIR OWN EXPENSE (?).[157]

Wellhausen (72): "Wenn Sie (die Juden von den Gläubigen) zu Frieden aufgefordert werden, dass sie ihn schliessen und annehmen sollen, so sollen sie es tun; und wenn sie die Gläubigen zu ähnlichem auffordern, so haben diese ihnen gegenüber die gleiche Pflicht, ausgenommen den Krieg wegen der Religion. Jeder hat sein Teil, das ihm zunächst obliegt". He wonders whether the clause prescribes that the Jews or the believers should end their hostilities when one of the parties asks the other party to do so, and concludes that it is rather unlikely that the believers agreed to this. Or perhaps it speaks of hostilities between the Jews and the believers. Indeed, *ṣulḥ* does not mean peace in the narrow sense, but good friendly relations in general. In this case the clause is a weak version of an earlier one (namely §52).

Wensinck (59–60): "Whenever they (the Jews) are summoned to conclude and to accept a peace treaty, then they shall conclude and accept it. And whenever they (the believers) [*sic* — M.L.] summon to the like of that, then they have the right for this vis-à-vis the believers except whoever makes war on account of religion (upon whom none of the regulations of this section is applicable). Everyone has his share from their side which is directed towards him". He adds: "That is to say, everyone must assume his particular responsibilities"

Watt (225): "Whenever they are summoned to conclude and accept a treaty, they conclude and accept it; when they in turn summon to the like of that, it is for them upon the believers, except whoever wars about religion; for (? incumbent on) each man is his share from their side which is towards them".

Serjeant (37, 38, in three separate clauses): "When they are called upon to make and adopt a truce they will make that truce and adopt it"; "If they call for the same (i.e. a truce) the *Mu'minūn* owe it to them (to adopt it)"; "Indeed, those who are at war for religion, each (group of) people is responsible (i.e. to defend) their share of their sector lying in front of

---

[157] A smoother version to the final phrase *min jānibihimi lladhī qibalahum* is found in Abū 'Ubayd: *mina l-nafaqa*; but it may be a *lectio facilior*.

them". He remarks on the first two clauses (according to his division of the document): "These clauses bind the parties not to enter into a separate peace, thus preserving their own interests at the expense of the rest".

Ḥiṣṣa towards the end of the clause may provide the key to its interpretation. It means "portion", "share", but not necessarily an equal one. For example, it means the uneven shares of members of the *ʿāqila*, each of whom carries a different burden according to his place in the *ʿāqila*, being at the same time entitled to a different share in the blood money for one of them.[158]

Rather than matters of war and peace, this clause refers to the settlement of blood feuds. The term *ṣulḥ* and several other derivatives of *ṣ-l-ḥ* relate to a wide variety of agreements. The one most appropriate here is "a settlement concerning a blood feud between two tribal groups".[159] While excluding the polytheists, the Kitāb stipulates co-operation in the settlement of blood feuds between the Jews who participated in it and the Muʾminūn. Suppose a Muʾmin kills someone and the Jews, be they from the murderer's *ʿāqila* (i.e. Arab converts to Judaism) or from another participating group,[160] are called upon to take part in the settlement of the ensuing blood feud. They will do so, and the same will happen if the Jews call upon the Muʾminūn to participate in the settlement of a blood feud involving one of them. However, *man ḥāraba fī l-dīn* among the Muʾminūn or those engaged in fighting "for religion" are exempt from participating in a blood feud settlement initiated by the Jews.

§57. *wa-inna yahūda l-aws mawāliyahum wa-anfusahum ʿalā mithl mā li-ahl hādhihi l-ṣaḥīfa maʿa al-barr al-muḥsin*[161] *min ahl hādhihi l-ṣaḥīfa*

THE JEWS OF AWS, THEIR ALLIES AND THEIR PERSONS, HAVE THE SAME STANDING AS THE PEOPLE OF THIS TREATY, TOGETHER WITH THE RIGHTEOUS AND SINCERE OF THE PEOPLE OF THIS TREATY.

---

[158] Abū ʿUbayd, *Gharīb*, II, 161: *li-kull wārith an yaʿfuwa ʿani l-dam min rajul awi mraʾa, fa-idhā ʿafā baʿḍuhum saqaṭa l-qawad ʿani l-qātil wa-akhadha sāʾiru l-waratha ḥiṣaṣahum mina l-diya*. Also *ibid.*, I, 283–84, interpreting the saying *wa-l-maʿdin jubār*, or "the mine is a thing for which no penalty is exacted": *... illā annahum idhā kānū jamāʿa ḍamina baʿḍuhum li-baʿḍ ʿalā qadr ḥiṣaṣihim mina l-diya*.

[159] ʿAskarī, *Awāʾil*, I, 37, for example, says that *jamma* means *al-jamāʿa yamshūna fī l-dam wa-l-ṣulḥ*; Lane, I, 449b ("a company demanding a bloodwit", etc.). For *iṣṭalaḥa* and *ṣālaḥa* in the context of a blood feud see the story of al-Mughīra b. Shuʿba in *Sīra ḥalabiyya*, III, 15:11: *wa-ṣṭalaḥū ʿalā an yaḥmila...ʿurwa* [b. masʿūd] *thalātha ʿashrata diya...*; *wa-ṣālaḥa banī mālik ʿalā thalātha ʿashrata diya....*

[160] For the discussion of Yahūd Banī so-and-so see above, 49f.

[161] In most versions we find: *maʿa l-birri l-maḥḍ*.

Wellhausen (72): "Die Juden der Aus, ihre Beisassen und sie selber, haben die gleiche Stellung wie die Genossen dieser Schrift, bei reinster Lauterkeit von den Genossen dieser Schrift".
Wensinck (60): "The Jews of al-Aws, their clients and they themselves, have the same rights as the people of this document, in pure honesty on the part of the people of this document". He thinks that the clause deals with "clients who were not properly treated in the previous sections".
Watt (225): "The Jews of al-Aws, both their clients and themselves, are in the same position as belongs to the people of this document while they are thoroughly honourable in their dealings with the people of this document".
Serjeant (37): "The Jews of the Aws, their clients and themselves, are on the same (basis) as the people of this sheet, with sincere/complete observation (i.e. of its stipulation) on the part of the people of this sheet".

Instead of *al-maḥḍ* read: *al-muḥsin.* The latter reading is supported by §64 that has *al-barr al-muḥsin.*

§58. *al-barr dūna l-āthim*

THE RIGHTEOUS MAN WILL RESTRAIN THE SINNER.

§59. *lā yaksibu kāsib illā ʿalā nafsihi*

HE WHO OFFENDS, OFFENDS ONLY AGAINST HIMSELF.

Wellhausen (73): "Wer sich etwas zuzieht, zieht es sich selber zu".
Wensinck (61): "Every person who becomes guilty loads the guilt only upon himself".
Watt (225): "A person acquiring (? guilt) acquires it only against himself".
Serjeant (37): "...He who commits a breach (of this treaty) commits it against himself alone".

A similar concept can be traced in §§28 and 34: ...*illā man ẓalama wa-athima, fa-innahu lā yūtighu illā nafsahu wa-ahl baytihi.* Similar formulations are found in the Qurʾān.[162]

[162]For instance, Qurʾān 4,111: *wa-man yaksib ithman fa-innamā yaksibuhu ʿalā nafsihi...*, "And whosoever earns a sin, earns it against himself only..."; (Arberry, 89). Also Qurʾān 6,165: *wa-lā taksibu kullu nafsin illā ʿalayhā wa-lā taziru wāziratun wizra ukhrā...*, "Every soul earns only to its own account; no soul laden bears the load of another..." (Arberry, 142). Cf. *Mufaḍḍaliyyāt*, I, 620:13 (LXXXIX, 18), II, 254: *fa-yā li-llāhi lam aksib athāman wa-lam ahtik li-dhī raḥimin ḥijābā*, "Yea, by God! I never incurred the guilt of any crime, nor did I ever rend the veil of one of my own kin".

§60. *wa-inna llāh ʿalā aṣdaq mā fī hādhihi l-ṣaḥīfa wa-abarrihi*

ALLĀH GUARANTEES THE MOST LOYAL AND MOST RIGHTEOUS FULFILMENT OF THIS TREATY.

§61. *wa-innahu lā yaḥūlu hādhā l-kitāb dūna ẓālim wa-āthim*

THIS COMPACT DOES NOT INTERVENE TO PROTECT AN UNJUST MAN AND A SINNER.

Wellhausen (73): "Diese Urkunde schützt keinen, der offen oder geheim Unrecht begeht".
Wensinck (61): "This writing does not protect him who practices evil or treachery".
Watt (225): "This writing does not intervene to protect a wrong-doer or traitor".
Serjeant (39): "This writing does not intervene between a wrong-doer and one committing a criminal act".

The phrase *ḥāla dūna*[163] means intervening between something or someone and one who wants to take or harm it or him.[164] The clause is a warning that the Kitāb will not intervene between unjust men and sinners, and those who will punish them. Zamakhsharī interprets this clause[165] saying: should one act transgressively in contrast to what is written in the Kitāb, and should he claim that he is included among its people, his inclusion among them will not protect him from punishment for his transgression.[166]

A similar phrase appears in the clause concluding the Prophet's treaty with the Ghifār: *wa-inna hādhā l-kitāb lā yaḥūlu dūna āthim.*[167] The Ghifār treaty was above all an *amān* or a guarantee of security;[168] however, it did not provide security to an *āthim*. *Ḥāla dūna* is also found in the Prophet's

[163]Above, 126.

[164]A verse by Sāra al-Quraẓiyya regarding the affair of Mālik b. al-ʿAjlān has it that had there been a proper declaration of war, a heavy and great battle would have prevented the enemy from harming her fellow tribesmen, *wa-law adhinū bi-amrihim la-ḥālat hunālika dūnahum ḥarbun radāḥu*; Samhūdī, I, 182.

[165]Which he quotes in a different form: *lā yaḥūlu l-kitāb dūna ẓulm ẓālim wa-lā ithm āthim.*

[166]Zamakhsharī, *Fāʾiq*, II, 26: *lawi ʿtadā muʿtadin bi-mukhālafat mā fīhi wa-zaʿama annahu dākhil fī jumlat ahlihi lam yamnaʿhu dukhūluhu fī jumlatihim an yuʾkhadha bi-jināya.*

[167]*Wath.*, 268 no. 161 (vocalized *ithm*).

[168]*Wa-inna l-nabī ʿaqada lahum dhimmata llāh wa-dhimmat rasūlihi ʿalā amwālihim wa-anfusihim.*

treaty with Ayla that was similarly an *amān* treaty.[169] The people of Ayla received a guarantee of security for their ships and caravans, but some Aylīs were excluded: *wa-man aḥdatha ḥadathan fa-innahu lā yaḥūlu māluhu dūna nafsihi*, "Whosoever murders, his money will not protect him" (literally: it will not intervene between himself and the retaliators).[170]

§62. *wa-innahu man kharaja āmin wa-man qaʿada āmin,*[171] *illā man ẓalama wa-athima*

HE [of the Jews] WHO GOES OUT [opting not to participate in the compact] IS SAFE AND HE WHO STAYS IS SAFE, EXCEPT HE WHO ACTS UNJUSTLY AND SINS.

Wellhausen (73): "Wer zu Felde zieht geniesst Sicherheit, und wer zu Haus Bleibt, geniesst Sicherheit in der Medina, ausgenommen wer offen oder geheim Unrecht begeht".
Wensinck (61): "He who goes out as well as he who remains is safe in the city except he who does wrong or acts treacherously".
Watt (225): "He who goes out is safe, and he who sits still is safe in Medina, except whoever does wrong and acts treacherously".
Serjeant (39): "He who goes out is secure, and he who stays is secure in Medina, except one who does wrong or commits a criminal act". He adds: "This proviso may mean that a person leaving Medina is not to be attacked until he reaches his place of safety (*balagha maʾmana-hu*)".

This is a typical concluding clause stipulating that anyone who does not wish to be part of the treaty may leave unharmed.

The clause is addressed to the Jews rather than to *ahl hādhihi l-ṣaḥīfa*. No parallel from a treaty of Muḥammad was found, but in treaties from the period of Conquests the verb *kharaja* (coupled with *aqāma* instead of *qaʿada*) refers to secondary groups.[172] The same is true of this clause that

[169] *Hādhihi amana mina llāh wa-Muḥammad....*

[170] Wāqidī, III, 1031; Abū ʿUbayd, *Amwāl*, 258 no. 514; *Wath.*, 117–18 no. 31.

[171] The word *bi-l-Madīna* is a gloss; the Kitāb calls it Yathrib, see §§1, 49 and 55.

[172] The surrender treaty of Alexandria stipulated that whosoever of its (Byzantine) inhabitants wished to go to Byzantium could do so, and those wishing to stay could stay; ʿAskarī, *Awāʾil*, II, 10: *wa-qālū: ...ʿalā an yakhruja minhum man yashāʾu ilā l-rūm wa-yuqīmu man shāʾa bi-l-iskandariyya.* The treaty of Adharbayjān stipulated: *wa-man aqāma fa-lahu mithl mā li-man aqāma min dhālika, wa-man kharaja fa-lahu l-amān ḥattā yaljaʾa ilā ḥirzihi*; Ṭabarī, IV, 155 [I, 2662]. The treaty of Egypt similarly stipulated that the Byzantines and Nubians could leave unharmed or stay, having the same rights and duties: *wa-man dakhala fī ṣulḥihim mina l-rūm wa-l-nūb fa-lahu mithl mā lahum wa-*

concludes the treaty of the Jews. The Jews are given the option not to join and leave Yathrib.

§63. *wa-inna llāh jār li-man barra wa-ttaqā wa-muḥammad rasūlu llāh*

ALLĀH IS THE PROTECTOR OF HIM WHO IS RIGHTEOUS AND GOD-FEARING AND SO IS MUḤAMMAD, THE MESSENGER OF GOD.

§64. *wa-inna awlāhum bi-hādhihi l-ṣaḥīfa l-barru l-muḥsin*

THE MOST WORTHY OF THEM [the Jews] TO PARTICIPATE IN THIS TREATY ARE THE RIGHTEOUS AND SINCERE.[173]

ʿalayhi mithl mā ʿalayhim, wa-man abā wa-khtāra l-dhahāb fa-huwa āmin ḥattā yablugha maʾmanahu aw yakhruja min sulṭāninā; Ṭabarī, IV, 109:9 [I, 2588].

[173]Cf. *Manāl al-ṭālib*, 233: *wa-inna awlāhum, yaʿnī qurayshan wa-l-anṣār, an yaʿmalū bi-mā fī hādhihi l-ṣaḥīfa, wa-hiya l-kitāb, l-barru l-muḥsin minhum.*

Appendix A

When Was the Kitāb Concluded?

Buhl dates the conclusion of the Kitāb to around the middle of AH 2 on the basis of an historical analysis: for the time being the Prophet gave up the conversion of the Jews of Medina and changed his tactics, attempting to unite the whole population and guaranteeing religious freedom.[174]

But more cogent evidence points to the first year after the *hijra*. Gil (49) observes correctly that "the traditions of the *Sīra* place its composition among the very first acts undertaken by the Prophet after his arrival to Medina". Quoting Ibn Hishām (II, 150) he argues that the Kitāb was written before the "fraternization" or *mu'ākhāt* between the Muhājirūn and the Anṣār, while from Samhūdī (I, 267) Gil learns that the "fraternization" took place five or eight months after the *hijra*, when the Prophet was building his mosque. According to other versions, the "fraternization" was concluded (shortly) before or after the building of his mosque.[175]

It was also Abū 'Ubayd's opinion that the Kitāb was concluded shortly after the Prophet's arrival at Medina (*wa-innamā kāna hādhā l-kitāb fīmā narā ḥadathān maqdam rasūli llāh ṣ al-madīna*). He went on to say that this had been before Islam became victorious and strong and before God ordered the Prophet to levy poll-tax from the People of the Book. Abū 'Ubayd mentioned in this context the three main Jewish tribes since he believed, like many others, that they were the Jews mentioned in the Kitāb.[176] Abū 'Ubayd apologetically attempted to justify the position of the Jewish participants in the Kitāb. An early date for the Kitāb served his apologetic purposes, but should be upheld nonetheless.

---

[174] Buhl, *Leben*, 211–12. In *EI*^{2}, s.v. Muḥammad (F. Buhl—A. T. Welch) it is said of Ibn Isḥāq's version of the Kitāb: "This version appears not to date from Muḥammad's first year in Medina, as is sometimes claimed, since it reflects the later, strained relationship between the Prophet and the Jewish people of the settlement".

[175] Ibn Junghul, I, 225b, says with regard to AH 1: *wa-fī hādhihi l-sana ʿaqada rasūlu llāh ṣ l-ulfa bayna l-muhājirīna wa-l-anṣār bi-l-kitābi lladhī amara bihi fa-kutiba baynahum bi-l-mu'ākhāti llatī amarahum bihā wa-muwādaʿatihi l-yahūda lladhīna kānū bi-l-madīna wa-hum banū qaynuqāʿ wa-banū l-naḍīr wa-banū qurayẓa.*

[176] *Amwāl*, 266 no. 519.

Appendix B

The Unity of the Kitāb

The possibility that part of the Kitāb was added to it after its conclusion was raised many years ago. With regard to *wa-inna yahūda l-aws...* (§57) Wellhausen (73) says:

> Der Paragraph ist ohne Zweifel ein Nachtrag und deshalb an das Ende gestellt, während sonst von den Juden und Judengenossen in §25–35 [§§28–39] gehandelt wird. Von den "Genossen dieser Schrift" können die Juden der Aus nebst ihren (dieser Juden) beisassen nur dann so wie hier unterschieden werden, wenn sie nicht von vornherein zu ihnen gehörten, wie die anderen Juden in §25–35, sondern erst nachgehens hinzu kamen.[177]

Watt is of the opinion that the Kitāb "as we have it contains articles from two or more different dates".[178] He says elsewhere regarding the unity of the Kitāb: "The document is composite, as is shown by repetitions. In its present form it was seen to belong to a date after the Ḳurayẓa affair in 5/627, but some of its articles may go back to the Pledge of War at al-ʿAḳaba".[179]

Watt (226–28) bases his argument on the following presumed inconsistencies:

1. The believers are mostly spoken of in the third person, but sometimes they are "you" and sometimes "we".

"You" (§26: *mahmā khtalaftum...*) relates to the contracting parties with reference to their internal affairs. "We" (§18: *man tabiʿanā min yahūd...*;

[177]See also Muir, *The life of Moḥammad*, 184 n. 3: "There are some references to the hostility of Mecca and also anticipatory allusions to religious wars — additions made apparently at a later time". He continues: "As there is no reason to believe that the original or any copy was preserved, we can only regard the treaty as transmitted by memory, and this will account for spurious clauses and loose expression".

[178]Watt, 226. Denny argues in this respect: "This position is commonly held now and has been strengthened further by the important discussion of R.B. Serjeant, 'The Constitution of Medina'"; Denny, "*Ummah* in the Constitution of Medina", 39 n. 3.

[179]*EI*², s.v. al-Madīna, 996. Similarly, Goto (16) says that the document is "a composite form of several documents of various dates".

§20: *kull ghāziya ghazat maʿanā...*) relates to the contracting parties with reference to their dealings with foreign elements.

2. The Kitāb speaks mostly of "believers", but twice they are "Muslims".

§1 has Mu'minūn and Muslimūn as two distinct groups. §§28 and 44 refer to Muslimūn, not Mu'minūn.

3. Following Wellhausen, Watt mentions that articles 24 (§27) and 38 (*wa-inna l-yahūd yunfiqūna maʿa l-muʾminīna mā dāmū muḥāribīna*) are repeated.

The clause was duplicated due to a scribal error. It is not found in Abū ʿUbayd's recension and is missing in some versions of Ibn Isḥāq's recension.

4. There are similarities between different articles of the Kitāb. Watt observes, however, that one set of articles is spread, according to his division of the Kitāb, between articles 16 and 30 and another set between articles 37 and 46. According to Watt, this is sufficient to justify an examination of the possibility that the document as we have it contains articles from two or more different dates.

The Kitāb, while forming one document, includes two distinct parts, the treaty of the Mu'minūn and the treaty of the Jews; each of the parts has its proper ending. Watt remarks that articles no. 23 (§26) and 42 (§52) "say that disputes are to be referred to Muḥammad, though article 42 is more precise". There is no repetition here. §§26 and 52 are arbitration clauses belonging to different parts of the Kitāb. There is no question of precision: the clauses differ considerably according to their context.

5. Nos. 20 (§23) and 43 (§54) are both directed against Quraysh.

The clauses appear in different parts of the Kitāb and are addressed to different groups.

6. "The points about Jews in articles 16 (§18) and 24 (§27) are similar to those in articles 37 (§44) and 38 [the repeated clause *wa-inna l-yahūd yunfiqūna maʿa l-muʾminīna...*]; and indeed articles 24 and 38 are identical".

The clauses of the first pair do not resemble each other and the second pair appeared above under no. 3.

7. Nos. 30 (§33: *wa-inna li-yahūd banī l-aws...*) and 46 (§57: *wa-inna yahūda l-aws mawāliyahum wa-anfusahum...*) both deal with the Jews of the Aws.

This is a valid point. As we have just seen, Wellhausen argued that the latter clause was an addendum. Comparable to some extent is the case of the Yahūd Banī Thaʿlaba: at some distance from the clause that mentions them, their *mawālī* are added (§§34 and 38).

8. Finally Watt argues:

> It seems probable... that the three main Jewish groups are not mentioned in the document. If that is so, the document in its present form might belong to the period after the elimination of Qurayẓa. The difficulty that much attention is given to Jewish affairs at a time when there were few Jews in Medina could be explained by the hypothesis that the document in its final form was intended as a charter for the Jews remaining in Medina and included all relevant articles from earlier forms of the Constitution of the city.

Indeed, the main Jewish clans are not mentioned in the Kitāb. However, this is not due to omission — they were simply not part of it. A later "editing" of the text is highly unlikely. The Kitāb is too vague and too limited to serve as a charter; it reflects the state of affairs in Medina shortly after the *hijra*.

On the whole there is no case for arguing that the Kitāb is inconsistent.

Serjeant dedicated to the Kitāb two studies, respectively published in 1964 and 1978. The latter begins as follows (1):

> For almost a decade I have taught the "Constitution of Medina" at Cambridge as the eight distinct documents it comprises, issued on various occasions over the first seven years or so, of Muḥammad's Medinan period, using a typescript text of these documents, designated A to H.

Already in his 1964 article Serjeant mentioned his method of discerning the different documents (8):

> First of all I split up the "Constitution" wherever the language itself dictates a division — namely wherever there is to be found a terminating formula such as, "*Wa-ʾinna llāh ʿalā abarri hā<u>dh</u>ā*" or "*Wa-l-birru dūna ʾl-ithm*". In the case of document "B",

> as I have termed it, the concluding phrase runs, "*Wa-innakum mahmā 'khtalaftum fīhi min shay'in, fa-inna maradda-hu ila 'llāhi... wa-ilā Muḥammad*".

Gil did not accept Serjeant's theory and has confirmed his position in a recent study.[180] Referring to the strong connection between the elements of the Kitāb, Gil (48) says:

> As a rule, when an ancient literary source is submitted to the "method of the sources", the burden of proof should be on those who argue against its unity and genuineness. Repetitions, abrupt and unexpected entries of new elements, and linguistic variations cannot serve as adequate arguments in such a case, certainly not where Muḥammad is concerned, for they are peculiarities of his style, well known from the Qur'ān.[181]

Rubin (5 n. 2) remarks disapprovingly: "Serjeant, who completely ignored Wellhausen's study, cut the 'Constitution' into no less than 8 separate 'documents' in what seems to be a highly arbitrary manner".[182] Simonsen has misgivings about Serjeant's theory,[183] which also met little favour with Ṭibāwī[184] and Hoyland.[185] Even a student of Serjeant expressed his doubts

---

[180] Gil, "The Medinan Opposition to the Prophet", 65 n. 1.

[181] Simonsen, *Studies in the Genesis and Early Development of the Caliphal Taxation System*, 167 n. 23, offers an alternative interpretation: "It is... more likely that evidences of repetition in the Constitution are attributable to the transmission strata prior to al-Zuhrî. He merely collated the information he could find about the individual provisions that originally appeared in the agreement, in this way duplicating some points because they were conjoined in a different order in the older transmission". Simonsen argues (*ibid.*, 40) that Zuhrī was also the source of Ibn Isḥāq's text.

[182] Serjeant's more recent article was nonetheless included in Rubin, *The Life of Muḥammad*, 151–92.

[183] Simonsen, *Studies in the Genesis and Early Development of the Caliphal Taxation System*, 41: "Serjeant's conclusion is... methodically doubtful as in fact it is only ibn isḥâq's text [and not Abū 'Ubayd's — M. L.] which can be so subdivided".

[184] Tibawi, "Second Critique", 17–18.

[185] Who, while accepting Watt's argument that parts of the Kitāb may have been drafted at different times, calls Serjeant's division of it into several documents "excessive"; Hoyland, "Sebeos, the Jews and the Rise of Islam", 100, n. 33.

about it.[186] Another student of Serjeant, Rahman,[187] takes his conclusions for granted:

> Soon after the *hijra* the Prophet arranged the affairs of his newly created confederation on the basis of two pacts....

Elsewhere, with reference to Gil and Stillman,[188] she argues that their analyses

> suffer from faults similar to those of the Muslim medieval traditionists. Stillman's conclusion that it was "merely an interim step to be abandoned" (p. 11) while the document contains references to events that would happen 9 years after the *hijrah* would explain why he failed to understand the idea of the organization of the *ummah* and with it events concerning the Jewish tribes in Medina. M. Gil's attitude towards the very same problem is puzzling even more. While accepting the validity of the *ʿahd* and its interpretation, as presented by R.B. Serjeant, he would not accept the fact that there had been a treaty between Muḥammad and the Jews.[189]

[186]Zein al-Abdin, "The Political Significance of the Constitution of Medina", 146: "There are good arguments to suppose that the Constitution was written in parts and over a period of time; nevertheless, any exact number for these parts or any definite date for them remains an unverifiable hypothesis". Serjeant defended his theory in his review of R. Simon's *Meccan Trade and Islam*, Budapest 1989, in *Der Islam* 70 (1993) 317–18, claiming that "Simon is in fundamental error in dismissing the analysis of the so-called 'Constitution of Medina' and the division of it into 8 separate documents, which he still considers as a single document. The title given this document is only a 19th century interpretation of it. Of my preliminary analysis of it he is quite justified in saying that 'the author raises some insufficiently proved aspects and divides the Constitution of Medina into eight parts on the basis of purely formal criteria'. But he seems unaware of my detailed study of it in the *BSOAS* for 1978 to which there has been no challenge worthy of mention up to date". Several years earlier, in his review of R. Bell's *A Commentary on the Qurʾān*, in *JSS* 39 (1994), 128, Serjeant remarked that he had returned to his 1935–36 notes of Bell's lectures; he found "that Bell had suggested the so-called 'Constitution' consisted of a number of separate documents. It is a pity that Bell did not follow up this line of enquiry for by applying the same critical methods he employed with the Quranic text he could have arrived at the division of it into eight documents and worked out their relation to certain Quranic passages".

[187]See her "*Jibt, Ṭāghūt* and the *Taḥkīm* of the *Umma*", 53, 54 n. 16.

[188]See his *The Jews of Arab Lands*, 11, 115–18.

[189]Rahman, "The Conflicts between the Prophet and the Opposition in Madina", 277 n. 66. I could not find in her two articles any reference to Watt.

Giannakis[190] agrees with Serjeant: "This is a collection of documents issued on various occasions during Muhammad's Medinan period". Goto, who gives Watt credit for his suggestion that the text of the Kitāb is a composite one, discusses the document "assuming that it is composed of several differently dated documents".[191] Donner refers to the Kitāb as "a group of documents collectively known as the 'Constitution of Medina'".[192] Jones mentions "the treaty documents now known as the Constitution of Medina".[193]

Let us look into Serjeant's arguments. Without referring to Watt he mentions inconsistencies in the Kitāb:[194]

> The "constitution", then, divided itself into eight distinct documents — but while the division at once resolved the inconsistencies apparent when you regard it as a single document, it immediately raised a series of formidable new problems. Fortunately, however, I regard these problems as ultimately soluble by close study of the early literature.

Serjeant also remarks: "Close study of the internal evidence of the several documents reveals many indications of a difference in date".[195] He notes that in document B the Prophet is named Muḥammad followed by *ṣallā llāhu ʿalayhi wa-sallama* (admitting, however, that the expression may not be original to the document), whereas in documents F and H he is designated *rasūl allāh*. Serjeant draws the following conclusion: "From this it may be inferred that his claim to the title of 'Apostle of God' was not accepted by all parties to the first contract — as in fact we know from the Sīrah itself that this was contested by many of the Medinans".

However, references to the Prophet as *nabī* or *rasūlu llāh* and the *ṣlʿm* formula do not provide firm grounds for claiming that the Kitāb is inconsistent, since scribes are most likely to differ over them.[196] Scribes also followed different conventions concerning Allāh's appellations.

---

[190] "The Concept of Ummah", 104.

[191] Goto, 6. (Only Serjeant's earlier article was available to Goto when he wrote the original Japanese version of his article.)

[192] Donner, *The Early Islamic Conquests*, 54, 61. See also *idem*, "From Believers to Muslims", 29, where the Kitāb is described as "a set of documents setting down agreements reached between Muhammad and the people of Yathrib sometime after the *hijra*".

[193] Jones, "The Word Made Visible", 5.

[194] "The 'Constitution of Medina'", 9. See also Serjeant, "Ḥaram and Ḥawṭah", 48.

[195] "The 'Constitution of Medina'", 10.

[196] See the variants to every mention of Muḥammad in the Kitāb, for example in the arbitration clauses §§26 and 52. Ḥamīdullāh, "Aqdam dustūr", 110, observes that the

Serjeant's "terminal formulae" are indeed peculiar, but can by no means serve as markers for the division of the Kitāb into separate documents.

Two of them, §14: *wa-inna l-muʾminīna l-muttaqīna ʿalā aḥsan hudan* [read: *hādhā*] *wa-aqwamihi*, and §26: *wa-innakum mahmā khtalaftum...*, appear in the first part of the Kitāb. The other seven: §§37 and 58: *wa-inna l-birr dūna l-ithm* [read: *wa-inna l-barr dūna l-āthim*]; §: 43: *wa-inna llāh ʿalā abarr hādhā*; §47: *wa-l-birr dūna l-ithm* [read: *wa-l-barr dūna l-āthim*]; §53: *wa-inna llāh ʿalā atqā mā fī hādhihi l-ṣaḥīfa wa-abarrihi*; §60: *wa-inna llāh ʿalā aṣdaq mā fī hādhihi l-ṣaḥīfa wa-abarrihi*; and §63: *wa-inna llāh jār li-man barra wa-ttaqā wa-muḥammad rasūlu llāh* [*ṣ*], appear in the second part of the Kitāb or the treaty of the Jews.

Only one of these formulae is a genuine concluding clause, namely the arbitration clause §26 that ends the first part of the Kitāb or the treaty of the Muʾminūn: *wa-innakum mahmā khtalaftum....* But Serjeant divides the first part into two separate documents, A and B, because of §14. Another clause, §63, is semi-final: according to Serjeant it concludes the Kitāb; but both Ibn Isḥāq and Abū ʿUbayd have after it another final clause, §64: *wa-inna awlāhum bi-hādhihi l-ṣaḥīfa l-barru l-muḥsin.*

Serjeant's argument is inconsistent. Since he declared one arbitration clause, §26, a terminal formula, he should also have declared the other arbitration clause, §52, a terminal formula. Instead, it is found in the middle of document F according to Serjeant's division of the Kitāb.

The first so-called terminal formula, §14, is the only terminal formula that has Muʾminūn as its subject, whereas four of the so-called terminal formulae in the second part of the Kitāb have Allāh as their subject. This clearly demonstrates the one and only division of the Kitāb into the treaty of the Muʾminūn and the treaty of the Jews.

Most of the list of Jewish tribes in the Kitāb forms in Serjeant's analysis (26–27) a separate document, namely document C. This division leaves two groups, *mawālī thaʿlaba* and *biṭānat yahūd*, in another document (29). If

words *al-nabī*, *rasūlu llāhi* and the *ṣlʿm* formula that follow the name Muḥammad in the latter part of the Kitāb were added by the scribes "for the sake of form" (*taʾadduban*). However, Ḥamīdullāh allows for the possibility that the Prophet himself added the words *al-nabī* or *rasūlu llāh* and the Jews, although they did not recognize him as a prophet, did not dare to object because of their precarious political and military situation. See on this point Donner, "From Believers to Muslims", 39–40. (For a rare example of the *ṣlʿm* formula being used while addressing the Prophet see Muṣʿab, *Nasab*, 266: *yā rasūla llāh ṣallā llāh ʿalayka....*)

indeed, as has been argued above, the *yahūd banī thaʿlaba* and the *mawālī thaʿlaba* relate to the same Thaʿlaba, then their appearance in two separate documents is untenable.

Appendix C

The Recensions of the Kitāb

Ibn Isḥāq and Abū ʿUbayd

Serjeant (9) bases his study of the Kitāb on Ibn Isḥāq's recension, remarking that Abū ʿUbayd's text is defective. Crone believes that Abū ʿUbayd's recension is later than Ibn Isḥāq's.[197] However, she remarks (203 n. 16): "Ibn Hishām knew of another recension which may well have been Abū ʿUbayd's: he tells us that some have *al-birr* [read: *al-barr*] *al-muḥsin* for *al-birr al-maḥḍ*, which is precisely what Abū ʿUbayd has".

Abū ʿUbayd's recension has an *isnād* going back to Zuhrī, who died roughly a quarter of a century before Ibn Isḥāq. But this should not lead to the conclusion that it is earlier than Ibn Isḥāq's recension, because the latter also received it from an informant of Zuhrī's generation.[198]

Abū ʿUbayd's recension is indeed much shorter than Ibn Isḥāq's and many clauses are missing in it; however, in some minor points it is superior. For instance, *minhum* in the list of Arab participants (§§4–11) appears in Abū ʿUbayd throughout and must reflect the original reading.[199]

Zuhrī

Zuhrī's recension is preserved in Abū ʿUbayd's *Kitāb al-amwāl*. It is quoted from Zuhrī via two slightly different chains of transmitters:

[197] *Slaves on Horses*, 7.

[198] Crone argues that in some respects Abū ʿUbayd's version is the more archaic one. It lacks the invocation; where Ibn Isḥāq later qualifies Muḥammad as *rasūl allāh*, Abū ʿUbayd by contrast calls him *nabī* (but the opening clause in Abū ʿUbayd has: *min muḥammad al-nabī rasūli llāh* — M. L.); and it was presumably Ibn Isḥāq who omitted the Jews from the clause on *ṣulḥ* (§56) rather than Abū ʿUbayd who inserted them. She observes (7) that Abū ʿUbayd's version "is a typical product of written transmission: it has copyists' mistakes, interpolations, several of the by now unintelligible clauses have been omitted, and it has also been equipped with an *isnād*; but otherwise the text is the same".

[199] Serjeant (40) argues regarding two of the clauses that Abū ʿUbayd inserts *minhum*.

1. At one point (166 no. 328) Abū ʿUbayd records a fragment of the Kitāb with the following *isnād*: Abū ʿUbayd ← ʿAbdallāh b. Ṣāliḥ[200] ← al-Layth b. Saʿd[201] ← ʿUqayl b. Khālid al-Aylī[202] ← Zuhrī.

2. Abū ʿUbayd had yet another text of the Kitāb (166 no. 329) with the same *isnād* but for his immediate source who was not ʿAbdallāh b. Ṣāliḥ but Yaḥyā b. ʿAbdallāh b. Bukayr.[203]

Abū ʿUbayd gained access to Zuhrī's recension in Egypt. Both his immediate informants, ʿAbdallāh b. Ṣāliḥ and Yaḥyā b. ʿAbdallāh b. al-Bukayr, were Egyptians. Abū ʿUbayd must have received Zuhrī's recension after his arrival in Egypt with Yaḥyā b. Maʿīn in 213/828.[204]

Having carefully compared the versions of Zuhrī's recension that he received from the two informants, Abū ʿUbayd arrived at the conclusion that they were almost identical. Therefore he adduced the full text of the Kitāb (260–64 no. 518) on the authority of both ʿAbdallāh b. Ṣāliḥ and Yaḥyā b. ʿAbdallāh b. Bukayr (← al-Layth b. Saʿd ← ʿUqayl b. Khālid ← Zuhrī). His meticulous comparison of the versions is reflected in his remark that while ʿAbdallāh's version had *ʿalā r.b.ʿātihim* (§§3–11), in Yaḥyā's version the long vowel was placed differently: *ʿalā r.bāʿ.tihim*. The latter reading was more reliable, he remarked (*wa-hādhā ʿindī huwa l-maḥfūẓ*; 166 no. 329).

In sum, at the beginning of the third century of Islam at least two nearly identical versions of the Kitāb in Zuhrī's recension were circulating in Egypt.

Ibn Jurayj

Abū ʿUbayd also adduces a small fragment of the Kitāb going back to Ibn Jurayj[205] that the former received from Ḥajjāj, i.e. Ḥajjāj b. Muḥammad al-Miṣṣīṣī.[206] One assumes that Ibn Jurayj transmitted the whole Kitāb, although Abū ʿUbayd only adduces from it a clause including a unique reading (§12, *mafdūḥ* instead of *mufraḥ*). The quotation appears in the section of

[200] D. 223/838, the *kātib* of al-Layth b. Saʿd; *GAS*, I, 104.

[201] Below, 200n. Printed erroneously: *al-Layth ʿan Saʿd*.

[202] D. 141/758; Lecker, "Biographical Notes on Ibn Shihāb al-Zuhrī", 26–27, 56.

[203] D. 231/845; *GAS*, I, 460; *Tahdh.*, XI, 237–38 no. 387.

[204] *Tahdh.*, VIII, 315 no. 572; Gottschalk, "Abū ʿUbaid al-Qāsim b. Sallām", 272.

[205] ʿAbd al-Malik b. ʿAbd al-ʿAzīz, d. 150/767; *GAS*, I, 91.

[206] D. 206/821; see an entry on him in *Tahdhīb al-kamāl*, V, 451–57 no. 1127; *GAS*, I, 31, 91.

Abū ʿUbayd's book dealing with male and female enemy captives.[207] The small fragment we have from Ibn Jurayj's recension includes the introduction and §12.[208] Zuhrī was one of Ibn Jurayj's teachers and may have been the source of the latter's recension.

[207]For Abū ʿUbayd it was not a matter of theory: for eighteen years he functioned as *qāḍī* in Ṭarsūs; *Tahdhīb al-kamāl*, XXIII, 362; Gottschalk, "Abū ʿUbaid al-Qāsim b. Sallām", 272. At some point Abū ʿUbayd quotes Zuhrī's recension in full, whereas in the section on the enemy captives he only adduces the relevant clause (*wa-hum yafukkūna ʿāniyahum*).

[208]See Abū ʿUbayd, *Amwāl*, 166–67 no. 330: …*ʿani bn jurayj qāla fī kitābi l-nabī ṣ bayna l-muslimīna wa-l-muʾminīna min quraysh wa-ahl yathrib wa-mani ttabaʿahum fa-laḥiqa bihim wa-jāhada maʿahum: inna l-muʾminīna lā yatrukūna mafdūḥan minhum an yuʿṭūhu bi-l-maʿrūf fī fidāʾ aw ʿaql.*

Appendix D

The Preservation of Ibn Isḥāq's Recension

ʿAlī and ʿUmar

In early Islam the preservation of the Kitāb became a bone of contention between Sunna and Shīʿa; the assumption was that the person whom Muḥammad entrusted with the Kitāb was also his heir. As usual when the leading figures of the Islamic community are involved, there is little hope of finding out "what really happened"; but the tracing of the opposing views is illuminating nevertheless.

The claim that ʿAlī preserved important official documents from the time of Muḥammad is not restricted to the Kitāb.[209] On the whole, the Shīʿite claim regarding ʿAlī is more widespread than any rival claim.[210] The Shīʿite case is argued in a well-crafted report about the document kept by ʿAlī, probably for frequent reference, in the scabbard of his sword.[211] Qays b. ʿAbbād, on whose authority the report is transmitted, and al-Ashtar, asked ʿAlī whether the Messenger of God had entrusted him with something he had denied the others (*hal ʿahida ilayka rasūlu llāh ṣ ʿahdan lam yaʿhadhu ilā l-nās kāffa?*) "No, but...," was the answer, the exception being a *ṣaḥīfa* that ʿAlī pulled out of the scabbard of his sword.[212] This is the Shīʿite claim

[209] A treaty reportedly concluded between the Prophet and "the Jews" after the assassination of Kaʿb b. al-Ashraf of the Naḍīr was kept after the Prophet's death by ʿAlī. For reports on the *kitāb ʿAlī* see e.g. Ṭūsī, *Tahdhīb al-aḥkām*, VI, 140–41 (Abū ʿAbdallāh ← his father: *qaraʾtu fī kitāb ʿalī anna rasūla llāh ṣ wa-ālihi kataba kitāban bayna l-muhājirīna wa-l-anṣār...*); *ibid.*, X, 280 (← Abū ʿAbdallāh: *inna fī kitāb ʿalī: law anna rajulan qaṭaʿa farja mraʾa ...*); also 292 (← Ibn Faḍḍāl: *ʿaraḍtu kitāb ʿalī ʿalā abī l-ḥasan fa-qāla: huwa ṣaḥīḥ, qaḍā amīru l-muʾminīna fī diyat jirāḥati l-aʿḍāʾ kullihā...*, which is followed by a long list); 295–308; ʿAbd al-Razzāq, IX, 263.

[210] Cf. Kohlberg, "Authoritative Scriptures", 300–302. See also the extensive note on ʿAlī's *ṣaḥīfa* in Kister, "Sifrut ha-sira", 215–16; the note appeared in abridged form in *idem*, "The *Sīrah* Literature", 352 n. 1.

[211] Abū ʿUbayd, *Amwāl*, 241 no. 495 (*jafn sayfihi*).

[212] The two Companions could read in it the following: *al-muslimūna takāfaʾu dimāʾuhum wa-yasʿā bi-dhimmatihim adnāhum, wa-hum yad ʿalā man siwāhum, lā yuqtalu muʾmin bi-kāfir wa-lā dhū ʿahd fī ʿahdihi, man aḥdatha ḥadathan aw āwā muḥdithan fa-ʿalayhi laʿnatu llāh wa-l-malāʾika wa-l-nās ajmaʿīna.*

regarding the Kitāb, slightly disguised as a negative answer.[213] In addition, a document dictated by the Prophet and preserved by ʿAlī is often quoted in connection with questions of inheritance.[214]

The protagonist of the rival claim, which is rare, is ʿUmar b. al-Khaṭṭāb. Unaware of the dispute over the preservation of the Kitāb, Serjeant says: "There is no reason to suspect the Tradition which says that ʿAlī b. Abī Ṭālib, in his capacity as Muhammad's secretary, wrote the original document and kept it in his sword-case".[215] Serjeant argues that the "obvious source" of the Kitāb was ʿAbdallāh b. Ḥasan b. Ḥasan b. ʿAlī b. Abī Ṭālib. According to Serjeant, "Ibn Isḥāq was exclusively devoted" to him; on the other hand, "ʿAbdallāh... was the chief of the ʿAlawīs in his day...; and in whose hands, were it preserved at all, would it more likely be found than in those of the chief of the ʿAlawīs?" The text adduced by Serjeant to prove that Ibn Isḥāq "greatly relied upon him" is taken from Yāqūt's *Muʿjam al-udabāʾ*: Ibn Isḥāq would come to ʿAbdallāh and say: *athbit hādhā* [printed: *hādhihi*] *fī ʿilmika, fa-yuthbituhu wa-yarwīhi*[216] *ʿanhu*. Serjeant's translation runs as follows: "'Confirm this from your information', and he would verify it, and Ibn Isḥāq would transmit it on his authority".[217] But *athbit hādhā* means "record it in your *ʿilm*" or *ḥadīth*. ʿAbdallāh would record it and transmit it on the authority of Ibn Isḥāq, not the other way round.[218]

[213] Cf. *Lisān al-ʿarab*, XIII, 54, s.v. *b-ṭ-n*.

[214] *Ṣaḥīfat kitābi l-farāʾiḍ* said to be *imlāʾ rasūli llāh* in the handwriting of ʿAlī; Ṭūsī, *Tahdhīb al-aḥkām*, IX, 247; *ṣaḥīfat al-farāʾiḍ*; IX, 273, 285, 306. Elsewhere it is referred to as *farāʾiḍ ʿAlī*; IX, 294; *kitāb ʿalī*; IX, 211, 269, 308, 324, 325–26. The details provided about the *ṣaḥīfat al-farāʾiḍ* give the impression that it was an old document written on parchment: it was a *ṣaḥīfa mithl fakhidhi l-baʿīr... kitāb ghalīẓ yuʿrafu annahu min kutubi l-awwalīna*; IX, 271.

[215] "Early Arabic Prose", 134. See also Ṭabarī, II, 486 [I, 1367]: *wa-qīla inna fī hādhihi l-sana* [i.e. AH 2] *kataba rasūlu llāh ṣ l-maʿāqil fa-kāna* [*l-kitāb* is missing here] *muʿallaqan bi-sayfihi*. Cf. *The history of al-Ṭabarī*, VI, trans. Watt and McDonald, 92: "It is said that in this year the Messenger of God wrote the *Maʿāqil*, which was suspended from his sword".

[216] Serjeant offers an alternative, "less likely", reading: *wa-yurwīhi*, which he suggests to render "he would make him transmit it on his authority"; but this reading is impossible. In the addenda to his article (Serjeant, *Studies in Arabian History and Civilization*, 4), Serjeant remarks: "Dr J. Burton has pointed out to me that the usual formula is *A-thabuta* not *athbit*, i.e. 'Is this correct according to your information?'". However, Serjeant's original reading is smoother.

[217] Serjeant, "The 'Constitution of Medina'", 53; Yāqūt, *Udabāʾ*, VI, 2419 no. 995.

[218] For *athbata* see, for example, the following passage: *wulida lī walad fa-ataytu ʿaliyyan fa-athbatahu fī miʾa*; Abū ʿUbayd, *Amwāl*, 303–304 no. 586. In other words, ʿAlī ordered that the newborn baby be registered among those who received an annual pay of 100

The claim in support of ʿUmar is presumably as old as the one supporting ʿAlī if not older, although it could only be found in relatively late sources. ʿUmar b. al-Khaṭṭāb's descendants are said to have preserved the Kitāb together with a document issued by ʿUmar himself, thereby implying that ʿUmar was entrusted by Muḥammad with the Kitāb. Ibn Hishām quotes the Kitāb from Ibn Isḥāq without an *isnād*. However, two of the sources that quote Ibn Isḥāq's recension begin it with an *isnād*. These are Ibn Taymiyya (d. 728/1328) and his student, Ibn Qayyim al-Jawziyya (d. 751/1350).[219] The introduction to the Kitāb found in these sources is fuller than the one found in Ibn Hishām and elsewhere. It runs as follows:

> Muḥammad b. Isḥāq said, i.e. [a gloss; regarding the events that took place — M. L.] shortly after the Prophet's arrival at Medina: "The Messenger of God wrote a treaty between the Muhājirūn and the Anṣār in which he made a non-belligerency treaty with the Jews and made a pact with them, permitting them to remain in their former religion and keep their orchards intact and stipulated their obligations and rights".

To this point the text (exclusive of the gloss) also appears in Ibn Isḥāq.[220] The following is new:

---

dirhams. See also Lane, I, 329a, s.v. *athbata*: "He wrote it, set it down, registered it, or recorded it, i.e. a man's name, *fī l-dīwān*, in the register of soldiers or pensioners or accounts". Also *Naqāʾiḍ*, Glossary, 299, *athbata*: "to put in writing". Crone, in her review of C. Hillenbrand's translation of *The History of al-Ṭabarī*, XXVI, in *JSS* 35 (1990), correctly renders (339) *ithbāt ṣaḥābatika*, "inscribing your friends in the *dīwān*". *Wa-uthbita fī l-dawāwīn* in Ṭabarī, VIII, 119 [III, 464], is correctly translated in *The history of al-Ṭabarī*, XXIX, trans. Kennedy: "established him in the *dīwān*, interpreted as "he was given a regular salary, recorded in the official list, or *dīwān*". Cf. *Tahdhīb al-kamāl*, XXIV, 413: *kāna bn Isḥāq min aḥfaẓi l-nās fa-kāna idhā kāna ʿinda l-rajul khamsat aḥādīth aw akthar jāʾa fa-stawdaʿahā muḥammad b. isḥāq, qāla ḥfaẓhā ʿalayya fa-in nasītuhā kunta qad ḥafiẓtahā ʿalayya.* See also Bosworth, "Abū ʿAbdallāh al-Khawārazmī on the Technical Terms of the Secretary's Art", 143. Serjeant returned to this topic in a more recent article: "There is no reason to suspect the Tradition which says that ʿAlī b. Abī Ṭālib, in his capacity as Muhammad's secretary, wrote the original document and kept it in his sword-case.... The document was probably kept by one of ʿAlī's descendants and copied by Ibn Isḥāq..."; "Early Arabic Prose", 134. These comments reveal a certain naivety, considering the nature of early Islamic historiography.

[219] Ibn Taymiyya, *Ṣārim*, 62; Ibn Qayyim, *Aḥkām*, II, 835.

[220] *Qāla muḥammad b. isḥāq, yaʿnī fī awwal mā qadima l-nabī ṣ l-madīna: wa-kataba rasūlu llāhi ṣ kitāban bayna l-muhājirīna wa-l-anṣār wādaʿa fīhi yahūd wa-ʿāhadahum wa-aqarrahum ʿalā dīnihim wa-amwālihim wa-shtarṭa ʿalayhim wa-sharaṭa lahum*; above, 141.

> Muḥammad b. Isḥāq said: "'Uthmān b. Muḥammad b. 'Uthmān b. al-Akhnas b. Sharīq transmitted to me the following: 'I took this letter from the family of 'Umar b. al-Khaṭṭāb. It was attached to the letter of taxation (*ṣadaqa*) that 'Umar wrote to the tax collectors'".[221]

'Uthmān b. Muḥammad was a great-grandson of the Prophet's contemporary al-Akhnas b. Sharīq of the Thaqīf, who was a client (*ḥalīf*) of the Quraysh subdivision of Zuhra.[222] No details on 'Uthmān b. Muḥammad were found. One could argue that the repetition of the name 'Uthmān is the result of a scribal error and that the latter "'Uthmān" in the pedigree should be replaced with "al-Mughīra":[223] 'Uthmān b. Muḥammad b. al-Mughīra b. al-Akhnas b. Sharīq was a traditionist from the Ḥijāz who could have been Ibn Isḥāq's source.[224] He is identical to the 'Uthmān b. Muḥammad al-Akhnasī quoted by Wāqidī several times.[225] But it is probably better not to introduce this emendation and wait until new evidence about 'Uthmān b. Muḥammad b. 'Uthmān emerges; the more so since Ibn Isḥāq is known to have quoted, at least once, 'Uthmān's son, al-Mughīra.[226]

"I took this letter from the family of 'Umar b. al-Khaṭṭāb" does not imply that Ibn Isḥāq's informant actually took the original document from 'Umar's family; he merely copied it. There is nothing unusual in the claim that 'Umar's descendants preserved documents from his term in office. Letters

---

[221] *Qāla bn isḥāq: ḥaddathanī 'uthmān b. muḥammad b. 'uthmān b. al-akhnas b. sharīq, qāla: akhadhtu min āl 'umar b. al-khaṭṭāb hādhā l-kitāb, kāna maqrūnan bi-kitābi l-ṣadaqati lladhī kataba 'umar li-l-'ummāl, kataba: bi-smi llāhi l-raḥmāni l-raḥīm....*

[222] On al-Akhnas see *Iṣāba*, I, 38–39 no. 61; *Usd al-ghāba*, I, 47–48, s.v. Ubayy b. Sharīq; above, 116.

[223] See the recent edition of *al-Ṣārim al-maslūl* by al-Ḥalawānī and Shawdarī, Beirut: Dār Ibn Ḥazm, 1417/1997, II, 129 n. 3 (*jā'a fī kutubi l-tarājim bi-annahu...*).

[224] See *Tahdhīb al-kamāl*, XIX, 488–89 no. 3859, who lists among his pupils 'Abdallāh b. Ja'far al-Zuhrī al-Makhramī (d. 170/786); on 'Abdallāh see *Tahdhīb al-kamāl*, XIV, 372–76 no. 3203 (Wāqidī was among those who transmitted his *ḥadīth*).

[225] Wāqidī, I, 359–60 (a report on 'Umar — of particular interest for us here — which Wāqidī quotes from 'Uthmān through 'Abdallāh b. Ja'far); II, 491 (← 'Abdallāh b. Ja'far); III, 883 (two reports going back to 'Uthmān, one of which is transmitted via 'Abdallāh b. Ja'far).

[226] Ibn Kathīr, *Bidāya*, III, 213–14, regarding the first sermon delivered by Muḥammad after his arrival at Medina: ... ← Yūnus b. Bukayr ← Ibn Isḥāq ← al-Mughīra b. 'Uthmān b. Muḥammad b. 'Uthmān b. al-Akhnas [printed erroneously *wa-l-Akhnas*] b. Sharīq ← Abū Salama b. 'Abd al-Raḥmān b. 'Awf.

exchanged between the governor of Egypt, ʿAmr b. al-ʿĀṣ, and the caliph ʿUmar may have remained in the possession of the former's descendants.[227]

Some comparative evidence can be added that relates to the preservation of other documents from the reigns of Muḥammad and ʿUmar.[228] Having been appointed as a tax collector, Zuhrī came to ʿUmar's grandson, Sālim b. ʿAbdallāh b. ʿUmar, who read out for him the *kitāb al-ṣadaqa*. Then Zuhrī went to Abū Bakr b. Muḥammad b. ʿAmr b. Ḥazm, who read out for him the *kitāb al-ʿuqūl*. In other words, these documents were still extant in the Umayyad period[229] and were considered relevant to Zuhrī's duties as a tax collector.[230] I have previously identified this *kitāb al-ʿuqūl* with our Kitāb,[231] but I now realize that *ʿuqūl* in this context are "rates of compensation for murder and bodily injuries",[232] and hence the document that ʿAmr b. Ḥazm's descendant read out for Zuhrī must have been Muḥammad's letter to ʿAmr. The following seems to be a clear reference to the same document: the Prophet wrote a letter (*kitāb*) to Ibn Ḥazm concerning the *ṣadaqāt*; it included matters of *ṣadaqāt* and *diyāt*.[233] Zuhrī quotes from it several passages dealing with blood money.[234]

Abū Bakr b. Muḥammad b. ʿAmr b. Ḥazm, who preserved this letter, was Zuhrī's contemporary and died several years before Zuhrī.[235] At the

---

[227] Lecker, "The Estates of ʿAmr b. al-ʿĀṣ in Palestine", 33 n. 88; *Futūḥ miṣr*, 90, 168, 169. Cf. Bravmann, "The State Archives in the Early Islamic Era".

[228] Cf. Lecker, "On the Preservation of the Letters of the Prophet Muḥammad".

[229] Which should be taken into account in the study of Islamic law.

[230] Lecker, "Biographical Notes on Ibn Shihāb al-Zuhrī", 38–39. See also Qurṭubī, *Tafsīr*, VI, 32–33, interpretation of Qur'ān 5,1: *qara'tu kitāb rasūli llāh ṣ lladhī katabahu li-ʿamr b. ḥazm ḥīna baʿathahu ilā najrān, wa-fī ṣadrihi: hādhā bayān li-l-nāsi mina llāh wa-rasūlihi, 'yā ayyuhā lladhīna āmanū, awfū bi-l-ʿuqūdi', fa-kataba l-āyāt fīhā ilā qawlihi: 'inna llāha sarīʿu l-ḥisābi'* (Qur'ān, 5,1–4). See also in Dārimī, II, 188 (*kitāb al-diyāt*), a report going back to Zuhrī ← Abū Bakr b. Muḥammad b. ʿAmr b. Ḥazm ← his father ← his grandfather; above, 128. Other quotations from the document follow in the same section of Dārimī.

[231] "Biographical Notes on Ibn Shihāb al-Zuhrī", 39.

[232] *Wath.*, 210–11 no. 106.

[233] *Tahdhīb al-aḥkām*, X, 291. This is a quotation from the document: *fī l-ʿayn khamsūna wa-fī l-jā'ifa l-thulth wa-fī l-munaqqila khamsa ʿashrata wa-fī l-mūḍiḥa khams mina l-ibl.*

[234] *Qara'tu fī kitāb rasūli llāh ṣ li-ʿamr b. ḥazm ḥīna baʿathahu ilā najrān wa-kāna l-kitāb ʿinda abī bakr b. ḥazm, fa-kataba rasūlu llāh ṣ fīhi: hādhā bayān mina llāh wa-rasūlihi... hādhā kitābu l-jirāḥ: fī l-nafs mi'a mina l-ibl...*; Abū Dāwūd, *Marāsīl*, (ed. Arnāwūṭ), 211–12. Ḥammād b. Salama saw a copy of this document; *ibid.*, 128 (the passages adduced here concern the taxation of livestock).

[235] *Tahdh.*, XII, 38–40 no. 154.

time of ʿUmar b. ʿAbd al-ʿAzīz, Abū Bakr was both the *qāḍī* of Medina and its governor.[236]

Saʿīd b. al-Musayyab (d. 95/714) doubted that ʿAmr b. Ḥazm's letter originated from the Prophet. According to Saʿīd, the practice initiated by ʿUmar b. al-Khaṭṭāb of paying different rates of blood money for the loss of different fingers ceased to exist when Muḥammad's alleged letter was discovered with ʿAmr b. Ḥazm's family.[237] Zuhrī reported (← ʿUmar's grandson, Sālim b. ʿAbdallāh ← his father, Ibn ʿUmar) that the Prophet had written the *kitāb al-ṣadaqa* but never sent it out to his governors; rather, he attached it to his sword (*fa-qaranahu bi-sayfihi*). Abū Bakr acted according to it and so did ʿUmar.[238] This contradicts the claims of ʿAmr b. Ḥazm's offspring: if the Prophet's letter was never sent, their claim is false.[239]

The *kitāb al-ṣadaqa* that Zuhrī received from ʿUmar's grandson, Sālim b. ʿAbdallāh b. ʿUmar, concerned taxation. ʿIkrima b. Khālid, who was in charge of levying the *ṣadaqa* taxes of the ʿAkk,[240] reported that ʿUmar's great-grandson, Abū Bakr b. ʿUbaydallāh (b. ʿAbdallāh b. ʿUmar b. al-Khaṭṭāb) had copied for him a *ṣaḥīfa* bound to the scabbard of ʿUmar's sword.[241]

---

[236]Horovitz, "The Earliest Biographies", no. 2, 23: Abū Bakr was the judge of Medina from AH 86, the year in which ʿUmar b. ʿAbd al-ʿAzīz became its governor; it was caliph Sulaymān b. ʿAbd al-Malik who in AH 93 added to his judgeship the office of governor. He also held this office under ʿUmar b. ʿAbd al-ʿAzīz. Yazīd b. ʿAbd al-Malik dismissed him from the governorship, but for some time he continued to officiate as a judge.

[237]Ibn Ḥajar, *Maṭālib*, II, 127–28 no. 1845, quoting the *Musnad* of Isḥāq b. Ibrāhīm b. Makhlad, also known as Isḥāq b. Rāhūya (*GAS*, I, 109–10): ... *ḥattā wajadnā kitāban ʿinda āl ʿamr b. ḥazm yazʿumūna annahu min rasūli llāh ṣ, fīhi....* Saʿīd also reported (Ibn Ḥajar, *Maṭālib*, II, 127 no. 1844) that ʿUmar's differentiated rates for the fingers were made equal when ʿUthmān found a letter that Muḥammad had written to ʿAmr b. Ḥazm establishing equal rates for all of the fingers. From Isḥāq b. Rāhūya's *Musnad* (quoted in Ibn Ḥajar, *Maṭālib*, I, 231 no. 809) we learn that ʿAmr b. Ḥazm's letter was also transmitted by his grandson, Abū Bakr to Qays b. Saʿd al-Makkī (d. 119/737; *Tahdhīb al-kamāl*, XXIV, 47–50 no. 4907), who in his turn transmitted it to Ḥammād b. Salama (d. 167/784; *Tahdhīb al-kamāl*, VII, 267–68).

[238]Ibn Zanjawayh, *Amwāl*, II, 804 no. 1392.

[239]Cf. the letter suspended from a spear that was held by the supporters of Yazīd b. al-Walīd when they called upon the supporters of the deposed caliph al-Walīd b. Yazīd to submit to the Qurʾān and *sunna* of the Prophet and form a *shūrā*; Ṭabarī, VII, 249 [II, 1804]: *wa-kāna maʿa aṣḥāb yazīd b. al-walīd kitāb muʿallaq fī rumḥ fīhi innā nadʿūkum....*

[240]Ibn Abī Shayba, *Muṣannaf*, III, 127.

[241]Abū ʿUbayd, *Amwāl*, 500 no. 1108: *kataba lahu kitāban nasakhahu min ṣaḥīfa kānat marbūṭa bi-qirāb ʿumar b. al-khaṭṭāb.* There follows a clause from the *ṣaḥīfa* regarding the taxation of *dirhams*: *wa-fī l-riqa rubʿu l-ʿushr idhā balaghat riqatu aḥadihim khams awāqī.* For the term *riqa* see *Lisān al-ʿarab*, s.v., X, 375. Abū Bakr b. ʿUbaydallāh (who was one

When ʿUmar b. ʿAbd al-ʿAzīz ascended the throne, he looked for the Prophet's letter concerning taxation (*ṣadaqāt*) and ʿUmar's letter (on the same matter). He found the Prophet's letter with ʿAmr b. Ḥazm's descendants, while ʿUmar's similar[242] letter was found with ʿUmar's descendants. Both letters were copied for him. The source of this report is Muḥammad b. ʿAbd al-Raḥmān al-Anṣārī (d. 124/742), ʿUmar b. ʿAbd al-ʿAzīz's governor in Yamāma.[243]

ʿAmr b. ʿAwf al-Muzanī and the Kitāb

Gil (47) discovered a new *isnād* attached to the Kitāb, one that according to him is the *isnād* missing in Ibn Hishām:

> Serjeant[244] has suggested that the document might have come into the possession of ʿAbdallāh b. al-Ḥasan, then the chief of the ʿAlids, who seems to have been the main authority of Ibn Isḥāq. In fact, the *isnād* of the document, which is missing in Ibn Hishām, is given by Ibn Sayyid al-Nās,[245] who has it brought back to Kathīr b. ʿAbdallah b. ʿAmr (b. ʿAwf) al-Muzanī. It is interesting to note that the Muslim authorities considered the traditions of Kathīr to be *ḍaʿīf*. However, there was a tradition that it is Kathīr who was the nominee of the Prophet over the *ḥaram* of Medina.[246] His father, ʿAbdallāh, was held in great esteem by the Prophet. His grave was one of the only five that

of Zuhrī's teachers) died at the time of Marwān b. Muḥammad; *Tahdh.*, XII, 32 no. 145; *Tahdhīb al-kamāl*, XXXIII, 119–21 no. 7246. The Egyptian transmitter al-Layth b. Saʿd (d. 175/791) reported on the authority of Nāfiʿ, the *mawlā* of Ibn ʿUmar (d. in 117/735 or later), that the clause concerning the taxation of *dirhams* is found in *kitāb ṣadaqat ʿumar*. ʿUmar's letter concerning the *ṣadaqa* was also seen by Mālik b. Anas who read in it the above-mentioned clause; Abū ʿUbayd, *Amwāl*, 500–501 nos. 1109–11.

[242] Or identical, *mithl*.

[243] Ibn Zanjawayh, *Amwāl*, II, 800 no. 1389. See also *Mustadrak*, I, 394–97. On Muḥammad b. ʿAbd al-Raḥmān see *Tahdh.*, IX, 298. Fragments from Muḥammad's and ʿUmar's letters were adduced by Abū ʿUbayd and by his pupil, Ibn Zanjawayh, in the relevant chapters of their books; see e.g. Abū ʿUbayd, *Amwāl*, 500 no. 1106; Ibn Zanjawayh, *Amwāl*, II, 800 no. 1389; 810 no. 1404; 813 no. 1409; 852 no. 1496.

[244] "The 'Constitution of Medina'", 4.

[245] I, 197 (read: 198). The existence of this version was known to Buhl; see his *Leben*, 209 n. 24.

[246] Gil refers to *Tahdh.*, VIII, 127; read: 85 no. 127, s.v. ʿAmr b. ʿAwf al-Muzanī.

> the Prophet ever visited.[247] One of the Prophet's first places of prayer was in the proximity of the area of this clan.[248] As a matter of fact the *ḥadīth* ascribed to him echoes elements of our document in the clause repeated several times saying that alliances shall be concluded between Muslims only, and that no group shall conclude a separate peace.

Gil's assumption that Kathīr who was declared *ḍaʿīf* or "weak" in the transmission of *ḥadīth* was a Companion of the Prophet is unfounded.[249] Gil confuses Kathīr b. ʿAbdallāh b. ʿAmr b. ʿAwf, a transmitter who died in the middle of the second century AH, with his grandfather, the Companion ʿAmr b. ʿAwf. It was ʿAmr b. ʿAwf al-Muzanī, and not his grandson Kathīr, who according to Wāqidī was put in charge of the *ḥaram* of Medina and died during Muʿāwiya's reign.[250]

ʿAmr's appointment in charge of the *ḥaram* is at the background of ʿAmr's report (Kathīr ← his father ← his grandfather, ʿAmr) that the Prophet declared Medina a *ḥimā* (here synonymous with *ḥaram*) covering an area of one postal stage (four parasangs, ca. 24 km.) on each side.[251] The choice of a Muzanī for this task was not accidental. Muḥammad put a Muzanī called Murāwiḥ in charge of *ḥimā al-Naqīʿ* not far from Medina. In addition, he gave the ʿAqīq to Bilāl b. al-Ḥārith al-Muzanī; these measures may indicate a partiality for the Muzayna on Muḥammad's part.[252]

Ibn Sayyid al-Nās quotes Ibn Abī Khaythama (d. 279/892) — probably in his *Kitāb al-taʾrīkh*[253] — who in his turn quotes Aḥmad b. Janāb Abū

[247] Reference to Samhūdī, III, 897: *lam yanzil fī qabr aḥad qaṭṭu*; however, this indicates an active role of the Prophet in ʿAmr b. ʿAwf's burial rather than a visit to his grave. For details on the practice see later in the same source, where we find how the Prophet entered the grave of Fāṭima bint Asad, ʿAlī's mother, viz. while she was being buried.

[248] Samhūdī, III, 780–82.

[249] Cf. *EI*², s.v. al-Djarḥ wa-ʾl-Taʿdīl (J. Robson): "The Companions of the Prophet were considered reliable, so *djarḥ* could not apply to them; but traditionists of later generations were subject to investigation".

[250] *Tahdh.*, VIII, 85 no. 127. On ʿAmr see *Iṣāba*, IV, 666–67 no. 5928; *Usd al-ghāba*, IV, 124–25 (the remark *ḥadīthuhu ʿinda awlādihi* indicates that it was transmitted via family *isnāds*).

[251] *Anna l-nabī ṣ ḥamā l-madīna barīdan min kull nāḥiya*; Ṭabarānī, *Kabīr*, XVII, 21. Kathīr (erroneously vocalized: Kuthayyir) is one of the sources quoted in Wāqidī, I, 40, for the battle of Badr. His grandfather is said here to have been one of the *bakkāʾūna*. Kathīr also reports on the battle of the Ditch; Suyūṭī, *Durr*, V, 186:1.

[252] Lecker, *Banū sulaym*, 237–38.

[253] *EI*², s.v. (Ch. Pellat); Yāqūt, *Udabāʾ*, I, 262 no. 84. For the assumption that this is the book in question see already Goto, 3. Zurqānī, IV, 169:14, quotes Ibn Sayyid al-Nās

l-Walīd al-Miṣṣīṣī (d. 230/845)[254] ← ʿĪsā b. Yūnus al-Sabīʿī (d. 187/803 or 191/807)[255] ← Kathīr b. ʿAbdallāh b. ʿAmr [b. ʿAwf][256] ← his father[257] ← his grandfather. In short, the *isnād* found in Ibn Abī Khaythama ends with a family *isnād* that goes back to the Prophet's Companion ʿAmr b. ʿAwf al-Muzanī.

Gil's assumption that "the *isnād* of the document, which is missing in Ibn Hishām, is given by Ibn Sayyid al-Nās" is not borne out by the evidence,[258] besides clashing with the rival *isnād* mentioned above, namely ʿUthmān b. Muḥammad b. ʿUthmān b. al-Akhnas b. Sharīq ← ʿUmar's family. Ibn Isḥāq's recension was similar to that of Ibn Abī Khaythama, but these were two distinct recensions. Having quoted the Kitāb according to Ibn Isḥāq, Ibn Sayyid al-Nās says: "Thus Ibn Isḥāq reported it. Ibn Abī Khaythama mentioned it with this *isnād*...."[259] In his short interpretation of the Kitāb

on this point: *qāla bn sayyid al-nās: wa-asnadahu bn abī khaythama ʿan ʿamr al-muzanī*. Ibn Abī Khaythama's recension of the Kitāb was mentioned by Ḥamīdullāh, "The Earliest Written Constitution", 12; also, many years earlier, by Sprenger, *Leben*, III, 20n.

[254] *Tahdh.*, I, 21–22 no. 25.

[255] *Ibid.*, VIII, 237–40 no. 439.

[256] Kathīr died between AH 150 and AH 160; *Tahdh.*, VIII, 423. Ibn Saʿd, V, 412 (who calls him Kathīr b. ʿAbdallāh b. ʿAwf, omitting his grandfather ʿAmr) includes him in the sixth generation of transmitters from Medina, together with people who died in the sixties and seventies of the second century AH.

[257] On Kathīr's father ʿAbdallāh see *Tahdh.*, V, 339–40 no. 579; *Iṣāba*, IV, 194 no. 4851 (s.v. ʿAbdallāh b. ʿAmr b. ʿAwf); Wāqidī, II, 799 (Muḥammad's messengers to the Muzayna before the conquest of Mecca were Bilāl b. al-Ḥārith and ʿAbdallāh b. ʿAmr al-Muzanī); II, 800, 820; III, 896 (the banner carriers of the Muzayna during the conquest of Mecca and at Ḥunayn were Bilāl b. al-Ḥārith, al-Nuʿmān b. Muqarrin and ʿAbdallāh b. ʿAmr b. ʿAwf); Wāqidī, Index, III, 1198, s.v.

[258] Serjeant (9 n. 36) remarks on the *isnād* that Gil quoted from Ibn Sayyid al-Nās that "it seems to have no special evidential value and is not to be regarded as an *isnād* missing from Ibn Isḥāq who, in fact is quoted by Ibn Sayyid al-Nās as an authority in his own right".

[259] *Hākadhā dhakarahu bn isḥāq. Wa-qad dhakarahu bn abī khaythama fa-asnadahu: ḥaddathanā... anna rasūla llāh ṣ kataba kitāban bayna l-muhājirīna wa-l-anṣār, fa-dhakara bi-naḥwihi*. The words *fa-dhakara bi-naḥwihi* are found in MS Staatsbibliothek Berlin (Sprenger 122), 61a; but it appears that *fa-dhakarahu bi-naḥwihi*, as in Ibn Sayyid al-Nās^2, I, 320, is a better reading. Zurqānī, IV, 169:15, has an additional word that no doubt belongs to the copy of Ibn Sayyid al-Nās that he himself used: *fa-dhakarahu muṭawwalan bi-naḥwihi*. In other words, according to Ibn Sayyid al-Nās, Ibn Abī Khaythama has an extensive (perhaps even a full) recension of the Kitāb. The words *fa-dhakarahu bi-naḥwihi* seem to indicate that Ibn Abī Khaythama's recension is similar to that of Ibn Isḥāq. According to Goto, 3, Ibn Sayyid al-Nās, having quoted Ibn Isḥāq's text, "relates that the same text was recorded by Ibn Abī Khaythama"; but later (4) he correctly qualifies

Ibn Sayyid al-Nās quotes a gloss from *kitāb al-muzanī*, i.e. the Kitāb in the recension of Kathīr b. ʿAbdallāh al-Muzanī.[260]

Various fragments from the Kitāb appear as short *ḥadīth*s attributed to different transmitters.[261] In two cases the *ḥadīth* of Kathīr b. ʿAbdallāh (← his father ← his grandfather, ʿAmr b. ʿAwf) echoes, or remotely echoes, the Kitāb in the form of utterances ascribed to the Prophet.[262]

---

this by saying that we have no way of knowing whether Ibn Abī Khaythama's version is exactly the same as Ibn Isḥāq's.

[260]*Al-r.b.ʿa*: *al-ḥālatu llatī jāʾa l-islām wa-hum ʿalayhā*; *min kitābi l-muzanī*; Ibn Sayyid al-Nās, I, 198, 199.

[261]Similarly, sections of the Prophet's speech at the "Farewell Pilgrimage" appear as independent *ḥadīths*; see Buhl, *Leben*, 343. Cf. the classification of the early Shīʿite *ḥadīth* collections (*al-uṣūl al-arbaʿumiʾa*), in order to make them more accessible, into their components and the distribution of individual *ḥadīths* among various works according to subject matter; Kohlberg, "Shīʿī *Ḥadīth*", 303–304.

[262]Ṭabarānī, *Kabīr*, XVII, 23 (*man tawallā ghayr mawālīhi... man qatala ghayr qātilihi... wa-man aḥdatha ḥadathan aw āwā muḥdithan...* — only the last component resembles an expression found in the Kitāb), 24 (*lā yutraku mufraj* [*sic*] *fī l-islām*; one of the sources adds: *ḥattā yuḍamma ilā qabīla*).

Appendix E

The Term *Muwādaʿa*

Much of the diplomatic history of Muḥammad is linked to the term *muwādaʿa* which is synonymous with several other terms but is probably the most widespread.[263]

Serjeant (15) argues: "It is... most important to take into account the precise wording of Ibn Isḥāq/Ibn Hishām introducing the documents". But he goes on to render the verb *wādaʿa* in Ibn Isḥāq's introduction to the Kitāb: "He made a peace".[264]

With regard to the Prophet's treaty with the Qurayẓa, Kister observes that "the expressions *ʿaqd* and *ʿahd* do not define clearly the nature of the treaty and its contents. A more precise term is the *muwādaʿa*, usually concluded with the unbelievers; it denotes a treaty of non-aggression, of renunciation of violence... a treaty of peaceful co-existence".[265] But since a *muwādaʿa* always included a time limit, its definition should refer to this

[263]The term *muwādaʿa* appears in a variety of contexts: — the *ayyām al-ʿarab*: *Naqāʾiḍ*, 326:4,11; Ḥimyarī, *Rawḍ*, 260a:16, s.v. al-Dhanāʾib; — the relations between Persia and Byzantium: a *muwādaʿa wa-hudna* between Anūshirwān and Byzantium; Ṭabarī, II, 148–49 [I, 958]; Ibn al-Faqīh, 116:4 (a *muwādaʿa* involving the payment of *itāwa*); Ibn al-Faqīh 137:5; Ibn Qutayba, *Maʿārif*, 655:5 (where *wādaʿa* and *tāraka* are synonymous); — internal struggle between rival Muslim factions: Ibn Ḥabīb, *Muḥabbar*, 290:6 (a *kitāb muwādaʿa* between Ṭalḥa and Zubayr which was to remain in power until ʿAlī's arrival); Ṭabarī, III, 245 [I, 1874] (the *ridda* rebels propose a *muwādaʿa*); Ṭabarī, V, 5 [I, 3274] (*muwādaʿatu l-ḥarb* between ʿAlī and Muʿāwiya in Muḥarram AH 37).

[264]In a footnote Serjeant quotes, without further comment, Ibn al-Athīr, *Nihāya*, V, 167, s.v. *w-d-ʿ*: *wādaʿa banī fulān, ay ṣālaḥahum wa-sālamahum ʿalā tarki l-ḥarb wa-l-adhā.* A more accurate rendering of the verb can be found in Serjeant's earlier article, "The 'Constitution of Medina'", 7, where the expression *wādaʿathu yahūd kulluhā* is rendered: "... the Jews, all of them, made a truce (*ṣulḥ*) [! — M. L.] with him". Wellhausen (73, 74) renders the same expression: "... traten die sämtlichen Juden mit ihm in Vertrag", whereas he translates *fa-arāda rasūlu llāh stiṣlāḥahum kullahum wa-muwādaʿatahum*: "Der Bote Gottes wollte... Friede und Ordnung... herstellen und mit allen einen Friedensvertrag schliessen". Donner, "Muḥammad's Political Consolidation", 238, renders *muwādaʿa*: "treaty of friendship". Those with whom the Muslims have a *muwādaʿa* live in *dār al-muwādaʿa*; see e.g. Sarakhsī, *Sharḥ kitāb al-siyar*, V, 1699 no. 3383.

[265]Kister, "The Massacre of the Banū Qurayẓa", 82.

element: "a non-belligerency treaty for a certain period of time", or "a temporary cessation of warfare by agreement between the belligerents".

Throughout his Medinan period Muḥammad concluded many such agreements with a variety of parties. The non-belligerency pact with the Ghaṭafān leader ʿUyayna b. Ḥiṣn[266] is referred to both as *muwādaʿa* and *mudda*. It was concluded in 5/626 for a period of three months. This occurred when heavy drought pushed ʿUyayna out of his tribe's territory and onto grazing grounds not far from Medina.[267]

The basic ingredient of all the *muwādaʿa* treaties is a reciprocal guarantee of security. Sometimes the *muwādaʿa* is even said to be the equivalent of *amān*.[268] The explicit mention of *amān* could be replaced by a reciprocal undertaking of each party not to attack the other party, or by terms to the same effect.

In the context of the Prophet's treaties a *muwādaʿa* is always a truce with non-Muslims. A Muslim no longer needed a treaty to secure his life and property from other Muslims. Thus Ibn Isḥāq reports that when the Prophet came to Medina, he concluded a *muwādaʿa* with the Jews since they refrained from "following him" (i.e. they did not embrace Islam).[269]

---

[266] On whom see *EI*², s.v. (M. Lecker).

[267] Masʿūdī, *Tanbīh*, 249; Ibn Saʿd, *al-Ṭabaqa al-rābiʿa*, II, 551; Ibn Saʿd, II, 63; Ṭabarī, II, 564 [I, 1463]; Wāqidī, II, 422 (where the truce is called *mudda*); Rubin "*Barāʾa*", 16. Rubin's statement (29) that "the treaties of Muḥammad's pagan allies were not temporary ones, but rather unlimited in time" is imprecise. For *mudda* associated with *amān* see Wāqidī, II, 593:14 (at Ḥudaybiyya, Muḥammad made this suggestion to the Quraysh: *fa-in shāʾū mādadtuhum mudda yaʾmanūna fīhā*). The term *ajal* was connected with the non-belligerency treaty said to have been concluded between Quraysh and the Anṣār at the ʿAqaba meeting: it granted Muḥammad *amān* and *dhimām* and was supposed to remain valid for four months; Lecker, "Did the Quraysh Conclude a Treaty with the Anṣār", 163, 169.

[268] Cf. ʿAbd al-Razzāq, V, 394: *fa-saʾaltuhu an yaktuba lī kitāb muwādaʿa āmanu bihi.* See also above, 143.

[269] *Fatḥ al-bārī*, VII, 214:4. This "following" (*ittibāʿ*) is also behind the famous *ḥadīth* of the Prophet: "Had ten Jews followed me, every Jew on the surface of the earth would have followed me" (*lawi ttabaʿanī ʿashara mina l-yahūd lam yabqa fī l-arḍ yahūdī illā ttabaʿanī*); Suhaylī, II, 292:4; see also Suyūṭī, *Durr*, II, 267:-8 (*law ṣaddaqanī wa-āmana bī wa-ttabaʿanī...*). For an *ittibāʿ* that does not involve conversion to Islam see *Durr*, II, 286:5 (← al-Suddī): *kāna rajulāni mina l-yahūd akhawāni yuqālu lahumā bnā ṣūriyā qadi ttabaʿā l-nabī ṣ wa-lam yuslimā....*

Bibliography

ʿAbd al-Jabbār, *Tathbīt* — al-Qāḍī ʿAbd al-Jabbār b. Aḥmad al-Hamadhānī. *Tathbīt dalāʾil al-nubuwwa*, ed. ʿAbd al-Karīm ʿUthmān, Beirut 1966–68. 2 vols.

ʿAbd al-Malik b. Ḥabīb. *Taʾrīkh*, ed. J. Aguadé, Madrid 1991.

ʿAbd al-Razzāq, al-Ṣanʿānī. *al-Muṣannaf*, ed. Ḥabīb al-Raḥmān al-Aʿẓamī, Beirut 1390/1970–1392/1972. 11 vols.

Abū ʿAwāna. *Musnad*, Hyderabad 1362/1943–1386/1966. 5 vols.

Abū Dāwūd, Sulaymān b. al-Ashʿath. *Marāsīl*, Cairo 1310/1892.

—, *Sunan*, ed. Aḥmad Saʿd ʿAlī, Cairo 1371/1952. 2 vols

Abū Nuʿaym al-Iṣbahānī. *Dalāʾil al-nubuwwa*², ed. Muḥammad Rawwās Qalʿajī and ʿAbd al-Barr ʿAbbās, Beirut 1406/1986.

Abū ʿUbayd al-Qāsim b. Sallām. *Kitāb al-Amwāl*, ed. Muḥammad Khalīl Harrās, Cairo 1396/1976.

—, *Gharīb* — *Gharīb al-ḥadīth*, Hyderabad 1384/1964–1387/1967. 4 vols.

—, *al-Gharīb al-muṣannaf*, ed. Mohamed Mokhtar Labidi, Carthage 1989–1996. 3 vols.

—, *Kitāb al-nasab*, ed. Maryam Muḥammad Khayr al-Darʿ, Damascus 1410/1989.

Aghānī — Abū l-Faraj al-Iṣfahānī. *Kitāb al-aghānī*, Būlāq 1285/1868. 10 vols.

Aghānī (Dār al-Kutub) — Cairo 1345/1927–1394/1974. 24 vols.

Aḥmad — Aḥmad b. Ḥanbal. *Musnad*, Cairo 1313/1895. Reprint Beirut. 6 vols.

Aḥmad² — ed. Aḥmad Muḥammad Shākir, Cairo 1368/1949–1377/1957. Reprint Cairo 1414/1994. 16 vols.

Akhṭal, *Dīwān* — *Shiʿr al-Akhṭal*, ed. Fakhr al-Dīn Qabāwa, Ḥalab 1391/1971. 2 vols.

al-Anbārī, Muḥammad b. al-Qāsim. *Kitāb al-aḍdād*, ed. Muḥammad Abū l-Faḍl Ibrāhīm, Kuwait 1960.

Arazi, A. "Matériaux pour l'étude du conflit de préséance entre la Mekke et Médine", in *JSAI* 5 (1984), 177–235.

Arberry, A.J. *The Koran Interpreted*, London 1964.

al-ʿAskarī, Abū Hilāl. *al-Awāʾil*, ed. Muḥammad al-Miṣrī and Walīd Qaṣṣāb, Damascus 1975. 2 vols.

AʿU — Abū ʿUbayd.

al-ʿAwtabī, Salama b. Muslim. *al-Ansāb*², ʿUmān, 1410/1990–1412/1992. 2 vols.

Ayalon, D. "The Nubian Dam", in *JSAI* 12 (1989), 372–90.

al-Azraqī, Muḥammad b. ʿAbdallāh. *Akhbār Makka*, ed. Rushdī Malḥas, Beirut, n. d.

Badʾ — al-Maqdisī, Muṭahhar b. Ṭāhir. *al-Badʾ wa-l-taʾrīkh*, ed. Cl. Huart, Paris 1899–1919. 3 vols.

Bahjat al-maḥāfil — ʿImād al-Dīn Yaḥyā b. Abī Bakr al-ʿĀmirī. *Bahjat al-maḥāfil wa-bughyat al-amāthil fī talkhīṣ al-muʿjizāt wa-l-siyar wa-l-shamāʾil*, Cairo 1330–31 A.H. Reprint Medina n. d.

Bakrī — Abū ʿUbayd al-Bakrī. *Muʿjam mā staʿjama*, ed. Muṣṭafā al-Saqqā, Cairo 1364/1945–1371/1951. 2 vols.

—, *Simṭ al-laʾālī fī sharḥ amālī l-Qālī*, ed. ʿAbd al-ʿAzīz al-Maymanī, Cairo 1354/1936. 2 vols.

Balādhurī, *Ansāb* — Aḥmad b. Yaḥyā b. Jābir al-Balādhurī. *Ansāb al-ashrāf*, I, ed. Muḥammad Ḥamīdullāh, Cairo 1959; V (Sā'ir furū' Quraysh), ed. I. 'Abbās, Beirut 1417/1996; MS Süleymanie Kütüphanesi, Reisülküttap Mustafa Efendi, 597, 598.

—, *Futūḥ al-buldān*, ed. M.J. de Goeje, Leiden 1863–66.

al-Bayḍāwī, 'Abdallāh b. 'Umar. *Anwār al-tanzīl wa-asrār al-ta'wīl*, Cairo 1375/1955.

al-Bayhaqī, Aḥmad b. al-Ḥusayn. *Dalā'il al-nubuwwa*, ed. 'Abd al-Mu'ṭī Qal'ajī, Beirut 1405/1985. 7 vols.

Blau, J. "Arabic Lexicographical Miscellanies", in *JSS* 17 (1972), 173–90.

Bosworth, C.E. "Abū 'Abdallāh al-Khawārazmī on the Technical Terms of the Secretary's Art", in *JESHO* 12 (1969), 113–64. Reprinted in *idem*, *Medieval Arabic Culture and Administration*, London: Variorum, 1982, no. XV.

Bravmann, M.M. *The Spiritual Background of Early Islam*, Leiden 1972.

—, "The State Archives in the Early Islamic Era", in *Arabica* 15 (1968), 87–89. Reprinted in *idem*, *Spiritual Background*, 311–14.

BSOAS — *Bulletin of the School of Oriental and African Studies.*

Buhl, F. *Das Leben Muhammeds*[2], trans. H. Schaeder, Leipzig 1930. Reprint Heidelberg 1955. The Danish original appeared in 1903.

Caskel — W. Caskel and G. Strenziok. *Ǧamharat an-Nasab: Das genealogische Werk des Hišām ibn Muḥammad al-Kalbī*, Leiden 1966. 2 vols.

CHALUP — A.F.L. Beeston, T.M. Johnstone, R.B. Serjeant and G.R. Smith (eds.). *The Cambridge History of Arabic Literature: Arabic Literature to the End of the Umayyad Period*, Cambridge 1983.

Cook, D. "The Prophet Muḥammad, Labīd Al-Yahūdī and the Commentaries to *Sūra* 113", in *JSS* 45 (2000), 323–45.

Crone, P. *Slaves on Horses: The Evolution of the Islamic Polity*, Cambridge 1980.

al-Dāraquṭnī, 'Alī b. 'Umar. *al-Mu'talif wa-l-mukhtalif*, ed. Muwaffaq b. 'Abdallāh b. 'Abd al-Qādir, Beirut 1406/1986. 5 vols.

—, *Sunan*, ed. 'Abdallāh Hāshim Yamānī al-Madanī, Medina 1386/1966. 2 vols.

Dārimī — *Sunan*, ed. Muḥammad Aḥmad Duhmān, n. p. n. d.

Denny, F.M. "The Meaning of *Ummah* in the Qur'ān", in *History of Religions* 15,i (1975), 34–70.

—, "Some Religio-Communal Terms and Concepts in the Qur'ān", in *Numen* 24,i (1977), 26–59.

—, "*Ummah* in the Constitution of Medina", in *JNES* 36 (1977), 39–47.

al-Dhahabī, Muḥammad b. Aḥmad. *Siyar a'lām al-nubalā'*, ed. Shu'ayb al-Arnāwūṭ *et al*, Beirut 1401/1981–1409/1988. 25 vols.

Donner, F.M. *The Early Islamic Conquests*, Princeton 1981.

—, "From Believers to Muslims: Confessional Self-Identity in the Early Islamic Community", in *al-Abḥāth* 50–51 (2002–2003), 9–53.

—, "Muḥammad's Political Consolidation in Arabia up to the Conquest of Mecca", in *The Muslim World* 69 (1979), 229–47.

EI[2] — *The Encyclopaedia of Islam*, 2nd. ed., Leiden 1960 f.

Elad, A. "The Southern Golan in the Early Muslim Period: The Significance of Two Newly Discovered Milestones of 'Abd al-Malik", in *Der Islam* 76 (1999), 33–88.

Fākhir — al-Mufaḍḍal b. Salama. *al-Fākhir*, ed. 'Abd al-'Alīm al-Ṭaḥāwī and Muḥammad 'Alī al-Najjār, Cairo 1380/1960.

al-Fākihī, Muḥammad b. Isḥāq. *Akhbār makka*, ed. ʿAbd al-Malik b. ʿAbdallāh b. Duhaysh, Mecca 1407/1987. 6 vols.

Fatḥ al-bārī — Ibn Ḥajar al-ʿAsqalānī. *Fatḥ al-bārī sharḥ ṣaḥīḥ al-Bukhārī*, Būlāq 1301/ 1884. 14 vols.

Fierro, M.I. "La *Fahrasa* de Ibn al-Ṭallāʿ", in *Estudios Onomástico-Biográficos de al-Andalus*, II (1989), 277–97.

Friedmann, Y. *Tolerance and Coercion in Islam: Interfaith Relations in the Muslim Tradition*, Cambridge 2003.

Futūḥ miṣr — Ibn ʿAbd al-Ḥakam. *Futūḥ miṣr wa-akhbāruhā*, ed. Ch. Torrey, New Haven 1922.

GAL — C. Brockelmann. *Geschichte der arabischen Litteratur*, Leiden 1943–1949.

GAL S — *GAL, Supplementbände.*

GAS — F. Sezgin. *Geschichte des arabischen Schrifttums*, Leiden 1967 f.

Gharāʾib al-qurʾān — al-Ḥasan b. Muḥammad al-Qummī al-Naysābūrī. *Gharāʾib al-qurʾān wa-raghāʾib al-furqān*, on the margin of Ṭabarī, *Tafsīr.*

Giannakis, E. "The Concept of Ummah", in *Graeco-Arabica* 2 (1983), 99–111.

Gil — see Gil, "The Constitution of Medina".

Gil, M. "The Constitution of Medina: A Reconsideration", in *IOS* 4 (1974), 44–66.

— "The Medinan Opposition to the Prophet", in *JSAI* 10 (1987), 65–96.

—, "The Origin of the Jews of Yathrib", in *JSAI* 4 (1984), 203–24. Reprinted in Peters (ed.), *The Arabs and Arabia on the Eve of Islam*, 145–66.

Goitein, S.D. *Studies in Islamic History and Institutions*, Leiden 1968.

Goldziher, I. *Muslim Studies* — (*Muhammedanische Studien*, Halle 1889–90), ed. S.M. Stern, trans. C.R. Barber and S.M. Stern, London 1967–71. 2 vols.

Goto — see Goto, "The Constitution of Medina".

Goto, A. "The Constitution of Medina", in *ORIENT* (Report of the Society for Near Eastern Studies in Japan) 18 (1982), 1–17. (Originally published in Japanese in 1977.)

Gottschalk, H. "Abū ʿUbaid al-Qāsim b. Sallām: Studie zur Geschichte der arabischen Biographie", in *Der Islam* 23 (1936), 245–89.

Guillaume, A. *The Life of Muhammad: A Translation of Ibn Ishaq's Sīrat Rasūl Allāh*, Oxford 1955.

al-Hamdānī, al-Ḥasan b. Aḥmad b. Yaʿqūb. *Kitāb al-iklīl*, X, ed. Muḥibb al-Dīn al-Khaṭīb, Beirut 1407/1987.

Ḥamīdullāh, M. "Aqdam dustūr musajjal fī l-ʿālam: wathīqa nabawiyya muhimma", in *Islamic Scholars Conference* 1 (1937), 98–123.

—, "The Earliest Written-Constitution of a State in the World: A Document of the Time of the Prophet", in *Majallat al-Azhar* Rajab 1389/September 1969, 11–16.

—, *Le Prophéte de l'Islam*, Paris 1378/1959. 2 vols.

—, "Sources of Islamic Law - a New Approach", in *Islamic Quarterly* 1 (1954), 205–11.

Harawī, *Gharībayni* — Abū ʿUbayd Aḥmad b. Muḥammad al-Harawī. *Kitāb al-gharībayni*, ed. Maḥmūd Muḥammad al-Ṭanāḥī, Cairo 1390/1970.

Ḥassān b. Thābit. *Dīwān*, ed. W. ʿArafat, London 1971. 2 vols.

Ḥilyat al-awliyāʾ — Abū Nuʿaym al-Iṣfahānī. *Ḥilyat al-awliyāʾ wa-ṭabaqāt al-aṣfiyāʾ*, Cairo n. d. Reprint Beirut 1387/1967. 10 vols.

al-Ḥimyarī, Muḥammad b. ʿAbd al-Munʿim. *al-Rawḍ al-miʿṭār fī khabar al-aqṭār*, ed. I. ʿAbbās, Beirut 1975.

Hinds, M. *Studies in Early Islamic History*, J. Bacharach, L.I. Conrad and P. Crone (eds.). Princeton 1996.

Hinds, M. and H. Sakkout. "A Letter from the Governor of Egypt to the King of Nubia and Muqurra Concerning Egyptian-Nubian Relations in 141/758", in *Studia Arabica & Islamica: Festschrift for Iḥsān ʿAbbās on his sixtieth birthday*, ed. W. al-Qāḍī, Beirut 1981, 209–29. Reprinted in Hinds, *Studies in Early Islamic History*, 160–87.

Hirschberg, H.Z. *Yisraʾel be-ʿarav* (Hebrew), Tel-Aviv 1946.

Horovitz, J. "The Earliest Biographies of the Prophet and their Authors", in *Islamic Culture* 1 (1927), 535–59 (no. 1); 2 (1928), 22–50 (no. 2), 164–82 (no. 3), 495–526 (no. 4).

Hoyland, R. "Sebeos, the Jews and the Rise of Islam", in Nettler, R.L. (ed.), *Medieval and Modern Perspectives on Muslim-Jewish Relations*, Oxford 1995, 89–102.

Humphreys, R.S. *Islamic History: A Framework for Inquiry*², Princeton 1991.

Ibn ʿAbd al-Barr, Yūsuf b. ʿAbdallāh al-Namarī. *al-Inbāh ʿalā qabāʾil al-ruwāt*, Cairo 1350 A.H. (bound with *idem*, *al-Qaṣd wa-l-amam*).

Ibn Abī Shayba. *Muṣannaf*, ed. ʿAbd al-Khāliq al-Afghānī, Bombay 1399/1979–1403/1983. 15 vols.

Ibn ʿAdī, ʿAbdallāh al-Jurjānī. *al-Kāmil fī ḍuʿafāʾ al-rijāl*, Beirut 1404/1984. 7 vols.

Ibn ʿAsākir. *Taʾrīkh madīnat Dimashq*, ed. ʿUmar b. Gharāma al-ʿAmrawī, Beirut 1415/1995-1419/1998. 70 vols.

Ibn al-Athīr, ʿAlī b. Muḥammad, ʿIzz al-Dīn. *al-Kāmil fī l-taʾrīkh*, Beirut 1385/1965–1386/1966. 13 vols.

Ibn al-Athīr, al-Mubārak b. Muḥammad, Majd al-Dīn. *al-Nihāya fī gharīb al-ḥadīth wa-l-athar*, ed. Ṭāhir Aḥmad al-Zāwī and Maḥmūd Muḥammad al-Ṭanāḥī, Cairo 1385/1965. 5 vols.

Ibn al-Ḍiyāʾ, Abū l-Baqāʾ Muḥammad b. Aḥmad al-Makkī. *Taʾrīkh Makka l-musharrafa wa-l-masjid al-ḥarām wa-l-Madīna al-sharīfa wa-l-qabr al-sharīf*, ed. ʿAlāʾ Ibrāhīm al-Azharī and Ayman Naṣr al-Azharī, Beirut 1418/1997.

Ibn Durayd, Muḥammad b. al-Ḥasan. *al-Ishtiqāq*, ed. ʿAbd al-Salām Hārūn, Cairo 1378/1958.

Ibn al-Faqīh, Aḥmad b. Muḥammad al-Hamadhānī. *Kitāb al-buldān*, ed. M.J. de Goeje, Leiden 1885.

Ibn Ḥabīb. *Kitāb al-muḥabbar*, ed. I. Lichtenstaedter, Hyderabad 1361/1942.

—, *Kitāb al-munammaq fī akhbār Quraysh*, ed. Khūrshīd Aḥmad Fāriq, Beirut 1405/1985.

—, *Mughtālīna — Asmāʾ al-mughtālīna*, in *Nawādir al-makhṭūṭāt*², ed. ʿAbd al-Salām Hārūn, II, Cairo 1393/1973.

Ibn Ḥajar, Aḥmad b. ʿAli al-ʿAsqalānī. *al-Maṭālib al-ʿāliya bi-zawāʾid al-masānīd al-thamāniya*, ed. Ḥabīb al-Raḥmān al-Aʿẓamī, Kuwayt 1393/1973. 4 vols.

—, *Taqrīb al-tahdhīb*, ed. ʿAbd al-Wahhāb ʿAbd al-Laṭīf. Reprint Beirut 1395/1975. 2 vols.

Ibn Ḥazm, ʿAlī b. Aḥmad al-Andalusī. *Jamharat ansāb al-ʿarab*, ed. ʿAbd al-Salām Hārūn, Cairo 1382/1962.

—, *Jawāmiʿ al-sīra al-nabawiyya*, Cairo n. d.

—, *al-Muḥallā*, Cairo 1349/1928–1352/1933. Reprint Beirut n. d. 11 vols.

Ibn Hishām — Ibn Hishām, ʿAbd al-Malik. *al-Sīra al-nabawiyya*, ed. al-Saqqā, al-Ibyārī and Shalabī, Beirut 1391/1971. 4 vols.
—, *Kitāb al-Tījān fī mulūk Ḥimyar*. Reprint Ṣanʿāʾ 1979.
Ibn Ḥudayda, Muḥammad b. ʿAlī al-Anṣārī. *al-Miṣbāḥ al-muḍīʾ fī kuttāb al-nabī*, ed. Muḥammad ʿAẓīm al-Dīn, Beirut 1405/1985. 2 vols.
Ibn al-Jawzī, *Muntaẓam* — Ibn al-Jawzī, ʿAbd al-Raḥmān b. ʿAlī. *al-Muntaẓam fī taʾrīkh al-mulūk wa-l-umam*, ed. Muḥammad ʿAbd al-Qādir ʿAṭā and Muṣṭafa ʿAbd al-Qādir ʿAṭā, Beirut 1412/1992. 17 vols.
Ibn Junghul — *History*, abridged by Ibn al-Mulla, MS Br. Lib. Or. 5912.
Ibn al-Kalbī, Hishām b. Muḥammad. *Jamharat al-nasab*, ed. Nājī Ḥasan, Beirut 1407/1986.
—, *Nasab Maʿadd wa-l-yaman al-kabīr*, ed. Nājī Ḥasan, Beirut 1408/1988. 2 vols.
Ibn Kathīr, Ismāʿīl b. ʿUmar. *al-Bidāya wa-l-nihāya fī l-taʾrīkh*, Cairo 1351/1932–1358/1939. Reprint Beirut 1974. 7 vols.
Ibn Mākūlā, ʿAlī b. Hibat Allāh. *al-Ikmāl*, ed. ʿAbd al-Raḥmān b. Yaḥyā al-Yamānī, Hyderabad 1381/1962. 6 vols.
Ibn Manẓūr. *Mukhtaṣar taʾrīkh Dimashq li-Ibn ʿAsākir*, ed. Rūḥiyya al-Naḥḥās *et al.*, Damascus 1404/1984-1409/1989. 15 vols.
Ibn al-Nadīm. *Fihrist*, Cairo 1347 A.H. Reprint Beirut 1398/1978.
Ibn al-Najjār, Muḥammad b. Maḥmūd. *al-Durra al-thamīna fī taʾrīkh al-Madīna*, printed as an appendix to al-Fāsī's *Shifāʾ al-gharām bi-akhbār al-balad al-ḥarām*, Cairo 1956, II, 318 f.
Ibn Qayyim al-Jawziyya. *Aḥkām ahl al-dhimma*, ed. Ṣubḥī al-Ṣāliḥ, Beirut 1401/1981. 2 vols.
Ibn Qudāma, Muwaffaq al-Dīn ʿAbdallāh al-Maqdisī. *al-Istibṣār fī nasab al-ṣaḥāba min al-anṣār*, ed. ʿAlī Nuwayhiḍ, Beirut 1392/1972.
Ibn Qutayba. *al-Maʿārif*, ed. Tharwat ʿUkāsha, Cairo 1969.
—, *Taʾwīl mushkil al-qurʾān*, ed. Aḥmad Ṣaqr, Cairo 1393/1973.
Ibn Rusta — *al-Aʿlāq al-nafīsa*, ed. M.J. de Goeje, Leiden 1892.
Ibn Saʿd — Ibn Saʿd, Muḥammad. *al-Ṭabaqāt al-kubrā*, Beirut 1380/1960–1388/1968. 8 vols.
—, *Qism mutammim* — *al-Ṭabaqāt al-kubrā, al-qism al-mutammim li-tābiʿī ahl al-Madīna wa-man baʿdahum*, ed. Ziyād Muḥammad Manṣūr, Medina 1408/1987.
—, *al-Ṭabaqāt al-kubrā: al-ṭabaqa al-rābiʿa min al-ṣaḥāba*, ed. ʿAbd al-ʿAzīz ʿAbdallāh al-Salūmī, Taif 1416/1995. 2 vols.
Ibn Sayyid al-Nās. *ʿUyūn al-athar fī funūn al-maghāzī wa-l-shamāʾil wa-l-siyar*, Cairo 1356 A.H. 2 vols.
Ibn Sayyid al-Nās^2 — ed. al-Khaṭrāwī and Mittū, Medina–Beirut 1413/1992. 2 vols.
Ibn Shabba, ʿUmar. *Taʾrīkh al-madīna al-munawwara*, ed. Fahīm Muḥammad Shaltūt [Mecca 1399/1979]. 4 vols.
—, *Taʾrīkh al-Madīna*^{2}, ed. ʿAlī Muḥammad Dandal and Yāsīn Saʿd al-Dīn Bayān, Beirut 1417/1996. 2 vols.
Ibn Shahrāshūb — *Manāqib āl Abī Ṭālib*, Najaf 1376/1956. 3 vols.
Ibn al-Ṭallāʿ, Muḥammad b. Faraj. *Aqḍiyat rasūli llāhi*, ed. Muḥammad Ḍiyāʾ al-Raḥmān al-Aʿẓamī, Cairo–Beirut, 1398/1978.

Ibn Taymiyya, Aḥmad b. ʿAbd al-Ḥalīm. *al-Ṣārim al-maslūl ʿalā shātim al-rasūl*, ed. Muḥammad Muḥyi l-Dīn ʿAbd al-Ḥamīd, Ṭanṭā 1379/1960. Reprint Beirut, Dār al-Fikr, n. d.

Ibn Zanjawayh, Ḥumayd. *Kitāb al-amwāl*, ed. Shākir Dhīb Fayyāḍ, Riyāḍ 1406/1986. 3 vols.

II — Ibn Isḥāq.

IOS — *Israel Oriental Studies.*

ʿIqd — Ibn ʿAbd Rabbihi. *al-ʿIqd al-farīd*, ed. Aḥmad Amīn Aḥmad al-Zayn and Ibrāhīm al-Ibyārī, Cairo 1359/1940–1372/1953. 7 vols.

Iṣāba — Ibn Ḥajar al-ʿAsqalānī. *al-Iṣāba fī tamyīz al-ṣaḥāba*, ed. ʿAlī Muḥammad al-Bijāwī, Cairo 1392/1972. 8 vols.

Istīʿāb — Ibn ʿAbd al-Barr, Yūsuf b. ʿAbdallāh al-Namarī. *al-Istīʿāb fī maʿrifat al-aṣḥāb*, ed. ʿAlī Muḥammad al-Bijāwī, Cairo n. d. 4 vols.

al-Jāḥiẓ. *al-Bayān wa-l-tabyīn*, ed. ʿAbd al-Salām Muḥammad Hārūn, Cairo, 1395/1975. 2 vols.

JAOS — *The Journal of the American Oriental Society.*

al-Jāsir, Ḥamad. "Muʾallafāt fī taʾrīkh al-madīna", in *al-ʿArab* 4, ii (1969), 97–100 (no. 1); *al-ʿArab* 4, iii (1969), 262–67 (no. 2); *al-ʿArab* 4, iv (1970), 327–35 (no. 3); *al-ʿArab* 4, v (1970), 385–88, 465–68 (no. 4).

JESHO — *Journal of the Economic and Social History of the Orient.*

JNES — *Journal of Near Eastern Studies.*

Jones, A. "The Word Made Visible: Arabic Script and the Committing of the Qurʾān to Writing", in Ch. Robinsion (ed.), *Texts, Documents and Artefacts: Islamic Studies in Honour of D.S. Richards*, Leiden 2003, 1–16.

JSAI — *Jerusalem Studies in Arabic and Islam.*

JSS — *Journal of Semitic Studies.*

al-Jumaḥī, Muḥammad b. Sallām. *Ṭabaqāt fuḥūl al-shuʿarāʾ*, ed. Maḥmūd Muḥammad Shākir, Cairo 1394/1974. 2 vols.

Kanz al-ʿummāl — al-Muttaqī al-Hindī. *Kanz al-ʿummāl fī sunan al-aqwāl wa-l-afʿāl*, ed. Ṣafwat al-Saqqā, Beirut 1399/1979–1407/1986. 18 vols.

Kashf al-ẓunūn — Ḥājjī Khalīfa. *Kashf al-ẓunūn*, ed. Şerefettin Yaltkaya and Rifat Bilge, n. p.: Maarif Matbaasi, 1360/1941–1362/1943. 2 vols.

Kennett, A. *Bedouin Justice*, London and New York 1925. Reprint London 2000.

Khadduri, M. *War and Peace in the Law of Islam*, Baltimore 1962.

Khalīfa b. Khayyāṭ. *al-Ṭabaqāt*, ed. Akram Ḍiyāʾ al-ʿUmarī, Riyāḍ 1402/1982. Reprint of the 1387/1967 edition.

al-Khaṣṣāf, Aḥmad b. ʿAmr al-Shaybānī. *Aḥkām al-awqāf*, Cairo 1322/1904.

Khāzin, *Tafsīr* — al-Khāzin, ʿAlāʾ al-Dīn ʿAlī b. Muḥammad al-Baghdādī. *Lubāb al-taʾwīl fī maʿānī al-tanzīl*, Cairo 1381 A.H. 4 vols.

Khizāna — ʿAbd al-Qādir b. ʿUmar al-Baghdādī. *Khizānat al-adab*, ed. ʿAbd al-Salām Hārūn, Cairo: al-Khānji, 1387/1967–1406/1986. 13 vols.

Khulāṣat al-wafā — al-Samhūdī. *Khulāṣat al-wafā bi-akhbār dār al-muṣṭafā*, Medina 1392/1972.

Khushanī — Abū Dharr al-Khushanī. *Sharḥ al-sīra al-nabawiyya*, ed. P. Brönnle, Cairo 1911.

Kister, M.J. *Concepts and Ideas at the Dawn of Islam*, Aldershot: Variorum, 1997.

—, "The Massacre of the Banū Qurayẓa: A Re-examination of a Tradition", in *JSAI* 8 (1986), 61–96. Reprinted in *idem*, *Society and Religion from Jāhiliyya to Islam*, no. VIII.

—, "On Strangers and Allies in Mecca", in *JSAI* 13 (1990), 113–54. Reprinted in *idem*, *Concepts and Ideas at the Dawn of Islam*, no. I.

—, "Sifrut ha-sira (ha-biyografia shel ha-navi Muḥammad)", in *idem*, *Meḥqarim be-hithavvut ha-islam* (*Studies on the Emergence of Islam*), Jerusalem 1998, 215–37. (A collection of previously published articles in Hebrew translation.) This is an extended version of *idem*, "The *Sīrah* Literature".

—, "The *Sīrah* Literature", in *CHALUP*, 352–67.

—, *Society and Religion from Jāhiliyya to Islam*, Aldershot: Variorum, 1990.

—, "Some Reports Concerning al-Ṭā'if", in *JSAI* 1 (1979), 1–18. Reprinted in *idem*, *Studies in Jāhiliyya and Early Islam*, no. XI.

—, *Studies in Jāhiliyya and Early Islam*, London: Variorum, 1980.

—, "*al-Taḥannuth*: An Inquiry into the Meaning of a Term", in *BSOAS* 31 (1968), 223–36. Reprinted in *idem*, *Studies in Jāhiliyya and early Islam*, no. V.

Kohlberg, E. "Authoritative Scriptures in Early Imāmī Shī'ism", in É. Patlagean and A. Le Boulluec (eds.), *Les retours aux écritures: fondamentalismes présents et passés*, Louvain 1993, 295–312.

—, "Shī'ī *Ḥadīth*", in *CHALUP*, 299–307.

Kowalski, T. "Zu dem Eid bei den altern Arabern", in *Archiv Orientalni* 6 (1934), 68–81.

Krehl, L. *Das Leben des Muhammed*, Leipzig 1884.

Lane, E.W. *Arabic-English Lexicon*, Cambridge 1984. Reprint in two vols. The original edition appeared in London, 1863–93.

Lecker, M. "Abū Mālik 'Abdallāh b. Sām of Kinda, a Jewish Convert to Islam", in *Der Islam* 71 (1994), 280–82.

—, "'Amr b. Ḥazm al-Anṣārī and Qur'ān 2,256: 'No Compulsion is There in Religion'", in *Oriens* 35 (1996), 57–64. Reprinted in *idem*, *Jews and Arabs*, IV.

—, *The Banū sulaym: A Contribution to the Study of Early Islam*, Jerusalem 1989.

—, "The Bewitching of the Prophet Muḥammad by the Jews: A Note à propos 'Abd al-Malik b. Ḥabīb's *Mukhtaṣar fī l-ṭibb*", in *al-Qanṭara* 13 (1992), 561–69. Reprinted in *idem*, *Jews and Arabs*, no. XII.

—, "Biographical Notes on Abū 'Ubayda Ma'mar b. al-Muthannā", in *Studia Islamica* 81 (1995), 71–100. Reprinted in *idem*, *Jews and Arabs*, no. XVIII.

—, "Biographical Notes on Ibn Shihāb al-Zuhrī", in *JSS* 41 (1996), 21–63. Reprinted in *idem*, *Jews and Arabs*, no. XVI.

—, "Did Muḥammad Conclude Treaties with the Jewish Tribes Naḍīr, Qurayẓa and Qaynuqā'?", in *IOS* 17 (1997), 29–36.

—, "Did the Quraysh Conclude a Treaty with the Anṣār Prior to the Hijra?", in *The Biography of Muḥammad: The Issue of the Sources*, ed. H. Motzki, Leiden 2000, 157–69.

—, "The Estates of 'Amr b. al-'Āṣ in Palestine: Notes on a New Negev Arabic Inscription", in *BSOAS* 52 (1989), 24–37.

—, "Ḥudhayfa b. al-Yamān and 'Ammār b. Yāsir, Jewish Converts to Islam", in *Quaderni di Studi Arabi* 11 (1993 [1995]), 149–62. Reprinted in *idem*, *Jews and Arabs*, no. V.

—, "Idol Worship in Pre-Islamic Medina (Yathrib)", in *Le Muséon* 106 (1993), 331–46. Reprinted in *idem*, *Jews and Arabs*, no. I. Also reprinted in Peters (ed.), *The Arabs and Arabia on the Eve of Islam*, 129–44.

—, *Jews and Arabs in Pre- and Early Islamic Arabia*, Aldershot: Variorum, 1998.

—, "Judaism Among Kinda and the *Ridda* of Kinda", in *JAOS* 115 (1995), 635–50. Reprinted in *idem*, *Jews and Arabs*, no. XIV. Hebrew translation: "Ha-yahadut be-qerev shevet Kinda ve-ha-'ridda' shel Kinda", in *Taymāʾ* 6 (1998), 1–28.

—, "Kinda on the Eve of Islam and During the *Ridda*", in *JRAS* (1994), 333–56. Reprinted in *idem*, *Jews and Arabs*, no. XV.

—, "King Ibn Ubayy and the *Quṣṣāṣ*", in H. Berg (ed.), *Methods and Theories in the Study of Islamic Origins*, Leiden (forthcoming).

—, "The Levying of Taxes for the Sassanians in Pre-Islamic Medina (Yathrib)", in *JSAI* 27 (2002), 109–26. (Festschrift Sh. Shaked.)

—, "Muḥammad at Medina: A Geographical Approach", in *JSAI* 6 (1985), 29–62. Reprinted in *idem*, *Jews and Arabs*, no. VIII.

—, *Muslims, Jews and Pagans: Studies on Early Islamic Medina*, Leiden 1995.

—, "A Note on Early Marriage Links Between Qurashīs and Jewish Women", in *JSAI* 10 (1987), 17–39. Reprinted in *idem*, *Jews and Arabs*, no. II.

—, "On Arabs of the Banū Kilāb Executed Together with the Jewish Banū Qurayẓa", in *JSAI* 19 (1995), 66–72. Reprinted in *idem*, *Jews and Arabs*, no. X.

—, "On the Markets of Medina (Yathrib) in Pre-Islamic and Early Islamic Times", *JSAI* 8 (1986), 133–47. Reprinted in *idem*, *Jews and Arabs*, no. IX.

—, "On the Preservation of the Letters of the Prophet Muḥammad", in *idem*, *People, Tribes and Society*, no. X.

—, *People, Tribes and Society in Arabia around the time of Muḥammad*, forthcoming (Variorum Collected Studies Series.)

—, "A Pre-Islamic Endowment Deed in Arabic Regarding al-Waḥīda in the Ḥijāz", in *idem*, *People, Tribes and Society in Arabia* (forthcoming).

—, "Wāqidī's Account on the Status of the Jews of Medina: A Study of a Combined Report", in *JNES* 54 (1995), 15–32. Reprinted in *idem*, *Jews and Arabs*, no. VII. Also reprinted in Rubin (ed.) *The Life of Muḥammad*, 23–40.

—, "Was Arabian Idol Worship Declining on the Eve of Islam?", in *idem*, *People, Tribes and Society*, no. III.

—, "Were Customs Dues Levied at the Time of the Prophet Muḥammad?", in *al-Qantara* 22 (2001), 19–43.

—, "*Yahūd/ʿuhūd*: A Variant Reading in the Story of the ʿAqaba Meeting", in *Le Muséon* 109 (1996), 169–184. Reprinted in *idem*, *Jews and Arabs*, no. VI.

Lichtenstaedter, I. "From Particularism to Unity", in *Islamic Culture* 23 (1949), 251–80.

Lisān al-ʿarab — Ibn Manẓūr, Jamāl al-Dīn. *Lisān al-ʿarab*, Beirut 1968. 15 vols.

Madelung, W. *The Succession to Muḥammad: A Study of the Early Caliphate*, Cambridge 1997.

Maghānim — Majd al-Dīn Muḥammad b. Yaʿqūb al-Fīrūzābādī. *al-Maghānim al-muṭāba fī maʿālim Ṭāba*, ed. Ḥamad al-Jāsir, Riyāḍ 1389/1969.

Majmaʿ al-zawāʾid — ʿAlī b. Abī Bakr al-Haythamī. *Majmaʿ al-zawāʾid wa-manbaʿ al-fawāʾid*, Beirut 1967. 10 vols.

Manāl al-ṭālib — Majd al-Dīn al-Mubārak b. Muḥammad Ibn al-Athīr. *Manāl al-ṭālib fī sharḥ ṭiwāl al-gharāʾib*, ed. Maḥmūd Muḥammad al-Ṭanāḥī, Mecca [1399/1979].

Manāqib mazyadiyya — Abū l-Baqā' Hibat Allāh al-Ḥillī. *al-Manāqib al-mazyadiyya*, ed. Ṣāliḥ Mūsā Darādika and Muḥammad ʿAbd al-Qādir Khrīsāt, Amman 1404/1984.

Manāsik — *Kitāb al-manāsik wa-amākin ṭuruq al-ḥajj wa-maʿālim al-jazīra*, ed. Ḥamad al-Jāsir, Riyāḍ 1401/1981.

al-Maqrīzī, Aḥmad b. ʿAlī Taqī al-Dīn. *Imtāʿ al-asmāʿ bi-mā li-l-nabī mina l-aḥwāl wa-l-amwāl wa-l-ḥafada wa-l-matāʿ*, Muḥammad ʿAbd al-Ḥamīd al-Namīsī, Beirut 1420/1999. 14 vols.

Maʿrifa wa-ta'rīkh — Yaʿqūb b. Sufyān al-Fasawī. *Kitāb al-maʿrifa wa-l-ta'rīkh*, ed. Akram Ḍiyā' al-ʿUmarī, Beirut: Mu'assasat al-Risāla, 1401/1981. 3 vols.

al-Marzūqī, Aḥmad b. Muḥammad. *Sharḥ dīwān al-ḥamāsa*, ed. Amīn and ʿAbd al-Salām Hārūn, Cairo 1371/1951–1373/1953. 4 vols.

Massignon, L. "L'*umma* et ses synonymes: notion de 'communauté sociale' en islam", in *REI* (1941–46), 151–57.

al-Masʿūdī, ʿAlī b. al-Ḥusayn. *al-Tanbīh wa-l-ishrāf*, ed. M.J. de Goeje, Leiden 1894.

Mawrid al-ẓam'ān — Fā'id b. al-Mubārak al-Ibyārī. *Mawrid al-ẓam'ān ilā sīra al-mabʿūth min ʿAdnān*, MS Staatsbibliothek Berlin (Sprenger 146).

al-Mawṣilī, Abū Ḥafṣ ʿUmar b. Muḥammad. *Kitāb al-Wasīla* (*Wasīlat al-mutaʿabbidīn ilā mutābaʿat sayyid al-mursalīn*), Hyderabad 1392/1973–1397/1977.

Mufaḍḍaliyyāt — Ch. J. Lyall. *The Mufaḍḍalīyāt: An Anthology of Ancient Arabian Odes*, Oxford 1921–24.

Muir, W. *The Life of Moḥammad*, Edinburgh 1912.

Muqtaḍab — Yāqūt al-Ḥamawī. *al-Muqtaḍab min kitāb jamharat al-nasab*, ed. Nājī Ḥasan, Beirut 1987.

Muranyi, M. *Beiträge zur Geschichte der Ḥadīṯ- und Rechtsgelehrsamkeit der Mālikiyya in Nordafrika bis zum 5. JH. D.H.*, Wiesbaden 1997.

—, "Fiqh", in H. Gätje (ed.). *Grundriss der Arabischen Philologie*, II, Wiesbaden 1987, 299–325.

Muṣʿab b. ʿAbdallāh al-Zubayrī. *Kitāb nasab Quraysh*, ed. E. Lévi-Provençal, Cairo 1953.

Mustadrak — al-Ḥākim al-Naysābūrī. *al-Mustadrak ʿalā l-ṣaḥīḥayni fī l-ḥadīth*, Hyderabad 1335/1917–1342/1923. Reprint Riyāḍ, 1968. 4 vols.

Naqā'iḍ Jarīr wa-l-Farazdaq, ed. A.A. Bevan, Cambridge 1905. 3 vols.

Nashwān, *Shams al-ʿulūm* — *Die auf Südarabien bezüglichen Angaben Našwān's im Šams al-ʿulūm*, ed. ʿAẓīm al-Dīn Aḥmad, London: Gibb Memorial Series, 1916. Reprint Beirut 1407/1986.

Naṣr b. ʿAbd al-Raḥmān al-Fazārī al-Iskandarānī. *al-Amkina wa-l-miyāh wa-l-jibāl wa-l-āthār*, MS Br. Lib. Add. 23,603

Nathr al-durr — Abū Saʿd Manṣūr b. al-Ḥusayn al-Ābī. *Nathr al-durr*, ed. Muḥammad ʿAlī Qarna *et alii*, Cairo 1980–90. 8 vols.

van Nieuwenhuijze, C.A.O. "The *ummah* — an Analytic Approach", in *Studia Islamica* 10 (1959), 5–22.

Nöldeke, Th. *Die ghassânischen Fürsten aus dem Hause Gafna's*, Berlin 1887.

Nūr al-Nibrās — Burhān al-Dīn al-Ḥalabī. *Nūr al-nibrās ʿalā sīrat Ibn Sayyid al-Nās*, MS Staatsbibliothek Berlin (Sprenger 124, 125).

Nuwayrī, *Nihāyat al-arab* — Shihāb al-Dīn al-Nuwayrī. *Nihāyat al-arab fī funūn al-adab*, Cairo 1923–1998. 33 vols.

Orthmann, E. *Stamm und Macht: Die arabischen Stämme im 2. und 3. Jahrhundert der Hiğra*, Wiesbaden 2002.

Ossendorf-Conrad, B. *Das "K. al-Wāḍiḥa" des ʿAbd al-Malik b. Ḥabīb.* Edition und Kommentar zu Ms. Qarawiyyīn 809/40 (Abwāb al-Ṭahāra), Beirut 1994.

Paret, R. S.v. "Ummah", in H.A.R. Gibb and J.H. Kramers (eds.), *The Shorter Encyclopaedia of Islam*, Photomechanical Reprint, Leiden 1974, 603–604.

Peters, F.E. (ed.). *The Arabs and Arabia on the Eve of Islam*, Aldershot 1999.

Powers, D. *Studies in Qur'ān and* Ḥadīth, Berkeley 1986.

Qalyūbī — Aḥmad b. Aḥmad al-Qalyūbī. *al-Nubdha al-laṭīfa*, ed. Saʿīd ʿAbd al-Fattāḥ, Riyāḍ 1417/1997.

Qasṭallānī — *al-Mawāhib al-laduniyya bi-l-minaḥ al-muḥammadiyya*, ed. Ṣāliḥ Aḥmad al-Shāmī, Beirut: al-Maktab al-Islāmī, 1412/1991. 4 vols.

al-Qayrawānī, ʿAbdallāh b. Abī Zayd. *Kitāb al-jāmiʿ*, ed. Muḥammad Abū l-Ajfān and ʿUthmān Baṭṭīkh, Beirut–Tunis 1402/1982.

Qurṭubī, *Tafsīr* — al-Qurṭubī, Muḥammad b. Aḥmad. *al-Jāmiʿ li-aḥkām al-qur'ān*^{3}, Cairo 1387/1967. Reprint. 20 vols.

Quṭrub, Muḥammad b. al-Mustanīr. *Aḍdād*, ed. Ḥannā Ḥaddād, Riyadh 1405/1984.

Rahman, H. "The Conflicts Between the Prophet and the Opposition in Madina", in *Der Islam* 62 (1985), 260–97.

—, "*Jibt, ṭāghūt* and the *taḥkīm* of the *umma*", in *Arabica* 29 (1982), 50–59.

al-Rāzī, Muḥammad b. ʿUmar. *al-Tafsīr al-kabīr*, Cairo n. d. Reprint Tehran. 16 vols.

REI — *Revue des Études Islamiques.*

Robin, Ch. "Le royaume Ḥujride, dit 'royaume de Kinda', entre Ḥimyar et Byzance", in *Comptes rendus des séances: Académie de inscriptions & belles-lettres*, 1996, 665–714.

Rubin — see Rubin, "The 'Constitution of Medina': some notes".

Rubin, U. "*Barā'a*: A Study of Some Quranic Passages", in *JSAI* 5 (1984), 13–32.

—, "The 'Constitution of Medina': Some Notes", in *Studia Islamica* 62 (1985), 5–23.

—, (ed.), *The Life of Muḥammad*, Aldershot: Variorum, 1998. (The Formation of the Classical Islamic World, 4.)

Samʿānī — ʿAbd al-Karīm b. Muḥammad al-Samʿānī. *al-Ansāb*, ed. ʿAbdallāh ʿUmar al-Bārūdī, Beirut 1408/1988. 5 vols.

al-Samarqandī, Naṣr b. Muḥammad. *Bustān al-ʿārifīna*, on margin of *idem*, *Tanbīh al-ghāfilīna*, Cairo n. d.

Samhūdī — *Wafā' al-wafā bi-akhbār dār al-muṣṭafā*, ed. Muḥammad Muḥyī al-Dīn ʿAbd al-Ḥamīd, Cairo 1374/1955. Reprint Beirut 1401/1981. 2 vols.

al-Sarakhsī, Muḥammad b. Aḥmad. *Sharḥ kitāb al-siyar al-kabīr li-Muḥammad b. al-Ḥasan al-Shaybānī*, V, ed. ʿAbd al-ʿAzīz Aḥmad, Cairo 1972.

Serjeant — see Serjeant, "The *Sunnah Jāmiʿah*" ....

Serjeant, R.B., "The 'Constitution of Medina'", in *Islamic Quarterly* 8 (1964), 3–16. Reprinted in *idem*, *Studies in Arabian History and Civilization*, no. V.

—, "Early Arabic Prose", in *CHALUP*, 114–53.

—, "Ḥaram and Ḥawṭah, the Sacred Enclave in Arabia", in *Mélanges Taha Husain*, ed. ʿAbd al-Raḥmān Badawī, Cairo 1962, 41–58. Reprinted in *idem*, *Studies in Arabian History and Civilization*, no. III.

—, *Studies in Arabian History and Civilization*, London: Variorum Reprints, 1981.

—, "The *Sunnah Jāmiʿah*, Pacts with the Yathrib Jews, and the *Taḥrīm* of Yathrib: Analysis and Translation of the Documents Comprised in the So-called 'Constitution of Medina'", in *BSOAS* 41 (1978), 1–42. Reprinted in *idem*, *Studies in Arabian History and Civilization*, no. VI. Also reprinted in Rubin (ed.), *The Life of Muḥammad*, 151–92.

—, "Sunnah, Qur'ān, 'Urf", in *Law and the Islamic World Past and Present*, Ch. Toll and J. Skovgaard-Petersen (eds.), Copenhagen: The Royal Danish Academy of Sciences and Letters/Munksgaard, 1995, 33–48. Reprinted in *idem*, *Society and Trade in South Arabia*, Aldershot: Variorum, 1996, no. VII.

Sharon, M. "*Ahl al-bayt* – People of the House", in *JSAI* 8 (1986), 169–84.

—, *Revolt: The Social and Military Aspects of the ʿAbbāsid Revolution*, Jerusalem 1990.

Sijistānī, *Waṣāyā* — Abū Ḥātim al-Sijistānī. *Kitāb al-waṣāyā*, ed. ʿAbd al-Munʿim ʿĀmir, Cairo 1961 (bound with *idem*, *al-Muʿammarūna*).

Simonsen, J.B. *Studies in the Genesis and Early Development of the Caliphal Taxation System*, Copenhagen: Akademisk Forlag, 1988.

Sīra ḥalabiyya — ʿAlī b. Burhān al-Dīn al-Ḥalabī. *Insān al-ʿuyūn fī sīrat al-amīn al-maʾmūn*, Cairo 1320 A.H. 3 vols.

Sīra shāmiyya — Muḥammad b. Yūsuf al-Ṣāliḥī al-Shāmī. *Subul al-hudā wa-l-rashād*, III, ed. ʿAbd al-ʿAzīz ʿAbd al-Ḥaqq Ḥilmī, Cairo 1395/1975.

Sprenger, A. *Das Leben und die Lehre des Moḥammad*, Berlin 1869. 3 vols.

Stillman, N.A. *The Jews of Arab Lands*, Philadelphia 1979.

al-Suhaylī, ʿAbd al-Raḥmān b. ʿAbdallāh. *al-Rawḍ al-unuf*, ed. Ṭāhā ʿAbd al-Rāʾūf Saʿd, Cairo 1391/1971. 4 vols.

al-Suyūṭī, Jalāl al-Dīn. *al-Durr al-manthūr fī l-tafsīr bi-l-maʾthūr*, Cairo 1314/1896. 6 vols.

—, *al-Khaṣāʾiṣ al-kubrā*, ed. Muḥammad Khalīl Harās, Cairo 1387/1967. 3 vols.

Ṭabarī — Abū Jaʿfar Muḥammad b. Jarīr al-Ṭabarī. *Taʾrīkh al-rusul wa-l-mulūk*, ed. Muḥammad Abū l-Faḍl Ibrāhīm, Cairo 1380/1960–1387/1967. 10 vols. References to the European edition (ed. M.J. de Goeje *et al.*, Leiden 1879–1901) are added between square brackets.

—, *The history of al-Ṭabarī*, VI, trans. W.M. Watt and M.V. McDonald, New York 1988.

—, *The history of al-Ṭabarī*, VII, trans. W.M. Watt and M.V. McDonald, New York 1989.

—, *The History of al-Ṭabarī*, IX, trans. I.K. Poonawala, New York 1990.

—, *The History of al-Ṭabarī*, X, trans. F.M. Donner, New York 1993.

—, *The History of al-Ṭabarī*, XI, trans. Kh.Y. Blankinship, New York 1993.

—, *The History of al-Ṭabarī*, XIV, trans. G. Rex Smith, New York 1994.

—, *The History of al-Ṭabarī*, XX, trans. G. Hawting, New York 1989.

—, *The History of al-Ṭabarī*, XXIX, trans. H. Kennedy, New York 1990.

Ṭabarī, *Tafsīr* — Abū Jaʿfar Muḥammad b. Jarīr al-Ṭabarī. *Jāmiʿ al-bayān fī tafsīr al-qurʾān*, Būlāq 1321/1903–1330/1912. 12 vols.

—, *Tahdhīb al-āthār* (Musnad ʿAlī), ed. Maḥmūd Muḥammad Shākir, Cairo [1402/1982].

al-Ṭabarānī, Sulaymān b. Aḥmad. *al-Muʿjam al-Kabīr*[2], ed. Ḥamdī ʿAbd al-Majīd al-Salafī, Cairo 1400/1980–1405/1985. 10 vols.

al-Ṭabrisī, al-Faḍl b. al-Ḥasan. *Iʿlām al-warā bi-aʿlām al-hudā*, Beirut 1985.

Tahdh. — Ibn Ḥajar al-ʿAsqalānī. *Tahdhīb al-tahdhīb*, Hyderabad 1325/1907. 12 vols.

Tahdhīb al-kamāl — Abū l-Ḥajjāj Yūsuf al-Mizzī. *Tahdhīb al-kamāl fī asmāʾ al-rijāl*, ed. Bashshār ʿAwwād Maʿrūf, Beirut 1405/1985–1413/1992. 35 vols.

Takmilat al-ikmāl — Ibn Nuqṭa. *Takmilat al-ikmāl*, ed. ʿAbd al-Qayyūm ʿAbd Rabb al-Nabī. Mecca 1987–2002. 7 vols.

Tawḍīḥ al-mushtabih — Ibn Nāṣir al-Dīn. *Tawḍīḥ al-mushtabih*, ed. Muḥammad Naʿīm al-ʿAraqsūsī, Beirut 1407/1986–1414/1993. 10 vols.

al-Tāzī, ʿAbd al-Hādī (ed.). "al-Nuṣūṣ al-ẓāhira fī ijlāʾ al-yahūd al-fājira, ta'līf Aḥmad b. Abī l-Rijāl (1029-1092/1660-1681[!])", in *Majallat al-majmaʿ al-ʿilmī al-ʿirāqī* 32 (1981), 378–400.

al-Thaʿālibī, Abū Manṣūr ʿAbd al-Malik b. Muḥammad. *Thimār al-qulūb fī l-muḍāf wa-l-mansūb*, ed. Abū l-Faḍl Ibrāhīm, Cairo 1384/1965.

al-Thaqafī, Ibrāhīm b. Muḥammad. *al-Ghārāt*, ed. Mīr Jalāl al-Dīn Ḥusaynī Urmawī, Tehran 1395/1975. 2 vols.

Tibawi, A.L. "Second Critique of English-Speaking Orientalists and Their Approach to Islam and the Arabs", in *Islamic Quarterly* 23 (1979), 3–50.

al-Ṭūsī, Abū Jaʿfar Muḥammad b. al-Ḥasan. *Tahdhīb al-aḥkām*, Beirut 1406/1985. 10 vols.

ʿUmdat al-akhbār — Aḥmad b. ʿAbd al-Ḥamīd al-ʿAbbāsī. *ʿUmdat al-akhbār fī madīnat al-mukhtār*, ed. Muḥammad al-Ṭayyib al-Anṣārī and Asʿad Ṭarābzūnī, n. d., n. p.

Usd al-ghāba — Ibn al-Athīr, ʿAlī b. Muḥammad, ʿIzz al-Dīn. *Usd al-ghāba fī maʿrifat al-ṣaḥāba*, Cairo 1280/1863. 5 vols.

Wakīʿ, Muḥammad b. Khalaf. *Akhbār al-quḍāt*, ed. ʿAbd al-ʿAzīz Muṣṭafā al-Marāghī, Cairo 1366/1947. Reprint Beirut n. d. 3 vols.

Wāqidī — Muḥammad b. ʿUmar al-Wāqidī. *Kitāb al-maghāzī*, ed. M. Jones, London 1966. 3 vols.

Ward, S. "A Fragment from an Unknown Work by al-Ṭabarī on the Tradition 'Expel the Jews and Christians from the Arabian Peninsula (and the Lands of Islam)' ", in *BSOAS* 53 (1990), 407–420.

Wath. — M. Ḥamīdullāh. *Majmūʿat al-wathāʾiq al-siyāsiyya li-l-ʿahd al-nabawī wa-l-khilāfa al-rāshida*[5], Beirut 1405/1985.

Watt — see Watt, *Muhammad at Medina.*

Watt, W.M. "Economic and Social Aspects of the Origin of Islam", *Islamic Quarterly* 1 (1954), 99–103.

—, *Muhammad at Medina*, Oxford 1956.

Wellhausen — J. Wellhausen. *Skizzen und Vorarbeiten*, IV=*Medina vor dem Islam*, Berlin 1889.

—, *The Arab Kingdom and its Fall*, trans. M.G. Weir, Calcutta, 1927. Reprint Beirut 1973.

Wensinck — A.J. Wensinck. *Muhammad and the Jews of Medina, with an Excursus: Muhammad's Constitution of Medina, by Julius Wellhausen*, trans. and ed. by W.H. Behn, Freiburg im Breisgau 1975 (=*Mohammed en de Joden te Medina*, Leiden 1908).

World Survey of Islamic Manuscripts, ed. G. Roper, London 1992–94. 4 vols.

Wright, W. *A Grammar of the Arabic Language*[3], Cambridge 1896–98. 2 vols.

al-Yaʿqūbī, Aḥmad b. Abī Yaʿqūb. *Buldān*, ed. M.J. de Goeje, Leiden 1892.

—, *Taʾrīkh*, Beirut 1379/1960. 2 vols.

Yāqūt — Yāqūt al-Ḥamawī. *Muʿjam al-buldān*, Beirut 1957. 5 vols.

Yāqūt, *Udabā'* — *Mu'jam al-udabā'*², ed. I. 'Abbās, Beirut 1993. 7 vols.
Zād al-ma'ād — Ibn al-Qayyim al-Jawziyya. *Zād al-ma'ād fī hady khayr al-'ibād*, on margin of al-Zurqānī.
al-Zamakhsharī, Maḥmūd b. 'Umar. *al-Fā'iq fī gharīb al-ḥadīth*, ed. 'Alī Muḥammad al-Bijāwī and Muḥammad Abū l-Faḍl Ibrāhīm, Cairo 1971. 4 vols.
Zein al-Abdin, al-Tayib. "The Political Significance of the Constitution of Medina", in *Arabian and Islamic Studies: Articles presented to R.B. Serjeant on the Occasion of his Retirement etc.*, London and New York 1983, 146–52.
al-Zubayr b. Bakkār. *Jamharat nasab Quraysh*, I, ed. Maḥmūd Muḥammad Shākir, Cairo 1381.
al-Zurqānī, Muḥammad b. 'Abd al-Bāqī. *Sharḥ 'alā l-mawāhib al-laduniyya*, Cairo 1329/1911. 8 vols.

Index

SLAEI **Studies in Late Antiquity and Early Islam**

LAWRENCE I. CONRAD, EDITOR

Published Titles

1. *The Byzantine and Early Islamic Near East* (proceedings of the workshops on Late Antiquity and Early Islam):

   I. *Problems in the Literary Source Material* (Papers of the First Workshop on Late Antiquity and Early Islam), edited by Averil Cameron and Lawrence I. Conrad. 1992. xiv, 428 pp. ISBN 0-87850-080-4

   II. *Land Use and Settlement Patterns* (Papers of the Second Workshop on Late Antiquity and Early Islam), edited by G.R.D. King and Averil Cameron. 1994. xiv, 317 pp. ISBN 0-87850-106-1

   III. *States, Resources and Armies* (Papers of the Third Workshop on Late Antiquity and Early Islam), edited by Averil Cameron. 1995. xvi, 491 pp. ISBN 0-87850-107-X

   VI. *Elites Old and New* (Papers of the Sixth Workshop on Late Antiquity and Early Islam), edited by John Haldon and Lawrence I Conrad. 2004. xi 316 pp. ISBN 0-87850-144-4

2. Robert Schick, *The Christian Communities of Palestine from Byzantine to Islamic Rule: A Historical and Archaeological Study*. 1995. xviii, 627 pp. ISBN 0-87850-081-2

3. Albrecht Noth, *The Early Arabic Historical Tradition: A Source-Critical Study*. Second edition in collaboration with Lawrence I. Conrad; translated from the German by Michael Bonner. 1994. xi, 248 pp. ISBN 0-87850-082-0

4. Martin Hinds, *Studies in Early Islamic History*. Edited by Jere Bacharach, Lawrence I. Conrad, and Patricia Crone, with an Introduction by G. R. Hawting. 1996. xix, 262 pp. ISBN 0-87850-109-6

5. Uri Rubin, *The Eye of the Beholder: The Life of Muḥammad as Viewed by the Early Muslims*. 1995. ix., 289 pp. ISBN 0-87850-110-X

6. Jean Maurice Fiey, *Saints syriaques*. Édité par Lawrence I. Conrad. In French. 2004. xx, 224, pp. ISBN 0-87850-111-8

7. Elizabeth Savage, *A Gateway to Hell, A Gateway to Paradise: The North African Response to the Arab Conquest.*
1997. x, 200 pp. ISBN 0-87850-112-6

8. Suliman Bashear, *Arabs and Others in Early Islam.*
1997. viii, 161 pp. ISBN 0-87850-126-6

10. Milka Levy-Rubin, *The* Continuatio *of the Samaritan Chronicle of Abū l-Fatḥ al-Sāmirī al-Danafī.* 2002. xiii, 203 pp. ISBN 0-87850-136-3

11. Josef Horovitz, *The Earliest Biographies of the Prophet and their Authors.*
2002. xxxviii, 158 pp. ISBN 0-87850-118-5

13. Robert Hoyland, *Seeing Islam as Others Saw It: A Survey and Evaluation of Christian, Jewish, and Zoroastrian Writings on Early Islam.*
1997. xviii, 872 pp. ISBN 0-87850-125-8

14. Fred M. Donner, *Narratives of Islamic Origins: The Beginnings of Islamic Historical Writing.* 1998. xv, 358 pp. ISBN 0-87850-127-4

17. Uri Rubin, *Between Bible and Qur'ān: The Children of Israel and the Islamic Self-Image.* 1999. xiii. 318 pp. ISBN 0-87850-134-7

19. Josef W. Meri, *A Lonely Wayfarer's Guide to Pilgrimage: 'Alī ibn Abī Bakr al-Harawī's* Kitāb al-Ishārāt ilā Maʻrifat al-Ziyārāt.
2004. xli, 308 pp. ISBN 0-87850-169-X

20. James E. Lindsay, ed. *Ibn 'Asākir and Early Islamic History.*
2001. xii, 157 pp. ISBN 0-87850-120-7

21. David Cook, *Studies in Muslim Apocalyptic.*
2003. xii. 472 pages ISBN 0-87850-142-8

22. Andreas Görke, *Das* Kitāb al-Amwāl *des Abū 'Ubaid al-Qāsim b. Sallām: Entstehung und Überlieferung eines frühislamischen Rechtwerkes.* In German. 2003. ix, 204 pp. ISBN 0-87850-146-0

23. Michael Lecker, *The "Constitution of Medina": Muḥammad's First Legal Document.* 2004. x, 227 pp. ISBN 0-87850-148-7

Published by:
The Darwin Press, Inc.
Box 2202, Princeton, NJ 08543
www.darwinpress.com
books@darwinpress.com